Advance Praise for *Landing Page Optimization: The Definitive Guide to Testing and Tuning for Conversions, Second Edition*

I love it when someone who's obviously a true expert shares almost everything he knows. [Well, you've got to save something for your paying clients, don't you?] And I can't think of anyone who shares more than Tim Ash. I can't believe the amount of useful information and actionable insights he's crammed in here.
> —STEVE KRUG, Author of *Don't Make Me Think*

Tim has figured out what so many people don't understand: your website can (and should) get better. Every single day.
> —SETH GODIN, Author of *Meatball Sundae*

Tim combines science, art, and psychology to show you how you can make your website both more usable and more profitable. Real-world examples and illustrations make each point clear. This book isn't just for big budget click buyers—every page of every website is a potential landing page. Landing Page Optimization *is the ultimate guide to making web pages that get results, and it's an essential addition to every marketer's bookshelf.*
> —ROGER DOOLEY, Author of *Brainfluence* and founder of Dooley Direct

You know that landing page optimization is important. What's missing is a manual that tells you exactly how to go out and get results. Fear not—here it is. Buy this book. Go rock it!
> —AVINASH KAUSHIK, Digital Marketing Evangelist at Google, and author of *Web Analytics 2.0*

Do you hear that sound? That is the sound of visitors bouncing away from your site without doing what you wanted them to do. Want a better melody? Tune your site to the sound of visitors giving you their money. Tim's Landing Page Optimization *is a must-have for your bookshelf.*
> —BRYAN EISENBERG, *New York Times* and *Wall Street Journal* bestselling author

Today's diverse and ever-changing Internet marketing environment can require daily, hourly, and even minute-by-minute fine tuning. Tim does an excellent job of explaining common pitfalls, how to avoid them, and how to execute advanced tactics. This book is a must-read for the modern Internet marketer.
> —KEVIN M. RYAN, CEO, Motivity Marketing, *Digital Next* columnist

A solid, business-focused approach to turning viewers of a website into customers. This is a book written by and for business. It's not about design: it is about increasing sales, gaining customers, and retaining them. Learn how to do the measurements; learn how to conduct experiments. Revise your website by analyzing what visitors actually do. It is always good to see a former student succeed: Tim Ash provides a wonderful example. This is the best business-focused, measurement-based guide to website design I have seen.

—DON NORMAN, Cofounder of Nielsen Norman Group, former director of Northwestern's MBA plus MEM program in design and operations, author of *Living with Complexity*

Landing Page Optimization

The Definitive Guide to Testing and Tuning for Conversions

Second Edition

Tim Ash

Rich Page

Maura Ginty

WILEY

John Wiley & Sons, Inc.

Senior Acquisitions Editor: WILLEM KNIBBE
Development Editor: SARA BARRY
Production Editor: DASSI ZEIDEL
Copy Editor: LIZ WELCH
Editorial Manager: PETE GAUGHAN
Production Manager: TIM TATE
Vice President and Executive Group Publisher: RICHARD SWADLEY
Vice President and Publisher: NEIL EDDE
Book Designer: FRANZ BAUMHACKL
Compositor: KATE KAMINSKI, HAPPENSTANCE TYPE-O-RAMA
Proofreader: REBECCA RIDER
Indexer: TED LAUX
Project Coordinator, Cover: KATHERINE CROCKER
Cover Designer: RYAN SNEED
Cover Image: © COLIN ANDERSON/BRAND X PICTURES/JUPITER IMAGES

Dear Reader,

Thank you for choosing *Landing Page Optimization: The Definitive Guide to Testing and Tuning for Conversions, Second Edition*. This book is part of a family of premium-quality Sybex books, all of which are written by outstanding authors who combine practical experience with a gift for teaching.

Sybex was founded in 1976. More than 30 years later, we're still committed to producing consistently exceptional books. With each of our titles, we're working hard to set a new standard for the industry. From the paper we print on, to the authors we work with, our goal is to bring you the best books available.

I hope you see all that reflected in these pages. I'd be very interested to hear your comments and get your feedback on how we're doing. Feel free to let me know what you think about this or any other Sybex book by sending me an email at nedde@wiley.com. If you think you've found a technical error in this book, please visit http://sybex.custhelp.com. Customer feedback is critical to our efforts at Sybex.

Best regards,

NEIL EDDE
Vice President and Publisher
Sybex, an Imprint of Wiley

To my parents, Tanya and Alexander, for your love and sacrifices to get me here.

To my brother, Artyom, for your open heart and unfolding wisdom.

To my wife, Britt, for being my love and perfect partner on this wondrous journey.

To my children, Sasha and Anya, for showing me that joy is endless.

—TIM

To all those many thousands of websites that need optimizing!

To all my family and friends who motivated me to write this book and stuck with me through the many long hours of writing it.

—RICH

To all the people who taught me that words are fun.

—MAURA

Acknowledgments

My appreciation to the professional team at Wiley/Sybex for being flexible and accommodating during the difficult and long gestation of this second edition. Special thanks to Acquisitions Editor Willem Knibbe for having the patience to put up with my antics and repeated deadline slips.

I am grateful to the whole amazing SiteTuners team and our clients for inspiring me and making every workday an exciting adventure of learning and fun. To my business partner and dear friend Robyn Benensohn, what can I say … through three start-up companies and seventeen years I have enjoyed your love and support. What a long, strange trip it's been—I would not be here without you. Thank you for everything.

I would like to thank my amazing wife, Britt, for her patience and support throughout my entrepreneurial journey. Sweetheart, I know that it has been difficult at times, but I expected no less from my spirit warrior woman. I love you so much— you will always be my true north. My dearest children Sasha and Anya, I marvel daily at the unfolding miracles that are your lives. I am so grateful to be able to share with you the fleeting time we have before you go forth to shine your beautiful light and spirits upon the world. I will always be with you in my overflowing heart.

—TIM

A huge thanks to my friend and mentor Tim Ash, who placed his faith and trust in me to help write the 2nd edition of this book. It's been a real privilege and an honor to work with you on it. And a special thanks to two of my biggest blogging and writing inspirations: Avinash Kaushik, who got me hooked on web analytics with his eye-opening *Web Analytics: An Hour a Day* book, and Bryan Eisenberg, who turned on many optimization lightbulbs for me with his fantastic *Call to Action* book.

—RICH

Thanks to Tim, for asking me to work on this book. Thanks to Umaru, for always being patient, especially when I'm working too much. Thanks to my family and friends who helped me get to any point of patience and skill to explain anything to anyone else.

—MAURA

About the Authors

Tim Ash is author of the original bestselling first edition of the book *Landing Page Optimization*. The book has been reprinted numerous times and has been translated into six languages. Tim is the CEO of SiteTuners, a firm that specializes in improving website conversion rates through landing page diagnosis and redesign, conversion consulting, landing test plan creation, and internal client training/mentoring. Since 2002, SiteTuners has improved conversion rates for over 850 clients large and small, including Canon, Google, Expedia, CBS, Sony Music, Facebook, Nestle, Verizon Wireless, Texas Instruments, Cisco, Intuit, and Coach.

Tim is a highly regarded keynote and conference presenter, and the chairperson of Conversion Conference—the first international conference series focused on improving online conversions. He has published hundreds of articles about website usability, best practices in landing page design, and tactics to improve website conversion rates, and is the host of the *Landing Page Optimization* podcast on WebmasterRadio.fm.

After attending the University of California, San Diego on a U.C. Regents full academic scholarship, he received his B.S. in Computer Engineering and Cognitive Science "with highest distinction." Tim also completed his M.S. and C.Phil. degrees during his PhD. studies in Computer Science (specializing in neural networks and artificial intelligence) at U.C. San Diego.

He lives and works in San Diego, California, with his wife and two children. In his nonexistent spare time, Tim is an avid photographer, artist, and a certified Tai Chi Chuan instructor. He dreams of the long-ago days when he still had time to Salsa dance. Tim can be reached by e-mail at tim@sitetuners.com.

Rich Page has been analyzing and improving websites for over 10 years and is currently working as a conversion solution specialist at Adobe, helping Fortune 500 clients improve their testing and optimization strategies. Previously he worked for Disney Online on their web analytics and optimization team and graduated with a Masters in Information Technology from the University of San Diego. He has been blogging about web analytics and optimization topics for five years and is currently in the process of writing *Website Optimization: An Hour a Day*, which is slated for summer 2012 release from Sybex.

He currently lives in London, where he returned after spending nearly 10 years in Southern California. In his spare time, he is a passionate classic rock fan and loves to sing karaoke and play tennis.

Maura Ginty is a search, content, and social media strategy expert with 13 years in online marketing. She started Autodesk's first centralized search engine optimization (SEO), web content, and social media programs.

She is a member of the Google Technology Advisory Council and a frequent speaker at leading industry events such as Dreamforce, Search Engine Strategies, SMX, Online Marketing Summit, and Conversion Conference. Her previous online adventures ran through JupiterMedia, Lonely Planet, Symantec, and various nonprofits.

Contents

Introduction   *xv*

Part I   **Understanding Landing Page Optimization**   **1**

Chapter 1   **Setting the Stage**   **3**

What Is a Landing Page? 4

A Few Precious Moments Online 4

Your Baby Is Ugly 6

Your Website Visitors: The Real Landing Page Experts 6

Understanding the Bigger Online Marketing Picture 8

The Myth of Perfect Conversion 17

Chapter 2   **Understanding Your Landing Pages**   **19**

Landing Page Types 20

What Parts of Your Site Are Mission Critical? 22

What Is Your Business Model? 28

The Types of Conversion Actions 30

Chapter 3   **The Matrix—Moving People to Act**   **35**

The Matrix Overview 36

Roles 36

Tasks 38

The Decision-Making Process 39

Awareness 40

Interest 43

Desire 45

Action 53

Part II   **Finding Opportunities for Site Improvement**   **63**

Chapter 4   **Common Problems—The Seven Deadly Sins of Landing Page Design** **65**

A Sober Look 66

Unclear Call-to-Action 66

Too Many Choices 73

Visual Distractions 76

Not Keeping Your Promises 83

Too Much Text 86

Asking for Too Much Information 87

Lack of Trust and Credibility 93

Real-World Case Study: CREDO Mobile 106

Chapter 5 Conversion Ninja Toolbox—Diagnosing Site Problems   111

You Are Not as Good as You Would Like to Believe. 112

Focus on the Negative 113

Web Analytics Tools 114

Visual Analysis Tools 125

Feedback and Survey Tools 131

Website Performance Tools 133

Competitive Analysis Tools 135

Usability Testing Tools 136

E-mail Enhancement Tools 139

**Chapter 6 Misunderstanding Your Visitors—Looking for
Psychological Mismatches   141**

Empathy: The Key Ingredient 142

Researching the Whole Story. 143

Demographics and Segmentation 144

Welcome to Your Brain 148

Cognitive Styles. 152

Persuasion Frameworks 157

Cultural Differences 165

Part III   Fixing Your Site Problems   169

Chapter 7 Conversion Improvement Basics   171

Web Usability Overview 172

Visual Presentation 173

Writing for the Web. 192

Usability Checks 197

Chapter 8 Best Practices for Common Situations   201

Homepages 202

Information Architecture and Navigation. 205

E-commerce Catalogs 211

Registration and Multiple-Step Flows 234

Direct Response Pages 243

Mobile Websites 246

Chapter 9   The Strategy of What to Test   251

How to Think About Test Elements 252

Selecting Elements to Test 261

Testing Multiple-Page Flows 264

Timeless Testing Themes 267

Price Testing 273

Part IV   The Mechanics of Testing   279

Chapter 10   Common Testing Questions   281

Lies, Damn Lies, and Statistics 282

Crash Course in Probability and Statistics 286

Have I Found Something Better? 293

How Sure Do I Need to Be? 295

How Much Better Is It? 298

How Long Should My Test Run? 300

Chapter 11   Preparing for Testing   305

Overview of Content Management and Testing 306

Content Management Configurations 308

Common Testing Issues 313

Chapter 12   Testing Methods   325

Introduction to Testing Terminology 326

Overview of Testing Methods 331

A-B Split Testing 332

Multivariate Testing 335

Variable Interactions 350

Part V   Organization and Planning   359

Chapter 13   Assembling Your Team and Getting Buy-in   361

The Usual Suspects 362

Little Company, Big Company 372

The Company Politics of Tuning 375

Strategies for Getting Started 378

Insource or Outsource? 380

Chapter 14 Developing Your Action Plan   **387**

Before You Begin... 388

Understand Your Business Objectives 389

What Is the Lifetime Value of the Conversion Action? 390

Assemble Your Team...................................... 401

Determine Your Landing Pages and Traffic Sources 403

Decide What Constitutes Success 405

Uncover Problems and Decide What to Test 407

Select an Appropriate Tuning Method....................... 410

Implement and Conduct QA 412

Collect the Data.. 416

Analyze the Results and Verify Improvement 418

Chapter 15 Avoiding Real-World Pitfalls   **421**

Ignoring Your Baseline 422

Collecting Insufficient Data............................... 422

Not Accounting for Seasonality 424

Assuming That Testing Has No Costs........................ 424

Not Factoring In Delayed Conversions 426

Becoming Paralyzed by Search Engine Considerations 433

Failing to Act.. 436

Appendix Landing Page Testing Tools   **437**

Enterprise Tools... 438

Free or Inexpensive Tools 440

Glossary   **443**

Index   *451*

Introduction

The train is pulling out of the station—will you be on it?

Landing page optimization is no longer a well-kept secret. It has rapidly become the most powerful method that smart Internet marketers use to build a lasting competitive advantage.

Well-optimized landing pages and websites can change the economics of your business overnight and turbocharge your online marketing programs.

Don't *guess* at what your visitors want. Turn your website or landing page into a dynamic laboratory to find out what they *actually respond to.*

But you must orient yourself quickly to learn a number of new skills:

- What is the real economic value of my landing page?
- Can I see the world from my visitor's perspective?
- How do I uncover problems with my website?
- What page elements should I change or test to get the best results?
- Can I build the necessary team and action plan for my optimization initiatives?
- What tools are available to help me optimize my website?
- How do I avoid the biggest pitfalls when running my test?

If any of these questions ring true, you have found the right book.

Who Can Benefit from This Book

If you are looking for an instant fix for your landing page, put down this book and look around for a "Top 10 ways to increase conversions" entry on someone's blog. You will not find any quick or easy prescriptions here. To truly benefit from this book, you will need to commit to understanding all of the important fundamentals of this challenging and rewarding field.

If you are involved in any way with making your company's Internet marketing programs more effective, this book is for you. If you have already gotten your feet wet in landing page optimization, this book will take you to the next level and provide you with a solid framework for repeatable future success.

This book will benefit people in the following roles:

- Conversion rate optimizer
- Landing page developer
- Web designer
- Media buyer
- Copywriter
- Webmaster

- User experience engineer
- Affiliate manager
- Web analytics manager
- Product manager
- Advertising manager
- Marketing manager
- Director of online marketing
- Media director
- VP of online marketing
- CMO

What's Inside

Landing page optimization does not fit neatly into any box on an organizational chart. It requires a truly diverse set of knowledge and perspectives in order to be effective. Among other topics, you need to be familiar with web development, human psychology, copywriting, visual design, usability, team building, and the scientific method.

This book is a guide to this strange and wondrous land. We have spent a lot of time exploring up ahead and we've come back with a comprehensive map. Like many pioneers, we have suffered setbacks and endured many painful lessons along the way. Our sincere hope is that this book can shorten your own learning curve and help you become a more effective conversion rate optimizer.

Here's what you will find inside.

Part I: Understanding Landing Page Optimization

- **Chapter 1: "Setting the Stage"**

  Helps you understand how landing page optimization fits into the larger picture of online marketing.

- **Chapter 2: "Understanding Your Landing Pages"**

  Helps you understand the different types of landing pages, key target audience segments, and conversion actions.

- **Chapter 3: "The Matrix—Moving People to Act"**

  Presents a disciplined framework for making sure that the important categories of people arriving on your landing page are able to complete their desired objectives in a systematic order.

Part II: Finding Opportunities for Site Improvement

- **Chapter 4: "Common Problems—The Seven Deadly Sins of Landing Page Design"**

  Takes you through the common pitfalls prevalent on almost all landing pages.

- **Chapter 5: "Conversion Ninja Toolbox—Diagnosing Site Problems"**

  Presents a number of powerful tools and techniques to help you uncover conversion problems.

- **Chapter 6: "Misunderstanding Your Visitors—Looking for Psychological Mismatches"**

  Deconstructs the basics of the human decision making, social interactions, and cognitive styles from the perspective of persuasion.

Part III: Fixing Your Site Problems

- **Chapter 7: "Conversion Improvement Basics"**

  Introduces the foundations of good usability, copywriting, and visual presentation.

- **Chapter 8: "Best Practices for Common Situations"**

  Examines specific applications such as e-commerce catalogs, direct response, registration and sign-up paths, and mobile.

- **Chapter 9: "The Strategy of What to Test"**

  Creates a framework for determining the most impactful changes to make to your landing pages.

Part IV: The Mechanics of Testing

- **Chapter 10: "Common Testing Questions"**

  Reviews important elements of testing, including the basics of the math behind it, required length of data collection, and confidence in the results found.

- **Chapter 11: "Preparing for Testing"**

  Surveys the common methods for creating and presenting test content, along with common testing issues.

- **Chapter 12: "Testing Methods"**

  Presents a framework for understanding different landing page testing approaches and the implications of using each particular method.

Part V: Organization and Planning

- **Chapter 13: "Assembling Your Team and Getting Buy-in"**

  Reviews all important stakeholder roles and company politics common to landing page testing. Suggests several strategies for getting started and discusses the decision to use in-house staff or outsource.

- **Chapter 14: "Developing Your Action Plan"**

  Lays out a detailed framework for putting your optimization plan into action.

- **Chapter 15: "Avoiding Real-World Pitfalls"**

  Describes several common pitfalls that can derail your testing program.

- **Appendix: "Landing Page Testing Tools"**

  Provides an overview of some currently available landing page testing platforms.

- **Glossary**

  Comprehensively covers important landing page optimization terms.

Please refer to the ConversionNinjaToolbox.com website for some additional landing page optimization resources described in this book.

Understanding Landing Page Optimization

I

All of us have our own unique perspectives and biases when dealing with landing page optimization and testing. The knowledge and belief systems that you bring to these processes will largely determine your success. As you study the topic of landing page optimization, you first have to get the right perspective. Part I of this book lays this groundwork. Leave all of your assumptions at the door, and let's get started. Part I consists of the following chapters:

Chapter 1   **Setting the Stage**

Chapter 2   **Understanding Your Landing Pages**

Chapter 3   **The Matrix—Moving People to Act**

Setting the Stage

Life is like a sewer...what you get out of it depends on what you put into it.

—Tom Lehrer, American humorist, singer, and songwriter

1

What is a landing page? What does one look like from your perspective? How does it fit into the overall marketing picture? Can you convince every single web visitor to take the desired action on your page? Are you devoting enough attention to your landing page? Is it the right kind of attention?

This chapter examines these questions and sets the stage for understanding landing page optimization.

Chapter Contents

What Is a Landing Page?
A Few Precious Moments Online
Your Baby Is Ugly
Your Website Visitors: The Real Landing Page Experts
Understanding the Bigger Online Marketing Picture
The Myth of Perfect Conversion

What Is a Landing Page?

In a nutshell, a landing page is any webpage on which an Internet visitor first arrives on their way to an important action that you want them to take on your site. The landing page can be part of your main website, or a stand-alone page designed specifically to receive traffic from an online marketing campaign.

Strictly speaking, it is not just the landing page that you should be optimizing, but rather the whole path from the landing page to important conversion actions (such as purchases, form-fills, or downloads) often happening somewhere deeper in your website.

So why pay so much attention to landing pages and important conversion paths instead of optimizing the whole website?

The famous 80/20 rule applies perfectly here—landing pages and paths represent your business-critical activities. They are the drivers of revenue and business efficiency. They are the "money" pages.

Of course if you plan to redesign your website from a clean slate, you should rethink everything and do so with conversion improvement primarily in mind. This kind of "best-practices" website blueprint approach has consistently resulted in significant performance improvements for SiteTuners' clients. But you will naturally find that only a few pages (or page templates) on the site require special thought, work, and care. These are the ones to focus on—the rest are merely supporting pages.

A Few Precious Moments Online

The following is a story that helps to paint a picture of why it's essential to focus on improving and optimizing landing pages.

Imagine that you are in charge of online marketing for your organization and the launch of its first website.

You have slaved for months to tune and optimize your campaigns. Countless hours and days have passed in a blur. You have created great pay-per-click (PPC) campaigns, bought additional banners and exposure on related websites, optimized your site for organic search engines, set up dedicated Facebook fan pages and Twitter accounts, created a powerful affiliate program with effective incentives, and set up the website analytics needed to track visitor behavior in real time.

You are standing by with a powerful series of e-mail follow-ups that will be sent to prospects or customers who respond to your initial offer or leave their contact information on your site. This approach should significantly increase the lifetime value of the relationship with your website visitor.

You feel pretty confident of the success that your marketing efforts will bring. Your website launches, and you log on to your web analytics tool to check what your visitors are doing. Much to your dismay, the first visitor arrives—and leaves in half a second. The next one lands on your site, clicks another link, and is gone as well. More and more visitors flash by—a virtual flood. Yet only a tiny percentage will take the action that you would like them to take.

Tim's Online Shopping Adventure

I was looking to buy a new camcorder online. First I used the Web to gather information about desirable features. Then I researched appropriate models. After deciding on the one for me, I invested hours of my time making sure that I bought the best possible one. I started looking for a place to buy it by typing the specific camcorder model name into a search engine. I got back a page of search results and began investigating the promising ones.

As I clicked on each link in my mission-oriented "hunter" mode, I looked in vain for intangibles that would cause me to stick around. One site was too cluttered with confusing links and options; another featured obnoxious colors and was plastered with banner ads; the next looked too cheesy and unprofessional. Other websites' failings were subtler: I could not readily tell the depth of their product or brand selection, and could not see at a glance which models were most popular or well received. I gave them a little more of my time and attention, but ultimately abandoned them as well. Click, backtrack, click, backtrack, click, backtrack—and so it went…until I found a company that was just right, and I bought my camcorder from them.

Sound familiar? The fact is that most of the companies that I had briefly visited sold the model that I wanted, had it in stock for quick shipping, and were in a similar price range. So why did one particular company get my money whereas most of the others got just a second of my attention? Helping to unravel this puzzle is what this book is all about. We want to make sure that your company is the one that is experienced as "just right" (or at least the best of the available choices) by more of your website visitors.

It's hard to figure out what went wrong since you only have your website visitors' fleeting attention for a split second. There is a lot that you do not know, including

- Who they are
- How they found you
- What they are thinking or feeling
- Why the vast majority of them leave so soon, without buying or "converting" in some other fashion

Luckily for you (and your job), you aren't the only one to be left in the dark. This type of situation plays out on thousands of new or redesigned websites and landing pages every month. This is because websites are usually built or designed with little thought for the visitor experience, and conversion rate optimization typically takes a back seat both to the visual design of the website and to driving traffic.

All of your hard work comes down to the few precious moments that your visitor spends on your page. During this fleeting interaction, all of your tools of persuasion need to be brought to bear in a powerful yet subtle fashion to achieve the desired result. This book will arm you step by step with all the important tools that you will need.

Your Baby Is Ugly

This book is not simply about learning new skills. It is about changing your relationship to your website and its visitors. Like a parent, you are probably very proud of your creation but you probably can't see it objectively. But let's get one thing straight. It's going to be painful to hear, but it's true.

Your baby is ugly.

Your landing page has significant and fundamental problems that affect its business performance.

Let's clarify. When we say "ugly," we don't just mean that it is lacking in artistic appeal (it may actually be very "pretty"). We are talking about the whole host of gross and subtle elements that contribute to your visitor's suboptimal total experience—often without your knowledge.

You are probably much invested in your role as a competent online marketing professional and are justifiably proud of your skills and experience. Other people in your organization are paying you for this knowledge and expect you to know what you are doing.

But let's take a look at the reality of the situation. Conversion rate optimization is a complicated activity requiring diverse skill sets. You are more than likely not trained in all the important skill sets necessary to become a world-class website optimizer.

Some of these skill sets include

- Usability principles and user-centered design
- Psychology and motivation
- Neuroscience
- Social psychology and persuasion
- Web analytics and statistics
- Direct-response copywriting
- Visual and website design

Even if you are trained and/or have experience in some of these skills, it's the well-rounded and deep *combination* of them all that is likely to produce results.

Please check your ego and your biases at the door. The first step is admitting that you have a problem.

Your Website Visitors: The Real Landing Page Experts

You can (within the limits of ethics and accuracy) represent yourself in any way that you want on the Internet. Your landing page is not written on stone tablets. In fact, it is the most ethereal of objects—a set of data residing on a computer hard disk that is accessible to the whole world. No one is forcing you to use the particular colors, page layout, pictures, sales copy, calls-to-action or headlines that comprise the page now.

> The only things stopping you from creating more compelling landing pages may be a lack of attention and imagination, and an intentional disregard of your intended audience.

The promise of better-performing landing pages is often tempered by a fear of making things worse than they already are. How are you to know in advance what will or won't work better? Yet you are supposed to be the "expert." Shouldn't your landing page already be perfect based on your extensive online marketing experience? What if your design knowledge was exposed as nothing more than subjective posturing and guesswork?

Don't be afraid. You have access to a real expert—in fact, thousands of them. You are interacting with them daily already, but you have mostly ignored their advice to date.

> The real experts on the design of your landing pages are your website visitors.

There is a lot of lip service paid in the profession of marketing to the "voice of the customer," when in reality we often ignore the customer and substitute opinions of people from our own company in their place. No matter how well intentioned, this policy is a big mistake.

Although you may never be able to answer why a *specific* person did or did not respond to your landing page, there are ways to determine what *more* of your website visitors would respond to. In fact, landing page testing can be viewed as a giant online marketing laboratory where your test subjects (your website visitors) voluntarily participate without being asked. Their very actions (or inactions) expose them and allow you to improve your appeal to a similar population of people that subsequently visit your page.

Websites and stand-alone landing pages have three properties that make them ideal as online laboratories. Let's look at each of these in turn:

A High Volume of Traffic With high website traffic volumes, statistical analysis allows you to find verifiably better landing pages and to be confident in your decision. The best landing page version from a valid head-to-head test is a proven winner. Unlike previous nontested designs, they are no longer based solely on subjective opinions. Nor are they the results of popularity contests within your company or chosen according to the highest paid person's opinion (HIPPO). Without enough traffic, you risk making decisions that are not representative enough of your true audience.

Accurate Tracking Tools Web analytics tools support the accurate real-time tracking and recording of every interaction with your website. Each visit is recorded along with a mind-numbing amount of detail. Reports can tell you the source of the visitors, the pages they most visit, their path through your site, the time that they spent lingering over certain content, and whether they were persuaded to act and to return in the future.

Ability to Easily Make Content Changes It can be easy to swap or modify the content that a particular visitor sees on your landing page. The content can be changed to show many variations of the same landing pages and can be customized based on the source of the traffic (referred to as *segmentation*). Different content can also be displayed based on the visitor's behavior on the page or their past history of interactions with your site (referred to as *behavioral targeting*). In nonweb environments, it is expensive or time-consuming to come up with an alternative version or prototype. On the Internet, countless website content variations can be created and managed at minimal cost for a landing page optimization test. The more easily you can make changes to your website, the more flexibility and options you will have at your fingertips when coming up with ideas for improving your landing pages.

Understanding the Bigger Online Marketing Picture

Before we focus on the specifics, let's get oriented and see where landing page optimization fits within the following three key activities of online marketing:

- **Acquisition** Getting people to your website or landing page
- **Conversion** Persuading them to take the desired action(s)
- **Retention** Deepening the relationship with your website visitors and increasing their lifetime value

Each step feeds into the next. The efficiency of each online marketing activity can be viewed as a set of funnels like the one in Figure 1.1.

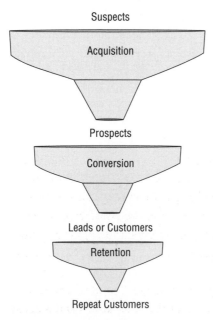

Suspects

Acquisition

Prospects

Conversion

Leads or Customers

Retention

Repeat Customers

Figure 1.1 The activity funnel

Inefficient acquisition activities will limit the traffic to your site. A confusing landing page with a low conversion rate will restrict the number of leads or customers. Uncoordinated retention follow-up will fail to extract added value from your current prospects or clients. Ideally, you would like each step to have the highest possible yield.

Conversion Is the Weak Link

In the marketing world, a lot of time and resources are spent in acquiring traffic from sources that are thought to provide more high-converting visitors. You buy media, track PPC campaigns, drive organic traffic via search engine optimization (SEO), and implement web analytics tools to properly track all channels. Dedicated in-house or agency staff craft keyword lists, write ad copy, and manage keyword bidding to achieve the proper profitability, cost per action (CPA), and return on investment (ROI). Copywriters adjust our sales copy to improve clickthrough rates (CTRs). Every aspect of performance can be scrutinized under a microscope.

Once someone converts, extensive retention e-mail campaigns are set in motion to persuade visitors to deepen their level of engagement. You worry about every single word in your e-mails as you test headlines and offers. You analyze bounce rates, open rates, and unsubscribe rates with almost religious fervor in order to extract the last penny of revenue and profit possible over the lifetime of your interaction with someone.

But you have almost completely ignored your website and landing page and how well they are converting visitors for the site's goals. Figure 1.2 perfectly illustrates the common and sad state of affairs.

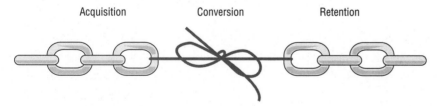

Acquisition   Conversion   Retention

Figure 1.2 The weakest link

What's wrong with this picture?

Sure, you occasionally do minor facelifts or even complete redesigns of your sites. But these changes are rarely tested and are simply assumed to improve the situation. They are just a cost of "doing business." And even though you may spend obscene amounts of money to buy traffic, the effort that you devote to the landing pages to which it is sent is negligible. A couple of hours of graphic designer and copywriter time are often all that the landing page merits. After a cursory review by the higher-ups, the landing page goes live.

Worse yet, you assume that the quality of the landing page cannot be changed, so you do not even look to it for improvements. You turn all the other knobs and dials at your disposal and continue to neglect the biggest profit driver under your control—the conversion efficiency of the landing page. And this is costing a lot of money in the form of missed opportunity. Double- or triple-digit conversion rate gains are routinely realized by conversion consultants and in-house optimization teams. Yet there is still a widespread perception among online marketers that their landing pages are already solid and can't be improved significantly.

 Your website and landing page conversion rates have been neglected for much too long—costing you a lot of money.

Because of the large amounts of money spent on acquisition and retention, sophisticated systems have been created to maximize the ROI of these activities. When you neglect the langing page, the money you spend on acquisition and retention is largely wasted, flushed down the proverbial toilet. Many companies are now beginning to understand that website and landing page conversion can have a dramatic impact on online marketing program profits. That's where the new battleground is in the coming years. As management guru Peter Drucker stated, finding keys to competitive advantage can be the difference between a mediocre company and an industry leader. Don't forget also that if you are one of the few in your industry to understand this weak link and fully optimize it, your company, your boss, and ultimately your career will certainly benefit.

Acquisition

Acquisition activities focus on generating traffic to your website or landing page. The goal is to create an awareness of your company or products and enough interest for your target audience to visit your site.

Web marketing experts use a variety of methods to drive traffic. They can be broadly grouped into online and offline methods, although there is often some overlap and mutual reinforcement between the two.

Online Acquisition Methods

Web marketers typically use the following *online* methods for driving traffic:

Search Engine Optimization (SEO) The process of making your website pages appear near the top in unpaid search engine results for important keywords relevant to your business is known as *search engine optimization*, or *SEO*. People using search engines show focus and a specific intention to act, so search engine traffic often has a high onsite conversion rate.

Pay-Per-Click (PPC) Pay-per-click (PPC) advertising continues to be a popular way to get seen on search engine results pages (SERPs) and content networks. Short paid advertisements appear side by side with traditional SEO results, with the highest bidder usually getting the top (most visible) spots on the page. While optimized PPC campaigns often convert at a high rate, competition for many commercial keywords may be high and result in increasing prices.

Banner, Text, and Rich Media Ads Banner ads, which were once the most common form of online ad, have seen a steady decline in CTRs due to banner blindness—the increasing tendency for site visitors to ignore these types of ads. Simple banners have evolved to rich media ads, including interactive, video, peel-back (like Figure 1.3), interstitial, and other ad types that often cost more but often perform better.

Figure 1.3 Example of a peel-back ad

Social Networking Sites Social networking sites allow people to connect in communities of shared interest. Within them, individuals and businesses can engage in powerful and often unguarded two-way conversations with other community members. In addition, many social networks allow a presence for companies and organizations (see the Conversion conference "Fan" page on Facebook in Figure 1.4) and offer segmented advertising opportunities based on the rich profile information of people on the network. Because of these features, social networks can often become a low-cost source of highly targeted, well-converting traffic.

Affiliates Affiliate programs allow a company to pay only on a success basis if someone refers traffic to its landing page. Traditional advertising makes you pay for exposure only (in the form of payment for number of page views that contain your ad or a clickthrough to your site).

The next logical step is to pay for some well-defined success metric (such as a free-trial sign-up or an actual purchase). Many companies have well-established affiliate programs through which performance-based partners direct traffic to the site and are credited on a commission basis if the desired conversion action takes place.

Figure 1.4 Conversion Conference fan page on Facebook

If affiliate programs are set up properly, they can help send targeted and qualified traffic to a landing page. If the activity of the affiliates is unregulated, the resulting traffic can often be of poor quality and experience significant and sudden changes in volume and composition.

In-House E-mail Lists An "in-house" mailing list is one that your company has collected over time in the normal course of its marketing activities. Its quality varies based on the exact activities used to collect the e-mail addresses (ranging from dropping cards in a fishbowl at a tradeshow booth, to free webinar registration, or contact request form-fills on your website).

If used properly, in-house mailing lists gathered from your own website can become an asset that grows in value over time. In-house mailing lists are at the core of retention activities and will be discussed in the "Retention" section later in this chapter.

Third-Party E-mail Lists Third-party lists are ones that you rent for the purpose of sending recipients information about your products or services. Typically the people on the list have no actual relationship to your company and did not specifically request any kind of communication from you.

Usually you do not have direct access to the e-mails on the list—you simply have the right to "drop" or e-mail to the list on a one-time or recurring basis. Often the list owner can filter the list based on additional demographic information associated with each e-mail address in order to more effectively target your intended audience.

The quality and targeting of third-party lists vary widely. Some are clearly low quality and will be perceived as spam by recipients. Others can provide a good overlap with your intended audience, as long as repeated mailing to the same list doesn't lead to burn-out and *list fatigue* (lower response rates over time).

Blogs The number of blogs continues to explode. Blogs exist on an uncountable range of topics and are often focused on deep subject matter coverage of very narrow niches. Once a blog author has a reputation as an expert, resulting exposure from a blog post may result in highly engaged traffic from their reader base. The traffic resulting from a blog post is usually spiky in nature. The vast majority of it will come within hours of the blog post, and a long tail of traffic will dribble in over time as others read the post in the archives section of the blog or discover it in search engines.

Collaborative Authoring and User-Generated Content Sites Certain websites are built for collaboration. Anyone can add content to them in the form of news and discussion forums, product reviews on e-commerce sites, or contributions on reference topics. Often there are communities of dedicated volunteers who police the behavior of other members to make sure they are contributing useful content and following official and informal community guidelines.

Some examples include Yelp's city guides (with restaurant reviews from their readers), Wikipedia (a collaborative encyclopedia completely written by its members), and eBay (the biggest online auction site where your reputation as a seller depends on the reviews of past purchasers). Links in these sorts of content entries can direct visitors to your website or landing page.

Video and Interactive Game Content This content type grew with the increased adoption of high-speed Internet connections. Many video clips now include promotional ties. As video production becomes less expensive, more small companies create rich media and larger companies create YouTube channels, ads, and contests. Many companies are also driving traffic by embedding links in online games and quizzes.

Offline Acquisitions Methods

People do not live strictly in the online realm. They have online experiences mixed with exposure to your brand in the physical world. The offline methods that you use to drive traffic will lead to a web visitor directly typing your URL into a browser. It is difficult to accurately credit the traffic coming from offline sources (with the exceptions noted in the following list). A single visitor may be driven to your site from multiple sources (both online and offline) and may have been "touched" (interacted with your content or at least noticed it) multiple times before arriving on your site.

Common effective *offline* tactics include the following:

Brand Awareness A direct traffic referral means that the person is specifically aware of and looking for your company, often due to its strength in an industry sector or category. Although not strictly an offline method, brand awareness traffic is usually achieved as a result of repeat exposure to your brand in diverse settings, including offline.

TV, Radio, Print, and Outdoor Advertising Traditional broadcast media are trying to adjust to the accountability inherent in the online marketing channels and become more trackable. Many of these broadcast ads specify a campaign-specific URL as one of the possible response mechanisms (for example, a TV campaign might direct viewers to http://*YourCompany*.com/tv). This is not foolproof, because many people may still drop the last part of the URL and simply type in the company name.

Public Relations and Media Coverage Various public relations activities can result in mentions of your company in print and broadcast media. Typically your site will experience a spike of coverage-related traffic after such events.

Industry Tradeshows and Events An opportunity to speak and exhibit in front of a targeted audience can generate highly targeted traffic. Many key influencers, analysts, and decision makers also attend or network at topical conferences.

Client Referrals Current and past clients can be excellent sources of additional traffic. If a company has a specific incentive program to reward existing and past clients for referrals, the mechanism for completing the referral transaction is done via the Web.

Direct Marketing and Catalogs Direct response marketing (from TV infomercials, to mailers and printed catalogs) has a long history of trackable success. Many of the conversion points for traditional marketing have moved online. This is accomplished either through specifying dedicated landing page URLs or by using "promo code" discounts that must be entered during online checkout.

The resulting mix of offline traffic hits a website at a number of places. Some visitors will arrive on your homepage, whereas others may land deep within your site, or even on specially designed single-purpose landing pages that are not connected to your main website at all.

Conversion

Since conversion is the main topic of this book, let's start with some definitions.

As explained earlier, a *landing page* is the point at which an Internet visitor lands on your website and is often the critical first point of contact. Landing pages can be stand-alone with no connection to your main website. They can also be part of a specialized microsite that is focused on a particular audience and desired outcome. The landing page can also be a specific page somewhere on your main company website.

A conversion happens when a visitor to your landing page takes a desired *conversion action* that has a measurable value to your business. The conversion action must be defined ahead of time, it must be trackable, and its business value must be clear (either directly calculated or estimated based on historical numbers).

The desired action can be a purchase, a download, a completed web form (a lead), or even a simple clickthrough to another page on your website. Conversions can also be measured by having someone interact with a particular feature of your site (such as taking a product demo tour, viewing a video, or submitting a product review). A conversion can also be considered in more subtle brand-interaction terms, such as reaching a certain threshold of page views per visit, repeat visits, return frequency, time spent on your site, or a high site rating response from survey tools.

Websites often have more than just one conversion action but usually will have a few main *macro conversions* that are the most important (such as a sale, free trial sign-up, or lead form completion).

Websites will also often have additional intermediate *micro conversion* points on the way to the macro conversions (such as a clickthrough to another important page, a download of informational materials, adding an item to a shopping cart in an e-commerce catalog, or the completion of a single page in a multistep process).

The basic definition of *conversion rate* is the percentage of visitors to your website or landing page who take a desired action, and it is usually calculated by dividing the number of conversions by the number of unique visits that occur during the same timeframe, as follows:

$$\text{Conversion rate} = \text{Number of conversions} \div \text{Unique visitors}$$

The full catalog of possible conversion actions is covered in detail in Chapter 2, "Understanding Your Landing Pages." You may also find Chapter 14, "Developing Your Action Plan," helpful in terms of calculating the economic value of your conversion actions and building the business case for your projects.

Conversion rates vary widely across different industries and even between competitors in the same industry. Often conversion rates can even vary significantly between different sources or segments of your traffic. For example, targeted PPC traffic sources and repeat visits will often convert higher than other segments.

Retention

Retention is the third key online marketing activity, and it is closely tied to conversion. Once someone has become aware of your company and made initial contact, you must deepen your relationship with them to extract any future value. In *Permission Marketing: Turning Strangers into Friends and Friends into Customers* (Simon &

Schuster, 1999), author Seth Godin accurately lays out the changing balance of power between consumers and companies. Consumers are in almost total control and are increasingly immune to traditional advertising assaults. They tune out most interruptions and focus only on what is important to them. If they notice you, they will give you limited "permission" to interact.

Retention programs should seek to build on the initial permission with anticipated, personal, and relevant ongoing communications. Over time, as you earn the consumer's trust and continue to provide value, you are granted higher levels of confidence.

Retention programs start immediately after the initial conversion action on your site has been taken. This initial action may have been an e-mail sign-up for your newsletter or a whitepaper download. It will often not be the actual initial purchase of your products or services. But you can leverage the right to contact the person by educating them via a set of automated e-mails and leading them closer to the ultimate desired action.

The basis for all retention programs is the ability for the user to receive information from your company on an ongoing basis. So the minimum requirement is that they have given you their e-mail address or phone number, or included you in their blog or news feed reader (also known as an RSS feed). Let's take a look at these sorts of communication channels:

E-mail E-mail is probably the most widely used of all retention media. Sophisticated e-mail campaigns can be set up to touch specific recipients with a preprogrammed sequence of messages and have recently proven successful in retaining and converting existing website visitors.

Automated e-mail content can be customized and modified based on interactions with previous e-mails or even webpages themselves. The key is to not lose your hard-earned subscribers' trust with unrelated offers or overly heavy sales pitches.

Newsletters Newsletters are a close cousin to and a specific use of e-mail retention marketing. Their main goals are to educate a prospect and offer news regarding promotions and new features, ultimately aimed at enabling the reader to make an informed buying decision at some point. Their editorial tone is generally neutral, and calls-to-action subtly nudge the reader to come back to the website and take the next step in the buying process.

Blogs and News Feeds The goal of news feeds is to get a reader to subscribe to and automatically receive updates from a blog or an accredited news source or publication. Unlike e-mail, newsletters, or news feeds, blogs allow for two-way interaction between the company and an audience. Often the real value of a solid blog is in the comment threads and discussions among its readers. This is one of the major reasons for a recent major shift toward public company blogs.

Rewards and Loyalty Various "points" programs give people incentives to act, such as frequent-flyer miles or "every fifth car wash is free." Online tracking allows retention marketers to reward granular events such as responding to e-mail promotions, participating in surveys, or referring others. All of these rewards are designed to get a user to engage and convert later for other goals that are more valuable to the company.

Retention marketing is critical to an online company's profitability. Effective programs can have a multiplier effect on revenues by increasing lifetime value of the client relationship. You will also typically have much higher profit margins with repeat customers because the incremental cost of marketing to them is minimal.

The Myth of Perfect Conversion

Don't make the mistake of assuming that every visitor is a potential prospect that will become a repeat, long-term buyer of your goods or services. That would be a delusion. The mythical 100 percent conversion rate simply does not exist.

There are three types of visitors to your website:

1. Noes—Those who *won't ever* take the desired action
2. Yesses—Those who *will always* take the desired action
3. Maybes—Those who *may* take the desired action

You should completely ignore the first two and concentrate on the last group. Let's examine this concept more closely.

Some visitors to your website are not prepared to take action. They may be unable to afford what you sell. They may work for your rival and are merely checking the competition. Or they may have been simply surfing the Web and thought that it was worth a second of their time to look at your landing page—kicking your website's tires, so to speak. There are countless reasons why someone will not take the desired action. The important realization is that there is *nothing that you can do to influence them to act*. For most landing pages, this group is by far the largest of the three.

There is also a group of visitors who will always take the desired action. There is ample evidence for this. People will put up with maddeningly difficult registration or checkout processes. They will seek out links and information that are buried deep within websites. In general, they will display a degree of tenacity that is staggering.

Why do they do this? Some are already sold on what you are offering due to outside influences. Still others have searched far and wide and have been able to find only your company as a viable answer to their immediate and burning needs. Others are just tired of looking further and have settled on your company as the best alternative that they have seen thus far. Regardless, short of a broken website, nothing will deter these people from taking the desired action on your landing page. The main point is that *these people do not need any convincing by you*.

The final group of undecideds contains a wide variety of people. Some of them are almost there—a small improvement in your landing page or website might get them over the hump and result in the desired action. Others may need significant additional persuasion and hand-holding in order to come around. Figure 1.5 shows the range of possible visitor dispositions toward the desired conversion action.

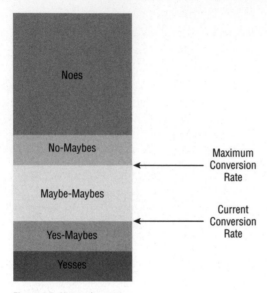

Figure 1.5 Visitor dispositions

Unless your website is truly ineffectual, you are already converting some of the maybes. This segment of "yes-maybes," along with your yesses, makes up your current conversion rate. However, even with the best landing page you will not be able to convert all the people in this group at once—they have contradictory needs. Landing page changes that sway a particular person might repel another. So at best, you can hope to convert only a portion of the undecideds. The remainder (the "no-maybes") will forever be out of your reach. So the maximum conversion rate improvement that is possible for your business is limited to capturing the rest of the "maybe-maybes" that are still up for grabs.

Of course, it is impossible to precisely measure or even estimate the sizes of these segments for a particular landing page or website. But you should understand that your actual conversion rate "ceiling" is well below 100 percent.

The next chapter defines different landing page types and discusses conversion goals in detail.

Understanding Your Landing Pages

Begin with the end in mind.

—STEPHEN R. COVEY, author of *The Seven Habits of Highly Effective People*

What is the purpose of your landing page?

This seems like a simple question. But the vast majority of us cannot answer it in a simple and cogent sentence.

Most of your websites and landing pages have become overgrown like a dense jungle. They have no clear purpose or unique value proposition and are instead a grab-bag of unrelated tidbits—each one hoping to compete for visitors' attention.

Let's take a close look at what your landing pages are and what they ought to be.

CHAPTER CONTENTS

Landing Page Types
What Parts of Your Site Are Mission Critical?
What Is Your Business Model?
The Types of Conversion Actions

Landing Page Types

The landing page is the first webpage that a visitor lands on as a result of your traffic acquisition efforts.

First, it's important to understand the types of landing pages that exist and the likely traffic sources for each:

Main Site Landing Page Main site landing pages are the most common type of landing page and are part of your main website. For example, such a landing page might be the homepage of your corporate website, a top organic search entry page, or a blog article page. The specific landing page might also be buried several layers deep within your site organization (for example, a product detail page in an online catalog).

Often the most important landing page on your website is the homepage, and it receives a combination of traffic. The mix includes direct-type-in (in other words, people who simply remember your company URL), bookmarks (from returning visitors who want to easily access your site again), social networking (such as links from your Facebook fan page or LinkedIn company page), or a variety of offline campaigns. Most traffic from offline sources is likely to end up on your homepage for the simple reason that visitors will not bother to type in a long and convoluted URL. Even if you give them a specific landing page, many visitors will shorten it and drop everything except your top-level domain name.

It's important to understand how search engine optimization (SEO) impacts the distribution of landing pages that you have on your main site. Let's use the case of an online shoe store to illustrate the likely location of your landing pages based on the corresponding keywords:

- "shoes"—Website homepage
- "women's shoes"—Women's shoes category page
- "hiking boots"—Hiking boots category page
- "reebok sneakers"—Reebok brand page
- "converse allstar"—Product detail page for a particular shoe model

As you can see, the popularity and number of SEO keywords for which your website ranks well will determine the distribution of traffic hitting your main site.

Microsite Landing Page Landing pages can be part of a *microsite* specifically designed for a single audience, marketing campaign, or purpose. This can be an adapted, focused, and smaller version of your website, or it can be a third-party website (such as the increasingly more common Facebook fan page or Twitter profile page).

A microsite often has one main call-to-action (such as a purchase or information request). All of the information on the site is designed to funnel the visitor back to this desired conversion action (which occurs either within the microsite or back on the main related website).

A microsite usually contains a few pages of supporting information that allow a visitor to make an educated decision about the topic in question, request further information, or buy something. Such information includes a detailed description of your product or service, buying guides or wizards, downloadable whitepapers, comparisons to similar products or services, case studies, testimonials, interactive communities full of product fans, and other validation. Such microsites represent a more advanced online marketing approach, and while they often have higher conversion rates, they are still far less common than landing pages on main sites.

Often, microsite landing pages are driven to by pay-per-click (PPC) or e-mail newsletters, because the copy of the ad can be created to exactly match the main purpose and conversion goal of the microsite. Some marketers even hide these microsites from search engines so that they do not compete with their main website's organic search rankings or create duplicate content issues that can have unpredictable effects on your main site's SEO efforts.

Stand-alone Landing Page Some landing pages are specifically designed for a particular marketing campaign and often have the highest level of conversion rates. Such pages usually have information related only to the offer or conversion action that you would like your visitors to take. They are even more focused than microsites and are devoid of any navigation links leading back to the main company website. Their lifespan is often short (to match the length of a specific promotional offer or online campaign that is driving traffic to the page).

Usually, there is a clear, single call-to-action, which is great for users because it doesn't confuse them or overwhelm them with choices. If the desired action is not taken, stand-alone landing pages may employ an exit pop-up window with a secondary desired action, or a repeat of the original call-to-action.

Single products or services are ideal for stand-alone landing pages. Many products have been successfully sold via the online equivalent of a direct-mail sales letter.

Stand-alone pages often do not rank well in search engines, because they typically contain duplicate content. Therefore, targeted paid advertising is usually the main way of attracting traffic to them.

Now that you know what the major types of landing pages are, let's focus on the most important types of pages on your website that will lead you to true optimization success.

What Parts of Your Site Are Mission Critical?

Mission-critical activities on your sites can easily be identified. All you have to do is ask yourself the following question:

 Would your business's performance grind to a halt if the content in question was removed from your website?

You must be very sober and ruthless in answering. Very little of the content on your site meets this definition. For the most part, only activities that drive business revenues and sales fall into this category. But before we show you some examples of less-critical pages, let's discuss the mission-critical parts—in essence, the 80/20 part of your website that you should be focusing on the most.

Here are examples of the most mission-critical parts of your website and the least mission-critical pages. Some of these mission-critical pages will be revisited in Chapter 8, "Best Practices for Common Situations," for specific optimization best practices.

Homepage

The homepages of main sites or microsites are of very high importance, because they are like the cover of a book—most visitors will judge (usually within a few seconds) the contents of the site by scanning just the homepage. And if it doesn't instantly convey what they are looking for or the site's unique value proposition (think "what's in it" for the visitor), or it's just not a good visitor experience, chances are high that the visitor will leave your site and never return.

Another reason that homepages are mission critical is because they get a tremendous amount of exposure in comparison to other pages—they are typically the most visited single page across the whole website and often represent the main entry page for repeat visits. Therefore, significant time should be spent on optimizing your homepage to gain the best user experience and highest conversion rate.

In terms of traffic, the most typical source of traffic to homepages is through bookmark or direct-typed traffic, usually from a repeat visitor. Another source of traffic is sometimes from an offline acquisition campaign such as a TV or magazine ad. See Figure 2.1 for an example of Amazon's homepage.

Top Organic Search Entry Pages

Search engines are usually going to be one of the top sources of traffic to your main website (and sometimes to microsites). Therefore, the pages that are visited the most from search engines are particularly important to understand, because they will have a high impact on the conversation rate and success of your website. In fact, the traffic from your top organic search entry pages often adds up to more traffic than your homepage gets.

Figure 2.1 Amazon.com homepage

The best way to find these top-performing organic search entry pages is to log into your web analytics tool, look at your top 10 keywords, and see which page each of them is arriving at. Some of the entries on the top 10 keyword list may indeed surprise you. Quite often there will be pages among your top organic entry pages that you don't expect, and you are probably losing conversions by not fully optimizing them.

Category Pages

Category pages are typically high-level aggregate pages and are predominantly found on main websites only. They're usually one or two levels deeper than your homepage— for example, the credit cards category page on a large bank website.

Category pages are often visited as a result of using the website's main navigation or by arriving from organic search engine results. These category pages are important to understand and optimize, because they are often used by visitors as a way of funneling and browsing the contents of a website. If visitors can't find the information they are looking for on these pages, they are more than likely going to end up leaving and visiting a competitor's site instead. Figure 2.2 shows an example of a category page from the website of Canon's Canadian online store.

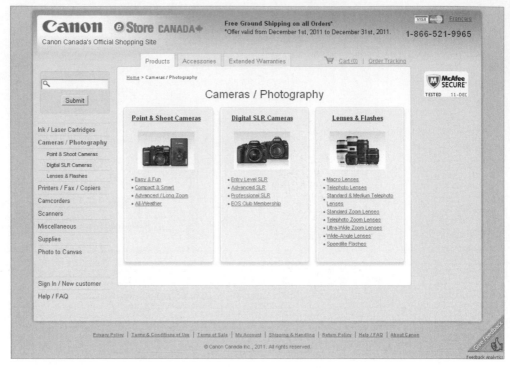

Figure 2.2 Canon Canada camera category page

Product and Information Pages

One of the key roles your website plays is to inform and engage its visitors. The pages that are the most important in your visitors' decision-making process are your product and information pages, and the performance of these pages often makes the difference between a dissatisfied visitor and an engaged and converted visitor. These product and information pages play a key role on main websites and microsites and often form the basis of stand-alone webpages.

These pages need to convey just enough information without overwhelming the visitor and offer an easy and simple way for them to continue in the decision-making process—for example, by adding a product to the cart or filling in a form for further information.

One of the common sources of direct traffic to product and information pages is via PPC or SEO. A Juicy Couture product detail page for a particular item is shown in Figure 2.3.

These pages are usually integral to the final stages of conversion, so optimizing them can have a significant impact on your conversion rates.

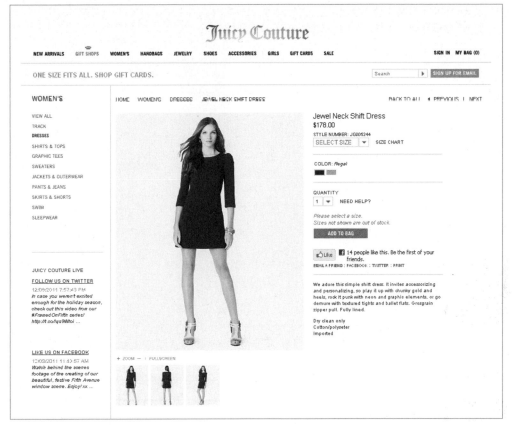

Figure 2.3 Juicy Couture product detail page

Checkout and Sign-up Pages

If you have a website that has conversion goals for lead generation or purchases, it's vital to examine and optimize the pages that visitors use to check out or complete a form. If these checkout or sign-up flow pages aren't well optimized, the rest of your visitor's experience up to that point, no matter how great, will have been wasted.

These types of pages can be found on all types of websites (including main websites, microsites, and stand-alone pages) and often vary in design across different websites. Some sites use single-page checkout or sign-up pages, whereas others use a multiple-page approach. Figure 2.4 shows a single-page version of the SEOmoz free trial signup. Luckily, there are plenty of ways to optimize these very important pages, and we will cover this in detail in Chapter 8.

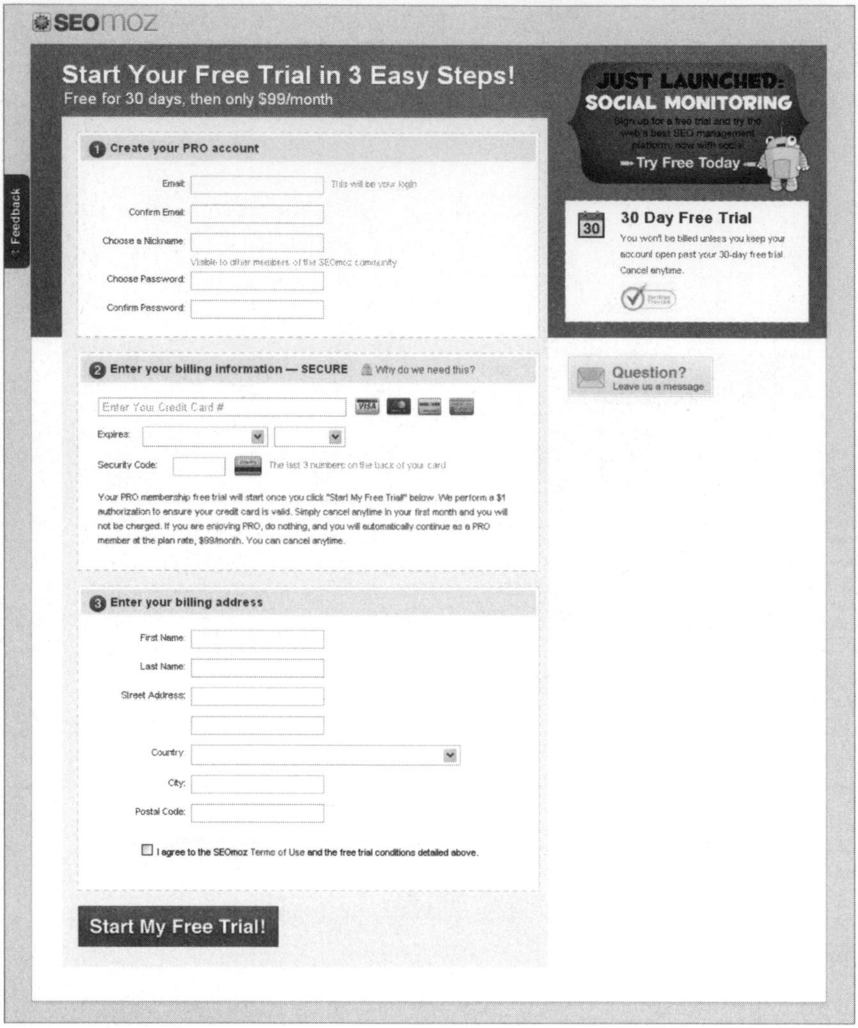

Figure 2.4 SEOmoz free trial signup

Internal Site Search Results Pages

After users first arrive at your website, if they can't find what they are looking for by scanning your homepage and high-level category pages, they usually give it one last shot before leaving your website. They do this by typing a keyword or phrase that they are looking for into your internal site search engine (usually found in the top right of your site).

Search users often look for ways to filter the search results by type, price, best-selling, top-rating, or best reviews. Therefore, to improve the chances of a successful search, you should implement this type of advanced search functionality (see the left column of the Helmet City search results page in Figure 2.5).

Figure 2.5 Helmet City search results page

While not as directly influential on the conversion rate, it's still important to optimize your search results pages if you have a large online catalog, since it serves as a gateway to finding product detail pages.

Not Mission-Critical Pages

Now let's contrast the previous page types against some examples of typical site content that is *not* usually mission critical:

- Investor relations
- Company mission statement and history
- Open job listings
- Management bios

Counter-examples can probably be found for each of these (such as job listings for a recruiting company or management bios for a professional services firm), but as a rule of thumb, supporting company information is not mission critical.

All other content on the site is at best irrelevant, or at worst a distraction from the mission-critical parts. As you will see later in this book, this deadwood content should be eliminated, or at least reduced in scope and emphasis as much as possible in order to streamline the important parts of your landing pages.

What you should be left with are the mission-critical parts that you will test and tune to improve conversion rates.

What Is Your Business Model?

Conversion actions are measurable events on your landing pages that move a visitor toward the mission-critical activities and business goals that you have identified.

Conversion actions will often vary by website type. By recognizing the under-lying business model behind your site, you can focus on optimizing the correct elements. Here are some common types of sites along with their main conversion actions:

E-commerce Websites Online stores are a common type of website and usually have conversion actions related to product purchase or download.

Conversion rates for e-commerce sites can be measured by looking for the percentage completion rate of visitors who start and finish the checkout process. Average conversion rates for most e-commerce websites are typically low—usually around 1–2 percent—due to the high commitment level needed from the visitor. Highly optimized sites can reach the 15–25 percent conversion rate range.

Lead-Generation Websites This type of website usually exists to promote some kind of service, with the main goal being to capture the visitor's e-mail address and other contact details (such as phone number) via online forms in order to complete a sale in the future. Sometimes lead generation also occurs on e-commerce sites that sell particularly expensive products or services and cannot "close" the sale on the initial visitor without additional nurturing of the relationship with the visitor over time. The visitor may need additional information, and personal persuasion may be required at some future point for the ultimate sale to be completed. Instead of getting the visitor to buy directly, the goal is to initiate a dialogue with the prospect.

Conversion rates for lead-generation sites are usually calculated based on the percentage of visitors who begin and complete the lead generation form or process. Average conversion rates are often higher for lead-generation websites since the commitment required (such as providing an e-mail address) is a lot lower than for an e-commerce purchase.

Media and Publishing Websites Media- and publishing-related websites are becom-ing increasingly common. These websites often don't have direct financial conversion actions and are centered more on improving engagement in order to increase advertis-ing revenue. Usually there is a mixture of several conversion goals that must be traded off against each other to maximize value. These can include increasing page views per visitor (and therefore increasing the on-page ads seen), ad clickthrough rate (CTR), visitor frequency, or videos viewed (often associated with companion video ads). Some of these websites also have related premium membership or magazine subscription signups, which represent more tangible conversion actions.

The conversion goal is to increase the average revenue per visitor based on a complicated weighted set of actions (such as clicks on content and ads, page views, and return visit frequency).

Support Websites This type of website is relatively rare, but as companies are becoming increasingly customer-centric, they are using support websites as a way of saving costs and creating efficiencies over traditional support media such as telephone call centers. The main conversion action for a support website seeks to drive visitors to resolve their issues online. Often the goal is to decrease the number of calls to the more expensive, toll-free support number.

Conversion rates are typically measured by the proportion of visitors who are successfully using self-service help tools or online support tickets (with the goal of maximizing self-service resolution of problems online).

Blog Websites Over the past several years, blogs have become more popular, not just for personal use but for corporate use as well. These types of websites are often hybrids of the previously described websites and often have few tangible conversion action points. Many blogs rely on advertising revenue or lead generation as their main conversion goals. Others rely on engagement-related conversion goals such as the number of comments per article and number of times each blog post is shared via social media, as well as the return frequency or number of people subscribed to the blog feed.

Brand-Related Websites Many larger companies have websites solely to support and deepen their brand engagement. These websites will often have few traditional conversion actions and usually rely on providing product education, achieving visitor engagement, or convincing people to share the brand's content on social networks such as Facebook or Twitter. Another common goal of brand websites is to get visitors to print out coupons that they can use in stores.

Social Community Websites Community websites exist to gather like-minded online users together around a particular common topic or interest, where they can meet fellow fans and colleagues to collaborate, discuss, and share content. These online communities can be intricate and form whole stand-alone websites, or be as simple as a Facebook fan page.

Common goals of these websites are to generate as many members as possible and a high level of repeat visitation, usually for the purpose of generating more advertising-related conversions (seeing and clicking on related ads). The success of these networks also depends on the propensity of members to contribute user-generated content of various types. This can include posting of original content (such as images or videos), commenting, rating and reviewing, or connecting with other members.

Review and Ranking Websites Thanks to the Internet, consumers are now armed with a greater knowledge of product and service information than ever before. As a result, many websites have been set up solely to organize information to help visitors make decisions regarding which products, services, or establishments to use. Examples include Yelp (restaurants, bars, and other local establishments), and Angie's List (home contractors and a range of personal services). The goal of these sites is to increase the number of vendors or establishments reviewed and rated, as well as to attract the number of free and paid members.

Auction and Bidding Websites Visitors to these websites bid for new or used items from individual sellers or from companies that also retail products directly. Conversion goals are related to increasing the number of items listed and the number of active members who are selling or buying.

Educational and Certification Websites These websites are set up with the purpose of teaching users about specific subjects, and often include some functionality related to testing or grading. Users first have to read relevant learning materials and then complete different sections or pass quizzes within a certain timeframe in order to complete their online education. These sites can be purely for first-time certification or degrees, or they can be for professional development or continuing education credits required to maintain membership in certain organizations. Conversion actions are measured by the percentage of visitors who sign up for online training, as well as by the completion rates of various courses or modules.

You'll learn how to optimize these types of websites in subsequent chapters, but for now let's take a closer look at the various types of conversion actions and how they are measured.

The Types of Conversion Actions

The key criteria for defining conversion actions is that they be measurable and have a clear value. (See Chapter 14, "Developing Your Action Plan," for details on how to calculate and estimate this value.)

Here are some examples of conversion actions along with their measurement and efficiency metrics:

Advertising This is usually the main conversion action of media and publishing sites such as ESPN.com or LAtimes.com. It involves the strategic placement of various advertisements on the website, such as banners, text ads, rich media ads (like peel-backs and video ads), and sponsored links within content.

Measuring advertising effectiveness usually involves a weighted mix and a variety of optimization criteria, depending on the business model of the site. This typically entails tracking the number of times that an ad was seen (based on the number of ad impressions and the average number of page views per user visit), the ad's CTR percentage, the size of the website audience, and the frequency and likelihood of return visits (which strongly influences the lifetime value of a visitor).

Research Some websites have conversion actions that require a lot of up-front information gathering. They provide resources and online guides to fully explain their products and services. If the education of visitors is your primary goal, the key metrics are the time spent on your educational pages and the number of page views. Common conversion actions include downloading guides and/or background information.

Downloads and Printouts Some websites want visitors to take away free content without having to leave behind any personal information. Visitors may be able to download and print (where applicable) any number of items from your site: whitepapers, coupons for offline use, samples, or computer software. The download or printout rate of the desired content is the best measure of efficiency.

Form-Fill Rate One of the most common conversion goals involves gathering data about the visitor, either for lead-capture or purchase purposes. These contact details are then used to follow up with the visitor (usually by e-mail) to try to influence future conversion actions. This can range from a single-input-field form with a minimum of data (such as an e-mail address for an online newsletter), to full disclosure of detailed personal information (such as a lengthy online application for a mortgage loan).

The form-fill rate is used to measure the efficiency of this process. The key influencers in this rate are the complexity, ordering, and number of fields in the process, sensitivity of information requested, as well as the staging and number of pages that the process spans.

A high form-fill rate is usually a key determinant of website success.

Commenting, Ratings, and User-Generated Content A great way to increase the success of a website is to allow contributions from the site's visitors, through commenting on, rating, or reviewing information on the site. Often, the informational content on the site is also created by visitors (via posting articles and videos, or by creating online avatars and characters).

This conversion action can be in the form of submitting product ratings and reviews on e-commerce websites or comments on blog posts, and can even form the basis of entire websites like Yelp.com or ezinearticles.com. Common ways of measuring the success of these conversion actions include average comments per post, average reviews per product, or percentage of visitors who engage in these activities.

Account Creation A key way to get visitors to engage and return to your site is to encourage them to create a profile, membership, or account. Profiles and membership are usually public on websites and allow visitors to interact with other registered members on your website.

The rapid growth in accounts is often viewed as proof of a website's success, as well as a reason for others to join.

Subscriptions Another type of conversion action is getting visitors to subscribe to a service or product. This can be in the form of paid subscriptions, free subscriptions, or *freemium* subscriptions (where the user can pay to upgrade from the free basic or limited level to get more features or content).

Subscriptions are found on many different types of websites, including photo-sharing websites (like flickr.com), e-mail services (like yahoo.com), online pharmacies (like drugstore.com), and premium media services (like the online *Wall Street Journal*). These websites are becoming more popular with the decline of traditional advertising revenue.

Purchase E-commerce purchase measurement seems simple at first—all you need to do is to count the number of sales. This is fine if you sell a single product. However, if you sell an array of products at different prices, you must also take the purchase amount (average order value) into account and optimize revenue per visitor. Often even this is not enough. Since some products have very different profit margins, you should be calculating your profit (also known as the gross margin contribution) per visitor. This strategy will allow you to make the correct decisions when balancing low-margin "loss leader" products versus the rest of your product line.

In reality, the repeat purchase rate often enters the picture and you have to estimate the value of this future revenue stream (based on historical data) and add it to the actual purchase amount.

Multiple Conversion Actions

The situation is often more complicated when multiple conversion actions are involved. For example, your site may sell a service, offer a free trial, and have a sign-up form for a free newsletter (which may eventually lead to future sales). These three conversion actions are all appropriate and roughly correspond to a visitor's position in the buying cycle. It is important to track and measure each of them. By assigning a financial value to each action, you can see if your overall value (or anticipated revenue) per visitor increases.

Sometimes visitors must make a mutually exclusive choice. For example, they may choose to fill out your information request form, start an online chat session with a customer support representative, or call your toll-free number. All three advance your agenda and allow visitors to select the most appropriate response medium for them. Each of these should also be assigned a specific financial value. That way, you can decide which page designs produce an increase in overall value per visitor.

Depending on your business model, the following conversion actions need to be considered:

- **E-commerce** Purchase or subscription, form-fill, review or rating, social media sharing

- **Lead Generation** Form fill, clickthrough to an important page, social media sharing
- **Media or Publishing** Advertising revenue per visitor, clickthrough (page view), comment or other user-generated content, social media sharing
- **Customer Support** Percentage of issues resolved online, download rate of supporting materials, customer satisfaction survey scores
- **Blog** Comments or other user-generated content, number of page views (for advertising supported sites), number of blog-feed subscriptions, social media sharing
- **Branding** Number of page views, downloads or printouts, social media sharing
- **Community** Profile or account creation, comments and user-generated content, social media sharing
- **Review and Ranking Websites** Profile creation, reviews and comments

Micro-Conversions

Many people view conversions as large-scale or "macro" events like the ones discussed earlier. Indeed, such conversions are very important. But we often overlook the fact that macro-conversions are not some kind of monolithic events. They can be decomposed into much smaller micro-conversion actions. The micro-conversions create small doses of psychological momentum that reduce friction and allow a visitor to continue moving toward your ultimate desired outcome. That outcome may not occur during their current visit and may be delayed for many months or even years, but the micro-conversions serve as the stepping-stones to eventually completing your intended macro-conversion action.

Micro-conversions vary by type of website and can be defined in many ways— for example, views of key pages or videos, time spent on the site, referring a friend, or proceeding to the next page of a checkout or sign-up process.

At the heart of many micro-conversions is the clickthrough. As discussed earlier, only a few parts of your website are mission critical and it's important to get as many visitors to these pages as possible. A clickthrough can measure the effectiveness with which you funnel visitors to the desired actionable pages, and through the conversion process. Clickthroughs can serve as an important intermediate gauge of progress. The CTR is often used to calculate conversion success.

Funnel analysis can be used to show the dropout rates for the clickthrough of multiple page flows (for example, clicks through a shopping cart checkout process). It is important to maintain momentum and continuity of intent through multiple page flows. This is often accomplished with prominent buttons, text calls-to-action, and attention-focusing design that directs people to the next step in the process.

Click-overlay heat maps (like those found in ClickTale and Crazy Egg) are useful for understanding visually what people are actually clicking on your web pages.

One great way to find pages with poor CTRs is to look for pages with high *bounce rates* (single page visits) or *exit rates* (the percentage of people who leave the site after visiting the page). Both of these metrics can be found in all common web analytics tools.

Still not sure whether something is a micro-conversion? Use this test:

Does the interaction create a meaningful moment that deepens your relationship or engagement with the visitor?

A meaningful moment simply means that you have been given a higher level of trust by the visitor, or that they have "invested" more time or effort in their interactions with you (thereby demonstrating more "skin in the game" and likely commitment in the future).

Taking a look at your website in detail to identify these more subtle micro-conversion points will help you to understand how your website and landing pages are converting, and will generate ideas for content that you can change to improve your conversion rate further.

In the next chapter we will lay out a powerful framework for understanding your website and its effectiveness.

The Matrix—Moving People to Act

A-I-D-A. Attention, interest, decision, action.

—BLAKE (played by actor Alec Baldwin in the
1992 movie *Glengarry Glen Ross*)

*People follow a similar mental trajectory when
they make decisions. If we are trying to persuade
them to act, we must have a firm grounding in the
basics of understanding their role, intent, and how
the decision-making process works.*

CHAPTER CONTENTS

The Matrix Overview

Roles

Tasks

The Decision-Making Process

Awareness

Interest

Desire

Action

The Matrix Overview

"The Matrix" framework was developed at SiteTuners to make sure that no important steps are overlooked when designing a conversion flow or website.

 The Matrix ensures that you have mapped out in detail how to guide the *right people*, through the *right activities*, in the *right order.*

The basic steps in creating The Matrix are as follows:

1. Define key visitor roles. From your understanding of your website visitors, you should have already identified the roles of people arriving on your site.

2. Define critical tasks for each role. A visitor in a particular role may have one of several activities or intentions in mind for their current visit to the website.

3. Define structured content to support each task. During each task, you will map out what specific help, information, and resources will be needed by the visitor to accomplish the required task.

Let's look at each of these steps in turn.

Roles

Depending on your business, your site may need to address the needs of very diverse types of visitors:

- Prospects
- Clients
- Information seekers
- Current or potential business partners
- Competitors
- Potential employees
- Members of the press
- Investors

The usual practice (especially if your landing page is your main site homepage) is to provide a comprehensive view of your company and to give all roles equal billing. This tendency to be even-handed is actually counterproductive. Everyone at your company may want real estate on the page, but they do not necessarily deserve it in equal measure (or at all).

Moreover, some visitors are more motivated to find the relevant information on your site. Job seekers will discover the page with available open positions no matter how deeply it is buried in your site. Likewise, potential affiliates will join your affiliate program regardless of whether you label the link "affiliates," "webmasters," "partners," or "referral program."

Reduce your conversion-related roles based on these criterion. The role breakdown can be basic, or it may need to be slightly more nuanced depending on your circumstances. We typically find that two to several roles are enough to capture the important classes of visitors from a conversion perspective.

Here are some examples of possible roles for different kinds of companies:

Plumbing-Supply Company Retail customers (who want to buy an individual replacement part), plumbing contractors (who need an array of parts for a specific customer job), wholesale buyers and real estate developers (who need large volume price breaks and extended payment terms)

Dating Service Prospective member (who has not signed up yet), new member (who has paid but has not set up a complete personal profile), experienced member (who has done multiple searches and contacted other members)

Educational Saving Plan Provider Future recipients (children under age 18), parents of recipients (who typically establish the plan), relatives and friends (who may contribute money to the plan)

Consumer E-tail Company New visitors (who have not been to your site before), returning visitors (who have been there but have not bought yet), first-time buyers (who are trying to complete their first purchase), repeat buyers (who already have their information stored in your system), e-mail list members (who have signed up to hear about special offers)

Roles vs. Personas

The personas of traditional advertising agencies are character sketches that help a project team better visualize the needs of their visitors or customers. They include a name, age, educational background, a description of the work and home environment, as well as interests and activities of the person. Several of these personas are usually developed and used to promote a sense of empathy and better understanding of the typical intended users of a product or service.

For our purposes, roles are different than personas.

In one sense, roles are more changeable. A persona is usually treated as a fully formed personality that does not change. In fact, most people play many different roles in their daily life. In each role, their skills, mental frameworks, and attitudes can shift dramatically. For example, you may

continues

Roles vs. Personas *(Continued)*

be confident, clear, and quick to make decisions during the workday. After work, you may leave the office to buy a present for a friend's birthday party. In this setting, you may become unsure of yourself, hesitant, and afraid to make the wrong decision. So even though you are the same person (and would presumably still be represented by the same persona), you behave completely differently in a business role and a gift-shopper role.

In some other circumstances, roles are actually more stable than personas. This is often the case in landing page testing. For example, regardless of the personalities involved, all website visitors to an e-commerce catalog site still need to complete the same functional tasks as part of their role as shoppers (such as placing items in a shopping cart and checking out). So the role of shopper can subsume the specific personas who might be functioning in this capacity.

The common definition of personas is often confused in online marketing circles with the notion of cognitive styles (see Chapter 6, "Misunderstanding Your Visitors—Looking for Psychological Mismatches," for additional discussion). Cognitive styles are a useful way to categorize people's preferred mode of behavior and method of gathering information. For example, one classification might contrast the needs of a fast-paced and task-oriented person versus the needs of a methodical people-oriented one. These kinds of distinctions are helpful and can often be used to design more effective web experiences.

Tasks

In user-centered design (UCD), tasks (also known as *use cases* or *scenarios*) represent a sketched-out problem statement that is implemented during a usability test. It is important that the tasks have measurable and quantifiable objectives and that these objectives are based on the high-priority goals of the business. For purposes of conversion rate optimization, individual features should not be tested (too narrow). Whole websites should not be tested either (too broad). Tasks should represent common activities that users might want to engage in that have significant value to the business.

Example tasks include the following:

Insurance Comparison Site Find three, $1-million term life insurance quotes for a healthy 30-year-old single man living in California.

Network Security Company Download and open the whitepaper on "Remotely Diagnosing Security Threats."

E-commerce Site Determine the cost of a Model-XYZ laptop computer when configured with the optional DVD drive.

Photo-Sharing Site Activate a free account and upload a picture from a local computer.

Notice that none of the tasks specify *how* a user is expected to accomplish them, only *what* needs to get done (i.e., they capture the visitor's intent).

The Decision-Making Process

In 1898, Elias St. Elmo Lewis pioneered a framework for describing stages of consumer interest and behavior. In effect, he created the modern concept of the sales funnel. All people were thought to progress through four stages covered by the acronym AIDA:

> Awareness (Attention)
>
> Interested
>
> Desire (Decision)
>
> Action

The key to properly applying this model is to make sure that there is continuity and flow to support a visitor's progress through each of the steps. None of the steps can be skipped, and all of them must happen in sequence. That is not to say that equal emphasis should be placed on each within your landing page, nor that visitors will spend an equal amount of time in each step. But there should be a clear path and the proper support to keep them moving forward toward your conversion goal.

In his book *Submit Now: Designing Persuasive Web Sites* (New Riders Press, 2002), Andrew Chak closely follows the AIDA model and applies it specifically to website visitors. He determined that the website or landing page should be designed for four main user types corresponding to the mind-set of each stage:

- **Browsers** May not know exactly what they want but have an unmet need
- **Evaluators** Know the available options and are comparing details
- **Transactors** Have made a decision and need to quickly complete their specific task
- **Customers** Have completed their transaction and need to stay satisfied until they transact again

It is also helpful to realize that AIDA often applies at radically different time-scales. If you are a consumer researching the next computer to buy, you may take days or weeks to make your decision. Yet your interaction with a particular website may be only one of dozens. You may have forgotten about the website by the time you make your ultimate decision (depending on when you visited it, what research you have conducted since, and why the website's offer is unique).

At the other extreme, the Web supports small-scale and short-duration micro-tasks that may happen in a fraction of a second. Sometimes the task that you want the user to perform is simply to clickthrough to another page on your site. Yet the same four AIDA steps must still happen during the visit for the conversion action to occur.

Your visitor will be asking the following questions in order to pass through all of the AIDA stages:

- Do you have what I want?
- Why should I get it from you?

This process may not happen during a single visit or interaction. The ultimate goal may be weeks or months away. But you must provide a clear path to that goal, as well as support along every step of the way. If your conversion action typically has a long delay, then try to provide mechanisms to record your visitors' progress. Restart them in the most recent and relevant state when they return to your landing page.

As you will see, the typical time spent in the awareness and interest stages on the Web is short. Most of the "Do you have what I want?" question is answered during the desire stage. However, without preceding attention and interest, desire cannot even happen. Similarly, although the bulk of "Why should I get it from you?" is answered during the action stage, it cannot even be reached without passing through the other three stages in order.

Awareness

Awareness and its close cousin attention are scarce commodities in our fast-paced world. We are constantly bombarded by information and sensory overload. Unceasing advertisements haunt us from our first waking moments to our exhausted end of the day. The pace of change keeps increasing and threatens to overwhelm us. The Internet has given us access to a vast wealth of information. Unfortunately, it has not helped us to organize or make sense of it very well to date.

> *What information consumes is rather obvious: it consumes the attention of its recipients. Hence, a wealth of information creates a poverty of attention and a need to allocate that attention efficiently among the overabundance of information sources that might consume it.*
>
> —HERBERT A. SIMON, noted interdisciplinary computational and social scientist

There is only one possible response: build walls. People learn to tune out. You can call them jaded or media savvy. But it boils down to the same thing—they have to get desensitized to survive. So it takes more and more effort for an advertiser to break through the clutter and the noise to reach their target audience.

> *You're not paying attention. Nobody is.*
>
> —SETH GODIN, *Permission Marketing*

As Seth Godin points out in his classic *Permission Marketing: Turning Strangers Into Friends and Friends Into Customers* (Simon & Schuster, 1999), this type of *interruption advertising* may still be necessary to make initial contact, but it should only be followed up with voluntary *permission marketing* once a visitor lands on your site. Permission marketing allows companies to trade things of greater value to the visitor in exchange for voluntary information and a deeper level of relationship with that visitor.

Permission marketing has the following three key attributes:

- **Anticipated** Your prospects actually want to hear from you.
- **Personal** Your messages are tailored to each person.
- **Relevant** Your messages relate directly to visitors' needs.

Let's look at the mind-set of visitors during the awareness stage. They have just arrived at your site. Their level of commitment is low and they may click away at any moment. They are looking for reassurance, recognition of their needs, and a clear path to follow. If something catches their eye, they may stay and explore further.

The Rules of Web Awareness

- If the visitor can't find something easily, it does not exist.
- If you emphasize too many items, all of them lose importance.
- Any delay increases frustration.

Unfortunately, instead of going into a permission marketing mind-set, most companies stay in interruption marketing mode on their landing pages. The page elements continue to scream, shout, and demand the visitor's attention. This is done through the use of bold color blocks, bright images and graphics, and large font headlines—all trumpeting different items to click on. In the next chapter, you'll see a sampling of the worst of these assaults as many companies try to trap a visitor through any means necessary.

Keys to Creating Awareness

There are three important keys to creating awareness:

Stop screaming at your visitors. Get out of the interruption marketing mind-set. Imagine your web visitors as guests who have just arrived at your home. Would you scream at them? Turn down the volume by eliminating gaudy and flashy visual elements. Everything on your landing page does not deserve special emphasis.

This does not mean that you should not have a larger headline or clear call-to-action. Your desired conversion action should be prominent and clear. But in the absence of elements loudly competing for attention, this will happen naturally. Create a Zen-like stillness on your page from which the call-to-action naturally emerges.

Eliminate unnecessary choices. Now that you have clearly defined your conversion action(s), you must take a hard look at your landing pages. Anything that does not directly support the conversion goal must be eliminated. If you have more than one conversion goal, you must emphasize the ones that have the highest value per visitor. These should receive a disproportionately large amount of screen real estate and prominence. Minor or supporting conversion goals should be minimized.

Unclutter what remains. Now it is time to become a word miser. Ruthlessly edit your remaining text copy. Simplify concepts and cut to the chase. Shorten prose paragraphs to easy-to-scan bullet lists. Organize information with short headlines and links so visitors do not have to read unwanted topics. Create room to breathe with lots of whitespace on the page.

These principles are demonstrated well in the homepage of software company 37Signals (www.37signals.com) shown in Figure 3.1. The page cleanly creates awareness of the four available software tools and their purpose. The page is rather Spartan and unembellished, but very functional and restrained (especially for a homepage).

Figure 3.1 37Signals homepage creates awareness of four side-by-side choices.

Interest

On the Web, interest is fleeting. A large number of other websites are just a mouse click away. The level of commitment to your particular site is low.

Interest is often tied closely to awareness. The attention of the person flits like a butterfly across your landing page—their awareness can be described as an ongoing scanning process. Interest is akin to the butterfly hovering for a moment over a particular flower. Interest can be viewed as a transient pull and concentration of the attention on a particular object.

Often, interest on the Web is expressed in a split-second decision. If the attention surge is strong enough, visitors will take the action of clicking. If not, their attention will subside back into scanning mode. If visitors' needs are not being met and they grow frustrated enough, interest can peak instead on a desire to leave the current webpage.

The key to creating the interest is to focus on the visitor. Elements of your landing page must be relevant to them, and they must self-select because they recognize this relevance.

The Rules of Web Interest

- Understand who the visitor is.
- Understand what the visitor is trying to accomplish.
- Clearly present the choices for visitor consideration.

Web interest comes in two main flavors: self-selection and needs recognition.

Self-Selection

In order to self-select, you must be given a choice of specific roles and the appropriate path to follow. In effect, the visitor has to raise their hand and say, "Yes, I identify with this label." Figure 3.2 shows the homepage for Tim Ash's alma mater University of California, San Diego (ucsd.edu). The main navigation menu across the top of the page contains a list of roles, enabling a visitor to self-select:

- Prospective Students
- Current Students
- Parents & Families
- Faculty & Staff
- Alumni
- Friends & Visitors

Figure 3.2 University of California San Diego homepage showing self-selection by role in the top navigation bar

Needs Recognition

Another way to increase interest is to have people identify with a specific need that they currently have or a task that they are trying to complete on the current visit. Needs may change more quickly than roles. The highlighted portion of the Delta Airline homepage in Figure 3.3 (www.delta.com) shows needs-based navigation.

The main menu box near the upper left offers visitors four choices:

- Book a trip
- My trips
- Check in
- Flight status

It would not have been enough simply to break down by roles (prospective travelers and booked traveler), since the last three tasks all apply to booked travelers.

Figure 3.3 The Delta Airlines homepage needs recognition by task.

Desire

The mind-set and attention span of the visitor in the desire stage is different from those in the preceding stages. Whereas the attention and interest stages may have lasted only a few seconds, visitors in the desire stage may give you their full attention for minutes or even hours. They are in research mode and are willing to take more time.

With visitors in the desire stage, you get the precious gift of having them spend time on your landing page or website. You have piqued their interest and are now engaged in a subtle seduction to increase your visitor's desire.

However, seduction is a tricky and tenuous activity. You can't move too fast without turning off visitors. Yet we see this all the time on the Web. Have you ever visited a site and been pushed to act before you even understood the context?

Unfortunately this situation is very common on the Internet. LegalSteroids pushes you to buy directly off of their homepage shown in Figure 3.4 (www.LegalSteroids.com). It is highly unlikely that anyone would buy powerful and potentially dangerous compounds to put into their body without first finding out more about the products and the company that stands behind them. Yet the only call-to-action available to the visitor is to "BUY NOW."

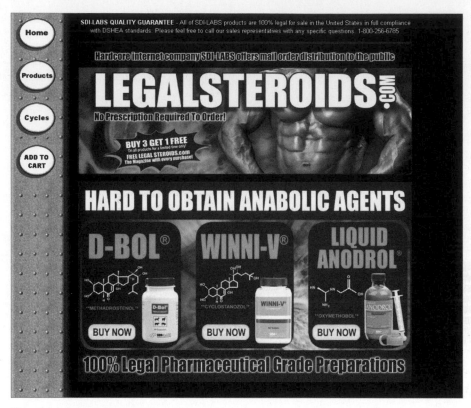

Figure 3.4 LegalSteroids homepage

This kind of "greedy marketer syndrome" can be seen as premature and inappropriate. So what should you do instead? Follow these basic rules for building desire:

The Rules of Web Desire

- Make the visitor feel appreciated.
- Make the visitor feel safe.
- Understand that the visitor is in control.

Make the visitor feel appreciated. The Web allows you to provide your visitors with all kinds of useful information, which, if properly presented, can make them feel knowledgeable, powerful, and understood.

Make the visitor feel safe. The Web is a scary place, and your homepage is often a first-time introduction. You must do everything you can to let visitors get to know you better. It is important to be completely open, honest, and transparent. You can help alleviate their fears by transferring credibility from others in the form of testimonials, awards, and trust symbols.

Understand that the visitor is in control. Visitors should be able to dictate the terms of the relationship with you. This includes the timescale of the interaction, the order in which things get done, the option to stay anonymous for as long as possible, and the ability to look for information in whatever format is easiest and most appropriate for them.

As they explore whether you have what they want, a typical visitor may engage in any of the following common activities:

- Research
- Comparing
- Getting details
- Socializing
- Customizing

Although the following examples are drawn mostly from e-tailing, the principles and steps are the same for all calls-to-action.

Research

During the research activity, people may have only vague notions of what they want. It's likely they don't know all of the lingo that you as a specialist know. They are looking for a guide or a knowledgeable expert to help them get oriented. Once they better understand the lay of the land, they can compare the available options against their perceived needs. These needs themselves may evolve as your visitors learn, as new preferences arise, and as early assumptions are abandoned.

To adapt to these changes, you must prioritize what features of the product or service are important to visitors. Rank their importance as must-have, nice-to-have, and nonessential. As long as your information is useful and objective, you get to define the rules of the game. You can differentiate key features that are a source of competitive advantage.

This information can be presented in a variety of formats:

- **Whitepapers and How-to Guides** Informational articles to educate prospects about important and complex topics
- **Buying Guides** Articles written to educate consumers about important features and differences among a certain class of products or services
- **Comparison Charts** At-a-glance feature lists or tables that serve as a quick way to narrow down the choices or understand key differences between them

- **Wizards** Automated tools that help visitors zero in on the right solution by asking them a series of simple questions related to their specific task
- **Demonstrations** Videos, animations, or presentation slides that showcase a particular product or service

For large e-commerce catalogs, faceted search (the ability to refine what you are looking for using a number of different filters) is often critical. The Shoes.com website (www.shoes.com) references 11,558 types of shoes available in the men's department.

Let's look at an example of how to use the "narrow by" faceted search on this site. It is easy to specify the following:

- Men's
- Dress shoes category
- Cap toe design
- Size 10.5
- Wide width
- Black color

If you select a specific combination of the filters above, this process quickly reduces the number of matching shoes to a very manageable 29, as shown in Figure 3.5 (with the active selected filters appearing just above the shoes).

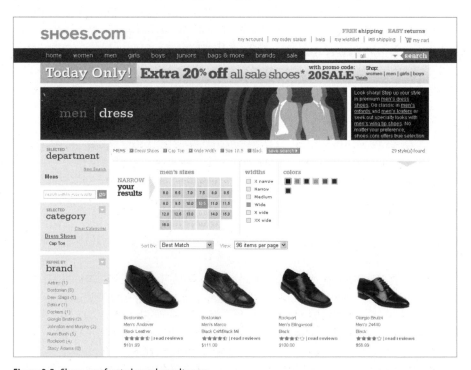

Figure 3.5 Shoes.com faceted search results page

Although the site's narrowing functionality is simply an advanced form of search, it is so useful that it qualifies as a wizard for the product-selection task. Several features combine to make it more powerful than the sum of its parts, as described here:

- **Flexible Search Options** Several ways of searching are provided, including department, category, brand, size, width, color, and free-form text search. The only obviously missing search parameter is price limit.

- **Context Sensitivity** All of the search options are "aware" of each other. For example, if certain brands or sizes were not available, this would be reflected in the shoe size chart. This allows for iterative drilldown and refinement.

- **Order Independence** Any of the category-narrowing methods can be used in any order.

- **Reversibility** A visitor to this site can easily undo any of their prior choices and rewiden the scope of their search.

The end result is radically different than simply offering multiple advanced search options on a website.

Some companies make searching so difficult (or do not provide any search functionality at all!) that visitors must spend a lot of time looking through seemingly endless and clearly inappropriate search results. It is safe to assume that no one will want to step manually through a large number of matching results pages by using the Previous Page and Next Page links.

The proper solution is to detect this information overload situation and help guide the visitor to a smaller number of items before displaying any potential matches in more detail. You want to provide them with door-to-door service—not drop them off within a few miles of their destination and have them walk the rest of the way.

Giving visitors too many choices and forcing them to wade through them is the web equivalent of being sprayed with a fire hose. Giving them no matching search results is admitting your incompetence in providing useful guidance.

Is it slightly more difficult and time consuming to provide thoughtful support during the search step? Of course it is. But you must do it to avoid a huge drop in conversion rate.

Comparing

Once visitors have been educated about the desirable features of the product or service, they usually find more than one acceptable alternative. The key must-have features have all been satisfied. So the decision to narrow their choice does not depend on the original criteria. They need additional "tie-breakers," although these may be less important than the core list. If the core needs are met, they serve as differentiators. Giving as much side-by-side detailed information as needed during this step is critical.

Because comparison sites are specialized and focused on this step, they obviously influence the ultimate decision. They fulfill one of the ultimate promises of the Internet: aggregating the full range of choices and helping to guide consumers. Most comparison sites also cover the research and desire steps, and seamlessly hand off to the tailored recommendation.

There are two ways that comparisons can be skewed: choice of features, and choice of competitors. We have all seen television car commercials, and we know that the comparison features are hand-picked and slanted in favor of the advertiser's product (for example, "Our car costs thousand less *and* has four more cup holders!"). Internet consumers generally don't fall for heavy-handed approaches like this. They are used to getting detailed objective information and can find it in a variety of places. To compete with comparison sites, single-brand or single-product sites must duplicate this deep and detailed content on their websites. Better yet, they can get the objective information from a trusted third party and feature the source prominently to lend extra credibility to their comparison. Include a wide range of realistic competitors. If possible, allow the selection of more than one alternative in your comparisons.

Despite the obvious benefit to consumers, the comparison step represents an internal tug of war for marketers. The instinct to carve out a competitive advantage through biased slanting is strong. Yet this is exactly the wrong impulse for the Internet environment and must be consciously resisted.

Some online marketers also live on a steady diet of self-inflicted in-house brainwashing and propaganda. They actually believe that their products are the "world-class leader" in their category. The consumer does not labor under this delusion. In fact, they seek out not only objective data and reviews, but also the opinions of third-party experts and existing users. Many online marketers would be shocked to find that their precious product claims are regularly savaged in peer-to-peer settings.

Much of this criticism is well deserved and should even be looked at as a source of ideas for improvement. Comparison information must be complete, objective, and easily digested by your target audience. The conclusion is unavoidable: If you don't provide support during the crucial comparison step, your competitor or some other influencer will.

Getting Details

Make sure that *you* understand everything about the total experience with the chosen product or service. Once visitors select a product or service from a list of finalists, they want to make sure they are making the right decision. At this step, all possible assurances should be made by including the following:

- Detailed description
- Features
- Specifications

- Compatibilities, standards compliance, and minimum requirements
- Configuration options
- Photos and/or diagrams
- Accessories and suggested add-ons
- Third-party media reviews and endorsements
- User reviews and client testimonials
- Case studies or survey results
- Suggested alternative products
- Delivery and setup options (shipping or installation)
- Service plans and customer-care levels
- Accurate costs and payment terms
- Availability and in-stock status

It is important to provide complete and objective information, even if this means reporting something negative. Chances are if someone is going to do their homework about your product or service on the Web, they will run across the negative information anyway. By presenting it yourself, you are seen as more trustworthy. You also have the opportunity to frame the concern on your own terms and partially mitigate its impact.

Socializing

Hesitant prospects are increasingly likely to turn to peer-to-peer sources to confirm their evaluation. Recommendations from existing customers are commonly valued as the most trusted advice, particularly users seen as similar or personally familiar to them. As Barry Schwartz points out in the book *The Paradox of Choice: Why More Is Less* (Ecco, 2003), anecdotal "evidence" even outweighs statistical proof. So, for example, if a person in your social circle presents a vivid account of their love for a certain photo-hosting site, that review will likely have more influence than statistically significant but distant independent analysis.

Aside from their vivid impact, user reviews are especially useful because they provide insights about real-world use in situations that a first-time buyer may not have considered. The reviews are not always flattering, but unless they are clearly false or offensive, they should be left on your site. Having negative reviews shows a well-rounded picture and indicates that the information on the site is more or less unfiltered (and therefore more trustworthy). When user-generated content reaches critical mass on these kinds of sites, they can serve as a defensible barrier to entry against other competitors (who may only feature stock descriptions or specs from the product manufacturer).

The trust factor only gains momentum on the flip side, when user-generated content is overwhelmingly positive. Peer reviews give voice to the passion of peer advocates, whose volunteer commentary often proves to be a successful, free form of marketing. If the feature portfolio is wide enough, quick ratings can substitute for a depth of reviews and reinforce a sense of user satisfaction.

Customizing

Once visitors have decided on a particular product or service, they should be given the opportunity to customize it. By personalizing the solution to their specific needs, they are vicariously "trying it on for size." This gets visitors involved in imagining exactly how they might use it in the future. Personalization and configuration put visitors in control and create momentum toward the action stage.

The laptop configurator on the Sony website (store.sony.com) allows a visitor to choose from a deep list of options (see Figure 3.6): CPU, memory, hard drive, optical disc drive, display, TV tuner, operating system, wireless local area network, battery, preinstalled software, music software, photo software, video software, finance software, other software, and service plan. A number of available accessories can also be added (adapters, batteries, carrying cases). The exact price and is subtotaled after every change and an order summary (with estimated shipping date) appears on the right side of the page.

Figure 3.6 Sony laptop configurator

If you get someone to actively engage in the customization process, they are also investing their time and effort (putting some "skin in the game"), thus becoming less likely to do so again on another, similar website.

Action

Desire and action are not distinct stages but rather a continuing give-and-take. Increasing desire pulls us to take successively larger steps toward the ultimate conversion goal. Each of these steps is in itself an action. After each action, we build on its momentum to create enough desire to jump to the next level of action and commitment.

Finding the best solution and finding the best provider for that solution are largely independent decisions. Just because you have gone to great lengths to help visitors research, compare, review, and customize a good solution does not mean that they will buy it from you. Especially if the item in question is a commodity, or widely available from a number of online and offline sources, many people will comparison-shop to find the best price and terms. There is growing evidence that online consumers are getting savvier, and that the median online purchase times for many industries are steadily increasing because of comparison shopping.

Consumers often use the Internet for a portion of their decision-making process but then prefer to conclude the transaction offline. In many instances, offline is in fact your biggest competitor in the action stage.

Tim Veers Offline

When my family was looking for a baby stroller, we researched it online and found the JoggingStroller.com website extremely helpful. We settled on a hard-to-find model made exclusively by a manufacturer in New Zealand. We then called a local retailer and, after determining that they had the right model and color in stock, decided to visit their store and examine it in person. We came well prepared and very much liked our physical test drive of the stroller. Even though it was slightly more expensive than online, we ended up purchasing it on the spot.

Were we disloyal to JoggingStroller.com? In a way we were. They did provide us with a free education, and yet we still did not buy from them. However, this is the harsh reality of Internet sales, and a significant reason why shopping cart abandonment rates will remain stubbornly high. But in our defense we also had a number of other considerations. We wanted to see the physical product and experience how heavy, solid, and maneuverable it was. It is difficult to convey this ergonomic information—even with the help of detailed product images and specifications. We were also excited by the prospect of our purchase and wanted to immediately take our baby for a walk in it. We were also consciously choosing to support a physical "brick and mortar" retailer who took the risk of carrying this manufacturer's product line in stock on the off chance that someone like us would walk into their store.

This does not mean that you should not bother to provide all of the preconversion supporting information on your landing page. By doing so, you narrow the range of your likely online competitors. Ones that do not have similarly deep and rich content will simply not be in the running because visitors are less likely to spend significant time on their websites. It then comes down to a decision of your company versus offline alternatives—and offline is not always an option. Unless you live in a large city, your choice of specialty products or services may be restricted (or nonexistent). In such circumstances, the best online company has a meaningful advantage.

There is a continuum of goods and services that ranges from concrete to vague. Many services fall toward the latter end of the spectrum. In his excellent book *Selling the Invisible: A Field Guide to Modern Marketing* (Business Plus, 1997), Harry Beckwith describes the fundamental difference between selling services and tangible products. When people buy services, they tend to look for specialized knowledge and expertise that they do not possess themselves. In the case of many professional occupations (such as lawyers, architects, or doctors), people only infrequently need the services and do not know how to objectively evaluate the merits of the service provider. But the consequences of making a poor decision are high. So they are forced to rely on the personal relationship, referrals, and any other tangible clues of quality that they can find.

It is important to remember that the landing page itself is simply a visual representation of a service promise that you are making to the visitor. These implied promises can be very different depending on your conversion actions:

- You will follow up on your contact request promptly (lead-generation forms).
- You will not spam visitors but will instead send them useful information (e-mail newsletter sign-up).
- The product they are seeing is accurately represented (online auction sites).
- Their purchase will indeed arrive before that special occasion (e-commerce).

Sometimes the desired ultimate conversion action is offline and the intermediate online steps are simply designed to pass the visitor on to a live person on the telephone, to schedule a callback, or to arrange for a subsequent face-to-face consultation or group event.

Brand Strength

Brands are very powerful. Well-known marketers Al Ries and Jack Trout correctly point out in their classic book *The 22 Immutable Laws of Marketing: Violate Them at Your Own Risk!* (HarperBusiness, 1994) that brands serve as a shortcut to decision making in our busy lives. Each product or service category only has room for a tiny number of established leaders, and they capture disproportionate value in their respective market categories. When a brand is firmly established in the mind of a person as a market leader, it becomes almost impossible to dislodge.

The halo provided by the brand's promise means that a person can devote much less attention to evaluating items related to the brand. The same presumption is not accorded to lesser-known or unknown competitors. Although their products or services may be objectively just as good, they require additional attention to evaluate. Because of this, they may be disqualified from consideration simply because people will not choose to spend the required time or effort investigating them.

Brands take enormous amounts of time and money to build. Take a hard look at your brand. Most likely it is not that strong. Even if your company is one of the online leaders in a particular category or niche, that does not mean that your brand awareness has spread to most people in your industry (or to the public at large for consumer products and services). The relative weakness of many online brands is the primary reason that their offline competitors often win the battle for the customer's mindshare. Since there is no short-term way to impact the strength of your brand, it is essentially outside of your control.

The Total Solution

Despite the attempt to neatly decouple the product or service from its provider, the separation is not always this clean. Often the two are enmeshed. For example, the product or service may be available from only one provider. In such "proprietary" cases, the provider, warts and all, must be considered as part of the solution.

Economist Herbert A. Simon coined a term for the related act of choosing to live with an imperfect but acceptable solution: *satisficing*. It is a combination of the words "satisfy" and "suffice." Most people do not want to invest additional time without a strong sense that they will find a better answer. As soon as they find a solution that is good enough, they often stop looking.

More commonly, the provider offers a number of value-added services or options that are not always available from others or that cannot be easily compared. Your visitor is thinking in terms of the total solution and is deciding based on that.

A total solution may involve the following elements:

- The base price
- The properly configured "out the door" price
- Additional costs such as shipping or installation
- Exchange and return policies
- Ease of setup and learning curve required
- Availability status and delivery date guarantees
- Service plans and options

- Ongoing costs to operate and maintain
- Convenient company physical locations
- Performance or level-of-service guarantees

There are a variety of ways that you can both reduce the anxiety that a visitor might feel about your solution, and at the same time build confidence and trust in your site. These are covered in the next chapter as the remedies to common landing page mishaps.

Transacting

Even if you have correctly done everything up to this point, remember that not everyone will act at this stage. They may not be able to afford your product. They may want to continue their search for alternatives. They may need the approval of others (such as coworkers or a spouse). They may not have the proper payment method or other credentials to complete the transaction. Some may simply want to sleep on the decision.

But let's assume that someone has finally built up enough desire to act. What is the best way to get that person to complete the transaction?

The Rules of Web Action

- Get out of the visitor's way.
- Make it easy for the visitor.
- Don't surprise the visitor.

Get Out of the Visitor's Way

The most criminal waste of attention at this point is focusing your visitors on extraneous tasks. One of the worst is making them register before checking out.

In forced registration, visitors are required to give their e-mail address and create a password before making a purchase. The merchant does this ostensibly to help the consumer on subsequent visits. The checkout information, such as shipping address and payment method, is stored. On their next visit, they are asked to enter the e-mail and password, and the stored data is auto-populated in the checkout process forms for them. Figure 3.7 shows the first page of the checkout process at Overstock.com (www.overstock.com).

Although the roles are clearly defined by the labels "Are you a new customer?" and "Are you an existing customer?", there are several ways that this step could be improved. Despite the fact that most people are likely to be new customers, both choices are given equal emphasis and screen real estate. The buttons both say "Continue," making it harder to differentiate their function.

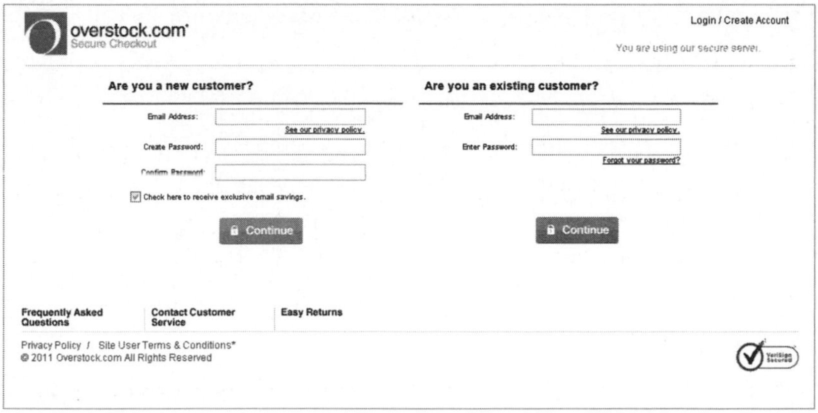

Figure 3.7 Overstock.com checkout process first step

It also creates unnecessary work for everyone by requiring a reconfirmation of the password for new customers. Only a few people will misspell the password that they had intended to enter. Even if they do, this can be easily dealt with by sending them an e-mail with a temporary password after their login attempt fails. Instead, extra data entry is forced on *all* potential customers.

Registration on your site may be a minor advantage to a small percentage of your visitors. But it is guaranteed to be an annoyance and hindrance to many more. If someone wants the convenience of not having to frequently reenter their personal data, they can set up a central user authentication account (that works across multiple websites), or activate their web browser's automatic form-fill capability. Many people may have no intention of transacting with you again and will not appreciate the extra work required to register. Others may object on privacy grounds to giving you their e-mail address since it is not an absolute requirement for completing an online transaction. Registration should never be forced and should be deemphasized in most cases. Even seemingly minor transactional friction such as filling out the e-mail and password may noticeably lower your conversion rates. If you must have the registration and login options first, the alternative mock-up in Figure 3.8 illustrates a cleaner approach.

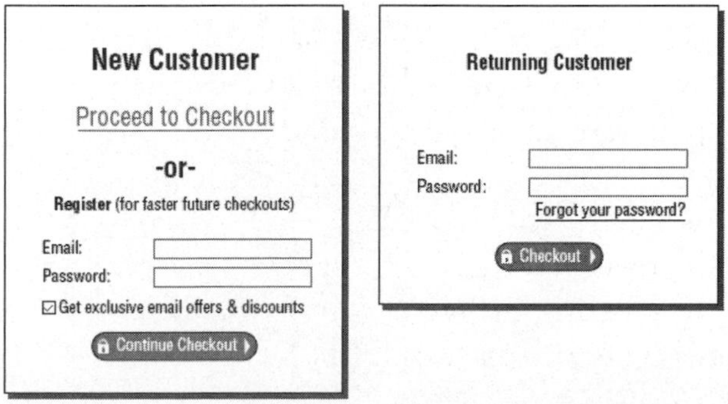

Figure 3.8 Mock-up of alternative to the Overstock.com checkout process

Note the following differences from Overstock's original version:

- **Emphasis** Most screen real estate supports new customers (usually the largest group by far). Within the new customer group, the main option is to proceed without registering.

- **Registration That Is Not Forced** New users can proceed immediately to the rest of the checkout process. The registration option describes the benefit of taking this step ("for faster future checkouts").

- **Minimal Data Entry** The password for new customer registrations is entered only once.

An even better approach would be to remove the optional new customer registration requirement from this page altogether. The same information can be collected easily near the end of the checkout process. At that stage visitors have significantly more invested in the transaction. They are less likely to abandon the process and more likely to supply the requested additional information.

Another common tactic during the transaction is to introduce last-minute upsells, cross-sells, or special offers. This is fine if it is handled before the checkout step (for example, by displaying accessories on a product detail page or in the shopping cart). Best Buy (www.bestbuy.com) does this in a seamless way by suggesting related accessories during a flat-screen TV add-to-cart by displaying them in a lightbox pop-over (see Figure 3.9). However, during the checkout process such tactics should be carefully considered.

Figure 3.9 BestBuy accessories upsell during a flat-screen TV add-to-cart

This same type of interruption should be avoided in any other setting where transactional form-fills are the primary goal, whether the secondary objective is a survey, subscription, or lead generation. Other examples involve coregistration (or "coreg" for short). This is a common online practice. During a transaction, you are invited (usually by simply checking a box) to participate in other (often unrelated) services or offers from co-marketing partners of the website. If you opt in, some of the information from your original transaction is then forwarded to the coreg partner for future promotional e-mails to you.

Many coreg programs are thinly disguised ways to gather and sell your e-mail to others. Since you are piggybacking the coreg on your own transaction, ultimately the impact of this will rub off on your own brand and credibility. Your primary transaction presumably has a lot more value than the incremental money you can make from coreg. So you must be careful about the potential risks (such as lower conversion rates or damage to your reputation). It is rarely a good idea to transfer some of the trust that you have built up (enough to complete the desired conversion action) to another company. As suggested earlier, if you are considering upsells or coregistration you should at least test the impact on your revenue per visitor.

Make It Easy for the Visitor

One of the keys to making the user experience easier is to remove choice and simplify the transaction process. An easy way to do this is to change or remove the navigation information available on the page. The main menu that is used during the earlier stages of the decision process is often no longer applicable during the action stage. Only information relevant to the transaction should be included in the new navigation. Everything else should be removed.

If your landing page is designed for a single conversion action, you should not use the navigation or page structure from your main corporate website. You should remove the navigation completely, or limit it to specific information related to your conversion action. This is especially the case if you are paying for the traffic stream directly (via PPC or banner ad purchases, for example). In such cases, we often recommend removing the navigation altogether. Sometimes you may still want to have your logo link back to your main site. But you should realize that this is a potential traffic leak, and that some people will wander off to your main site to never return. If you feel that your main site contains content that is necessary for the conversion action, you should copy it onto the landing page (or a supporting page on your stand-alone microsite). Do *not* link off to the main site for such supporting information.

Don't Surprise the Visitor

Form and checkout interruption are examples of last-minute surprises. And surprises are the last thing that you want your visitors to experience at the delicate point when they have finally decided to act. In fact, you should work very hard to provide context and reassurance during this critical time.

Many people already have an idea of how certain kinds of transactions should unfold. For example, a common checkout convention might be to go from shopping cart to order review to billing/shipping input to order confirmation. There should be a clear indication of where in the process the visitor is at any given time.

InsWeb allows people to get insurance comparison quotes (www.insweb.com). When you start a quote for auto insurance, a tab-based navigation bar appears at the top of the page (see Figure 3.10), showing you the steps in the quote process and your current position in it. The names on the tabs educate and reassure you about the upcoming steps. You are allowed to go back at any point (by clicking on a preceding tab) and review or modify the information from the previous steps. An even clearer reassurance would have been provided by a Back To Previous Page link next to the Continue button near the bottom-right corner of each screen.

Figure 3.10 InsWeb auto insurance quote first step

Most transactions have a final point-of-no-return. Usually this involves clicking a button after filling out form information. It is critical to provide last-minute reassurances on the page where this point occurs, such as the following:

- A recap or review of the information provided to complete the transaction (items ordered, personal information, billing, and price)
- Details of the fulfillment process (such as service levels, delivery dates, contact methods, and timeframes)
- Terms and conditions (the fine print)
- Spelling out exactly what will happen when the action is taken
- Validation and risk reducers (as discussed previously in the "Desire" section)

Let's take stock. In the first part of this book you have reviewed the necessary background and learned about landing pages, conversion actions, and The Matrix. In the next part of the book, you will learn how to identify site and landing page problems from a variety of perspectives.

Finding Opportunities for Site Improvement

II

This part of the book is about problems: seeing them clearly, having the right tools to identify them, and understanding their psychological roots. Before you can improve conversion rates, you must first see what is wrong or suboptimal. We encourage you to become a worrywart, a skeptic, and a cynic. Focus on both the subtle and gross issues with your landing pages. Only then can you soberly assess and address them. At the end of this journey lies the promised land of higher conversion rates, but you have to go through the valley of problems to get there. Part II consists of the following chapters:

Chapter 4   **Common Problems—The Seven Deadly Sins of Landing Page Design**

Chapter 5   **Conversion Ninja Toolbox—Diagnosing Site Problems**

Chapter 6   **Misunderstanding Your Visitors—Looking for Psychological Mismatches**

Common Problems— The Seven Deadly Sins of Landing Page Design

4

Chances are, your landing page is suffering from not just one, but several common deadly sins. Although much of this material is also addressed in other parts of the book, this chapter should serve as a solid overview of the most important conversion issues.

CHAPTER CONTENTS

A Sober Look

Unclear Call-to-Action

Too Many Choices

Visual Distractions

Not Keeping Your Promises

Too Much Text

Asking for Too Much Information

Lack of Trust and Credibility

Real-World Case Study: CREDO Mobile

A Sober Look

Landing page testing is the "gold standard" of conversion improvement. By tracking the actions (or inactions) of your visitors when they're presented with a certain version of your landing page, you can reliably determine which version they prefer. It is truly a case of "listening to the voice of the customer."

However, you do not need to run landing page tests to uncover many conversion issues. They are so common and so blatant that we have enshrined them as the "Seven Deadly Sins of Landing Page Design."

This chapter explores some common landing page problems. You may look at the extreme examples presented and laugh at the obvious problems with the pages.

However, even though you may deny it, chances are your own page suffers from many of the same deadly sins. We encourage you to look deeply and critically at your own pages, applying the material in this chapter. This is as close to a "silver bullet" as we will offer in this book, and many who have addressed these common sins have increased conversion rates significantly.

The sins are presented in no particular order, and commonly co-occur on a landing page.

In each of the following sections, we will ask a simple question. The questions are from the perspective of your website visitors, and we stand here as their advocates. If you cannot clearly answer the question presented, chances are you are committing the sin in question on your page, and it is costing you money.

Unclear Call-to-Action

What am I supposed to do on this page?

Your website visitor should be able to answer this question easily, yet it is often not so. Instead, your visitor must spend precious time deciding what to do, and then expend the mental energy required to do it. As a result, the visitor may get confused and frustrated, and leave your page in search of clearer experiences.

In the example shown in Figure 4.1, the visitor is confronted with a stark visual gateway page showing a large "image shot." But what is the actual call-to-action?

After staring at the idyllic beach scene, the visitor may click on it, or they may decide to hit the Back button on their browser. If no action is taken, the page will refresh and finally take the visitor to the homepage of the SandalWorld catalog. But by then, many visitors will be long gone. Amazingly, this page actually served as the landing page for a Google AdWords pay-per-click (PPC) campaign. To their credit, this company has gotten rid of the "splash page" (pun intended) in question, and now goes directly to the homepage of their catalog.

In the example shown in Figure 4.2, the call-to-action is also unclear.

Figure 4.1 Unclear call-to-action on the Sandal World homepage

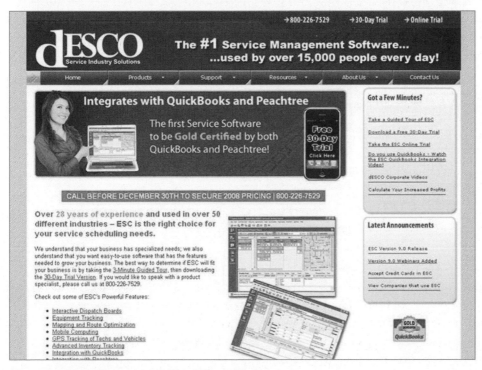

Figure 4.2 Unclear call-to-action on the Desco Software homepage

What are you supposed to do? Look at the picture of the model holding the laptop? Inspect the detailed report screenshots? "Call before December 30th" as instructed in the reverse-color text in the band near the center of the page?

In fact, the answer is "none of the above." The desired conversion action is to start a free 30-day trial by signing up online. Yet the only way to do this is to click on the small black iPhone picture. Unless you have an iPhone, chances are you would tune this image out completely. Even if you noticed the graphic, it is unclear that the image is clickable, rather than simply informational. Because of the hidden nature of the call-to-action, and the large number of visually dominant elements on the page, the desired conversion action is very unclear.

The preceding examples represent relatively small companies. But even larger ones commonly obscure the call-to-action.

The example in Figure 4.3 shows a product-detail page on the 1-800-flowers website.

Figure 4.3 1-800-flowers product detail page

There are many possible activities and visual priorities on the page: click on the banner ad and go to another product detail page on the site; look at the large rose image that is simply informational and shows you that you are in the Roses section of the website; or "Sign in now" (even though you have no reason to do so unless you are ready to purchase).

However, all of these other activities should be subordinated to the clear purpose of a product detail page: to be able to add the item in question to the shopping cart. The only page element designed to accomplish this is the tiny "Select Delivery Date" button at the bottom of the center column.

As a design exercise, SiteTuners created an alternative version of the page. All of the actual content about the product as well as the functional parts of the page had to be preserved. The objective was to clearly present the visual image of the product as well as create a single call-to-action.

Look at Figure 4.4. The call-to-action should be clear without much examination. Visitors are supposed to click the prominent "View Delivery Dates" button in the action block on the right side of the page.

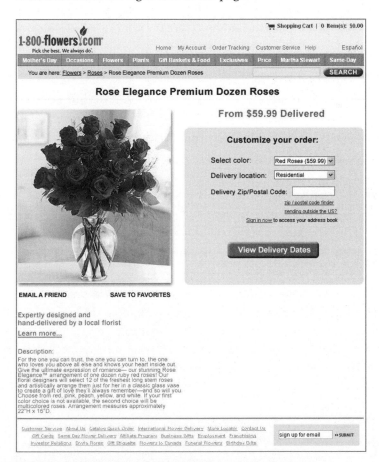

Figure 4.4 Alternative page mock-up for 1-800-flowers product detail page

All calls-to-action should be this obvious. In fact it is good to apply the "obvious standard": if your call-to-action is not obvious, you are losing money.

The new design incorporates several changes from the original. These included a darker header background color to separate it from the content of the page, removing the banner ad on top, removing the large graphic that represented the Roses category, and removing the dark text boxes within the content area with the reverse-color text.

This new design added the following elements to correspond to the best practices for controlling focus on a direct-response landing page (or a page on which a specific outcome is desired):

Clear Page Headline Each page on a website (and each stand-alone landing page) must be *about* something. It must have a clear purpose, and that purpose must be spelled out in a headline that spans the top of the page.

Well-Defined Action Block There should be a single place for the visitor to interact with your page, and that place should be visually called out with a subtle background color. This action block should draw the eye toward the desired activity on the page. The rest of the page should be plain and visually restrained. A white background for the content portion of the page is recommended unless there is a compelling need to use a different color.

Subheadline in Your Action Block The purpose of the action block must be clearly stated. What are you asking the visitor to do in the action block? What specifically is going to happen within it?

Clear Call-to-Action Within your action block, you must have a single clear call-to-action. The call-to-action must describe what happens next and what visitors can expect when they are done interacting with the action block. It should not be general or generic like the "Continue" or "Submit" text that is commonly used on websites. The wording of the call-to-action must be from the visitor's viewpoint, and not your company's. To put yourself in the visitor's shoes, try using button text that completes the following sentence: "I want to…."

Another way to validate the new design is to examine the visual focus of the two pages. To do this, you can use SiteTuners' very inexpensive AttentionWizard software (described in detail in Chapter 5, "Conversion Ninja Toolbox—Diagnosing Site Problems") to create an instant "attention heat map" of each page image. AttentionWizard is not eye-tracking or mouse-tracking, and it does not require the use of real people. It is a software prediction of where attention would be drawn during the first few seconds on the landing page, and can be used on a screenshot of a live web-page or a design mock-up that is not live.

As you can see from the attention heat map shown in Figure 4.5, the biggest "hot spot" on the page is on the bouquet of flowers. This is as it should be, since the picture represents the "hero shot" of the highly visual product and helps to sell it. However, the other four hot spot areas are on unrelated or non-actionable graphics. This is wasted attention. Because of the visual distractions on the page, none of the initial attention is expected on the call-to-action button. In other words, it is not clear at a glance exactly how to interact with the page.

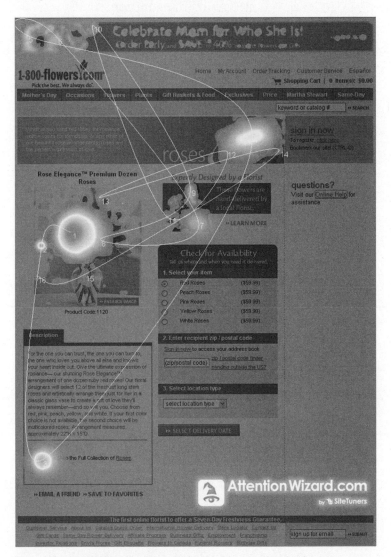

Figure 4.5 AttentionWizard heat map of the 1-800-flowers product detail page— no initial attention on the intended call-to-action

By contrast, the attention heat map of the new design in Figure 4.6 shows two primary areas of attention. The first hot spot is on the product image itself (enlarged from the original design to better show off the product). The second (and most intense)

hot spot is on the call-to-action button. This makes it clear what the desired action on the page is. Equally important is the fact that there are no attention hot spots (or "attention leaks") on any other parts of the page.

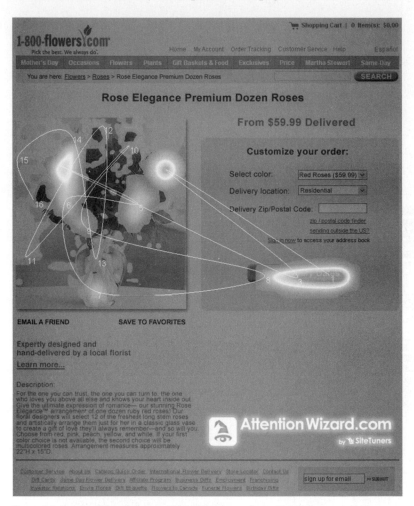

Figure 4.6 AttentionWizard heat map of the alternative mock-up of 1-800-flowers product detail page—clear initial attention on the call-to-action

Unclear Call-to-Action—The Fix

- The call-to-action should be clear and should draw the eye.
- The placement of the call-to-action should be above the fold.
- Competing visuals should be deemphasized.

Too Many Choices

What am I supposed to do first?

We often hear that choice is good. Many extol the virtues of the "long tail" concept: given more choice, some people will take advantage of it—exploring a wide variety of niche content. But this only applies to situations where someone really cares about the subject or task at hand, is knowledgeable about it, and has significant time and resources to expend in the discovery of novel and interesting alternatives.

Unfortunately that is rarely the situation when someone visits your landing page. Most people are in a hurry and do not have time, they don't care much about your website, and they know little about your subject matter. Under these circumstances, too many choices can cause paralysis and inaction. If visitors can't find a way to easily get closer to their goal, they will simply leave.

Consider Adorama's homepage (www.adorama.com), shown in Figure 4.7. It illustrates many of the issues with having too many choices.

Figure 4.7 Adorama homepage

Adorama sells a broad array of photography-related gear, and the visitor is presented with a bewildering array of choices. There are 146 clickable items on this page! Product shots feature a dozen disparate items that range in price from $24.95 to $799.95. Brightly animated graphical banner ads across the top and right side of the page clamor for attention, leading to specific items on the site. A scrollable news ticker and rotating banner ads draw the eye through motion.

Which of the following are visitors expected to do?

- **Read the scrolling news bar?** They probably did not come there for photo industry news.

- **Buy a replacement lithium-ion battery compatible only with certain Nikon cameras?** This is limited to a small segment of the visitors to the homepage (who already own the compatible models of cameras).

- **Click on the cryptic Photo Essentials category?** Even if they read down to the 13th position on the left navigation bar to reach this item, they would be hard-pressed to figure out what it meant.

- **Click on the Copiers/Printers/Fax Machines ad?** Most people would not have a compelling reason to buy these kinds of items from a company whose tagline is "The Photography People."

- **Read the "How to master dog photography" article by Bowser?** This is probably not a pressing concern for most visitors.

You can imagine that while sitting in a company staff meeting, somebody approved the addition of all of these items to the homepage. Each item may be useful to a subset of your audience and may be logical in its own right. But the cumulative effect of all this clutter is that you are squandering precious milliseconds of every visitor's attention. They are forced to wade through a lot of muck to even understand if there is any relevant information for them on your page. Will they do this? Probably not. Many will simply throw up their hands in frustration and try another website.

The main goal of a broad-selection online catalog should be to efficiently direct all visitors to a relevant set of product choices and to help them decide among them. The Adorama page does not do this effectively. A better alternative would be to focus on a smaller number of choices that apply to everyone and to funnel visitors deeper into the site.

Figure 4.8 shows the body of the homepage for B&H (www.bhphotovideo.com), a company similar to Adorama in its breadth and scope of product offerings.

Photography
Digital Cameras, Lenses, Flashes, Printers & Scanners See All Photo

Camcorders
High Definition, Shoot & Share, Sports & Helmet, 3D, Underwater
See All Consumer Video

Professional Video
Camcorders & Cameras, Production Equipment, Post Production, Audio for Video See All Pro Video

Photo Accessories
Film, Memory Cards, Tripods, Bags & Cases, Software, Underwater
See All Photo Accessories

Computers
Mac, PC, Tablets, Monitors, Storage, Software See All Computers

Pro Audio
Recording, Live Sound, ENG, EFP & Broadcast, Computer Audio
See All Pro Audio

Home Entertainment
TVs & Projectors, Home Theater In a Box, A/V Receivers, Speakers, Blu-ray Players DVD Players
See All Home Entertainment

A/V Presentation
Projectors, Projection Screens, Presenters and Visualizers, Furniture & Mounts
See All A/V Presentation

Lighting & Studio
Continuous Lighting, Strobe Lighting, Theatrical & Stage Lighting, Lighting Controls & Grip
See All Lighting & Studio

Portable Entertainment
iPods, MP3 Players, Headphones & Earphones, Portable DVD Players,
See All Portable Entertainment

Surveillance Video
Network Cameras, Analog Cameras, Lenses, DVR / NVR, Monitors
See All Surveillance

Optics
Binoculars, Telescopes, Spotting Scopes, Night Vision See All Optics

Figure 4.8 B&H Photo homepage body

It handles one critical task significantly better: The attention of the user is directed to the grid of high-level categories. Each main category is given equal weight, and the representative photos and descriptive text make it easy to see at a glance the breadth of the product line available on the site. Group shots representing the diversity of products in each category convey a sense of "categoriness." By combining multiple products in one image, they clearly show that this does not correspond to an individual item in the catalog, but rather to a group of items. Deeper navigation for knowledgeable visitors is also available via text link subcategories. The number of subcategories is restricted to a reasonable seven items (a short enough list to be effectively remembered in short-term memory) with a "See All" expansion for additional subcategories). The whole breadth of the product line is represented well, but without overwhelming complexity.

Too Many Choices—The Fix

- Don't present detail too early in the process.
- Group related choices into a smaller number of categories.
- Use visual shortcuts to reduce reading.

Visual Distractions

Since the Web is primarily a visual medium, you can think of your computer monitor as a window onto the world. A basic question is where your visitor should be looking shortly after arriving on your page.

Design can definitely influence conversion. Unfortunately, it is usually for the worse. Most of the responsibility can be laid at the feet of the internal creative team or outside interactive agency. Because of the limitations of their unique perspective, you have been forced to sacrifice conversions in the name of "coolness." So you have actually come to love your page and can no longer see it objectively.

Let's take a look at the origins of this situation, and begin with the end in mind. The "end" should be pretty obvious—to have the most efficient landing page or process possible. This requires putting aside your own corporate and personal needs and considering everything from the perspective of your visitors. Only they matter, and without them you would not have a business. In the past you may have paid lip service to the notion that "the customer is always right" but have probably not done anything about it.

 The key to effective landing page design is *clarity*.

The purpose of your landing page must be clear. The visitor should be focused on taking a simple path that leads to the desired conversion action. This simple path should arise out of the Zen-like stillness of your landing page.

Unfortunately, many landing pages are at the opposite end of the spectrum from this desired state. They scream and demand the visitor's attention. They visually assault the visitor, forcing them to determine for themselves which of the many strikingly visual elements on the page is the important one.

The situation can be pretty chaotic. Many pages range from simply annoying to downright repulsive. Gratuitous graphics clutter the page and are unrelated to the product or service in question. Strong and contrasting colors dominate the scene, and text styles are outlandish and baroque. There is no clear visual separation between page content and the page shell (header, navigation, backgrounds).

The page shown in Figure 4.9 is a perfect example.

Unfortunately, because this figure is in black-and-white, you must try to imagine the page in its full-color glory. The background colors of the boxes on the page are primarily red, orange, or green. The text is white and bright yellow. There is no clear focus or organization to the page. It is the visual equivalent of having someone fire a submachine gun at your face at point-blank range. Many people's reaction will be to immediately leave.

Figure 4.9 New York Barbells homepage

Graphics designers are rarely trained in maximizing conversion. The best designers pride themselves on their ability to be nonconformists, and their ability to "think outside the box." They are bored with doing regular production-oriented graphic design work, and like to keep themselves entertained by doing something new and interesting on every project.

Here is a short list of the more common visual transgressions found on landing pages:

Wild Background Colors Many landing pages use dark and dramatic color themes. Often the background of the page or large sections of it are black or fully saturated bright colors. Unfortunately, these kinds of color choices often create a dark and brooding atmosphere, or imply something so exotic that it would only appeal to teenage male adrenalin junkies who like to play video games.

Garish Text Page text and headlines are haphazardly placed on the page and often use large fonts in high-contrast colors. Font sizes are often enormous, and are further emphasized by the use of edging effects, drop shadows, color transitions and fades, and fill patterns.

Visual Embellishments and Flourishes Even simple page elements such as box edges are emphasized with drop shadows, glow, or other effects. Simple round disks in bullet lists are replaced by colorful graphical check marks or other icons. Neutral background space to the sides of the landing page is often filled in with intricate patterns or photographic images.

Animation or Video All of the other design sins on the landing page pale in comparison to the aggressive use of motion, animation, and video. Images and text pulsate or revolve, image slideshows use wild fly-in transition effects, intricate animation sequences draw the eye, and full-motion video autoplays on the page. These attention-grabbing tactics are powerful. Unfortunately, they are rarely tied to the desired conversion goal on the landing page and only serve to squander a few precious seconds of the limited visitor attention. The presence of these kinds of elements is not necessarily bad—in fact, it can increase conversion if handled properly (see Chapter 7, "Conversion Improvement Basics," for a detailed discussion). However, you should never deploy rich media on your page without testing it first to determine its impact on conversion.

The homepage of the Rushmore online casino shown in Figure 4.10 illustrates many of these problems. Online gaming sites often represent the excesses of competing visual attention, with the mistaken belief that re-creating the maddening cacophony of the real casino experience is somehow appropriate to the Web.

Figure 4.10 Rushmore Casino homepage

SpadeClub.com asked SiteTuners to redesign their homepage (shown in Figure 4.11). Although it was relatively visually tame by the standards of online gaming sites, the presentation still overwhelmed the business purpose. The goal of the page was get visitors to create an account and download the interactive software; however, the page suffered from many of the worst practices. These included a large (and irrelevant) photo of a model, icons next to each of the bullets in the Member Benefits section, and colorful avatar images in the Recent Winners and Testimonials areas. The background of the account-creation form was a deep burgundy color, and all form labels were in hard-to-read white text on this darker background.

Figure 4.11 SpadeClub's original homepage

As you can see in Figure 4.12, the redesigned homepage has a much cleaner look, with the only strong visual elements in the white content area being the "hero shot" (demonstrating a screenshot of the software) and the large call-to-action button. As a result of this redesign, the new page has a visual hierarchy and its conversion goal is clear.

Figure 4.12 SpadeClub's redesigned homepage

Graphic artists need to follow a minimalist visual aesthetic that focuses on conversion and not "window dressing." The new landing page may not be very exciting visually, but that's okay. In fact, it is desirable. On a toned-down page, the call-to-action emerges from the relative stillness of the page.

> "Boring" works. And it makes you a lot more money—that should make it much more exciting.

Banner Ads

A big awareness-thief is the third-party (or in-house) ad on your own landing pages. It is an invitation to throw away your visitors' attention and transport them to another website. Ads are specifically designed to grab awareness. Visual banner ads in particular are known for using bright, dramatic colors and provocative headlines. Many banner ads include animation and flashing colors to get noticed. Since most websites do not control the exact ads that will run on their pages, this is an invitation for disaster. A single banner ad can radically shift the attention away from your intended conversion action. Unless your primary business model is advertising supported, ads should be eliminated from your site, or at least radically deemphasized via location or editorial policies limiting the allowable formatting of the ads.

Entry Pop-ups

The absolute best way to destroy someone's attention is the use of entry pop-ups. These are floating windows that appear in front of your landing page as soon as it loads into the visitor's browser. Such pop-ups typically include a call-to-action such as filling out a form or clicking on a link leading to a special offer. Regardless of how they are technically implemented, they require an interaction by the visitor in order to deal with them. This means that the visitor must complete the intended action, or at least click on the pop-up in order to close and dismiss it from their computer screen. In effect, entry pop-ups prevent you from getting to the content of the landing page and are seen as an unwelcome surprise by most web users.

Entry pop-ups represent the most blatant kind of in-your-face interruption advertising. They will anger, annoy, frustrate, and distract your visitors before they even see your landing page. Worst of all, using entry pop-ups shows really poor thinking on the part of the marketer responsible for their creation. If the pop-up's desired conversion action is your most important one, then it properly belongs on the landing page itself. If the conversion action on the landing page is different than the one in the pop-up, then the two can be displayed on the landing page side by side, instead of resorting to the use of the pop-up. By emphasizing one or the other through the use of visual cues on the landing page, you can control their relative importance and steer people toward the more desirable one.

Entry pop-ups are an indication that your ability to prioritize is severely impaired and that you do not trust your actual landing page to get the job done on its own. It is absolutely unnecessary to compete with your own landing page and in the process alienate the vast majority of your visitors.

The page in Figure 4.13 is shown with a chat entry pop-up overlaid. The Chat dialog box popped up immediately (before the visitor even had a chance to view or read the page). It was also difficult to dismiss (by clicking on the small No Thanks link in the lower-right border of the pop-up window). The window appeared on the left edge of the screen and actually moved to the right. When it reached the right edge of the browser window, it reversed directions and moved to the left again. This kind of unwelcome and highly annoying surprise will probably cost a lot of money to the company in question.

Figure 4.13 Moving entry pop-up dialog box

Exit Pop-ups

The effect of exit pop-ups is not as clear. These are similar to entry pop-ups but appear only when someone is clicking *away* from your landing page or website. Exit pop-ups may try to entice you with a last-minute promotion, ask you to sign up for an e-mail newsletter in exchange for your contact information, or gather survey information about your reason for leaving. All of these can be seen as secondary conversion actions that have value to you. Since your primary conversion action did not happen, you can at least try to extract a little extra value from your visitor stream (especially if you are paying to get them there).

This may seem to contradict what we wrote earlier about competing for attention with your own landing pages. But in fact it does not—you are competing for attention with your web visitors' next destination. They have already made the decision to move on, and in a sense you have nothing to lose. So a final dose of interruption marketing may salvage a tiny fraction of these people. Of course, taken to an extreme this may frustrate people and leave them with a negative impression of your company. So be judicious in your use of exit pop-ups.

Not Keeping Your Promises

Does your landing page deliver what I expected?

Your visitor did not just materialize out of thin air. They came from somewhere. This "somewhere" could have been another page on your site, a search engine result, an e-mail newsletter, a link in a blog post, or a banner ad. Regardless of the origin, some kind of *expectation* had undoubtedly been set. Does your landing page keep the promise that your upstream traffic sources make?

It is critical to match the visitor's upstream expectation and *intent* on the landing page to maximize the conversion rate. The way to do this is to align your page with the messaging and promises made upstream, and create a clear information scent trail that makes visitors feel they are making progress toward their ultimate goal.

Creating a high degree of continuity and consistency with the upstream experience is critical. If you fail to do this, you visitor will feel lost, confused, and frustrated. This is especially the case where there is no actual access to information that had been previously promised, or an intentional "bait and switch" situation has occurred.

Let's explore a specific example. Imagine that you are looking for a new digital camera and are in the research stages of your search. You don't know much about the specific model to buy, or even what features it should have or what criteria it should meet. So you just do a Google search for "best digital camera" and get the PPC ad shown in Figure 4.14 on the search results page.

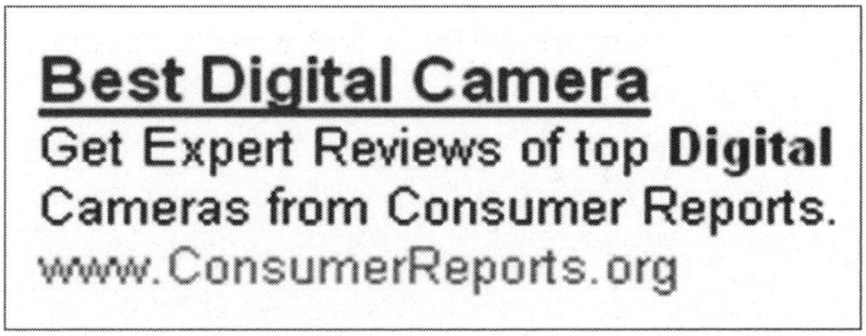

Best Digital Camera
Get Expert Reviews of top **Digital**
Cameras from Consumer Reports.
www.ConsumerReports.org

Figure 4.14 Google AdWords PPC ad

Imagine your state of mind and expectations. You are probably happy that the title of the result exactly matches your search query. The next two lines promise expert review of top digital cameras, which would definitely help you in your selection process. The source of these reviews is Consumer Reports, a highly regarded and well-established independent provider of information about the quality of consumer products. Your expectations are high—you expect to get expert reviews of top camera models from a trusted and familiar company.

When you actually clickthrough on the ad, you will arrive at the landing page shown in Figure 4.15.

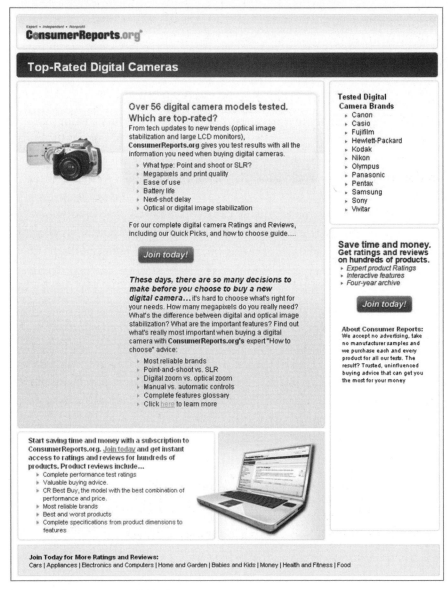

Figure 4.15 Consumer Reports PPC landing page

At first, there seems to be a high degree of continuity from the ad. The page title is "Top-Rated Digital Cameras." The headline asks: "Over 56 digital cameras tested. Which are top-rated?" The upper-right of the page lists "Tested Digital Camera Brands" and covers all of the major manufacturers.

However, the only apparent calls-to-action on the page are aggressively red buttons with the text "Join today!"

You were expecting expert camera reviews, but instead are being asked for money to join a subscription-based site before you get the promised camera reviews. This is a horrible, and completely avoidable, disconnect that will make most visitors to this site very mad. In the greedy rush on the part of the marketers to ask for the sale, they have actually blocked the site visitor from getting the information that they promised earlier. The chances of someone subscribing immediately after they feel that they have been duped are very low.

Here are some things that the Consumer Reports site could have done to avoid this situation:

Provide a sample review. This would show the visitor the depth and format of information and help to firmly establish Consumer Reports as a source of high-quality information. Since there are 56 models tested, it is unlikely that the visitor will buy the reviewed model without wanting to get the complete information on the rest of the models.

Provide non-review, value-added information. As it happens, there is already a small link in the body of the landing page that leads to a video buyers guide. This helpful guide explains in detail which camera features are important and why. This is valuable information that is already available for free but is buried on the landing page.

Be up-front in the upstream ad. Consumer Reports could have included the information that a subscription was required in the PPC ad itself. This would have probably resulted in a much lower clickthrough rate (CTR) on the ad, but it would have properly set the expectations of everyone visiting the landing page and increased the chances of those visitors buying the subscription in order to get access to the reviews.

Not Keeping Your Promises—The Fix

- Understand your important upstream traffic sources and their context.
- Match landing page content to the traffic source messaging and intent.
- Provide clear access to promised information or functionality, without strings attached.

Too Much Text

Do you really expect me to read all this?

Study after study has shown that people do not read online. Since the subject of writing for the Web is covered in detail in Chapter 7, we will only summarize this sin here.

No one reads full-paragraph text on the Web. People get lost if there is no clear hierarchy or flow to the organization of the text.

Figure 4.16 shows an example of a landing page for a PPC campaign. The page is stuffed with detailed, long-winded text and has dozens of hyperlinks along the sides. Chances are, it also pulls double-duty as a page for SEO. Even if this is the case, there is simply too much information. Most site visitors will be overwhelmed by the amount of text and won't read it.

Figure 4.16 Canyon Tours' text-heavy homepage

Too Much Text—The Fix

- Use a clear page title and headings.

- Use an "inverted pyramid" writing style, putting the important stuff first.

- Do not write in complete sentences—use short bullet lists whenever possible.

- Ruthlessly edit and shorten your text.

- Move long text to supporting pages or informational popovers.

Similarly, Figure 4.17 shows a very long page that features detailed information about rack-mounted computer servers. Even though this is a technical specialty, the amount of text on the page is simply too much. It would be better to segregate the detailed descriptions under "See details...."

Figure 4.17 Iron Systems' text-heavy page

Asking for Too Much Information

Why should I give you all this information?

In real life, we are careful to follow social rules and norms and to not act inappropriately. We give people their "space" and a high degree of privacy. In business transactions we also have a certain etiquette.

Online, however, we marketers often become greedy—possibly because of the anonymity of the Web. We start asking for information simply because it might be useful to us in the future, without considering the negative impact on conversion rates. For example, imagine walking into brick-and-mortar store and being greeted by a brusque clerk at the door who asks you if they may "hold onto your credit card while you browse the store." Such a request would most probably be met with disbelief or laughter. But online, equally inane behavior is often exhibited on landing pages.

As Seth Godin correctly points out in his book *Permission Marketing: Turning Strangers into Friends and Friends into Customers* (Simon & Schuster, 1999), the web visitors are in control. They decide the terms of their interactions with our landing pages. The marketer must make sure that the value scale tips in favor of the visitor. In other words, we must give as much as we can and ask for as little as possible in return at each stage of our deepening relationship with the visitor. We cannot expect them to endure hardships or a loss of control in order to supply us with information.

One SiteTuners client was a major research university healthcare system. Like many U.S. hospitals, they make most of their profits on elective surgeries and do everything they can to publicize their efficacy and availability. One of the tactics they used to market bariatric surgery (commonly called "gastric bypass" for cases of extreme obesity) was an online registration for an in-person seminar to be attended by prospective patients. The online registration form asked for the prospective patient's "BMI." Many people are not familiar with this acronym, but even if someone knew that it stood for Body Mass Index, chances are they would not know how to immediately calculate it. The form did supply a supporting link that showed the formula for calculating BMI, but why was all of this necessary? No one would subject themselves to an in-person two-hour seminar during the weekend on stomach-stapling surgery unless they were serious about the procedure. In any case, the seminar organizers could quickly eyeball an attendee and determine if they were a candidate for the surgery. Asking for the BMI information was completely unnecessary, and probably significantly lowered seminar sign-ups.

Another SiteTuners client, HearingPlanet, was collecting online leads by offering a free downloadable *Buyer's Guide to Hearing Aids*. However, in order to download the guide, the site visitor had to fill out the form on the landing page, as shown in Figure 4.18. This form included several fields for the physical mailing address of the person. This information was clearly unnecessary to simply download the guide.

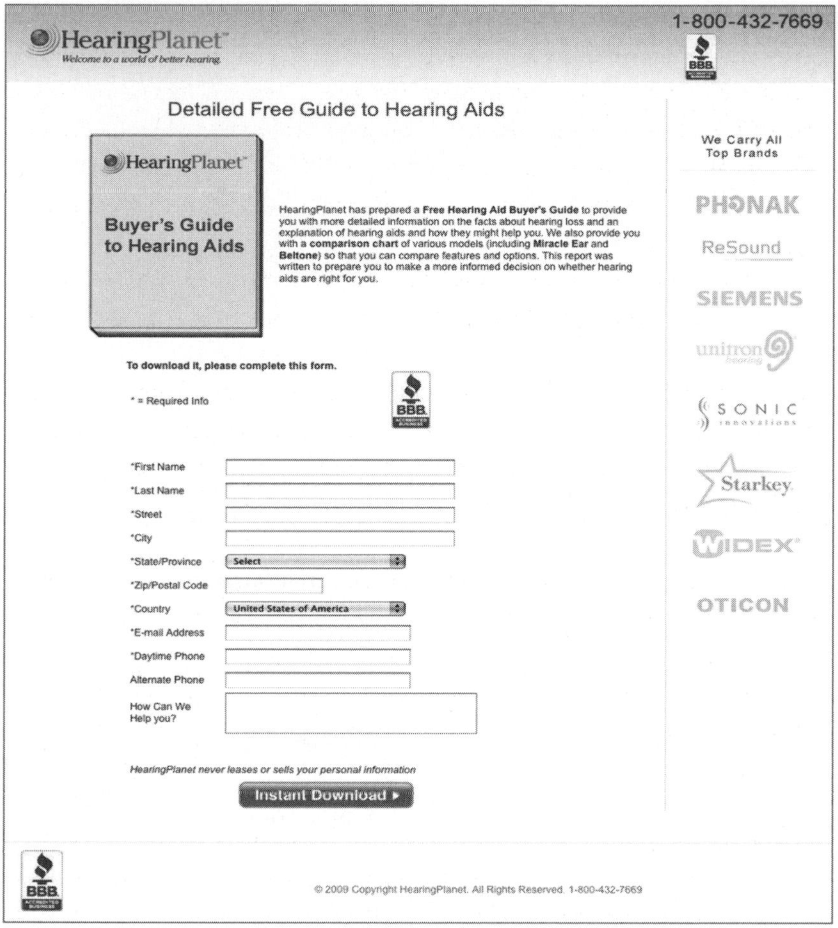

Figure 4.18 HearingPlanet e-book download page with street address form fields

When the address fields were removed from the form, as shown in Figure 4.19, the number of forms that were completed increased by 17 percent. The information that the company determined was important and therefore remained on the online form included first and last name, e-mail, daytime phone, state, and an optional comment field. However, this is not the minimum of information required to download the guide. Most marketers would still insist that you need a valid e-mail address, but this too is a product of the inappropriate online information-gathering greed that we suffer under. In fact, no data at all is necessary to download an electronic document.

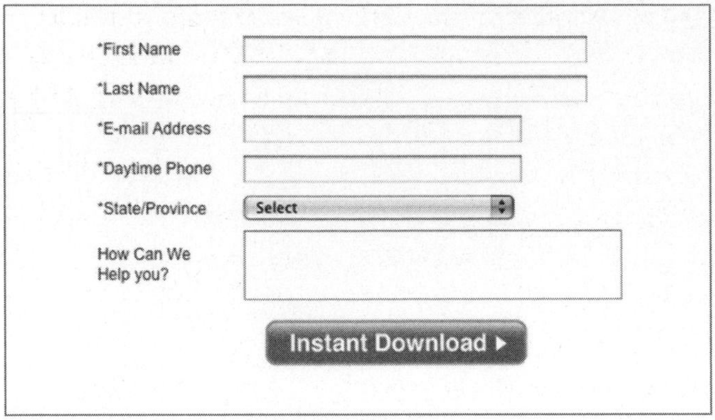

Figure 4.19 Alternative HearingPlanet form

In the case of HearingPlanet, it can be argued that the better option might be to let the download go viral and be spread as quickly as possible among prospects, their families, their caregivers, and their healthcare decision makers. In other words, even asking for the e-mail address may be too much. Nothing is really lost in the process, because the downloaded document contains links back to actionable landing pages. If a visitor finds the guide helpful, they will have a way to remember and get back in touch in the future. The only thing we marketers would lose in the process is a sense of control.

Forms should also be ruthlessly edited. A long and imposing form will turn many people away. The value of the incremental information gathered in a longer form will rarely outweigh the benefit of having many more people complete the process. Here are some quick ideas to improve your forms:

- Clarify form purpose with a clear and concise title that describes the benefit that the visitor will get if they expend the effort to complete the form.

- Keep all descriptive labels and explanatory text as short as possible.

- Organize form fields into logically labeled subgroups.

- The most important part of form creation is minimizing the number and complexity of form input fields. As a start, you should eliminate all "optional" fields.

 The Form Field Test: Is this information absolutely necessary to complete the current transaction?

You should only ask for information that you need right now—resist the temptation to ask for information that you may not need at all or that you can collect later in the process (after you have established more trust with the visitor). Also, you may want to avoid repeated data entry by having forms automatically uploaded into your sales force automation (SFA) or customer relationship management (CRM) systems, but do not insist on populating a complete record in these databases immediately. Such "nice-to-have" reasons do not meet the Form Field Test criteria.

A SiteTuners partner, SEM firm Engine Ready, was running a large-scale PPC campaign for a client in the debt-negotiation business. The client's goal was to collect qualified leads for telephone follow-up. The conversion action was the completion of the landing page form shown in Figure 4.20.

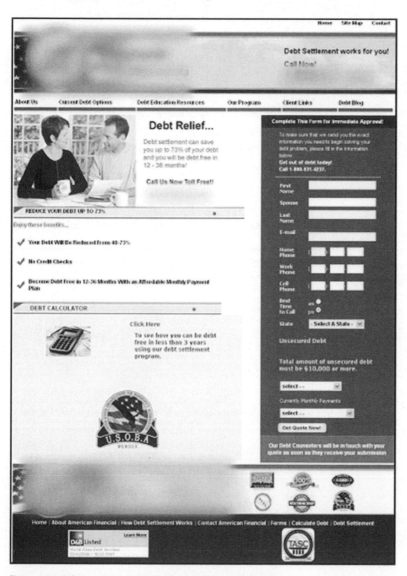

Figure 4.20 Debt negotiation original lead-generation landing page

After discussions with the client, we determined that not all of the fields on the original form were absolutely required—many of them could be collected during the follow-up phone call. A landing page test was conducted where the minimum number of fields was tested on the page along with a few other changes. The winning version is shown in Figure 4.21.

Figure 4.21 Winning alternative debt negotiation page

As you can see, the landing page was radically stripped down in terms of color, labels, and number of form fields. As a result, it looks much less imposing and is more likely to be completed. This winning landing page produced a 51 percent improvement in revenue per visitor over the original. The impact of this change was an estimated $48 million in additional annual revenue for the client.

Asking for Too Much Information—The Fix

- Ask only for information that is absolutely required.
- Collect additional information at a later date as trust is established.
- Shorten labels and unclutter form layout.

Lack of Trust and Credibility

Why should I trust you?

Human beings are social creatures who seek out companionship and relationships. Our map of reality can be viewed as a series of concentric circles, with those we trust most in the center and those we know and trust less further out.

We crave trust. Without it, we would be consigned to a world where we must examine everyone's actions with suspicion and assume they are working only for their purposes and not ours. Because of the sheer number of social interactions we have with complete strangers, we must extend some trust. Otherwise, many acts, both small and momentous, simply could not happen at all.

Even with total strangers in the "real world," we at least have their appearance and body language to go by. But what do you do online? Almost anyone can quickly create a website or landing page and masquerade as a wide variety of businesses. Many of these enterprises are untrustworthy. We are barraged by media reports about various scams perpetrated online and have our guard up.

As an online marketer, your job is difficult compared to your brick-and-mortar marketing counterpart. You must not only overcome anxieties, but do so in the most challenging of circumstances.

Online trust must be developed without any face-to-face contact, and it must be created instantly in the few precious seconds it takes a website visitor to evaluate your value proposition.

So how can you build instant trust online?

Appearance

First impressions matter. We do judge a book by its cover. Recent research indicates that people will form an initial impression of your landing page or website within 50 milliseconds. This is almost as fast as visual processing happens in the brain, and can be considered as an instantaneous and automatic response. In other words, we subliminally decide where the page falls on our "cheesy" to "professional" continuum. And this initial reaction extends to a more considered review of the page and will impact our likelihood of taking the desired conversion action.

Look at the screenshot in Figure 4.22 and answer the following question: Would you consider buying a grand piano from this company?

If you are like most people, the answer is probably a resounding "No!" The production quality of the site is at a very low level. The design is extremely dated and not up to the polish and professionalism standards of modern websites.

The same applies to the website shown in Figure 4.23. This company sells high-end luxury yachts. However, the website almost looks like an afterthought. Besides the dated logo, the only graphics on the page are an animated American flag that waves. We can charitably say that this site is not likely to contribute to high levels of confidence in the company or lead to sales of yachts.

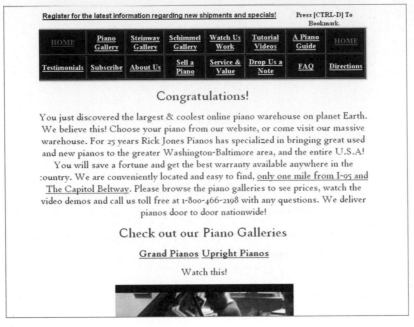

Figure 4.22 Rick Jones Pianos' homepage

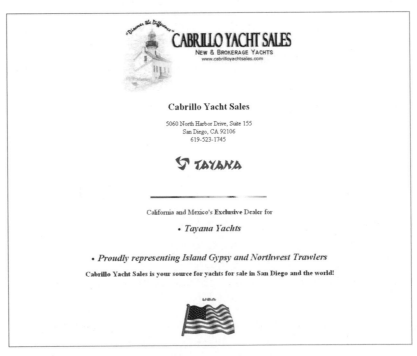

Figure 4.23 Cabrillo Yacht Sales' homepage

Here are some important elements that contribute to a good first impression:

Professionalism of Design Regardless of the intended audience or your business purpose, the visual design should be professionally executed. It should hang together and function as a single unified whole. Fonts, colors, and graphical elements must combine into a single visual "look."

Sparseness and Neatness Clutter can be your worst enemy, whether it is visual embellishments or dense, longwinded text. Less is more. Ruthlessly edit everything on the page until it is pared to its essence and has a natural and unforced feel. Give your page room to breathe.

Organization and Clarity Too many choices of what to do on the page can be paralyzing. Similarly, a disorganized page increases the visitor's "cognitive load" and forces them to spend time trying to figure out in what order they should digest the information you have presented. As the title of Steve Krug's excellent book on web usability so elegantly puts it: "Don't Make Me Think" (*Don't Make Me Think: A Common Sense Approach to Web Usability, 2nd Edition*, New Riders Press, 2005).

Transactional Assurances

Will we be spammed if we enter our e-mail in a form? Will the goods promised ever be delivered after we order from an online catalog? Will our very identity be stolen? Such questions are always in the background when we navigate around the Web. Even if we have decided to act or transact on a webpage, chances are there are a lot of concerns still swirling around in our heads.

Transactional assurances are especially critical during this moment of decision. They are risk reducers that lower a visitor's anxiety and help reassure the visitor that bad things are unlikely to happen.

Here are some common forms of transactional assurances along with their meaning to your visitor:

Guarantees If I don't like it, I can get my money back.

Policies The company has a no-hassle return policy.

Alternative Transaction Mechanisms I can also complete my transaction on the phone, by mail, or in person.

Trials and Introductory Offers If I don't like it, I can cancel before they charge my credit card.

Safe Shopping Symbols My personal information will not be stolen.

Privacy Symbols I will not be spammed by this company, and my e-mail won't be sold to spammers.

Transactional assurances need to be seen *before* the checkout process or conversion step itself, and as prominently as possible. Otherwise, the visitor may not feel comfortable enough to proceed.

Let's look at some examples. SmartBargains.com (www.smartbargains.com) lists a number of risk-reducing transactional assurance badges on their website. Unfortunately, they are placed in the footer of the page (see highlighted area in Figure 4.24). Because these symbols are well below the top of the page, they cannot be seen without scrolling. So the positive effect of displaying the trust symbols is significantly lower than it could be.

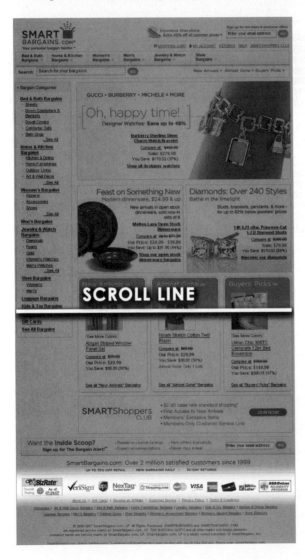

Figure 4.24 Smart Bargains' non-prominent transactional assurances

By contrast, PetSmart.com (www.petsmart.com) considers the ScanAlert HackerSafe trust mark (since renamed McAfee Secure) so important that they chose to display it in the upper-left corner—the most prominent and powerful position on any webpage. This area is usually reserved for the company's logo. In this case, PetSmart compensated for the change by displaying their logo in a large size and centered on the header. This format, shown in Figure 4.25, instantly transmits a two-part message to the visitor: "We're safe to buy from—we're PetSmart."

Figure 4.25 PetSmart homepage with trust symbol in upper-left corner

If possible, the safe shopping and privacy symbols should be the leading ones in their category; otherwise, there is an additional momentary pause and possible confusion as the visitor evaluates the validity and credibility of the less-familiar trust symbol itself.

Relieve point-of-action anxieties before they arise.

The mechanics of the conversion action matter. Whether you are trying to collect an e-mail for an online newsletter or have someone purchase an expensive item from you, reassurances are needed about the transaction.

Here are some conversion actions that can help reassure visitors about making an online purchase:

Forms of Payment and Delivery Many e-commerce catalogs only show acceptable forms of payment and return policies after the checkout process has been started. In fact, they must be seen before they are needed, and prominently displayed above the fold on every page. The same is true of well-known delivery and shipping methods.

Data Security and Privacy The site that you transact with must be certified as safe by outside experts in terms of its ability to protect your data. Having privacy policies and computer security trust symbols from well-known vendors will instantly show visitors that you have safeguarded their data properly.

Policies and Guarantees Often the transaction is not at issue—what happens afterward is the thing that concerns people. By prominently featuring your warranties, return policies, and guarantees, you can assuage these anxieties. Often, a visual seal can be created to draw the eye to these important elements.

Outside Experts and Media

Your visitors are not likely to have heard of you. Unless you represent a truly world-class consumer company, people are unlikely to know your brand promise. They do not know what you stand for.

Transactional assurances may lower a visitor's anxiety levels, but you can also raise your visitor's affinity level for your website or product with validation and credibility indicators. In effect, transactional assurances make the visitor feel "less worse," while evidence of third-party validation makes them feel "more better." Both are based on transferring goodwill from other people or companies to yours. No one wants to be the fool who fell for a ruse and had to deal with the consequences.

Third-party validation tells people that knowledgeable experts or reviewers have concluded that you have a quality service or product. This serves as a shortcut to decision making for your visitors.

Here are some examples of third-party validation:

- Industry or media awards (such as an editor's choice or fastest-growing company award)
- Media coverage (mentions in mainstream press, websites, or blogs)
- Inclusion in industry analyst reports
- Endorsements from trade organizations and associations
- Partnerships with other respected companies
- Studies and surveys (such as market share or customer satisfaction)
- Client lists and logos

Figure 4.26 shows the winning version of a landing page from a multivariate test for RealAge.com with the media mentions emphasized. The goal of the test was to increase the percentage of people who completed the "RealAge Test," which calculates your "real age" based on your lifestyle and how well you have maintained your body.

The questionnaire asks many personal questions about medical and personal history and habits. Despite this, the page shown in the figure performed 40 percent better than the original. Although a number of elements changed from the original page, one of the most prominent visual additions included the "As seen on" logos of media companies in the left column. These are well-known media brands and have a much higher recognition among consumers than RealAge. They provide a "halo effect" (credibility by association) and increase visitor trust.

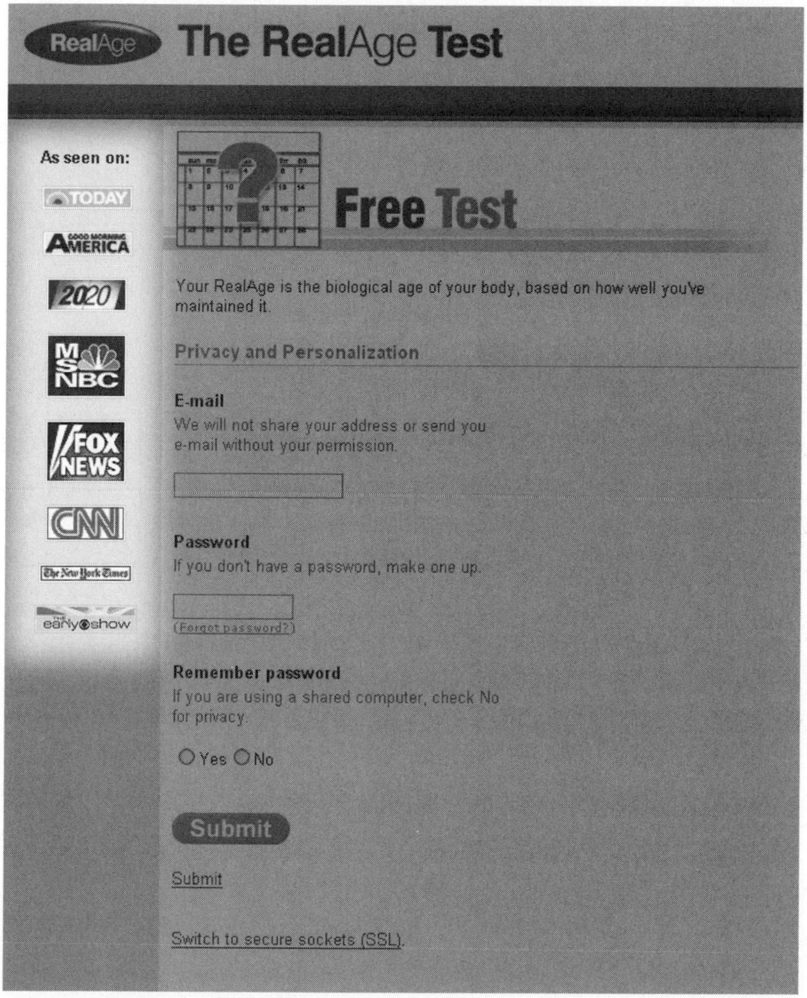

Figure 4.26 Winning page from RealAge landing page test

Another example of external validation is the PPC landing page for SF Video, shown in Figure 4.27. SF Video is a SiteTuners client that specializes in Blu-ray and DVD duplication and replication. Although the main purpose of the page is to get a visitor to fill out the online quote request form, most of the screen is taken up by logos of their marquee clients. In a business-to-business setting, your clients are often your most powerful asset. Chances are if you landed on this page, your internal thought process would sound like this: "Wow—this company works with a lot of very big and reputable companies. I hope that they will take on my itty-bitty little duplication job."

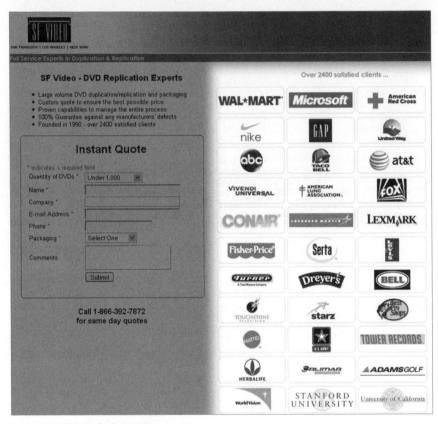

Figure 4.27 SF Video landing page

The presence of logos is critical for success. The page shown in the figure performed 58 percent better than another almost-identical page that only had six logos stacked in a single vertical column (see the "Variable Interaction" section of Chapter 12, "Testing Methods," for a more in-depth case study).

Trust is one of the few exceptions to the "less is more" guideline. It is often best to have as much visible trust reinforcement on the page as possible.

 Borrow trust from better-known brands.

Examples of outside authority include the following:

- **Reviews and Awards** Many services and products have won awards or at least been reviewed by relevant industry publications. Using the award seals or "Reviewed by" language can be very effective.

- **Paid Endorsements and Spokespeople** Paid endorsements can transfer the trust or at least the celebrity of the spokesperson to the product or service in question.

- **Marquee Clients** Using client logos with permission, or at least prominently featuring a written list of clients (unless specifically prohibited from doing so by contract language) will create powerful visual proof of your legitimacy. They confer an implicit halo effect: If you have worked with large companies, of course you can handle smaller companies as well.

- **Media Mentions** Media companies are experts at self-promotion and drumming their brands into our consciousness. Any association with them confers a notoriety and solidity to your landing page. Often "media outlets" can also be broadly defined as bloggers or authoritative voices in your specific niche.

There are several caveats to the use of expert and media logos. They must appear "above the fold" and be seen at the same time as the call-to-action (not below or after it) in order to provide the context for the content on the page.

On the other hand, they must be displayed subtly so they do not dominate the visual conversation. The logos are often well designed, distinctive, and instantly recognizable. So you may have to deemphasize their impact by reducing their size, decreasing their color saturation (possibly using grayscale), and decreasing the contrast with the background color chosen to display the logos.

Also, the use of rotating or animated lists of logos should be avoided, because the motion will draw an inordinate amount of attention, and the length of time required to view the entire list may be too long.

Consensus of Peers

We often follow the lead of people like ourselves. If we see many friends driving a particular make of car, we are more apt to consider buying it. If our circle of acquaintances turns us on to a new musical group, we are more likely to give the group a listen. Regardless of the actual cultural "tribes" that we belong to, our peers exert a strong influence on us.

When uncertain, people look outside of themselves to the actions of their peers under similar circumstances.

It almost does not matter what your tribes are (and all of us informally belong to many of them). BMW owners, iPhone users, Burning Man funksters, and hip-hop listeners are much more likely to tune into the behavior of like-minded people.

According to persuasion expert Dr. Robert Cialdini, the following two aspects of "social proof" (transferring trust from our peer group) are especially important:

The Many This implies that something is a hit or leader in your specific community or tribe. Once trends take off, the momentum of the leaders makes them hard to overtake. So any objective evidence of leadership within a particular tribe or subgroup is important.

The Comparable This is a sense of how similar someone is to you. You will not be influenced nearly as much by the actions of others with whom you do not identify. So the closer the marketing can be aligned with your specific circumstances, the better.

In a landmark study, Dr. Cialdini changed the messaging on bathroom hotel signs (across three different price points ranging from inexpensive to luxury brands). The signs asked the guests in the room to hang up their towels after use if they did not want them washed, and to leave them on the floor if they did.

Each request was identical except for the type of messaging used in the headline, as follows:

Recycle and do it for the environment. This was the standard control and resulted in 38 percent compliance during people's stay.

Cooperate and join us. This actually resulted in a lower 36 percent compliance, because it was perceived as a self-serving request on the part of the hotel to save on operating expenses. You can't *claim* partnership—you must *earn* partnership.

The majority of guests are reusing towels at least once during their stay. This appeal to "The Many" portion of the consensus principle resulted in a much improved 46 percent compliance with the request.

But how do you create a sense of comparability in this setting, when anonymous and random people stay at the hotel? What possible kinship of comparability can there be among them to further turbo-charge results? Well, as it turns out, even a tenuous kind of kinship is enough, as evidenced by the following:

The majority of people who stayed *in this room* are reusing towels at least once during their stay. This combination of "The Many" with "Comparability" resulted in a stunning 54 percent compliance rate.

So the use of relevant testimonials is often critical. And the testimonials should not just be from experts, but from our peers. They should change order depending on target audience or specific landing page and should not just be about the most favorable ones. Instead, lead with the most comparable ones.

A powerful example of using social proof for persuasion is shown on the Mozilla download page in Figure 4.28.

Imagine that you are considering installing the latest version of the Firefox browser. It is a popular choice, but it's only one of many viable alternatives. How do you decide?

This page combines both The Many and The Comparable into a potent one-two punch of social proof. First you see a prominent and large number "543,943,166," signifying the number of people who have downloaded the software in the two months since its release. Second, you are shown an interactive world map on which bright dots quickly blink on and off, signifying the latest download locations (presumably) in real time.

Figure 4.28 Mozilla download statistics page

The huge number of downloads provides compelling evidence for The Many. At the same time, a large number of flickering downloads in your area of the world shows that many Comparable people are taking action.

Figure 4.29 shows how social proof is used by the Internet radio station Pandora.

To the left of the main browser window, a Google Sidewiki pane is displayed. This Sidewiki is shown if you have a Google toolbar installed in your browser. Anyone with a valid Google account can comment on any website or page that they visit. Their comments are then displayed to any visitor to the same page and serve as a permanent record or context for the page. These comments demonstrate both large numbers of people (as inferred from the number of comments), as well as similar people (as evidenced by their visit to this particular page).

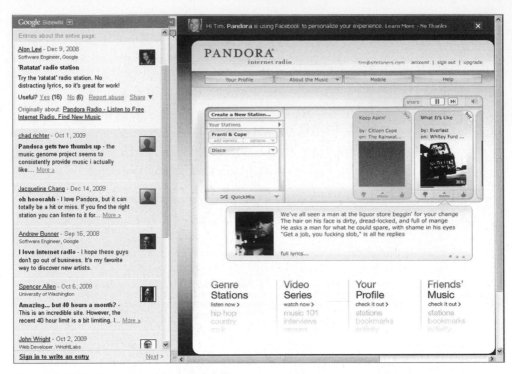

Figure 4.29 Pandora homepage with Google Sidewiki

Additionally, the top of the Pandora window shows integration with the Facebook social network: "Hi Tim, Pandora is using Facebook to personalize your experience." If a person visits a site that uses Facebook's open social integration features, they are asked if their Facebook profile information can be used by the site to personalize their experience. Although such disclosure on the part of the user is voluntary, many are choosing to allow such personal exposure in exchange for a better site experience. If the visitor agrees to the sharing of their Facebook profile information, the site operator gains access to their likes, their interests, and their friends' interests. This can be used in powerful ways to create a personalized and relevant site experience in the scope of the visitor's social activities. Since their friends are members of their cultural tribe, The Comparable is naturally what emerges.

Figure 4.30 shows the Pandora playlist for Tim Ash with the Facebook personalization features turned on.

The current artist in the playlist is Facebook "Liked" by a friend of Tim's (his wife in this case, as shown in the highlighted portion of the page). The familiar presence of a friend or relative in the context of Pandora creates positive feelings about the musical artist in question and increases the probability that the artist will in turn be given a "thumbs up" on Pandora or that their musical track will be purchased.

Figure 4.30 Use of Facebook personalization on Pandora

Support automatic compliance by demonstrating "social proof."

Here are two important ways to demonstrate social proof on your landing page:

Objective Large Numbers The Many can be demonstrated by showing how many people have bought, downloaded, or started a free trial. Numbers should be cumulative since the inception of the business or product. Spell out the digits of each number (for example, "Over 1,000,000 downloads"), and use larger fonts to draw additional attention.

Likeness Create affinity by demonstrating that the people taking action are similar to your website visitors. This can be done by picking appropriate colors, editorial tone, and graphics to make your visitors feel at home. You can also have several detailed testimonials that discuss common situations faced by similar people. Personalization via social networks is also a very powerful way to influence others.

Real-World Case Study: CREDO Mobile

SiteTuners' client CREDO Mobile is a socially conscious cell phone company based in San Francisco. They donate a portion of all revenues to progressive causes—groups that CREDO members help select. CREDO was interested in improving the performance of a landing page for a new e-mail campaign. The purpose of the campaign was to have recipients of the e-mail switch their phone plan to CREDO.

The original page is shown in Figure 4.31.

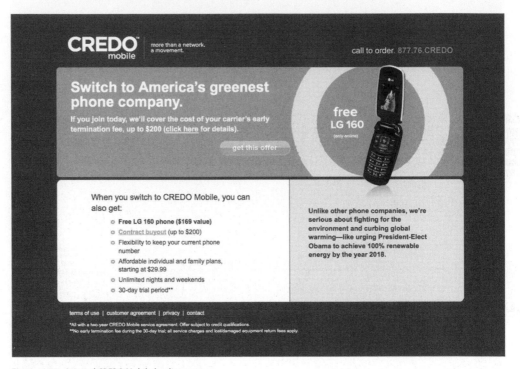

Figure 4.31 Original CREDO Mobile landing page

Most companies would have no hesitation launching a campaign with such a page. It has a professional design to a very high standard, and seems to have a clear call-to-action in the form of the button in the center of the page with the "get this offer" text. However, CREDO had SiteTuners conduct an online interactive Express Review of their landing page in order to identify major conversion issues, and four of the seven deadly sins were identified as follows:

Visual Clutter The page was strong visually, with a dark gray outside border, orange top rectangle, and white and gray lower rectangles.

Too Much Text The headline spanned two lines, there were six bullet points, and the text in the lower-right area was written in complete sentences.

Lack of Trust and Credibility The lack of trust and credibility is obvious. Unless you had already heard of CREDO, there was nothing on the page explaining who they were or borrowing trust from better-known organizations.

Unclear Call-to-Action At first glance, this might not seem to be a problem, because a green button (unlike anything else of that color) is placed near the center the page. However, a closer look at the AttentionWizard heat map shown in Figure 4.32 reveals a different story. The strong colors on the page and the shapes formed by the different-colored boxes and outlines of the design create artificial hot spots on the heat map that are simply artifacts of the design. In the midst of all the visual "noise," the green call-to-action button is lost and ignored.

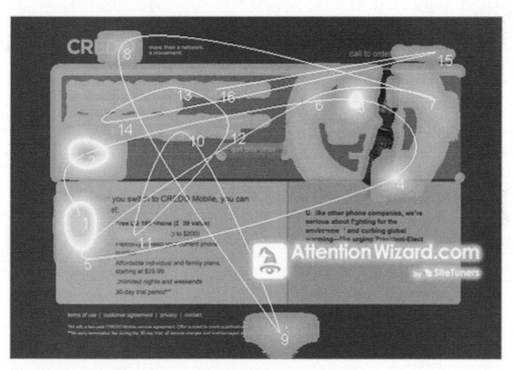

Figure 4.32 AttentionWizard heat map of the original CREDO Mobile landing page

After the Express Review, CREDO created a series of increasingly refined redesigns that incorporated our best-practices recommendations and additional ongoing consulting feedback. The final landing page is shown in Figure 4.33.

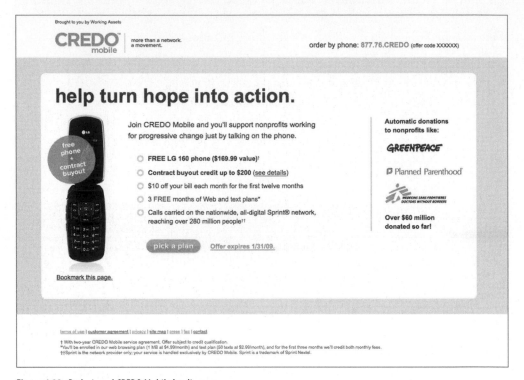

Figure 4.33 Redesigned CREDO Mobile landing page

Note that all four of the identified deadly sins were addressed as follows:

Visual Clutter The page center was changed to white, and a light seafoam green color was used for the border. This lowered the contrast of the page shell while maintaining brand consistency. The cell phone was retained as the main "hero shot" and overlaid with a bright orange round callout.

Too Much Text The headline was shortened to fit on one line, and the easy-to-scan bullet list is the only other significant remaining text on the page.

Lack of Trust and Credibility The logos of better-known organizations to which CREDO had donated large amounts from client revenue were added to the page in grayscale. These included Greenpeace, Planned Parenthood, and Doctors Without Borders.

Unclear Call-to-Action Besides the hero shot of the phone, the call-to-action button is the only bright graphical element on the page. The vibrant orange button is also set against a white background. The AttentionWizard heat map shown in Figure 4.34 confirms that there are appropriate amounts of attention on the hero shot, call-to-action, and the organizations that received donations.

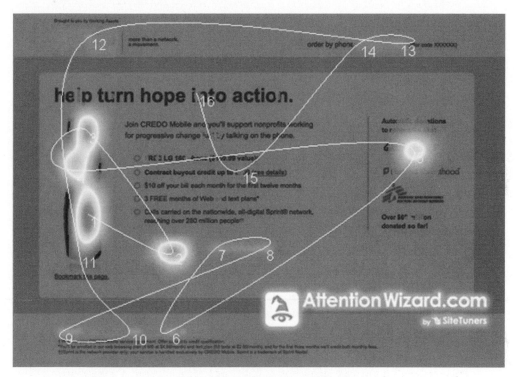

Figure 4.34 AttentionWizard heat map of the redesigned CREDO Mobile landing page

The results were stunning. In a head-to-head test, the new page performed 84 percent better than the original. The redesign of the page was done after a basic inventory and identification of the potential seven deadly sins. Correcting all of the relevant sins created a much more persuasive and effective page.

Now that you've surveyed the most common landing page problems, Chapter 5 will provide you with a number of powerful tools for identifying other problems.

Conversion Ninja Toolbox—Diagnosing Site Problems

5

Many methods are available for identifying landing page problems and seeing why they are not meeting the needs of your Internet visitors. You just need the guts to lift the veil of denial and to view these flaws and compromises objectively. To do that, you will need to arm yourself with an array of powerful tools and train yourself to be a ruthless and effective conversion ninja—fighting bad user experiences on behalf of your website visitors.

Chapter Contents

You Are Not as Good as You Would Like to Believe

Focus on the Negative

Web Analytics Tools

Visual Analysis Tools

Feedback and Survey Tools

Website Performance Tools

Competitive Analysis Tools

Usability Testing Tools

E-mail Enhancement Tools

You Are Not as Good as You Would Like to Believe

Imagine that you have been involved in designing or marketing websites and their landing pages for a long time. This typically involves holding fun brainstorming sessions, creating exciting graphical presentations of possible page designs, and writing persuasive offers and text copy.

Then comes the public unveiling and the first influx of visitors to your website. As the euphoria of the project starts to wear off, you inevitably start to see chinks in the armor of your beautiful and perfect creations: The text is too long, the intended audience is not identified clearly enough, there are no useful navigational cross-links if someone lands on a page deep within the site.

It gets worse.

Your dread may grow as objective evidence of poor design starts to mount: high shopping cart abandonment rates, extensive call-ins to the toll-free support number, high bounce rates on important pages, lower-than-expected conversion numbers.

Yet, in all of this gloom lies the way out of the mess too. After you take a step back and apply the tools and techniques in this chapter, you'll see exactly why your landing pages are at cross-purposes with the way that people take in and process information. Based on your honest analysis, you can prepare yourself for deciding exactly which elements to test and ultimately help improve.

> *Somewhere in the world is the world's worst doctor. And what's truly terrifying is that someone has an appointment with him tomorrow morning.*
>
> —COMEDIAN GEORGE CARLIN

The chilling thought above is brought to you by the deliciously twisted mind of the late master comedian George Carlin. What makes it so funny is that it is factually correct—there is somewhere by definition "the world's worst doctor." Of course, the consequences of being the world's worst landing page designer are not as severe. No one will die on the operating table. Your online marketing campaign will simply fail. If you are not the worst one, your campaign may simply bump along at a much smaller scale than it otherwise could. Besides, you can always go to your bosses and after throwing up your hands in frustration tell them all about how it is impossible to get cost-effective traffic to your site in the face of ever-increasing advertiser competition and rising prices.

Most online marketers do not want to admit that they are doing a poor job at conversion rate optimization. They liken themselves to the denizens of the mythical

Lake Wobegon from Garrison Keillor's *Prairie Home Companion* where "the women are strong, the men are good-looking, and the children are all above-average."

The whole field of decision-making theory is based on the understanding that people have warped perceptions of themselves and others. They do not make rational decisions. People consistently overestimate their own skills, influence, and importance. In one survey, 80 percent of participants reported that they were above-average drivers.

You have to let go of your own professional ego structure and become the most vicious and uncompromising critic of your own website.

Focus on the Negative

Instead of waiting only for good news, filter it out instead. Accentuate the negative. Focus on problems and things that are askew. The mind-set that I am describing is not some prescription to become a cynical person. It is a well-respected business approach called *managing by exception*. Assuming that you have set up your systems and procedures properly, you should have key indicators that tell you when things are going smoothly. During those times you should work on further strategic improvements to your business. Only if something goes wrong (as quickly flagged by your monitoring of key performance indicators in your web analytics tools) should your attention and resources be focused on the problem.

I do not mean to imply that if your online campaign is making money that you should be satisfied and smug. Unless every potential customer among your Internet visitors has already converted, you still have a lot of work to do.

The main point is to unflinchingly uncover and face problems with your landing pages and not to duck or hide from them. Remember that your baby is ugly and has significant problems—many of which may appear over time, as your market or competitors evolve. This spirit of continuous problem solving and improvement is at the heart of some of the most successful businesses on the planet. It should be an example for all of us to follow.

Now that you are prepared to look for landing page problems, you will be happy to discover we have created a conversion ninja toolbox to help you find the most important problems on your site with greater ease.

This toolbox includes many types of tools that you can deploy to uncover problems with your site—from simple web analytics tools to more advanced eye-tracking and web usability tools. Testing tool companies are addressed separately in the Appendix, "Landing Page Testing Tools."

We have summarized some of the best currently available tools in this chapter, but the Internet changes very quickly. Visit ConversionNinjaToolbox.com for an updated list of the latest ones.

Web Analytics Tools

One of the most important steps of landing page optimization is to first implement a tool that tracks all your website traffic and the actions of your visitors. Once you have collected historical data, you will be armed with much of the information that you need in order to effectively uncover issues and improve your website. The following tips will help you discover issues with your site. They can be performed using Google Analytics or a similar web analytics tool like Omniture SiteCatalyst, IBM Coremetrics, or Webtrends. We have chosen to show reports from and include instructions for Google Analytics because it is widely available and free.

Make Sure Your Mission-Critical Pages Are among Your Top 10 Pages

As discussed in Chapter 2, "Understanding Your Landing Pages," your mission-critical pages (like your key product pages and sign-up pages) are the most important on your site because they are involved in your conversion goals.

You can monitor your top 10 pages to see if the mission-critical ones are among them. To find this information, log into Google Analytics and click Content, and then select Content By Title. The results will look like those in Figure 5.1.

	Page Title	None	Pageviews ↓	Unique Pageviews	Avg. Time on Page	Bounce Rate	% Exit
1.	Website Conversion Optimization - Landing Page E...		28,253	20,956	00:01:27	43.53%	40.10%
2.	Multivariate Testing Website Optimizer		24,668	18,049	00:01:32	42.88%	39.70%
3.	Resources		8,285	5,981	00:00:55	57.80%	24.95%
4.	Conversion Consulting		8,093	5,811	00:00:40	42.00%	12.90%
5.	Conversion Improvement Specialists		7,896	6,117	00:00:27	34.42%	11.97%
6.	Landing Page Case Studies		6,820	3,999	00:00:48	54.48%	22.01%
7.	Express Review		5,947	4,738	00:02:23	64.57%	43.01%
8.	Landing Page Testing		5,846	4,453	00:00:35	48.23%	13.07%
9.	TuningEngine Landing Page Testing Tools		5,283	4,306	00:00:38	66.08%	21.84%
10.	About Us		4,303	3,357	00:00:39	34.31%	16.15%

Figure 5.1 Google Analytics top pages report

If your mission-critical pages do not show in the top 10 pages report, reconsider how you are promoting these pages on your site to make them more accessible. Consider placing prominent links on your most popular pages to generate more exposure for them, and tweak your navigation menu options for a similar effect.

You should also reconsider your SEO strategy for any of your mission-critical pages that do not show in your top 10 pages, and perform SEO adjustments on and off page in order to get them to rank higher in search engines for your most relevant targeted keywords.

Identify Top Entry Pages with High Bounce Rates

Examine the top pages that act as the entry point to your website, because these represent key moments where your visitor will make split-second decisions to stay or leave. The best way to identify problematic entry pages is to find pages with a high bounce rate—that is, exit pages where people arrive on your page and then leave immediately.

This usually happens because people do not find what they are looking for. In some cases, there is nothing you can do about this. But you can probably improve the page to provide more relevant information or better navigation, which will encourage visitors to stick with you at least a little longer.

To find these problematic top pages, select Content, and then click Top Landing Pages. You will see entrances, bounces, and bounce rates, as shown in Figure 5.2. Scan the top 20 or so pages and write down any of your pages with a bounce rate higher than 40 percent (definite room for improvement). These pages are perfect optimization candidates.

	Page	None	Entrances ↓	Bounces	Bounce Rate
1.	/		36,583	15,783	43.14%
2.	/conversions.html		3,139	1,986	63.27%
3.	/taguchi-method.html		2,710	2,063	76.13%
4.	/management.html		2,529	1,210	47.84%
5.	/express-consulting.html		1,992	1,281	64.31%
6.	/landing-page-case-study.html		1,349	751	55.67%
7.	/google-website-optimizer.html		1,011	534	52.82%
8.	/downloads.html		999	466	46.65%
9.	/a-b-split-testing.html		646	489	75.70%
10.	/conversion-consulting.html		515	225	43.69%

Figure 5.2 Google Analytics Top Landing Pages report

To fine-tune this report even further, consider your top organic search pages in particular, since they often form a significant bulk of high-quality traffic ripe for optimization. To find this in Google Analytics, drill down from the Top Landing Pages report you were just on. Use the drop-down filter menu at the top of your pages that says None, and then select Source and filter on the word *google* (or any other search engine) in the bottom left. The results will look like those in Figure 5.3.

	Page	Source	Entrances ↓	Bounces	Bounce Rate
1.	/	google	7,966	3,016	37.86%
2.	/conversions.html	google	2,425	1,464	60.37%
3.	/taguchi-method.html	google	2,171	1,656	76.26%
4.	/management.html	google	2,065	944	45.71%
5.	/landing-page-case-study.html	google	547	293	53.56%
6.	/google-website-optimizer.html	google.com	495	259	52.32%
7.	/express-consulting.html	google	393	243	61.83%
8.	/a-b-split-testing.html	google	325	256	78.77%
9.	/landing-page-optimization-design.html	google	314	239	76.11%
10.	/truth-about-taguchi-method.html	google	266	198	74.44%

Figure 5.3 Google Analytics top SEO pages

This is the 80/20 principle at work at its best. Identifying and fixing these problematic entry pages will give you the biggest kick-start in helping to optimize your website.

Consider the Depth of Interaction on Your Website and Main Sections

Identifying how many pages visitors usually consume on your site (average page depth) is a good way to uncover more general site problems and represent an overall barometer of your website health. For transactional websites, you should be looking to minimize the average number of page views. This, along with a high conversion rate, can be thought of as a measure of your website efficiency in quickly getting someone to their intended goal. By contrast, for advertising-supported content sites, the goal will be to increase the number of page views per visit.

Average page depth can be found for the site as a whole (shown on the main Google Analytics dashboard as Pages/Visit) and by content groups (by looking at Content Drilldown report). Page depth can be worked out by dividing page views by the number of visits (this is often also called *page views per visit*).

Set Up Goals for Your Conversion Points

To understand conversion rates for your key site goals (such as newsletter sign-ups, shopping cart completions, or whitepaper downloads), you need to examine your existing conversion goals, or set up new ones, in your web analytics tool.

We suggest you set up as many as possible for all your relevant site goals (both micro- and macro-level ones). To get an even more granular understanding of page flows leading to your goals, you can set up "goal funnels" for each of your goals. These allow you establish and track a series of pages leading up to the goal completion and the drop-off points between each step (for example, homepage to product page and then to checkout page). This technique is particularly good at identifying problematic pages and drop-off points for e-commerce shopping carts and forms that span multiple pages.

To examine your goal conversion rates and goal funnels, click Goals Report to see the screen shown in Figure 5.4. This screen breaks down your conversion rate for each goal and trends it over time, along with the goal value. Pay particular attention to conversion rates that seem low to you (this will vary significantly depending on your desired action, as discussed in Chapter 2)—they should be considered prime candidates for conversion improvement.

Flow visualization (shown in Figure 5.5) is another powerful way to see if your conversion funnels are working properly and to identify inefficiencies and point of high drop-off.

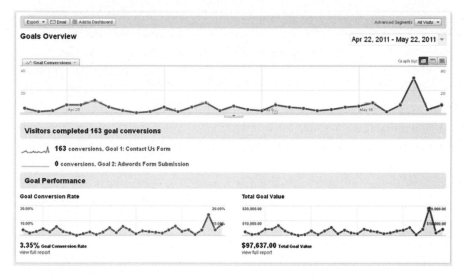

Figure 5.4 Google Analytics goal report

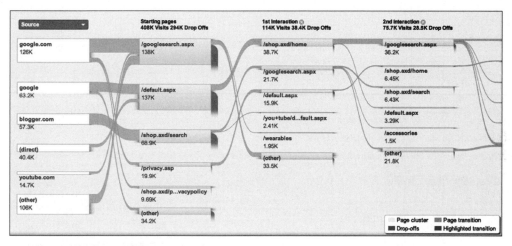

Figure 5.5 Google Analytics flow visualization

Analyze Your Main Traffic Sources

Your conversion rate will vary widely based on the type and quality of your traffic sources. To analyze your main traffic sources, navigate to Traffic Sources, and then select All Traffic Sources. Doing so pulls up a report that buckets your main types of traffic sources (for example, "google" and "direct") and gives you key metrics to determine their success—Pageviews Per Visit, Average Time on Site, % New Visits, and most importantly, Bounce Rate.

In particular, you should be looking for traffic sources that have bounce rates above 40 percent and time spent less than 30 seconds. Once you have identified these problematic sources, you can spend more time looking for reasons why they are underperforming. Two common sources of problems are pages ranking well in search engines for unintended keywords and a poor match between what the visitor clicks on and what they see on the landing page.

It's also important to compare your conversion rates for your goals (that we discussed in the previous section) for all your traffic sources. To do so, go to the list of all traffic sources as explained earlier. Then click on the Goal tabs shown above the list of traffic sources (similar to those in Figure 5.6). Any traffic sources that have a lower conversion rate than your average sitewide conversion rate should be examined and optimized.

Site Usage	Goal Set 1	Ecommerce			Views:
Visits **4,758** % of Site Total: 97.88%	**Goal1: Contact Us Form** **2.73%** Site Avg: 3.35% (-18.52%)	**Goal2: Adwords Form Submission** **0.00%** Site Avg: 0.00% (0.00%)	**Goal Conversion Rate** **2.73%** Site Avg: 3.35% (-18.52%)	**Per Visit Goal Value** **$16.37** Site Avg: $20.09 (-18.52%)	

	Source/Medium	None	Visits ↓	Contact Us Form	Adwords Form Submission	Goal Conversion Rate	Per Visit Goal Value
1.	(direct) / (none)		1,905	3.15%	0.00%	3.15%	$18.87
2.	google / organic		1,563	2.88%	0.00%	2.88%	$17.25
3.	google / cpc		288	0.35%	0.00%	0.35%	$2.08
4.	mthink.com / referral		231	2.16%	0.00%	2.16%	$12.97
5.	sitetuners.com / referral		98	1.02%	0.00%	1.02%	$6.11
6.	attentionwizard.com / referral		61	3.28%	0.00%	3.28%	$19.64
7.	landingpageoptimizationbook.com / referral		43	6.98%	0.00%	6.98%	$41.79
8.	bing / organic		34	0.00%	0.00%	0.00%	$0.00
9.	google.com / referral		33	3.03%	0.00%	3.03%	$18.15
10.	unbounce.com / referral		29	0.00%	0.00%	0.00%	$0.00

Figure 5.6 Google Analytics traffic sources report

Direct/Bookmark Traffic

Remember that direct/bookmark traffic usually arrives on your homepage via a bookmark or your website URL directly typed into the browser address bar by the visitor. If you find that the direct source has high bounce rates, your homepage most likely has significant conversion problems.

Having too much on the homepage is a common cause of high bounce rates. Homepage clutter can confuse the visitors and cause them to leave. Avoid turning your website into a Turkish bazaar; don't continue to add new content to your homepage without removing or prioritizing existing content.

A quick way to tell how cluttered your homepage is would be to run the free Clutter Test available at www.websitecriteria.com/index.html. Sample output from the Clutter Test is shown in Figure 5.7.

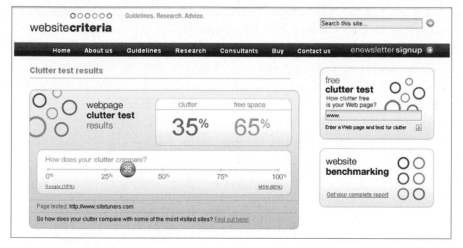

Figure 5.7 Clutter Test output for SiteTuners' homepage

Another common direct traffic issue might be poor navigation and not directing visitors properly deeper into the site. This issue is covered in more detail in the "Too Many Choices" section of Chapter 4, "Common Problems—The Seven Deadly Sins of Landing Page Design."

Referred Traffic

Referred traffic comes from other websites that link directly to a page on your site, and you can't control where it lands. However, you can do two important things to improve the performance of such traffic.

Visit the referring URL and review the specific landing pages on your site to make sure that they function well as a starting point for a visitor and are not a dead-end with no relationship to your desired conversion goals.

Understand the context in which your site was last seen by the visitor. In some cases it will be favorable ("this company is the greatest thing since sliced bread"). In other cases, your link will be buried in a long list of competitor sites. It is also possible that the link will be there for the purpose of belittling your company.

If you understand the mind-set of the visitors from important referral traffic sources, you can modify the landing page content (amplifying goodwill or neutralizing negative perceptions as appropriate).

SEO Traffic

SEO traffic (usually from Google, Yahoo!, or Bing) can often be a problematic traffic source. As we will discuss in Chapter 15, "Avoiding Real-World Pitfalls," there is often an inherent tension between getting high placement in search results and having a landing page that converts well. Search engine spiders prefer a lot of informational text centered on a coherent theme. But visitors who land on the page are often looking for something quick to click on and do not want to wade through a lot of text.

SEO performance can vary greatly depending on the keyword being used. Therefore, it's important to examine bounce rates for keywords in more depth. To do this, use the left-hand menu to click Traffic Sources and then Keywords. This will show you a report (see Figure 5.8) that lists your top keywords and their performance. It is particularly important to pay attention to keywords with bounce rates above 40 percent, since this could indicate a mismatch in visitor intent and landing page and should be modified and optimized.

Figure 5.8 Google Analytics search keyword report

By examining the most popular organic searches and corresponding landing pages, you can modify the content of the landing pages to make them more actionable. These pages may not have been part of the mission-critical page set that you previously identified in Chapter 2, but they may be important feeders for these pages. Consider whether they effectively transport incoming visitors from important keywords to the intended conversion path. In other words, you may not be giving the visitor a clear trail to follow to get to your conversion task's front door.

Paid Search Traffic

Paid traffic (whether from PPC, banner ads, text links, or other sources) has several desirable characteristics as a traffic source. It can be controlled (turned on and off, or increased or decreased) depending on the circumstances. It can be targeted (the traffic can be sent to its own specialized landing page). Its value and profitability can be tracked (by campaign, keyword, and even the version of the ad copy used).

Yet many companies do not take full advantage of these capabilities. The main obstacles and issues are improper traffic mapping and inappropriate landing page content.

By looking at paid search performance, you can see how your efforts are faring as a whole. More importantly, you can detect which paid keywords and traffic landing pages do not perform well (look for high bounce rates) and consider them as candidates for landing page optimization.

To find and examine the performance of your top paid keywords, click Traffic Sources, select Keywords, and click on the Paid link at the top of that report (see the results in Figure 5.9).

	Keyword ⌄	None ⌄	Visits ↓	Pages/Visit	Avg. Time on Site	% New Visits	Bounce Rate
1.	website review		577	1.68	00:01:14	89.95%	82.50%
2.	sitetuners		436	3.61	00:04:33	57.57%	39.45%
3.	site tuners		331	4.04	00:03:43	58.31%	33.53%
4.	conversion optimization		238	3.65	00:06:50	50.42%	46.22%
5.	tim ash		202	2.39	00:04:03	6.93%	55.45%
6.	conversion rate optimization		116	3.27	00:02:41	62.93%	44.83%
7.	website critique		114	1.73	00:00:46	92.98%	76.32%
8.	sitetuners com		106	3.09	00:05:16	70.75%	36.79%
9.	conversion specialist		58	1.33	00:00:22	100.00%	86.21%
10.	conversion specialists		58	1.50	00:00:55	98.28%	81.03%

Figure 5.9 Google Analytics paid keyword report

In many cases, paid search referral traffic is sent to the website homepage instead of the more appropriate pages deeper in the site. Or the traffic is sent to the most relevant page on the corporate site but should instead be sent to a stand-alone landing page that does not have all the navigation options and other distractions of the main website. Review traffic mapping for all high-value keywords to make sure it is being sent to the best possible pages. You may have to create new and more specific landing pages to receive the traffic from these keywords.

Social Media Traffic

Thanks to the rise of social media sites like Facebook and Twitter, you should pay particular attention to your social media traffic source performance. This source of traffic is often engaged in your brand or website and should therefore have low bounce rates and high conversion rates for your goals.

On the Referring Sites report, look for the major social media websites and examine their performance. In addition to Facebook.com and Twitter.com, look for the presence and performance of StumbleUpon, Digg, YouTube, and Del.icio.us, as these are also important social media sites as of this writing.

If your social media traffic sources aren't performing particularly well for your website or are simply not driving much traffic, reconsider your social media strategy efforts and optimize them.

Check Your Repeat Visit Rate

A lack of repeat visits is a tell-tale sign of a site that is not optimized to meet the needs of visitors. This is because unhappy visitors usually won't return (unless you have no competitors), whereas engaged, happy visitors will return much more often.

You can examine this repeat visit rate for the whole of your website by looking at the inverse of the % of New Visits metric on the main dashboard. You can also measure this by individual page, using the Custom Reporting option. Choose Page Title as the dimension, and then select the Pageviews and Repeat Visit % metric. This will show you a list of your top pages and their repeat visit rate. Look for any pages that have a low repeat visit rate—these are often prime candidates for improvement.

Another good barometer for understanding repeat visitation rate is by using return frequency, which is measured by calculating the average number of visits per monthly unique website visitor. This is especially effective for understanding the overall repeat visit health of your site or site sections; any time this metric is lower than 1.10, you could consider it problematic.

Don't forget, though, that since returning visitors have already been exposed to your message on their first visit, it may lose effectiveness on subsequent visits. Therefore, you may consider showing different website content or even a different offer to this group.

For example, returning visitors who have already acted once on your initial offer may not be eligible anymore and should be presented with an appropriate follow-up offer instead. For e-commerce sites, returning buyers should be accorded special status. At a minimum this means recognizing them and acknowledging their return to your site. Additional business rules can be added to display certain promotions based on customer loyalty (such as the number of purchases or total spending to date), or recommended products based on what they have purchased previously.

It is important not to neglect the other side of the coin, though—your new visit rate. If your website is heavily dominated by return visitors, you are not doing enough to drive and acquire new visitors. A return visit rate above 80 percent could also be considered problematic.

Check Your Top Internal Search Keywords for Relevancy and Quality

It's important to set up an internal (onsite) search tool on your website to help your visitors find what they are looking for (especially if you a have a complex or large site with many pages and diverse topics). However, it's even more important to analyze what they are searching for. Luckily, Google Analytics allows you to establish and analyze internal search tracking.

Once you have set up internal search tracking, you can take a look at your top internal search keywords. You can run each of the keywords through your internal search tool and check for the quality and number of relevant results. Doing so is important because research shows that many visitors will abandon a website if they do not find what they are looking for on the first page of results or are unsatisfied with the number of relevant results. Pay particular attention to top search results that yield no matching results—this indicates a mismatch between visitors' desires and expectations and the ability of a site to provide relevant content.

By taking a careful look at such empty search results, you can identify the type of information that is not effectively being found on your site. SiteTuners once helped a client in the wine business to significantly improve their search function by returning proper results for common misspellings of wine brands and specific product names. By insisting that the visitor must be able to type in searches correctly, the site was turning away business.

You can also autopopulate common empty search results with hand-picked search results pages. Alternatively, you can broaden the scope of the search to at least bring back close matches if exact results are not found.

If a search is common, it may be a candidate for inclusion in the site's permanent navigation. In other words, you may want to determine the amount of permanent visibility for that search query to help even more people find it.

Set Up Advanced Segments Based on Visitor Behavior

Another great way to uncover issues with your website is to create advanced segments (groups) of your visitors and analyze their patterns and performance. As we discussed earlier, a simple way to do this is by segmenting for conversion rate based on referring source, but you can get even more granular to dig even deeper for issues. Here are a few ideas for advanced conversion ninjas:

- Set up a segment for visitors who convert for your goals and a segment for visitors who don't convert. Then compare these two for patterns such as their top entry pages, top page flows, or top search keywords used. Based on what you find, you can tweak your site to promote page flows that mirror the user flow of visitors who always convert.

- Set up segments for returning visitors and new visitors and identify conversion rates for both. If either of these is particularly low, adjust your site's language and create pages or flows for each type of visitor (for example, create a page for new visitors and link to it from your homepage explaining the benefits of using the site).

- Set up segments for your most valuable visitors, such as those who order a high volume of products or visitors who have high engagement (high page views per visit, for example). You can then analyze their behaviors and tweak your site to match what these ideal website visitors seem to be doing.

Many analytics packages already have predefined segments, and you can always add your own. The overall traffic graph in Figure 5.10 shows the total traffic to a page and also breaks out new and returning visitors. The returning visitor line at the bottom is relatively stable, whereas the middle line showing new visitors shows significant variability. This variability is tied to various marketing activities. Breaking out the new visitors makes it easier to see the real impact of each campaign.

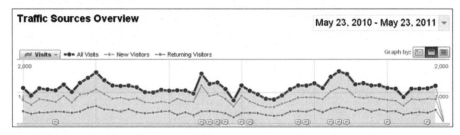

Figure 5.10 Google Analytics traffic sources by segment report

Analyze Your Visitor Demographics to Identify Missing Opportunities

Google Analytics can also be used to learn more about the demographics of your website visitors, in particular their location and native language.

To help optimize geographic aspects of your website, pull up the Map Overlay report (see Figure 5.11). You would expect lots of visitors near your physical location or where you market your site the most. If you notice any heavy concentrations around other regions, you can use this information to create specialized content specifically for certain regions or to adjust your customer service or business hours.

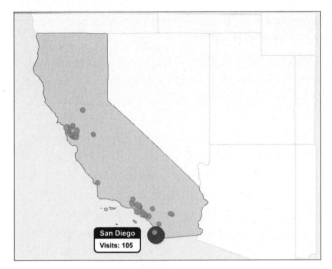

Figure 5.11 Google Analytics Map Overlay report

If a significant number of your visitors originate in other countries, you can determine whether you are ignoring their needs. Additional native-language and native culture–based content may be appropriate (see the discussion of international cultural issues in Chapter 8, "Best Practices for Common Situations," for additional background). You do not have to include a complete copy of your site in each applicable language. But if you intend to get conversions in other languages, at least the mission-critical tasks should be available in their native language.

Visual Analysis Tools

Web analytics tools mostly concern themselves with page-level issues. They may help identify behaviors related to the whole page (such as likelihood of bouncing), or help identify flows of people across pages on a website. However, they are not well suited for understanding the behavior of people *within* a page.

A new class of visual analysis tools allows you to understand site activity at a much more granular level. Since our experience of the Web is primarily visual (seen through a browser window), the nuances of our interactions with the page can provide a rich source of information about potential conversion problems. For example, you can track the movement of people's mice, see if they scroll the page, watch what they click on, see if they hover over objects without clicking, and see how forms are filled out. This information can be aggregated across many visitors or analyzed at the level of an individual user session.

CrazyEgg

CrazyEgg (www.CrazyEgg.com) monitors visitor activity at an individual page level. It installs with a small snippet of code on the target landing page on your website. After that, information is collected about visitors' interactions with that page. When enough people have visited the page, their information is combined into a series of simple visual reports.

One interesting use of CrazyEgg for conversion is to view a mouse-movement heatmap of the page). Since a small percentage of people will use their mouse as a pointer when they navigate the Web, a mouse-movement heatmap can serve as a quick-and-dirty substitute for eye-tracking. Of course this is different than true eye-tracking studies because those can capture very rapid (and often unconscious) eye movements, but it can provide insights into what people fixate on within the page and where their conscious attention is drawn. However, scientific research shows a high degree of correlation (around 84–88 percent) between the two.

The brighter areas on the heatmap overlay (shown in Figure 5.12) indicate areas where more mouse movement and hovering occurs.

Another useful report is the Confetti tool. This report shows your clicking behavior on the page. This can help identify visitor confusion (people clicking on page elements that are not clickable), or lack of prominence (visitors not clicking on clickable elements even though you may want them to).

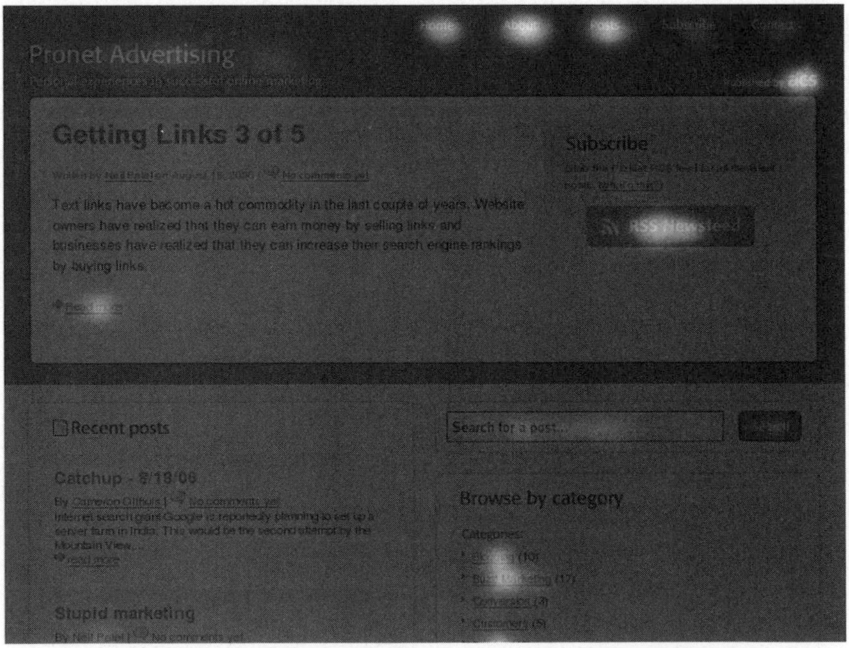

Figure 5.12 CrazyEgg mouse movement heatmap

The Confetti reports can be segmented by traffics source, browser resolution, and a number of other filters (see Figure 5.13).

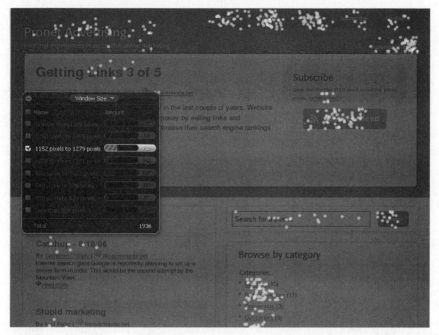

Figure 5.13 CrazyEgg Confetti report showing clicks on the page for a range of browser screen sizes

In particular, you should use this tool on your top entry pages and check what your visitors are clicking on the most. If they aren't clicking on your high-value links or navigation options on these pages, you can tweak their wording or layout to entice more clicks. This tool is inexpensive and can be deployed quickly.

ClickTale

ClickTale (www.ClickTale.com) offers a rich and robust set of tools for in-page web analytics. Its main components consist of the following.

- Mouse Tracking Suite (visitor recording, movement heatmap, click heatmap, real-time monitoring, and link analytics)
- Heatmap Suite (mouse movement, mouse clicking, attention, and scroll reach)
- Conversion Suite (conversion funnels, form analytics, advanced filtering and segmentation by business rules, and custom alerts)

This tool takes visual analysis one step further than CrazyEgg by recording and playing back your visitor's interactions with your website in real time. These recordings allow you to gain a wealth of insight about your visitor behavior, which may reveal possible issues. You can watch your visitors' mouse movements, what they hover on, how far they scroll down the page, and even which form fields they get stuck on the most.

ClickTale's recordings of your visitors interactions are especially valuable because the visitors don't know they are being recorded and act naturally, unlike in traditional web usability testing where the participants are fully aware they are being recorded and may act in different ways than usual, or may be prompted or guided by a moderator.

The results of these visitor session recordings are then automatically translated into aggregated static reports, allowing you to gain additional insights.

These reports offer unique insights. For example, the funnel report (often seen in web analytics packages) is taken to another level when intra-page information is examined. In Figure 5.14 the Conversion Report shows a progression of engagement with a form on a landing page:

- Visitors who landed on the page
- Visitors who interacted with the form
- Visitors who tried to submit the form
- Visitors who successfully submitted the form

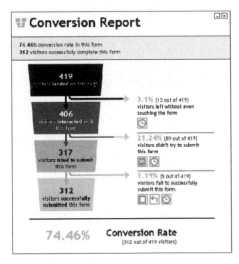

Figure 5.14 ClickTale intra-page conversion funnel report

The company offers a variety of reasonably priced plans and also has an enterprise-level offering for larger clients.

ClickTale was one of the pioneers of in-page analytics, but there are also other recent options, including tools that are more expensive but feature-rich like Tealeaf as well as less expensive but more basic tools like Userfly.

AttentionWizard

Visitor heatmaps and recordings are great for understanding visitor interaction with a live website, but what if you want to know how visitors are likely to interact with your page *before* you even launch it? An interesting new approach is to use a software algorithm to predict initial visual attention on the page. With advances in neuroscience and computational attention, it is possible to predict where a visitor to a website will focus during the first few seconds of their visit.

One example of such a service is the AttentionWizard tool (`www.AttentionWizard .com`) created and operated by SiteTuners. An image is cropped to simulate the "above-the-fold" experience on the page (so that no conscious volitional browser scrolling is required). The image is then uploaded into the web-based tool. See Figure 5.15 for an example of the original image.

Figure 5.15 Example input image for AttentionWizard

The corresponding AttentionWizard image is instantly produced showing both the predicted eye movement as well as the heatmap of attention for the page (See Figure 5.16).

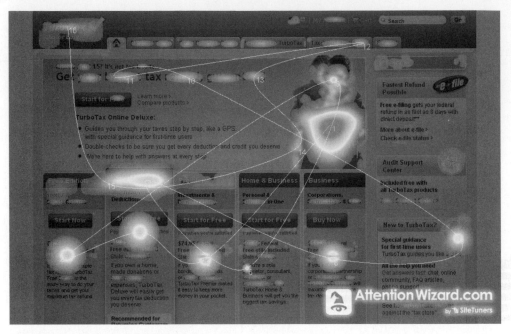

Figure 5.16 AttentionWizard heatmap example

Although not as accurate as eye-tracking, and slightly less accurate than mouse-movement heatmaps, the AttentionWizard approach has some compelling benefits:

- No real people (site visitors) are required.
- Results are available within a couple of minutes.
- AttentionWizard can be used on design mockups (that are not "live" yet).
- AttentionWizard can be used repeatedly to refine a design concept.

AttentionWizard can identify which page elements are being looked at and which are being ignored. A "busy" eye-gaze path and scattered heatmap with many hot spots is usually an indication that visual priorities of the page are not clear, which could cause visitor confusion and result in a lower conversion rate for your landing page.

Armed with this information, web designers can adjust the visual elements on a page to focus attention where it belongs, increasing the likelihood of conversion.

Attention heatmaps can be created several times during the design or redesign process to ensure that the visual refinements are having the intended effect. A heatmap that shows a relatively simple eye gaze path and a small number of hot spots focused on the desired conversion action is a good predictor of a page's clarity and effectiveness. The service helps you to understand and fix potential visual issues *before* you push a new website or page live.

AttentionWizard is available with inexpensive pay-as-you-go and subscription-based pricing options.

Feedback and Survey Tools

Although web analytics and visual analysis tools can be very powerful, they are not designed to easily uncover the motivations and attitudes of your visitors. You still have to guess *why* visitors are doing what they do. A great way of grasping the whys and uncovering issues visitors encountered is to get feedback directly from them. Many types of online tools allow you to do just that.

SurveyMonkey

One of the easiest ways to gather insight and feedback from your visitors is to set up an online survey for them to respond to. To generate feedback and uncover site issues, website surveys should at the very least ask the following questions:

- What was the purpose of your visit to this website?
- Did you find what you were looking for?
- If not, why not?

To gain more in-depth feedback from your visitors, you should create another set of more detailed questions if they wish to continue giving feedback. For example, "Please give feedback on how easy the checkout process was" or "Please describe any issues you have with our website."

SurveyMonkey (www.SurveyMonkey.com) was one of the pioneers in this space and still has great prices with a good feature set. There are many other tools now available to suit different needs. iPerceptions' 4Q tool (www.4qsurvey.com) is free but limited in functionality. OpinionLab (www.opinionlab.com) is an example of a more expensive, feature-rich online survey tool.

Kampyle

Kampyle gathers feedback from site visitors in two ways. An orange "Give Feedback" button or triangle permanently pins itself to a corner or side of the browser window on a website that has deployed Kampyle. The tool can also be configured to display a "Would you like to take our survey?" lightbox popover window to a small percentage of visitors.

Placing a feedback button that stays visible in the browser window of your website (see the triangle in the lower-right corner of Figure 5.17) allows your visitors to click and give feedback whenever they would like in a variety of formats. The simplest way is for them to rate your website on a scale of 1 to 5—a useful barometer of the overall visitor satisfaction of your website.

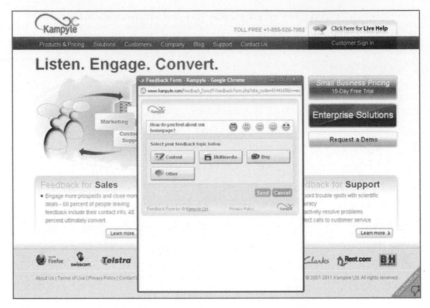

Figure 5.17 Kampyle feedback triangle example

Your visitors can also choose a feedback topic that they wish to respond to (for example Suggestion, Bug, or Complaint). This is a great way to gather insight about issues that visitors may be encountering on your website. You can then analyze the results by category to uncover ideas for improving your website.

When giving feedback with this tool, users also have the option to leave their e-mail address for you to respond to, therefore allowing you to form an ongoing dialogue with your respondents (particularly useful for discontented ones). Reasonably priced plans for small businesses are available as well as enterprise plans, making this a cost-effective way of gathering feedback for your website and uncovering problems.

UserVoice

Some of the best ideas for improving your website will come from the people who use your website often—your website visitors. UserVoice (www.UserVoice.com) is specifically designed to allow your website visitors to publicly submit and share their ideas, and also browse and vote on other visitors' ideas. This way, you can quickly generate a list of the top 10 things that visitors want to see improved or added to your website (for example, a new feature or improved navigation).

Many leading websites have implemented this tool (or similar ones) to help improve their websites. The company offers inexpensive subscription plans. This valuable tool is especially useful for websites that offer an online tool or service.

Velaro

Another way to discover possible issues with your website is by gaining quality feedback from your visitors during a live web chat session.

By installing and using Velaro (www.Velaro.com), you can proactively help your website visitors during key parts of the conversion process by popping up a message asking if they need help. For example, if a user seems stuck on the middle page of your shopping cart, you can pop up a message here and ask them if they need help. You can also actively assist them with co-browsing sessions (allowing you to help them fill out forms on your site).

After you have helped them, you can also ask visitors for additional general feedback and whether they encountered any other issues with your website.

These web chats are automatically documented and can be analyzed and grouped by the page on which they occurred, allowing you to identify where the most serious issues exist on your website. You can integrate this tool into Google Analytics for even better analysis results.

Velaro goes far beyond the usual chat functionality. It offers a rich suite of tools to dynamically change website content based on visitors' actions; it also effectively tracks conversions and integrates with popular customer relationship management (CRM) systems.

Website Performance Tools

Many websites often have basic, easily preventable site performance and technical issues that alienate visitors and significantly depress conversion rates. For example, many websites have slow-loading webpages or break when they are viewed in less common browsers or operating systems. Several online tools are available that you can use to diagnose and prevent these types of issues.

CrossBrowserTesting

Do you know if your website breaks or has issues with any of the various combinations of browsers, screen resolution sizes, and operating systems? And do you know whether vital information is not showing above the fold on common screen resolutions? Probably not, because the number of combinations that you would have to test is mind-boggling. Unfortunately, chances are fairly high that your website looks broken or subpar in a common configuration that you haven't seen before.

Screen resolution is particularly important to consider because it literally defines the visitor's window onto the Internet. Your page should look ideal at the most common minimum resolution in use at the time. But it must also look good at higher resolutions. As bigger computer monitors become more common, the standard will continue to shift, and your minimum resolution may need to be periodically adjusted.

Another important consideration is to understand the implications of what appears "above the fold." This term originated in the newspaper industry and referred to the main content that could be seen on the top half of the front page (without flipping the paper or opening it). On the Web it describes the content seen on the page without horizontal or vertical scrolling. What appears above the fold is influenced not only by screen resolution, but also by the size of the current browser window (which may be smaller than the whole screen), various currently visible browser toolbars (which take up vertical space), and the default size of the text chosen in the browser (larger font sizes will push content further down the page).

Although long landing pages are no longer the absolute no-no that they were several years ago, key information (for example, buttons or major calls-to-action) should still generally be above the fold. This guarantees that visitors can see all-important choices as they make their decision to click away or to stay longer on your site.

While Internet users are accustomed to scrolling vertically, studies have shown that they universally despise horizontal scrolling. Under no circumstances should your page require horizontal scrolling at common screen resolutions.

CrossBrowserTesting (`CrossBrowserTesting.com`) offers a variety of inexpensive plans that allow you to quickly identify and fix all of the issues just described.

YSlow

Remember that users will be quick to judge your website when first arriving on it. If a website takes more than a few seconds to load, research has shown that users will often prematurely abandon it (often to return to the search results and to find a competing website). Yahoo! has a great browser plug-in called YSlow that allows you to diagnose any load-time performance issues your site may be experiencing. It tests against 34 rules that have an impact on site performance, from CSS (cascading style sheets) to JavaScript usage.

It goes almost without saying that you should optimize your pages, graphics, and media files to be an appropriate size. A large number of Internet users still have slow connection speeds. Internet users are not very patient, and they will not generally wait for long downloads.

You should also be careful about anything requiring nonstandard browser plug-ins or technologies that are not widely supported. There are fewer experiences more annoying for the visitor than having to download a plug-in simply to see your landing page properly. At a minimum, always provide lower-tech alternatives (like a non-Flash site version), and never force visitors to download software that may be unfamiliar to them.

Competitive Analysis Tools

Benchmarking your website against your competitor can reveal valuable insights that will help you improve your conversion rates.

Compete and Quantcast

Both of these tools enable you to analyze key traffic metrics of your competitors—simply visit either Compete.com or www.Quantcast.com and perform a search for the URLs of your rivals. This free search will help you determine which of them are doing best—and hopefully enable you to analyze and learn from their success. In particular, you should look for competitor websites that have significantly higher monthly unique visitors than your site, a high return frequency, or high page views per visit—all of these are indicators of high engagement and satisfied visitors.

Once you know which rivals are performing the best (see Figure 5.18), you can visit their websites and look for features, content, or functionality that may be missing on your website. These websites might also give you ideas to help you differentiate your website from your competitors'—a key way of improving your website. Be aware, though, that these tools are not as accurate as regular web analytics tools like Google Analytics, because the traffic data they show is merely a sample based on their network of reporting sites.

Figure 5.18 Compete report example

Hitwise

Are you sure you are attracting the most targeted users from search engines? Are you performing SEO for the right keywords? These are important questions that need to be fully considered to build a well-oiled website that converts to its best potential.

A great way to see if you are missing out on critical keywords is to examine the ones that your competitors are using and generating the most traffic from. Without inside information from rival websites, this would be impossible.

Fortunately, a tool from Experian called Hitwise (www.hitwise.com) makes obtaining this information possible. After you gain access to this service, you can search for your competitors and see exactly which keywords they are gaining most of their traffic from and monitor them via automated reports. These reports may also give you ideas for new content or functionality on your website to help improve it.

Usability Testing Tools

Usability testing (covered in more detail in Chapter 7, "Conversion Improvement Basics") allows you to test your design ideas on representative users of your website. It can be an effective means of uncovering disconnects between users' expectations and your designs and therefore potential issues with your website and landing pages.

In the past, to conduct usability testing you had to use usability testing companies to help you recruit appropriate subjects, conduct the tests, and deliver detailed findings. However, thanks to recent improvements to online technologies and products, you can now conduct usability testing using online tools. These tools are also generally more cost effective.

UserTesting

UserTesting (UserTesting.com) allows you to define a specific usability task on your site and to get recorded videos of people trying to complete it. You start by completing an online task definition form (see Figure 5.19), which includes instructions for your test participants.

UserTesting then circulates your test to their panel of prescreened testers, and qualified ones respond. The people who agree to do the testing are generalists and usually do not have any kind of specific background required to understand more intricate websites. However, subject-matter experts are typically not necessary, and many website problems are more basic ones involving usability that can be uncovered by people with more general background.

All UserTesting testers are trained to speak out loud during their task completion and to record a video of their interactions with the website. The video is then delivered to the client. Typical response times are from a few hours to a couple of days.

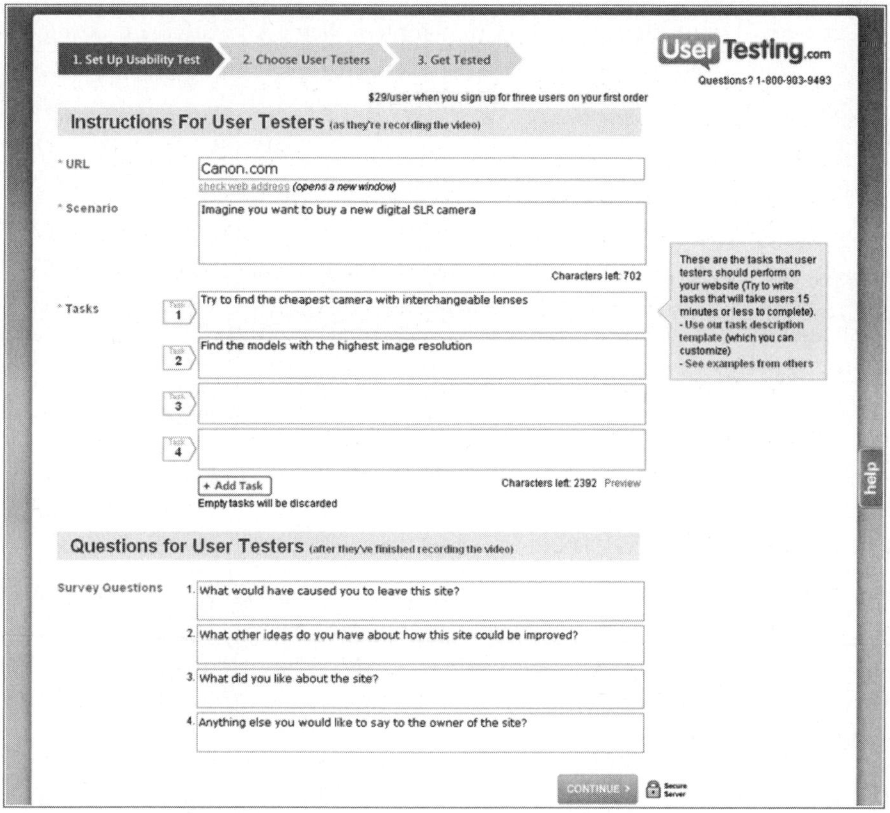

Figure 5.19 UserTesting task definition screen

This tool is great for gaining true visitor insight and finding possible issues with your website. UserTesting also provides you with a written summary describing the problems they encountered on your website—very valuable insight indeed, straight from the users' mouth.

UserTesting services are inexpensively priced on a per-tester basis. We recommend getting 5–8 user sessions to uncover most of your glaring conversion problems.

Loop11

Like UserTesting, Loop11 (Loop11.com) allows you to uncover issues with your website by asking testers to complete specific tasks. However, with Loop11 you recruit your own testers from the ranks of your website visitors. You can also survey many of your website visitors at once, as opposed to cherry-picking a few users who may not have seen your website previously.

Basically, you set up tasks for key goals on your website and invite your visitors (via pop-up or e-mail) to participate and try to complete them. An example task might be "Find our product demo request form." If the visitor completes the task, they click the Task Complete button, and if they can't complete it, they click the Abandon Task button. Figure 5.20 shows an example of a Loop11 task. You can then review task completion reports, come to a better understanding of task completion rates, and fix any parts of the task that the users find challenging.

Figure 5.20 Loop11 task header in a landing page usability test involving the Amazon homepage

We suggest that you create tasks relating to each of your major conversion goals and ask a few questions relating to them. This way, you can see which of your goals are most problematic.

A significant drawback of this tool is that it only gives you completion rates of tasks—it doesn't tell you why visitors aren't completing the tasks. That is why you should use this tool in tandem with UserTesting: to gain a more direct voice of the visitor.

Loop11 is available on a prepaid credit basis, allowing you to purchase as many test participants as you need.

Another option is to use a more advanced (but more expensive) website usability tool called UserZoom. This tool allows you to ask for additional feedback for each task so you can gain a better understanding of why a user was unable to complete a task. This tool also has other great features, like a basic online survey tool and a prototyping tool.

E-mail Enhancement Tools

For many companies, the conversion action on the website is not the ultimate sale. This is often the case in business-to-business large-ticket purchases, professional services, and consumer lead generation in a variety of industry vertical sectors. The ultimate conversion may be months off, or may be consummated via phone, or offline.

Since the decision times are so long, and the purchasing decisions are often complex, you should create an ongoing dialogue of some sort with the prospect in order to continue to move them through the sales funnel. A powerful way to do this is via e-mail. Since e-mail is central to the communication strategy, it is essential that it be used effectively. The following technologies help you to get the most value out of your e-mail.

LeadSpend

LeadSpend (LeadSpend.com) supports you in building a clean mailing list. This is critical because having a clean list reduces your bounce rates and helps you to avoid spam trap hits. Industry data from Return Path shows that if your "unknown user rate" is high, you will have a correspondingly low sender score (reputation among major Internet service providers). The practical effect of this is that you may have very low deliverability percentages (people actually getting your communications in their inboxes).

The best way to combat this is to "clean" your e-mail addresses in real time as you collect them. LeadSpend supports in-form validation of e-mail addresses entered on your pages without any perceptible delay to your visitors. This has the following impact on your e-mail collection program:

More Delivered E-mails Better deliverability percentage as a result of your higher sender score (as described earlier).

Grows Your List Faster Gives you a "second bite at the apple" (if you detect an invalid address, you can immediately ask for and often get a legitimate one).

Higher Form-Fill Rate Since you don't have to ask for annoying "confirm e-mail" information, your forms are more likely to be filled out.

In addition to real-time validation, LeadSpend supports API-based access and batch processing of existing lists. They have high verification rates (resolving over 97 percent of all e-mail addressed correctly without false positives). The company currently charges no up-front fees, and you only pay for each bad address caught (not ones that were valid to begin with).

SeeWhy

SeeWhy (SeeWhy.com) is a pioneer in e-mail abandonment recovery. In an e-commerce setting they can reliably recover a high percentage of people who started your shopping cart process and then bailed out. This technology can also be used for people who abandon multistep sign-up or registration processes.

If you get their e-mail address early in the process, a series of targeted follow-up e-mails will be sent by SeeWhy. Typically the timing involves three e-mails sent immediately, exactly 24 hours later, and exactly one week later. The exact messaging that you use will of course depend on your business. But the key to success is in the following features of the SeeWhy service:

Immediate Sending If you rely on batched or delayed sending of your follow-up sequences, your leads will quickly turn "cold" and the value of the follow-up will decrease dramatically.

Exceptional Deliverability SeeWhy has spent a lot of effort getting whitelisted by major ISPs, ensuring that the vast majority of their e-mails are delivered.

Intelligent Handling of Repeat Visitors If your visitor does return and complete the conversion, they will not get the rest of the follow-up e-mail sequence. This is critical because you do not want to get out of sync and offer special incentives to visitors after they have already returned and converted. This would just frustrate and anger them.

We recommend that you use SeeWhy as a supplement, and you do not rely exclusively on your ESP (e-mail service provider) for abandonment recovery.

We have covered a powerful array of weapons for any would-be conversion ninja. Remember to visit ConversionNinjaToolbox.com for the latest tools and updated information, and check out the Appendix for a list of landing page testing tool companies.

In the next chapter we will turn inward—toward the brains of your visitors in an effort to better understand who you are trying to persuade and how this can be accomplished.

Misunderstanding Your Visitors—Looking for Psychological Mismatches

I could be you, you could be me
I could walk a mile in your shoes…
And you could walk a mile in my bare feet

—Michael Franti and Spearhead,
"What I Be" song lyric

Who are you trying to influence? What are they like? Can you see the world from their perspective?

Now that you have identified areas where the site isn't performing well, it's time to figure out why. That requires looking at things through the eyes of your visitors. This chapter will give you that foundation.

CHAPTER CONTENTS

Empathy: The Key Ingredient

Researching the Whole Story

Demographics and Segmentation

Welcome to Your Brain

Cognitive Styles

Persuasion Frameworks

Cultural Differences

Empathy: The Key Ingredient

We are all familiar with the Golden Rule: "Do onto others as you would have them do onto you." This ethical guidepost exists in many variants among the world's major philosophies and religions. But it is missing an essential component by presupposing that everyone is the same. Moreover, it makes *your* behavior and beliefs the standard by which all conduct should be judged and measured.

There's one important thing missing from this powerful dictum: empathy. People are not all the same. If we want to understand them, we should try to step outside of our own needs and experience the world from their perspective.

> *Do unto others as they want done unto them.*
>
> —THE PLATINUM RULE, by Dr. Tony Alessandra

This chapter will help you get into the minds and hearts of your website visitors. All of the following frameworks require openness on your part. The more flexible, curious, and imaginative you are, the more powerfully you can wield these tools.

"You're Wrong"

After conducting hundreds of usability tests for a wide range of clients, Larry Marine, usability expert and founder of Intuitive Design & Research, delights in being constantly surprised by his audience. The viewpoint of a single person can never fully capture the perspective of others. During a talk in San Diego, Larry used the following presentation points to remind us about the difficulty of our task as online marketers:

- Everything you think you know about the user is probably wrong.
- The users aren't who you think they are.
- They do things differently than you think.
- They have different reasons for needing your product than you think.

But let's inject a note of warning: No matter how you might try to put yourself in others' shoes, you are bound to be wrong. You can never replicate their bodies, brains, or formative experiences. This realization requires a certain humility, wide-eyed wonder, and willingness to be constantly surprised. However, it is still important to understand the universal biological and psychological basics on which all of online marketing and persuasion are built.

Researching the Whole Story

Like a solid news reporter, you must understand the basics of the story and be able to articulate the following particulars about your audience:

- Who
- What
- Where
- When
- Why
- How

What does this mean in the context of a website or landing page? The following discussion should help you to get a better grounding:

Who is your audience? The *who* of your audience is defined by their demographics and segmentation. Because you can't meet every visitor to your site in person, you are limited to using aggregates. Through web analytics you can understand the traffic sources hitting your website and the specific landing pages. Extensive information is also available about these visitors and their behavior once on the site. From a landing page optimization perspective, it is important to understand this mix, because traffic segments can have radically different behavior and conversion potential.

What task is the visitor trying to complete? The *what* is the specific task that your visitor is trying to complete on your website. Tasks and how to properly define them are described more detail in Chapter 3, "The Matrix—Moving People to Act."

Where on your website does the interaction occur? The *where* of your visitor's experience depends on the context they arrived from, the specific landing page, and the path they take on your site to get to a mission-critical conversion page. Sometimes the where may be an offline call-to-action such as a phone call or an in-store sale, but the mechanism for it (e.g., displaying a special dedicated toll-free number, or creating a printable coupon for redemption in a store) is still part of the website.

When do your visitors make their decision? The *when* should be seen not as a specific time event, but as a position in a decision process. Some visitors are beginning to look around, trying to formulate a response to a vague concern they may feel. Others know exactly what they want, and may only be concerned with completing whatever transaction is required to obtain their desired product or service. As we discussed in Chapter 3, there needs to be appropriate supporting information for a visitor regardless of their place in the decision-making process.

Why do visitors behave the way they do? You do not have intimate and accurate information about your individual visitors, but the *why* can be understood by imagining the categories of cognitive styles. Many psychologists and philosophers have proposed fundamental archetypes or frameworks for describing the basic human temperaments and our consequently different ways of relating to the world. We'll examine this in more detail in the "Cognitive Styles" section later in this chapter.

How does your visitor operate on your site to complete their tasks? The *how* is the actual functional and aesthetic design of your website or landing pages. It is the medium through which each task must be accomplished. Specific page elements include layout, organization, and emphasis of key information, text copy, the call-to-action, and hundreds of other factors. All of them combine to influence the effectiveness of your landing page.

Demographics and Segmentation

Because almost everything on the Internet can be logged or recorded (see the discussion of web analytics tools in Chapter 5, "Conversion Ninja Toolbox—Diagnosing Site Problems," for more details), it provides a wealth of objective information. The goals of the effective online marketer is to determine which specific metrics are good predictors of success, and to monitor them in order to focus their programs in the right direction. As with all data, you should treat demographics with proper respect and be aware of data-gathering tools and their limitations. Depending on the exact technology used, web analytics tools will track the activities of your visitors differently and come up with different numbers for the same metrics.

Web Analytics

You already know a lot about your audience. Your website logs record information in mind-numbing detail about every request for information from your web servers:

- The Internet Protocol (IP) address of your visitors
- Which pages they viewed
- How long they spent looking at your site
- Which browser software they are using
- Whether they have been to your site before

As discussed in Chapter 5, all of this information is analyzed by web analytics packages, which have a wide range of capabilities and power. The simplest ones are glorified counters. High-end versions are powerful but often require months of laborious and expensive customization to create the right set of live online reports for key people on your staff. Such packages can tie into other systems within your company to give you a more complete picture of the ongoing interactions with your audience. For example, many analytics systems connect directly to a company's *customer relationship management (CRM)* systems.

In general, there are three main uses of web analytics software:

Canned Reports Specific reports can be generated (typically on the fly or at specified intervals) to report on a number of activities. The set of reports does not typically change. Some offer *clickstream analysis*—showing the popular sequences of clicks and pages that users take to navigate your site.

Data Mining Some systems have flexible reporting and scripting languages that allow you to construct your own specialized reports based on historical data. This supports open-ended discovery and ongoing questioning.

Dynamic Content Presentation Many web analytics systems support the ability to change content on the fly. They encode business rules within your webpages that can change specific portions of your content based on the actions of a particular user.

Web analytics tools have increased their focus on tracking the effectiveness of online marketing programs. They offer built-in reports for tracking separate marketing channels. Conversion details, ad source return on investment (ROI) comparison, and content insertion results are just a few examples of behaviors that can be tracked.

Traffic Sources and Their Variability

Your audience is not homogenous or uniform. Streams of diverse people visit your site as a result of your current and past marketing activities. None of these streams fit together very well, so it is dangerous and misleading to stitch them together into a unified picture. If your audience consisted of a 6-year-old in San Diego and a 74-year-old in New York City, it would be silly to describe your "average" visitor as a 40-year-old from Kansas. Yet similar conclusions are often drawn from web analytics data.

Try to keep your traffic sources separated and analyze them only within their peer group. The most appropriate segmentation may be to focus on specific roles and the tasks that you want your visitors to complete on the website. In other words, do not look at your overall site traffic, but focus instead on the demographics of the people who are interacting with the mission-critical parts of your site.

However, if you segment too finely, you may have problems as well. When you analyze within a particular traffic source or marketing segment, be sure that there is enough data to draw valid statistical conclusions. For testing, you should pay attention to a subset's stability and consistency over time.

Not only is your audience composition diverse, but these people act differently under different circumstances and conditions. Time of day can have strong cognitive effects. Someone browsing surreptitiously at work will spend less time on your site than the same person on the computer in her home during the evening. Time zones can cause a shift in your audience at different hours of the day, as more international visitors have *their* daytime. Although business decision makers are active during the workday, studies have shown that they are spending more time online outside of the 9–5 bracket.

Likewise, weekend behavior is different than that of the workweek. There are well-known differences in direct response e-mail marketing conversion rates based on the specific day of the week that a mail drop is done. However, the best days are completely different depending on the audience and the offer in question. So day of week turns out to be another unknown factor that must be considered in your testing.

Such effects can be mitigated by running conversion tests in whole-week units. But longer-term time variations such as external event-driven behavior or seasonality can also play a strong role and are much harder to deal with.

For example, a flower website will do a hugely disproportionate business in the two to three weeks leading up to Mother's Day every year. As the event date approaches, the audience becomes segmented and changes—all of the deliberate "planners" in the audience will have completed their transactions and secured the best prices and appropriate delivery dates. At the last minute, the less price-sensitive "procrastinators" will descend on the website and spend more money than they probably should in order to get what they want and have guaranteed express delivery.

Seasonal trends are also seen in many discretionary spending consumer e-tail categories, with the fourth quarter accounting for a majority of the year's sales. But even companies whose products have no natural seasonality to speak of may see slowdowns in the summer (when many people are away on vacation and do not have the same access to the Internet) or at other times.

Sometimes, your seemingly homogeneous audience is really not the same at all. For example, in the winter people from colder climates will tend to vacation in warmer places. In the summer this pattern reverses and Southerners head north to escape the heat. As a result, many travel-related sites have strong seasonality, coupled with a changing audience mix. In such circumstances it is difficult to conduct certain types of conversion testing (primarily having to do with your content or offers).

 Some websites have such extreme audience changes and vicious seasonality factors that content conversion tuning is simply not possible. The predicted best answer will simply not hold up over time.

However, even such difficult vertical industry sites can often derive some benefit from conversion optimization. Instead of focusing on the specifics of their business, the content changes can focus on the basic usability of their websites and effective and frictionless flow through the important tasks (such as booking a reservation or purchasing).

The TicketsNow website (www.ticketsnow.com) shown in Figure 6.1 will have the strongest conversion effects based on the contents of the highlighted featured offers. There is a limited supply of tickets for certain events, and the featured promotions change frequently. This would make it difficult to optimize the actual offers. However, the underlying page layout and site usability could be tuned independently of the featured offers. For example, you could test whether having two, three, or four featured offers on the page maximizes the revenue per visitor.

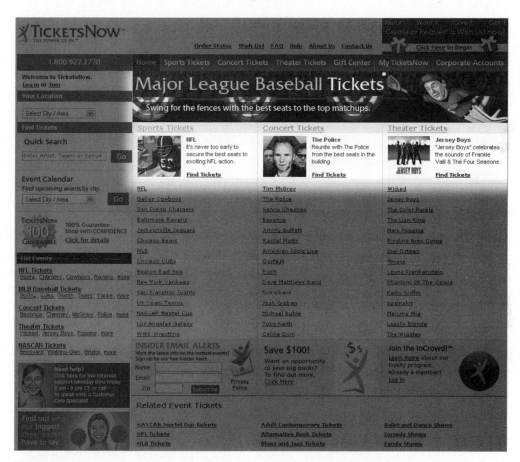

Figure 6.1 The TicketsNow homepage

When you look at the suitability of the traffic mix for conversion testing, watch for three important characteristics:

Recurring The traffic must come from a replenishable resource. For example, PPC or banner ad traffic is essentially endless—you can get more of it as long as you are willing to pay. This supply of "fresh meat" is important because you typically want to run conversion tests on new visitors. It is okay to have a high percentage of repeat visitors in your test, as long as the mix of visitors does not change and represents a roughly constant percentage of your traffic. However, nonrecurring traffic sources like e-mail have many drawbacks for traditional landing page optimization and must be used cautiously (if at all).

Controllable It is easy to control paid search and other online media buys. Unfortunately, other traffic sources are not under your command. For example, organic SEO depends on changes in the sometimes unpredictable ranking algorithms of the search engines. You also cannot control the context in which your site was seen or specify the pages on which the traffic will land. However, SEO traffic can still be used for testing if it has a record of being historically stable in terms of the volume and mix of landing pages.

Stable Even if your traffic is recurring and controllable, it may not be stable. For example, you may see a periodic traffic spike as one of your marketing partners pushes a special recurring campaign that drives visitors to your site. Or perhaps the turnover in the composition of your affiliate program results in a rapidly changing traffic mix. SEO traffic can also disappear overnight as the ranking algorithms are adjusted by the search engines.

Welcome to Your Brain

If what you've read so far is already sparking ideas of how to refine future web projects, you are relying on your higher-reasoning faculties to make these plans. But this is not the only mode in which your brain operates. Despite the fact that people can be very sophisticated and intelligent, we still carry a lot of our old evolutionary baggage with us.

A lot of the problems that we have with the Web in general (and landing pages in particular) are due to the limitations of our brains when trying to use this medium. There is a disconnect between how our brains evolved and how we are forced to use them on the Web. Much of the resulting friction stems from how we take in information, process it, learn, and make decisions. It is important for us to understand our own brains when designing better landing pages.

So let's take a moment to meet that very odd character: the human brain.

Your Three Brains

According to Paul MacLean, the former chief of the Laboratory of Brain Evolution and Behavior at the United States National Institute of Mental Health (NIMH), the older parts of the brain are still with us. MacLean developed a model of the brain based on its evolutionary development. According to his "triune brain theory," there are three distinct layers in the brain that evolved in turn to address new evolutionary needs.

Although each layer dominates certain separate brain functions, all three layers also interact in significant ways. MacLean said that the three brains operate like "three interconnected biological computers, [each] with its own special intelligence, its own subjectivity, its own sense of time and space and its own memory."

The Reptilian Brain

The first to evolve was the reptilian brain (also known as the archipallium, basal brain, or primitive brain). It was called the "R-complex" by MacLean and includes the brain stem and cerebellum. This kind of brain is the high point of development among lizards, snakes, and other reptiles (hence the origin of its name). This brain is mainly responsible for physical survival and maintenance of the body (including, circulation, breathing, digestion, and movement). It is the brain that takes over in fight-or-flight situations, and is responsible for establishing home turf, reproduction, and social dominance. Since it is responsible for autonomic functions such as breathing and the heartbeat, it is active even in deep sleep states. The reptilian brain is the basic program that allows animals to function. The reptilian brain can be viewed as obsessive, compulsive, rigid, and automatic. It is not adaptable or capable of change, and will repeat behaviors over and over—never learning from its mistakes.

The Limbic System

The second to evolve was the limbic system (also variously called the paleo-mammalian, intermediate, old mammalian, or mid-brain). It includes the hypothalamus, hippocampus, and amygdala. This type of brain is present in most mammals and is dominant in more primitive ones. The limbic system is the seat of our primary centers of emotion, attention, and affective (emotion-charged) memories. The amygdala is critical in creating the link between emotions and events, whereas the hippocampus plays the dominant role in storing and recalling memories.

The limbic system is in the driver's seat when it comes to value judgments. It decides whether we like something or are repelled by it. Because of this, the limbic system tends to dominate behaviors that involve the avoidance of pain and the compulsive repetition of pleasure (including feeding, fighting, sex, fleeing, bonding, and caretaking). In his book *The Compass of Pleasure* (Viking, 2011), Johns Hopkins University School of Medicine neuroscientist David Linden lays out the latest scientific research about pleasure circuits in the brain. The limbic system also determines the amount of attention that we give to something, and is responsible for much of our spontaneous and creative behavior.

The limbic system is connected downward to the reptilian brain and upward to the neocortex. Because it links emotions and behavior, the limbic system often inhibits or overrides the reptilian brain's habitual and unchanging responses. Similarly, the more complex emotions of bonding, attachment, and protective loving feelings connect it to the neocortex through rich pathways from the limbic system. According to MacLean, the limbic system decides how it feels about something, and the neocortex is often reduced to simply after-the-fact rationalizing that value judgment decision.

In many cases the self-reported verbal explanations of various experimental subjects were clearly at odds with the "true" internal reactions as recorded directly from their limbic systems. More of this is coming to light as direct measurements of the brain are being taken with the specific purpose of understanding how to convince and persuade people. Recent advances in real-time brain imaging and its applications to marketing are explored in Marin Lindstrom's book *Buyology: Truth and Lies About Why We Buy* (Crown Business, 2010), and in Roger Dooley's *Brainfluence: 100 Ways to Persuade and Convince Consumers with Neuromarketing* (Wiley, 2011). We also highly recommend Susan Weinschenk's book *100 Things Every Designer Needs To Know About People* (New Riders, 2011) for some very actionable takeaways for web designers from neuroscience research.

The Neocortex

The most recent brain to evolve is the neocortex (also called the cerebrum, cerebral cortex, neopallium, neomammalian brain, superior brain, or rational brain). It is composed of the two large hemispheres and some subcortical neuronal groups. This development is seen only in primates, and humans have by far the largest version (taking up more than two-thirds of total brain mass).

The neocortex contains specialized areas for controlling voluntary movement and processing sensory information. It is divided into two hemispheres (left and right), which control the opposite side of the body, respectively. There is some differentiation in function between the two. The left hemisphere is more linear, verbal, and rational, whereas the right hemisphere is more spatial, artistic, musical, and abstract. Higher cognitive functions are all centered in this brain (including language, speech, and writing). It supports logical thinking and allows us to see ahead and plan for the future. MacLean called the neocortex the "mother of invention and father of abstract thought."

Putting It All Together

It is clear that the three brains are connected via an extensive two-way network of nerves, though it's unclear exactly how and how much the three layers communicate. However, it is safe to assume that all three are active during most activities, with a particular one taking the lead in certain situations. The main point is that the neocortex does not dominate the lower levels. The limbic system often asserts its influence over higher mental functions. In times of extreme stress, even our reptilian brain can take over to accomplish seemingly superhuman tasks (such as lifting heavy cars under which people are trapped).

When we design landing pages for the Web, we must understand that we must often please the limbic system. We are being judged on the emotional gut reactions that our pages evoke. Our mid-brain knows what it likes and what it doesn't. After-the-fact logical rationalizations by the neocortex are just that. At some level, the whole point of large-scale statistical landing page testing is to tap directly into this hidden limbic system decision maker and unmask it by seeing its emotionally based underlying actions (unmediated by surveys, focus groups, or usability tests that require verbal and rational skills).

Learning Modalities

There are three major ways to get information into your long-term memory. Research has shown that no significant differences exist in the prevalence of these learning styles between the sexes or among different races:

- Learning by seeing (visual)
- Learning by hearing (auditory)
- Learning by doing (kinesthetic)

Research in teaching has determined that most people lean toward a dominant modality. Some have a more equal balance between two modalities, or even among all three. But there is no single best method for transmitting information. Depending on the specific person, different presentations or teaching techniques will have different levels of effectiveness.

Effective web persuasion requires a variety of methods that cover all three learning modalities. If people are aware of their preference, they can often assimilate information more efficiently by favoring certain kinds of learning tactics and focusing on specific features of your website. So make it easy for them by providing different ways of interacting with your site when appropriate. This is especially important during the desire stage of the decision process, when people are learning about your products or services.

Try to use the following types of information to address each learning modality more effectively:

Visual Guided imagery, demonstration, color coding, diagrams, charts, graphs, photos, maps, video clips

Auditory Audio clips, oral instructions or presentations, poems, rhymes, word association, video clips, live telephone support

Kinesthetic Games and interactive activities; associating emotions with concepts, props, or tangible examples; problem solving; role-playing

Keep in mind that this additional information should not be tacked on or gratuitous. But if there are key concepts that you want your audience to understand and remember, take the time to customize the experience for each modality and offer them the option of how they want to take in that information. For example, let's assume that you have a template for a product detail page in an e-commerce catalog. You may provide detailed specs and diagrams for your visual learners, a video clip overview of the product's main features and benefits for auditory learners, and a customization wizard (which lets the visitor pick colors and other options) that allows the kinesthetic learner to explore, construct, and interact with the product.

Educational psychologist Richard Mayer has identified several presentation rules that have a direct impact on landing page creation. He found that students remembered more about a topic when it was presented as words with tightly connected images. This worked better when the images where placed closely to the text reference. Memory worked best with moving images and a narrative (very much like our natural unfolding experience of the world), as opposed to static experiences.

Another means of enhancing memory is *pattern matching*, in which we create and fill in more general frameworks to better process and store meaning. In John Medina's *Brain Rules* (Pear Press, 2009), he discusses how we retain the gist of the meaning before we can recall any particular details. These generalized pictures feed into pattern matches.

This coding structure of association between concepts allows us to remember data points up to 40 percent more efficiently. When a common pattern match is employed, it may also help bind like audience groups to an affinity. For example, while specific references might alienate some, it will likely attract audiences that understand "the nod." The use of humor, idioms, and pop cultural references are examples of this high-risk, but potentially high-reward, meaning.

Cognitive Styles

Your audience can be spoken of in the collective, but in fact it is like a continual snowfall of individual visitors landing on your site—no two snowflake crystals are exactly alike. You do not have access to the individual thoughts, fears, or motivations of your visitors, yet you must try to understand them.

Since the individual level is not appropriate, some online marketers look for meaningful commonalities at a group level. One way to do this is by using cognitive frameworks. Cognitive frameworks sort people into exclusive categories based on observable cognitive styles or personality types. Cognitive styles are sometimes confusingly referred to as "personas" in online marketing circles (personas are briefly contrasted with roles in Chapter 3).

Any attempt to characterize your visitors is bound to be only partially accurate and too general, but that's okay. You are just trying to understand them well enough to come up with more effective landing pages. Within this limited scope and purpose, online marketers commonly turn to approaches that might help them to better understand their audience: Myers-Briggs, Keirsey-Bates, and the Platinum Rule. Remember, no single framework is definitive or complete. No one has a complete corner on "the Truth"—all you can hope for are better insights into your audience.

Cognitive frameworks are excellent tools in helping to understand a real-life person. Their focus is on improving an individual's self knowledge and approaches for interacting with others. Unfortunately, these frameworks have significant problems when applied to landing page testing. Landing page optimization deals with large numbers of visitors, so each major category of visitors within a cognitive framework will be represented in your audience. This means that you cannot tune for a specific category without making inevitable compromises that affect all others. We discussed a more appropriate framework for conversion improvement called The Matrix previously in Chapter 3.

Myers-Briggs

In 1923, noted Swiss psychiatrist Carl Jung wrote *Psychological Types* and outlined his classification of different types of people ("Theory of Personality Preferences"). According to Jung, many of the differences among people did not stem from mental illness, abnormalities, or problems. Rather, he suggested that people had more or less innate ways of relating to the world. These built-in filters would color every social interaction and dictate someone's effectiveness in a particular circumstance or environment.

This research was picked up and expanded in the 1930s by Katharine Cook Briggs and her daughter Isabel Briggs Myers. They worked through World War II to develop a specific testing tool that would classify people reliably according to Jung's basic theory. They culled through thousands of potential questions and were able to tease out ones that predicted personality types reliably. The final questionnaire and rating method was named the *Myers-Briggs Type Indicator* (MBTI).

The MBTI examines people on four independent scales. Each scale is anchored by two opposite extremes. Where someone falls on a particular scale is not supposed to change over the course of a lifetime. In other words, your basic personality type is pretty much set in stone. This does not mean that as you learn and grow you will not express your type differently. It only means that your underlying worldview shifts very slowly. Each of the scales (also called dichotomies) that follow indicates preferences and tendencies only. Very few people are the caricatures typically described by the two extremes of each scale. There are no value judgments associated with someone's innate type. Obviously, each evolved and took hold in a significant portion of the human population because it had some kind of evolutionary or survival value. None of the types are absolutely better or worse than others. The main goal of the Myers-Briggs method is to understand yourself. Through MBTI you can predict how you might perform in a specific environment or role. It also gives you the basis to find effective communications strategies with people of a different type.

It is beyond the scope of this book to go into detail about this field. The following sketches are meant simply to illustrate the basic concepts and taxonomy of the MBTI.

The Source of Energy: Extroverts (E) vs. Introverts (I) Extroverts draw their energy from the outside world and other people. They love social interactions and are gregarious and communicative. They expend a lot of personal energy and tend to speak before thinking.

Introverts prefer limited social relationships. They conserve their personal energy and are more internal and focused. Introverts are more reflective and notice their own internal reactions to events. They tend to think first and then speak.

Information Gathering: Sensors (S) vs. Intuitives (N) Sensors live in the present moment. They prefer orderly sequential planning and are practical people who pride themselves on being realistic. They insist on what is actual and specific.

Intuitives live in the future world of possibilities. They are conceptual and like to see the big picture. They are comfortable with randomness and disorder and are often viewed as impractical dreamers.

Information Processing: Thinkers (T) vs. Feelers (F) Thinkers tend to be objective. They prefer the clarity and detachment provided by firm rules, and they are not afraid to critique others.

Feelers are subjective and social. They prefer to be involved and operate based on harmony and social values. They try to mediate based on the changing circumstances and come to conclusions that are deemed to be humane and that maintain harmony.

Lifestyle Orientation: Judgers (J) vs. Perceivers (P) Judgers like control, definitiveness, closure, and structure. They plan, resolve, and decide the smallest aspects of their lives. They like to schedule their time and are comfortable meeting specific deadlines.

Perceivers prefer flexibility and a tentative, open-ended orientation to making decisions. They are adaptable and spontaneous and do not like to be hemmed in by deadlines.

The resulting four components can be combined in 16 individual personality types, or "role variants."

Keirsey-Bates

Whereas Myers and Briggs focused on people's *internal* mental states, David Keirsey and Marilyn Bates focused more on easily *observable* behavior patterns. This led Keirsey to develop a descriptive temperament framework that he later merged with the MBTI.

The letters (and concepts) from the MBTI were combined in different ways to provide a new framework for externally visible behaviors. He focused on the primary S-N (abstract-concrete) dimension, which he mapped to the "observant" and "introspective" qualities, respectively. These were combined with another dimension (cooperative-utilitarian) to create the four primary temperaments of the Keirsey Temperament Sorter:

- Artisans (SP): Tactical—Observant and pragmatic
- Guardians (SJ): Logistical—Observant and cooperative
- Idealists (NF): Diplomatic—Introspective and cooperative
- Rationals (NT): Strategic—Introspective and pragmatic

Jakob Nielsen has done a lot of groundbreaking work in web usability. The results of one particular experiment that he conducted (`www.useit.com/alertbox/fancy-formatting.html`) bear out strong evidence for the influence of temperament on the behavior of people on the Web. Figure 6.2 shows the eye-tracking results of four different users on the US Census website. All were trying to locate the current population of the United States. As you can see, there are radical differences in the gazing patterns and fixation (size of the circles correspond to a longer focus on that part of the page).

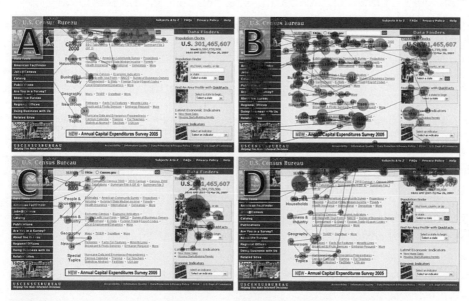

Figure 6.2 US Census website eye-tracking results showing evidence for different user cognitive styles

Although Nielsen has his own names for each of the type of people in the experiment, they basically correspond to the four primary temperaments described earlier:

A. "Search dominant" user can also be described as Rational (NT). After a short look at the top of the page content, this person focused on the left-hand vertical navigation column (and was pragmatic and efficient in their approach to finding information).

B. "Navigation-dominant" user can also be described as a Guardian (SJ). This cognitive style is methodical and this can be seen from their detailed and extended review of almost all page content.

C. "Tool-dominant" user can also be described as an Artisan (SP). This action-oriented and emotional person tended to focus on the drop-down navigation and the interactive form fields on the right of the page.

D. The "successful" user (the only one to correctly find the population information on the page) showed a pattern that could be expected of an Idealist (NF). They are conceptual big-picture people who are comfortable with some disorder. As a result, they were able to see past the non-conventional (large headline) style in which the population figure was presented.

Platinum Rule

Tony Alessandra states his Platinum Rule as follows: "Do unto others as *they* want done unto them." Like Keirsey, Alessandra focuses on observable behaviors (which characterize their operating styles), and provides us with two primary dimensions:

- Open vs. guarded
- Direct vs. indirect

The resulting quadrants form the four foundational styles. Like the MBTI, there are two additional scales to further subdivide each quadrant into 16 total styles (but these are beyond the scope of this summary). The primary styles are as follows:

- Relater—Indirect/open
- Thinker—Indirect/guarded
- Socializer—Direct/open
- Director—Direct/guarded

Table 6.1 provides an overview of the four basic styles.

▶ **Table 6.1** Four Foundational Styles of the Platinum Rule

	Director Style	Socializer Style	Relater Style	Thinker Style
Pace	Fast/Decisive	Fast/Spontaneous	Slower/Relaxed	Slower/Systematic
Priority	Goal	People	Relationship	Task
Seeks	Productivity Control	Participation Applause	Acceptance	Accuracy Precision
Strengths	Administration Leadership Pioneering	Persuading Motivating Entertaining	Listening Teamwork Follow-through	Planning Systematizing Orchestration
Growth Areas	Impatient Insensitive to others Poor listener	Inattentive to detail Short attention span Low follow-through	Oversensitive Slow to begin action Lacks global perspective	Perfectionists Critical Unresponsive
Fears	Being taken advantage of	Loss of social recognition	Sudden changes Instability	Personal criticism of their work efforts
Irritations	Inefficiency Indecision	Routines Complexity	Insensitivity Impatience	Disorganization Impropriety
Under Stress May Become	Dictatorial Critical	Sarcastic Superficial	Submissive Indecisive	Withdrawn Headstrong
Gains Security Through	Control Leadership	Playfulness Others' approval	Friendship Cooperation	Preparation Thoroughness
Measures Personal Worth By	Impact or results Track record and process	Acknowledgments Applause Compliments	Compatibility with others Depth of contribution	Precision Accuracy Quality of results
Workplace	Efficient Busy Structured	Interacting Busy Personal	Friendly Functional Personal	Formal Functional Structured

© Dr. Tony Alessandra, www.Alessandra.com, 1-760-603-8110. Reprinted with permission.

Persuasion Frameworks

Cognitive styles are merely descriptive—classifying people into groups based on their behavior or way of experiencing the world. To take this to the next level, we need actionable frameworks that give us insights on the fundamental principles of persuasion and how to move people to action.

The following frameworks in particular can be practically and powerfully applied to conversion on the Web. All of them describe the same basic operating principles for people from different perspectives. They are not meant to be exclusive, and you should use insights from all three when working on your conversion rate optimization projects.

BJ Fogg's Behavior Model

BJ Fogg is not your typical academic. In addition to founding the Stanford University's Persuasive Technology Lab, he works on many industry projects with companies that apply his powerful finding to practical real-world situations. Like Cialdini's work (described later in this chapter), his work is field tested. He coined the word "captology" to describe the intersection of persuasion and computer technologies, and also authored *Persuasive Technology: Using Computers to Change What We Think and Do* (Morgan Kaufmann, 2002).

Unlike some of the research, which merely describes how *attitudes* are changed and influenced, the core of Fogg's focus is on how to actually change people's *behavior*. He has developed the *Fogg Behavior Model (FBM)* to describe how behavior change happens. We have summarized it based on the information provided at www.behaviormodel.org. You can also check out the helpful Behavior Wizard at www.behaviorwizard.org for a taxonomy of various behavior types and how to create them.

As you can see in Figure 6.3, the FBM can be summarized in one simple concept: for a behavior to occur, three conditions must be present at the same time, motivation, ability, and an effective trigger. If the behavior does not occur, at least one of these elements must be missing.

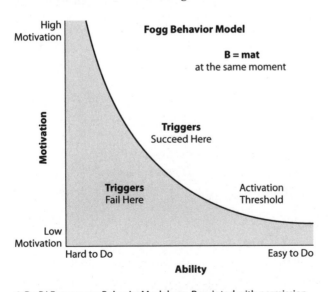

© Dr. BJ Fogg, www.BehaviorModel.org. Reprinted with permission.

Figure 6.3 The Fogg Behavior Model (FBM)

In other words, often the best way to get a desired behavior in the words of Fogg is to "put hot triggers in front of motivated people." Let's look at each of the components of the model in more detail.

Motivation

There are three basic human motivators. Each of them can be seen along a continuum. It is easiest to change behavior when you are able to affect someone as strongly as possible near one of the extremes.

Sensation The desire to feel pleasure, and the need to avoid pain. Pain avoidance is generally considered to be the stronger motivator.

Anticipation The hope that good things will occur in the future, and the dread or fear that bad things may happen. Fear is generally considered to be the stronger motivator.

Social Cohesion Our need for social acceptance, and the avoidance of social rejection. Ostracism and shunning are generally considered to be stronger motivators.

Ability

To perform a target behavior, a person must have the ability to do so.

There are two paths to increasing ability. You can train people, giving them more skills and more ability to do the target behavior. That's the hard path since people will generally avoid effort and tend to be lazy.

You can also **make the target behavior easier to do**. Fogg calls this approach *simplicity*. **By focusing on simplicity of the target behavior, you increase ability.**

Simplicity **is a function of your scarcest resource at that moment.** This resource can refer to time, attention, effort, money.

Triggers

Triggers tell people to "do it now!" Sometimes a trigger can be external, like the sudden sound of a car horn. Other times, the trigger can come from our daily routine: walking into your house reminds you to take off your shoes.

The FBM describes three trigger types to be used in the correct specific circumstances:

Facilitator If someone is motivated but is not responding because it seems hard (perceived lack of ability), use a "facilitator" trigger. It should include a call-to-action and some messaging that says "it's easy."

Signal If someone can do a task (has the ability) but is not motivated to do it, you should try to design a "spark" trigger. It should include a call-to-action plus some sort of motivator.

Spark If a person has both the motivation and ability to do something, they just need a straightforward "signal" trigger. This is essentially a "do it now" reminder. Don't try to motivate these kinds of people or emphasize simplicity or ease of doing the task.

Triggers can lead to a chain of desired behaviors. An effective trigger for a small behavior can lead people to perform harder behaviors.

Many designers make the mistake of asking people to perform a complicated behavior. A corresponding mistake is packing too much into a trigger. Neither path works well. Simplicity changes behavior.

SiteTuners' Unbalancing Scales

We want to tell you a quick story….

The Case of the Sleepy Dog

A tourist was driving on a deserted rural road and happened upon a cabin. An old man was smoking a pipe in his rocking chair on the porch while a droopy hound dog dozed by his side. The tourist got out of his car and struck up a conversation with the old man. Periodically as they talked the dog would let out a long plaintive howl and would then settle back down to sleep.

After this happened a few times, the tourist finally asked the old man, "What's wrong with your dog?"

The old man answered, "Oh, don't mind him—he's just lying on a nail."

The flabbergasted tourist asked, "Why doesn't he move?"

The old man thought for a minute and responded, "I reckon it don't hurt badly enough."

It is a well-known maxim in marketing that people who are comfortable enough with their current situation (like the hound dog in the story) are not good prospects for buying goods, services, or ideas—they simply don't care enough to make a change.

Direct marketers Bob Hacker and Axel Andersson have defined several key copywriting concepts that motivate us to act: fear, greed, guilt, exclusivity, anger, salvation, or flattery. Not one of these motivations is rational—all of them are rooted in our fundamental and unchanging emotional nature.

 The best way to get visitors to act is to appeal to their fundamental *emotional* motivations.

At SiteTuners we have developed a set of hierarchical scales to help us rate websites' persuasiveness. They are not precise instruments, but rather tools that help us to focus outward (on our website visitors) and then inward (on their emotional state). Each scale is a continuum of feelings and internal states.

Any proposed change to your landing page must be explainable within these scales and should attempt to "move the needle to the right." Your goal should be to unbalance the scales to the point where someone is moved to act. Although the scales are distinct, changes that affect one scale will have an impact on the others as well.

Anxiety vs. Trust

This is the most basic scale and addresses our feelings of safety and security. You would not think that sitting in front of a web browser would produce much anxiety, but you would be wrong. Giving up personal information, allowing people to contact us, and paying by credit card all have significant fears associated with them.

> We cannot expect someone to act unless we first guarantee their safety and security.

How will my information be used? Will I get on a spam list? Will I be the victim of identity theft? Will the purchase arrive undamaged and on time? Will I actually get what I ordered? Will unexpected fine print charges be added to my order without my knowledge? Will anyone respond if I have a problem after buying? Will it be easy to dispute or cancel my transaction?

As discussed in the "Lack of Trust and Credibility" section of Chapter 4, "Common Problems—The Seven Deadly Sins of Landing Page Design," anything that you can do to minimize anxiety will help conversion. This includes clear privacy policies, detailed shipping directions, unconditional return policies, client testimonials, certifications, and trust symbols that show that you conduct business with integrity.

Confusion vs. Clarity

Some sites are simple and intuitive. Most are akin to a busy marketplace with loud hawkers vying for your attention. You are assaulted with bright colors, boxes, and flashing advertisements. You are overloaded with too many choices and links. You are drowned in too much text displayed in tiny fonts. You are not sure how to navigate the site and find the information that you need.

Is this a button that I can click or just a graphic? Does "Buy it now" just put something in my shopping cart or does it actually charge me and place my order? Where am I in the site? How do I get back to the page that I read earlier? Which of these 20 links should I click? Why does this page text not address my particular needs?

Often too many internal company interests compete for real estate and prominence on important pages. Over time nothing ever gets taken away—new items are simply added to the webpage. Unfortunately, this often leads to a phenomenon know as "The Tragedy of the Commons." If too many shepherds have unrestricted access to the unregulated common grazing lands, the sheep will overwhelm the grass's ability to regenerate itself—destroying it for everyone. The individual self-interests of shepherds undercut the common good.

 By emphasizing too many items on a webpage, we destroy visitors' ability to find key information and paralyze them from making a decision.

Most sites and landing pages have poor information architecture and interaction design. Fixing major usability, coherence, and cognitive problems can have a major conversion rate impact.

Alienation vs. Affinity

Even if we get over our anxiety and confusion to find the information that we need, we still have to deal with affinity and alienation. We want to be understood, valued, and recognized for who we are. These are subtle issues of identity, tribalism, self-esteem, and belonging. We are members of many formal and informal tribes in our lives: fans of a specific sports team, employees of a certain company, drivers of a particular make of car, occupants of a specific zip code, and graduates of a certain school…the list is endless. Some of these tribes we chose consciously, others unconsciously. Still others chose us (such as the "tribe" of orphaned children, or being a member of a specific racial/ethnic group).

The editorial tone of the landing page needs to conform to the visitor's values and beliefs. Any images of people should also help them to self-identify. Graphics color schemes should match the appropriate palette for their sensibilities. Button text and calls-to-action should also use the language of the target community. By segmenting our visitors and personalizing information for them, we are much more likely to appeal to their sensibilities and move them to action.

Cialdini's Six Key Principles of Persuasion

In 1980, Robert Cialdini wrote the seminal book *Influence: The Psychology of Persuasion*, an analysis of human behavior that made a tremendous impact on marketing. By researching the tactics of salespeople, academics, religious groups, and others, he was able to distill several basic strategies that universally and reliably influence people. All of them have been shown to increase the rate at which a person or group complies with a request.

This tendency to comply is based on our species' built-in instinct and has been shown to operate across a variety of social structures and cultures. All animals have built-in fixed action patterns that are triggered by specific stimuli. Humans also have a number of these fixed action patterns. They are shortcuts that help us process our social environment more efficiently.

According to Cialdini, there are six "weapons of influence" that are most effective. These are outlined next along with thoughts on how they might apply to conversion rate optimization. Part III, "Fixing Your Site Problems," provides many additional ideas for what to test and improve on your landing page. These thoughts are for illustration only and are not meant to be exhaustive.

Reciprocation

When someone gives you an unsolicited gift, you feel indebted and incur an obligation to reciprocate. If we extend a small (even token) gift or gesture to someone, they will often respond positively and will even be more likely to return a disproportionately large gift (or concession).

On the Web, you should be first to offer "gifts" in as many situations as possible. This includes information, downloads, and samples of various kinds (especially for informational products or online services that have little or no incremental cost or effort to deliver).

Another related tactic called "reciprocal concession" involves asking for something unreasonable (more than you really expect), and then retreating and asking for a much smaller request. As long as this is viewed as a legitimate concession, the likelihood of the smaller request being accepted is a lot higher than if it had been asked for in isolation.

On the Web this kind of psychological "bracketing" is seen in displaying the most expensive products or options first. You may not expect someone to buy the expensive item, but it makes the following items seem reasonable in comparison.

Commitment and Consistency

Once a person has made a commitment, they are likely to follow through even if they know that acting consistently with that commitment will not be beneficial. The most powerful kinds of commitments are voluntary (not coerced), and also public.

The power behind commitment as a weapon of influence comes from the need for people to be consistent. Consistency is valued in social relationships. We want others to keep their word (it makes their behavior more predictable and not so chaotic or random) and to also be viewed by others as a person of high integrity. So once we have made a commitment, we subtly (or dramatically) shift our self-perception and image to become more consistent with our commitment. In other words, each time we comply with a request, even a trivial request, it modifies our attitudes and self-concept such that we will tend to act more consistently with that type of action.

On the Web this implies that as online marketers we should try to elicit small and public commitments of support or affirmation from our site visitors. From such small seeds, real attitude and behavior change can grow. It has been shown, for example, that someone who has "Liked" a Facebook fan page of a particular company is significantly more likely to become a customer in the future. They have started down the slippery slope of becoming more aligned with their initial seemingly inconsequential demonstration of support. This is closely related to the notion of "triggers" (see Fogg's Behavior Model earlier in this chapter).

Social Proof

We determine what is correct by finding out what other people think is correct. This is particularly true in the presence of uncertainty or in unfamiliar circumstances. We are particularly prone to follow the lead of people we perceive as similar to us. This "follow the herd" mentality is very powerful.

Two key components are needed to maximize the effect of social proof. A large number of people must all be acting in a certain way, and they must be as much like us as possible. If we can find circumstances where this is happening, we can put our brains on auto-pilot and use the behavior of others as a shortcut for our own decision making.

Demonstrating such social proof on landing pages is very effective. You can use large numbers (such as "over 20,000 happy customers") to demonstrate large numbers. You should also tap into similarity by using specific testimonials that are relevant (and show the same circumstances that your visitor is likely to be in). Product reviews/ratings of people who have purchased an item that we are also considering buying are powerful because we get to hear about their direct experience of a situation that we envision ourselves in.

Liking

The more we identify with someone else, finding common affinities, backgrounds, and even appearances, the more likely we are to agree to the same behavior or to be influenced by them. People prefer to say yes to the requests of people they know and like. So increasing the degree to which you are liked by someone will increase the probability that they will comply with your requests. We like people better and believe them more when they

- Are more attractive
- Are similar to us
- Like us
- Are familiar to us
- Are engaged in a cooperative effort with us
- Are associated with things we like
- Are present while we are eating a meal

It is a well-known technique in sales that the salesperson is supposed to find common ground with a sales prospect quickly and possibly mirror back those similarities in an effort to be more liked. On the Web this translates to the appearance of your site or landing page. It must have the right color scheme, content, and even editorial tone to appeal to your target audience (and seem as much like them as possible).

Authority

People create social hierarchies (social, political, and religious). We know our place in the hierarchy, and if we are not at the top we will often defer to those who are higher. Once someone has accepted you as an authority, they will follow your instructions even against their own judgment, ethics, and feelings. Even the appearance of authority (such as formal uniforms or displays of wealth) is enough to confer the power to influence others.

On the Web the appearance of authority can be used in a number of ways to confer trust and credibility and increase conversion rates. Visual badges or seals that indicate membership in professional organizations, logos of marquee clients (for business-to-business companies), media mentions, and even celebrity endorsements or reviews can all serve to convince people that your product or service is legitimate.

Scarcity

Finally, scarcity spurs us to pay more attention to or give more value to an item that we see as rare, forbidden, or difficult to replace.

Cultural Differences

In addition to our hardwired biological impulses and cognitive styles, there is clearly a cultural overlay in how we perceive the world. Although it is beyond the scope of this book to explore this in detail, we wanted to provide you with the following overview.

It has long been observed that search terms and phrases used by brands selling in multiple languages and markets often do not work in translation. For example, in Italian the regular translation of "cheap flights" ("voli economici") has only 33,000 local searches monthly in Google Italy. The Anglo-Italian search term "voli low cost" has nearly 8 times the search volume at 246,000 searches. Even within the same language there can be cultural differences between different countries. In Spain the most popular term for online gaming sites is "maquinas tragaperras" (translation: "online slot machines"). However, in Spanish-speaking Argentina the most popular term is the Anglo-Spanish "tragamonedas online" (translation: "slot machines *online*").

Likewise, many other elements of web design can be subject to subtle cultural nuances. By understanding these cultural preferences, you can provide a better experience for your customers in each market, leading to better engagement and more conversions.

However, cultural localization brings real challenges to web and content managers: if you have webpages that are templated across not just multiple languages, but across multiple alphabets, how can this content best be managed? What exactly are the benefits of localized design, and do they transcend the obvious economies of scale of a global template? Also, how do you identify this cultural difference in the first place?

There are cultural clues from the world of academia. Sociologists and anthropologists have long looked for evidence of cultural models in response to various visual stimuli. The theory of High vs. Low Context was developed by Edward T. Hall and is based on the notion that some cultures more than others rely on the nonverbal, implicit context of the message, such as shared beliefs and common knowledge, intonation, and body language, and are therefore high-context (such as Chinese or Japanese). Other cultures (such as German or Scandinavian) prefer a direct and explicit mode of communication. In website design, richer context is often provided through the use of animation and many graphics for high-context cultures, as opposed to a more textual and simple design for low-context cultures.

Another cultural model developed by Geert Hofstede in the 1980s divided cultures into *collectivist* or *individualist* societies. This distinction refers to the level of importance attached to being part of a group or organization, as opposed to loose ties among individuals. In design, this would be reflected in the emphasis on personal vs. group achievement, consumerism vs. socio-political agendas, novelty vs. tradition, differences in attitude to giving personal information online, and importance of community communication through chat rooms and forums.

A related concept is people's experience of and relationship to time. People in *monochronic* societies follow a strict time schedule and do one thing at a time, take time commitments and schedules seriously, are low-context and need information, are concerned about not disturbing others, are accustomed to short-term relationships, and show a great respect for private property.

By contrast, people in *polychromic* societies do many things at once, are easily distracted and subject to interruptions, are high-context and already have information, are committed to people and human relationships, change plans often and easily, borrow and lend things often and easily, and have a strong tendency to build lifetime relationships.

Let's now look at an example which perfectly illustrates these differences. Figure 6.4 shows two screenshots of the Japanese and German McDonald's homepages.

Japan is a high-context, mainly polychronic (with the exception when dealing with "foreigners" and with technology, when they shift to the monochronic side, according to Hall) and collectivist society. The Japanese website is busy with many graphics, icons, boxes and animations (suitable for high-context cultures). The navigation of the site is quite complex and animated with many links on each site—this is suitable for polychronic cultures. The large images scroll vertically (following the

Japanese traditional script, which is written in columns). There is also a prominent section dedicated to society, charity, family events, local community, as well as images of groups and families—thus addressing the collectivist needs.

Figure 6.4 McDonald's homepages in Japan (left) and Germany (right)

Germany is a low-context, monochronic and individualistic society. The German site is much simpler and direct—a large image of the food with a short message on the latest products and price deals —is a good representation of the low-context culture. The navigation menu is simple and static at the top of the site (monochronic culture). The section on nutrition is informative—and as such is the main role of the site. The main image can be scrolled horizontally, which reflects the reading/writing system from left to right. There is a clear focus on the products and the consumerist nature of the business (individualism).

As you are testing for cultural differences, explore the following:

Translation vs. Localization Sometimes direct translation is appropriate. For other cultures, a unique localized message needs to be created that will resonate better.

Font Families and Sizes There are significant differences in the font presentations that are desirable in different countries.

Colors Radical cultural differences exist in the use and meaning of colors.

Graphical Presentation As discussed Chapter 4, we generally recommend keeping visual clutter at an absolute minimum. However, this recommendation should be revisited for international audiences.

It is also important to question the importance or impact of the variable in its own right, since the absolute conversion rate and the particular impactful test elements can themselves vary widely by country.

Unless you already have deep internationalization and cross-cultural web development experience, we do not recommend tackling cultural topics alone. Oban Multilingual (`http://ObanMultilingual.com`) is a leading agency in multilingual and cross-cultural web marketing (including SEO, PPC, and CRO). They have developed the GlobalMaxer testing platform for cultural multivariate testing and international conversion optimization. Oban Multilingual also offers the Cultural Database, a rule-based engine that collects data on popular types of web design in each country, segmented by webpage type (cart page, homepage, product category page), country, and industry sector. It can be used to make suggestions on page elements to test by country.

Part III will focus on fixing your site problems, with an overview of conversion improvement basics, best practices for common situations, and a strategy for determining the most impactful changes you can make.

Fixing Your Site Problems

III

The painful work of diagnosis is over. Now we turn our attention to rebuilding and improving your landing pages and website. In this part of the book you will learn the keys to conversion improvement, best practices for specifics situations, and how to prioritize ideas for your landing page tests. Part III consists of the following chapters:

Chapter 7   **Conversion Improvement Basics**
Chapter 8   **Best Practices for Common Situations**
Chapter 9   **The Strategy of What to Test**

Conversion Improvement Basics

We all want the magic answer that will skyrocket profits. We have heard miraculous tales in which tiny landing page changes have a giant influence on the conversion rate. In reality, much of conversion rate improvement comes from not doing something very right, but rather from simply avoiding doing the wrong things. In this chapter we will examine the basic foundations of conversion optimization.

7

CHAPTER CONTENTS

Web Usability Overview

Visual Presentation

Writing for the Web

Usability Checks

Web Usability Overview

Good usability is properly managing people's expectations. Some of the overall goals of web usability are

- Decrease the time it takes visitors to finish tasks
- Reduce the number of mistakes visitors are likely to make
- Shorten visitors' learning time
- Improve visitors' satisfaction with your site

When you are considering usability for landing pages, you should always take into account the following picture of your visitor's typical mind-set and behavior:

- The visitor has extreme impatience and little commitment to your site.
- The visitor has a short fixation on only the more prominent items of interest.
- The visitor's typical desired next action is to click on something (probably a link or a button).
- The visitor doesn't read text; they scan it.
- The visitor will pay special attention to striking visual images and motion/animation.

When visitors come to your website, they are not a blank slate. They carry the sum total of their life experiences to date. This includes attitudes, irrational impulses, subtle anxieties, and conscious beliefs, as well as unconscious assumptions.

Our beliefs and assumptions have an enormous impact on how we behave. If you have just gotten a static electricity shock from a doorknob, you are going to be more consciously aware of other doorknobs and approach them with apprehension, based on the belief that another shock is possible. If you believe that the earth is flat (as most people did just a few centuries ago), you would not try to circumnavigate the globe and would be afraid of exploring based on the logical fear of falling off the edge.

Most of your visitors already have enormous experience with the Internet. Even recent or casual users have probably logged hundreds of hours interacting with websites. Out of that experience they have constructed a mental model of how the Web works.

Part of that mental model includes constraints (things that can't be done) and conventions (an understanding of and agreement with how things are commonly done).

> *A convention is a cultural constraint, one that has evolved over time. Conventions are not arbitrary: they evolve, they require a community of practice. They are slow to be adopted, and once adopted, slow to go away. So although the word implies voluntary choice, the reality is that they are real constraints upon our behavior. Use them with respect. Violate them only with great risk.*
>
> —Usability guru Don Norman

The visitor's mental model may not be exact or correct. For example, a disturbingly high percentage of people will type a URL into the Google search box instead of into their browser's address window. But it does not matter if the model is correct. As far as you should be concerned, the model is set in stone and not likely to change anytime soon.

In his excellent book *Don't Make Me Think* (New Riders, 2005), author and web usability expert Steve Krug suggests that you should have a firm grounding in common web design conventions and use them whenever possible. They make things easier for your visitors, and lessen the mental load and attention required for them to interact with your landing page.

Examples of powerful web conventions include:

- The company logo and home link appear near the upper-left corner.
- The navigation menu is near the top or on the left side of the page.
- The e-commerce catalog shopping cart link is near the upper-right corner of the page.
- Blue underlined text is a hyperlink.
- Brightly animated rectangular graphics are advertisements.

Visual Presentation

Visual presentation creates the powerful first impression that is responsible for many visitors leaving your site within the first few seconds of arriving. When they first get to your site, they have not had a chance to scan or digest most of your text message. They are mainly reacting emotionally to your page design. As mentioned in Chapter 6, "Misunderstanding Your Visitors—Looking for Psychological Mismatches," you can't fool or argue with the limbic system (your "emotional" mid-brain). If it does not like something, no logical argument can prevail against it (and the browser back button is an easy way to quickly exit any webpage).

Most of us can tell whether a landing page appeals to us or repels us. We can tell if a page is "cheesy" and unprofessional. This determination is made based on the page structure, color scheme, font variety, graphics and images, and the degree of visual clutter on the page.

But can people spot "cheesy" and unprofessional sites consistently? They absolutely can—and do so very quickly!

People make a judgment of a landing page's quality in 1/20th of a second, suggests 2005 research led by Dr. Gitte Lindgaard of Carleton University in Ottawa, Canada. In other words, the judgments were being formed almost as quickly as the eye can take in information. This process is subliminal and precise.

This first impression of the aesthetic quality persists and colors all subsequent judgments about visitors' experience with your site. You can't "fake out" this automatic ability of the brain to form accurate visual impressions. So make your site or landing page more visually appealing or suffer the consequences of lower conversion.

If you want to get a good laugh, visit "The World's Worst Website" (see Figure 7.1) at www.angelfire.com/super/badwebs/. This amusing compilation of suboptimal website elements and worst practices serves as an instructive list of what not to do.

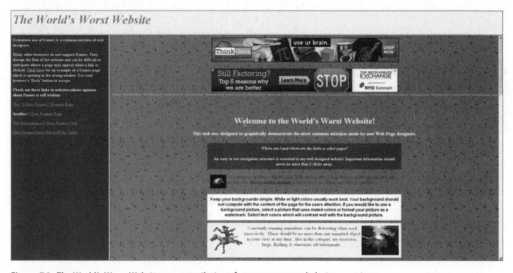

Figure 7.1 The World's Worst Website—a compilation of common poor web design practices

Instead, use the following guidelines to improve your visual design.

Page Layout

The main quality that your page design has to have is *coherence*. It must be well organized and hang together as a single unit. It is helpful to use a grid design to create your preliminary layout. Design the page around the visitor's task and the conversion action.

The balance of your design is created at this early stage and should be carefully preserved. The page should be simple and uncluttered and include enough whitespace for the eye to rest. Give the proper visual prominence to key elements. Group like items together.

Unless advertising is your primary source of revenue, seriously consider whether you should show any banner ads, or any visual elements that could be perceived as a banner. Banner ads are visually bold and may destroy the relative emphasis and coherence of the other page elements. The spaces on the page that banner ads take up also make it harder to create a clean page layout. In the end, the drop in conversion may end up costing you more money than the banner ad revenue can bring in.

The website for the *Law & Order* TV show is poorly organized and has low coherence (see Figure 7.2). Every available piece of screen real estate is stuffed with content along a confusing and unbalanced grid layout. Content is interspersed with advertising and navigation. The visual styles in different parts of the page vary widely and make it almost impossible to prioritize information or know in which order to consume it.

Figure 7.2 *Law & Order* TV show homepage—unorganized with no visual hierarchy

Never make the user scroll to find critical information like transactional buttons or important navigation links. Even if they are appropriate near the bottom of the page, include another copy somewhere above the fold.

Be wary of introducing any kind of horizontal rules, separators, or color changes into your design. Rules, or even abrupt changes in background color, serve to stop the eye from going further. Separators of any kind, including large amounts of vertical whitespace (which looks like the end of the page content), can discourage further exploration and reduce scannability.

Frames are composite pages created like a photo collage from several individual webpages and often pulled from several disparate sources. Frames have several significant practical problems and break the fundamental navigation paradigm of the Web. Basically, just say no to frames unless the framed content is critical to your site functioning and cannot be incorporated in any other way.

Page Shell Design

Independent of the content in the body of the page, several important guidelines should be followed in the design of the surrounding page shell.

Separation of Content from Page Shell

One of the key properties that a good webpage should have is a clear separation between page content and the rest of the page shell (which includes header, navigation, footer, supporting information, and page sides). Many pages make no meaningful distinction among these, requiring the user to spend valuable time discerning the different elements on the page.

One effective way to create this separation is to use nonwhite background colors for elements of the page shell. If this is not done, the results often look like the homepage of the J. Crew website (see Figure 7.3). In an attempt to look extra clean and pristine, the all-white page background actually destroys any sense of page structure and forces the user to identify elements of the page shell (such as navigation) by reading a lot of tiny text.

Centered Fixed-Width Designs

Another frequent page shell issue is the response of the page to changes in browser window size. Our recommendation is to create centered fixed-width designs for most situations.

The screen width that you should be designing for changes over time and should be occasionally revisited. As of this writing, we recommend designing for a 1024-pixel monitor width. Unless you have an old-fashioned and technology-averse demographic, most visitors can be expected to have a monitor at least this wide (you can confirm this by examining your web analytics reports).

Figure 7.3 J. Crew homepage—no clear separation of page content from the rest of the page shell

By allowing for a vertical browser scroll bar, and also by showing some of the page background beyond the side edges of the page, you imply that the actual content should be laid out on a grid between 950 and 980 pixels wide. Of course, if you have a significant audience segment on mobile phones or tablets, you will need to develop a separate mobile site based on the prevailing standards.

When you violate the guidelines above, the results are clearly suboptimal. For example, some fixed-width sites still left-justify the content part of the page on the screen. This is the case for top law firm Bingham McCutchen LLP (www.bingham.com). At narrow monitor resolutions their site may look okay (see Figure 7.4).

However, when viewed on a 24-inch 1920-pixel-wide monitor, it looks very odd (see Figure 7.5). The content is shoved to the left and someone seated in front of the monitor would have to rotate their head several degrees counterclockwise just to take it in.

The same problem can be seen on the website of the National Basketball Association (NBA; see Figure 7.6). The right half of the screen is simply filled in with a light gray background color and every visitor is expected to pivot their head to the left.

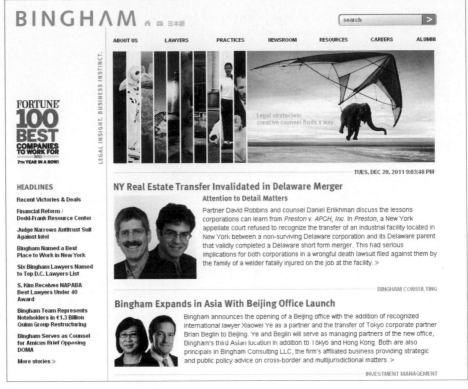

Figure 7.4 Bingham McCutchen's homepage—left-justified on a 1024-pixel screen—looks normal.

Figure 7.5 Bingham McCutchen homepage—left-justified on a 1920-pixel screen—looks lopsided and strange.

Figure 7.6 The NBA homepage—left-justified on a 1920-pixel screen—also looks lopsided and strange.

Stretching the middle of your page creates its own problems. The Sears homepage in Figure 7.7 is designed to have a fixed-width left navigation column and a stretchable right column. As a result, the images in the center of the page look very strangely spaced and are surrounded by large, empty background color blocks. The search input text field in the header has also been distorted into an unrecognizably long shape with a tiny magnifying glass button on its right edge as the only remaining clue to its intended purpose.

Figure 7.7 On the Sears homepage with its center section stretched on a 1920-pixel screen, the image background areas look odd.

Some websites adopt a hybrid approach—keeping the content fixed but stretching out the background images. This also presents significant problems. Figure 7.8 shows the Yahoo! News site at 1024 pixel width. Note that the darker header looks appropriate and properly caps the page (over the full width of the page contents). The light gray fade that ends just below the video player looks like a subtle and normal part of the design.

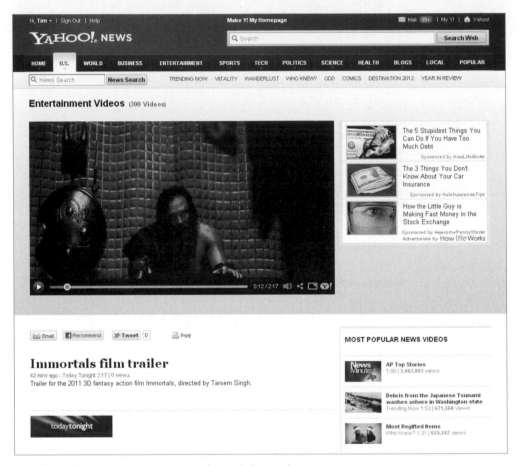

Figure 7.8 The Yahoo! News page on a 1024-pixel screen looks normal.

When viewed on a much wider monitor (see Figure 7.9), the effect of the design changes significantly. The stretchable header background now becomes an oppressive dark stripe that shoots its visual energy sideways in a "T" shape (we call this the dreaded "muffin top" of stretchable headers). And even the formerly subtle gray gradient becomes part of the design—creating visual interest on the sides of the page.

Figure 7.9 The Yahoo! News page on a 2400-pixel screen looks strange.

Some sites go to the other extreme—fixing both the width of the page and its height. This is usually based on too heavy-handed an effort to precisely control the whole visual experience. On the Toyota USA website, the page for the Yaris car model is fixed in both height and width. As you can see in Figure 7.10, the site looks diminutive on a 1920-pixel monitor. There is a distinct perception that the site is cramped and old-fashioned because it makes no meaningful accommodations for the larger screen.

Figure 7.10 The Toyota USA fixed-size page on a 1920-pixel screen looks tiny.

Another design approach with significant issues involves stretching the whole header (not just the background image). If you visit the Yaris car model website on a small screen (see Figure 7.11), you will see a normal-looking page. Note the Toyota branding in the upper left and the navigation bar above the content in the upper right of the header.

Figure 7.11 The Yaris car model homepage on a 1024-pixel screen looks normal.

However, when the same site is experienced at a width of 1920 pixels (Figure 7.12), the spatial relationships in the header get distorted beyond recognition. The Toyota branding is now almost completely out of the visual field of view in the upper left of the screen. Similarly, the navigation has now lost its proximal relationship to the page content and is floating disembodied in the upper-right corner.

Figure 7.12 The Yaris car model homepage on a 1920-pixel screen looks tiny.

Boring Page Sides

The content of your webpage should have all the attention when someone looks at it. If there is anything on the sides of the page that has visual interest, it should be removed. In general, the sides of your page should be a bit darker and should be a flat, even color. No patterns, textures, color gradients, or other visually interesting items are allowed in this area. Even a solid white color (which is very bright and would compete with the page contents, especially if there is no color change or boundary between them) should be avoided. Most importantly, you need to refrain from using illustrations or photographic images for page backgrounds. The sides of your page should be absolutely boring, so the visitor's brain can safely ignore them and focus on the content.

Figure 7.13 shows what happens when this guideline is violated. The Armani Exchange website uses giant, full-contrast models as enormous billboards that flank their own page content. In terms of visual impact, the sides of the page completely dominate the visual presentation and make it hard to focus on (much less consume) the page content.

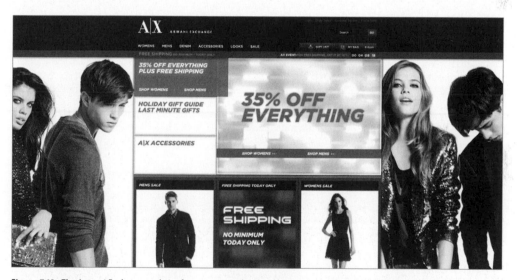

Figure 7.13 The Armani Exchange website features giant photographic images on the sides of the page.

There are rare exceptions to all these guidelines. The dark background and extreme contrast, lack of page containment, and stretchable design of the Gears of War 3 Xbox videogame website (see Figure 7.14) is designed primarily for teenage boys and young men who are already used to an immersive and visually rich videogame experience. But if your website is primarily designed for business or a normal cross-section of the adult population, such design liberties should be avoided.

All of the best practices guidelines we've described have been incorporated into the SiteTuners homepage shown in Figure 7.15.

Figure 7.14 Gears of War videogame homepage

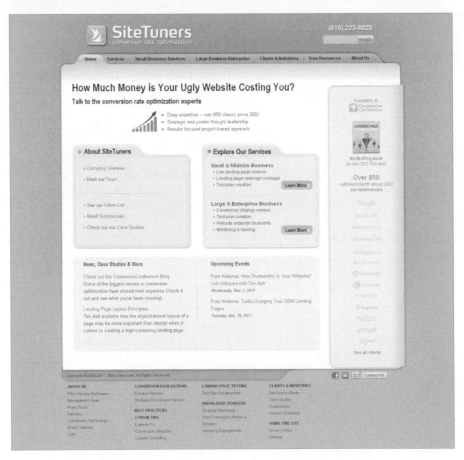

Figure 7.15 SiteTuners homepage

These best practices include:

- Fixed-width page (960 pixels wide) with a clearly delineated edge indicated by a color change and a step-off drop shadow
- Centering of the page on the screen
- Nonstretchable header contents
- Clear separation of page content (white high-contrast background) from the rest of the page shell (including header, navigation bar, footer, and page sides in off-white shades or mid-tones)
- Even neutral side color with no pattern, textures, or images of any kind

Graphics

Images on your landing page are a powerful, double-edged sword. When tightly coordinated with key messages, they support the path to desired actions. When used gratuitously or carelessly, they can distract visitors from the task at hand.

The best images support your visitor's task because they

- Relate to the content on the page
- Illustrate key concepts (are not simply used as window dressing)
- Show product views or details
- Contain pictures of friendly real people (not models)
- Have clear composition and tight cropping

However, images can also have a negative effect. They can serve as distractions or interruptions for your visitor if they

- Are generic and unrelated to the topic of the page
- Use clearly fake, staged, contrived, or slick stock art
- Contain bright, flashy elements that make the graphics look like advertisements
- Decrease readability if placed behind text or navigation menus

The following best practices should help you to effectively use images:

Use high-quality production graphics and images. Do not mix different visual styles (such as photos and clip-art cartoons).

Make sure all your image file sizes are small enough to load quickly. E-commerce visitors tend to leave a site that takes more than 2 seconds to load. The only possible exception to this is the product "click to enlarge" close-up. These images should be as large as possible while still fitting fully on the monitor.

Animation is almost universally annoying and should be generally avoided.
If animation is required to illustrate a concept, the user should be given the affirmative option of watching it and should not have it forced upon them. Similarly, Flash technology should be used only if there is a compelling need for it that would significantly improve the user experience. The move toward HTML5 as a standard should allow universal portability of animated, interactive, or video objects natively within webpages.

Color

Color has a strong emotional impact on people and can dramatically alter moods and attitudes. Since we are viewing projected colors on a computer screen, strong vibrant colors are particularly noticeable. So you should use full saturation primary color sparingly and conservatively. Our general advice is to follow the less-is-more approach and create a relatively benign visual environment, tending toward the mid-tones or lighter pastel shades. This applies not only to individual colors, but also to palettes of complementary colors chosen for the landing page's visual theme. Make sure that your colors look unified, professional, and appropriate for your target audiences.

Do not use inverse color schemes with dark backgrounds and light text colors. Most web browsers cannot print such pages very well. Stick to common color conventions. Use white (or very light) colors for text background areas (wild background patterns make it harder to read). Use colored text sparingly, and always use distinctive formatting for links (ideally blue underlined text or some other clearly different color that is not used for any other text on the page).

Video

As bandwidth and computer processing power increases, it is increasingly common to be able to stream high-quality video as part of the web experience.

We are often asked the question, "Does video work on the Web to increase conversions?" Of course the question is not a simple one, and the answer is not black and white.

One thing we do know is that motion and audio will grab the attention of visitors. The more important question is whether that captured attention is properly used to advance the conversion or is actually a powerful distraction.

Instead of thinking that video is inherently good or bad, you should realize that its exact parameters matter a lot more than its presence or absence. We have seen huge conversion gains from video as well as significant conversion drops.

Some important considerations for web video effectiveness include the following:

- Actor or actress used (gender and appearance can have a strong impact)
- Dress style and grooming (must be appropriate for your audience)
- Script contents and length
- Whether the video autoplays
- Whether the video starts with sound on or must be actively turned on by the visitor
- Whether the video replays automatically on subsequent reloads of the page or return visits
- Production quality
- Resolution and bandwidth required to view it
- Whether it is served from a public site or a dedicated media server

There are three primary ways to consume video on a webpage:

Embedded The software "viewer" window for the video is a fixed size and it is embedded in the page. The problem with this approach is that it takes up a lot of screen real estate while providing a small, often uncompelling visual experience.

Lightbox Popover The video is indicated by a small thumbnail graphic on the page (giving you a lot more design flexibility) and the video plays in popover window (with the page darkened in the background). The viewer window can be a lot larger than the embedded window.

New Window This approach is similar to the preceding one, but the video player runs in a completely separate browser window.

In addition to video clips, it is common to use a walk-on video spokesperson to briefly introduce your company and make a direct call-to-action (usually involving something on the page). The spokesperson can be seen from the waist up or full-body depending on the application. Figure 7.16 shows a video spokesperson on the Innovate Media homepage at the lower right of the screen.

The video spokesperson is just a part of the engagement strategy. Their call-to-action is to ask you to click on the "play video" button near the top right of the screen. This in turn starts a video in a lightbox popover and discusses Innovate Media's capabilities in more detail (see Figure 7.17).

Such a one-two-punch of spokesperson and introductory video can often lead to double-digit conversion improvement. With the cost of video production and serving rapidly falling, we recommend that you experiment with video to see if it can help.

Figure 7.16 Innovate Media homepage with video spokesperson

Figure 7.17 Innovate Media homepage with lightbox video

Information Architecture

Information architecture defines the way that information is organized on your website. This is typically hierarchical in nature (and looks like an extended outline on your sitemap page). However, it is important to remember that the Web is a hyperlink medium. People do not necessarily follow orderly or linear progressions (as they would when reading this book, for instance). They jump around and follow their nose. For this reason, some websites provide multiple navigation schemes to support their visitors' mental maps.

In general, your site navigation should

- Be immediately visible (not require scrolling or mouseovers to find key navigation)
- Support the visitor's task and intent (and not reflect your company's internal organization)
- Be consistent throughout the site (except when the context for the task changes, such as in an e-commerce catalog's linear checkout process)
- Use clear and distinct labels and groupings (so people know what to expect on the next page)
- Provide context (visitors need to know where they are in your site)
- Be tolerant of mistakes (allow visitors to easily reverse their last action and get back to their previous state)

Accessibility

Accessibility has to do with how easy information is to find and use properly. Accessibility is closely related to the concept of *affordance*. User-centered design originator Don Norman used the term to refer to the ability of people to easily discover the range of available actions possible in their interactions with computers or similar interfaces. Another way to think about accessibility or affordance is to ask "How easy would it be for someone to understand that something is possible on this webpage?"

The following are important concepts that together create good accessibility:

Availability Do visitors quickly see exactly what their options are? Is navigation clear, consistent, and placed in a conventional location?

Feedback When users take an action, do they get immediate feedback? Does the page change when they click on or mouse over important content?

Organization Is your content consistent, easy to scan, and based on the right visitor roles and tasks? Is it just a few easily digestible "chunks"?

Fault Tolerance Do you anticipate common user errors? Do you suggest meaningful alternatives to an apparent dead-end? Does your site support the easy reversal of actions?

Affinity Does your intended audience feel comfortable or anxious during their visit? Do they find your page to be professional and credible? Do their instincts tell them to trust you?

Legibility Are your fonts easy to read? Do text and background colors clash, or assault the senses? Are too many font types, sizes, and colors used?

Since most of our web experiences are currently based on reading, legibility requires special attention. Follow these web legibility guidelines:

Font Families Use *sans serif* fonts such as Arial, Helvetica, or Geneva. Do not use *serif* (with small lines at the end of characters) fonts such as Times Roman, Courier, or Palatino. At typical computer monitor resolutions, serif fonts are harder to read.

Font Sizes Use 10–12 point fonts for most body text. Larger and smaller fonts reduce reading speed. Consider increasing your font size by a couple of points if you are targeting an older audience, and make sure that you allow sufficient spacing between lines as well. If your audience is older (and may have visual problems), you should allow users to select larger fonts page-wide. Even though proportional page zoom is now built into many web browsers, many people are still unaware that they can easily magnify the page and zoom in and out at will.

Font Styles Do not use a wide range of font styles, colors, or sizes. Avoid using text in all capital letters, because it is harder to read. Likewise, as noted earlier, avoid using reverse-colored text (lighter text on a darker background).

Underlines and Hyperlinks Do not underline text that is not clickable. Blue underlines (purple after a click) are a strong default convention for hyperlinks. If you must emphasize nonlink text, consider changes in size, style, or color.

If you have a list-heavy site (such as a large directory or detailed informational portal), it is an exception to the rule. Huge amounts of underlined text on the page are annoying to the visitor and are also unreadable. However, if you decide not to underline your text links in such a situation, you should make sure that the link text color that you have chosen is not used elsewhere on your site to indicate nonlinked text.

Another exception involves sites with lots of cross-linked content in full sentences and paragraphs. In such cases the flow of reading would be disrupted by frequent font color changes and underlining.

Justification Do not create equal-length lines of text. The jagged ends of unjustified lines help increase reading speed and comprehension. Always use uncentered, left-justified text unless you are indicating headlines or subheadlines (which may be centered).

Line Length Blocks of text over 50 characters wide are harder to read. Consider putting in forced carriage returns (also called "hard breaks") so that screen size variations don't warp layout and the eye can easily find the beginning of the next line.

Contrast High contrast between text and background increases legibility. However, as stated earlier, this applies only to darker text on a lighter background. Use of reverse-color text (lighter on a dark background) decreases readability and should be avoided.

Buttons

Buttons are often the main visual call-to-action on a landing page. The following guidelines should help you to make them more effective.

Prioritize Your Buttons

Ideally you should have a single, clear call-to-action button on your page. If you have more than one, you need to create a visual hierarchy so that their importance is clear to your web visitor. One way to do that is to change the color or size of the nonprimary buttons to something visually less interesting (make those buttons duller and smaller). If you have two side-by-side buttons, remember that the one on the right is by convention considered the default one (most likely to be clicked on). You may consider demoting some of your secondary buttons to text links.

Experiment with Format

The exact format of the button matters. Experiment with a wide range of button shape parameters to see what works best. Possible changes to the button include

- Shape (amount of rounding and corner "radiasing," or having them remain square)
- Dimensionality (drop shadows and curves)
- Color (contrasting and being ideally unique on the page)
- Visual embellishments (adding small triangles or chevrons to indicate action)
- Size (try radically smaller or larger versions)

Be Specific and Manage Expectations

Buttons should accurately describe the intended action. Make sure that the button describes exactly what will happen when it is clicked. For example, many e-commerce sites mistakenly put "Buy It Now!" buttons next to products when the actual action is "Add to Cart."

Another common mistake is to use the label "Order Now" when you really mean "Proceed to Checkout." This causes unnecessary stress and anxiety for visitors as they try to figure out the threat or opportunity presented by your button. It is always best to remove the hesitation and assure them that taking the next step is a small and safe action.

Use unambiguous standard language for all button labels. Do not try to be funny or cute. The attempt will often be lost on the audience, especially when you consider the international nature of Internet traffic. Most people from other cultures who are non-native speakers will find it difficult to process and understand unfamiliar button labels.

Label from the Perspective of Your Visitors

Button text should always be written from the perspective of your visitors and address their intentions and desires. In many cases you should try to complete the thought in the mind of the visitor: "I want to…" Appropriate examples of possible completions for this sentence include "Download The Whitepaper," "Start My Free Trial," "Get Details," or "Select This Plan." This formulation is unlikely to work with commonly seen button text such as "Submit," "Create Account," or "Reset."

Writing for the Web

> *How Users Read on the Web:*
>
> *They don't.*
>
> —Web usability expert Jakob Nielsen

Even though the words above were written in 1997, they still hold true. Jakob Nielsen's pioneering work in this area has been confirmed by a lot of subsequent research. The vast majority of Internet users do not read any webpage word by word. They scan it and focus on individual words, phrases, or sentences, often the words most tightly connected with their task. They are often seeing your company for the first time, and they do not know how much trust to place in your information. They are used to being assaulted with promotional messages and will tune out most of your attempts to overtly market to them. They are task-oriented and are on your site to get something specific accomplished.

Most of the adaptations that you need to make to your writing have a single purpose: to reduce the visitor's cognitive load. Instead of being forced to pay attention to how the information is presented, they can devote more focus to getting their intended task accomplished. By getting out of their way, you empower them to be faster, more efficient, and more effective. This will lead to higher conversion rates for you, and higher satisfaction for your web visitors.

Headlines

Headlines are your biggest chance to wrestle for the reader's attention, and you will win or lose that battle within seconds. A Nielsen study evaluated site copy by how quickly readers could identify a content relationship from just the first two words of the headline. Remember that visitors may arrive on your site from any number of links and may not have a lot of context about your page. Headlines are the top-scanned item for users to orient themselves before they decide what to do next. In fact, 8 out of 10 people will only read the headline.

It is beyond the scope of this book to explore the rich field of effective copywriting and headline writing, but we highly recommend that you read and subscribe to Brian Clark of Copyblogger.com and also read the book *The Copywriter's Handbook: A Step-by-Step Guide to Writing Copy That Sells* (Holt Paperbacks, 2006) by Robert W. Bly.

Body Copy

Effective web body copy integrates the following elements:

- Inverted pyramid structure
- Brevity
- Hype-free copy

Let's take a look at each element in turn.

Use Inverted Pyramid Structure

The preferred structure for most web writing is the *inverted pyramid*. In this style of writing, you put your conclusions and key points first. Less important and supporting information should be placed last. This is critical since most readers will choose not to read very far.

Most of this is probably not earth-shaking insight in the world of journalism. Newspaper editors have had a similar audience makeup for centuries: casual visitors who scan for information that competes for their attention and consider the source as a transient and disposable resource. Because of this, print journalists have developed a powerful structural model that should be emulated by web content authors. Headline size and prominent positioning indicate the importance of articles. The lead paragraph summarizes the whole story, and supporting detail is further down.

By using this structure, you maximize the chances that visitors will come away with the information that you consider most valuable. Make sure that you only have one main idea per paragraph. If you bury a second idea lower in a block of text, it will probably be missed as the reader jumps down to scan the lead-in text of the subsequent paragraph or subheading. Even if it's not missed, you're burdening the reader to determine the connection, which doesn't work well with their highly activated mode of scanning for information.

The inverted pyramid even applies to bullet lists or lists of navigational links—put the important ones on top. Each idea gets its own slice as the pyramid gets smaller. The same structure should be used for creating online audio or video clips for your site.

Keep It Short

Keep your pages short. There is evidence to show that significantly shorter text results in higher retention and recall of information and is more likely to lead to conversion actions. Your page should only contain important information for its topic and level of detail. You can move longer supporting text to other pages or informational lightbox popover windows and create links for the more dedicated readers. Nielsen studies find a significant drop-off in the percentage of the total page read after the length exceeds 200 words.

However, there is an occasional exception to the shorter-is-better guideline. Some single-product consumer websites have long direct-response pitch letters that significantly outperform shorter alternatives. They draw the reader in and encourage them to spend a lot of time on the page. After a certain point the visitor's attention investment gets high enough to build momentum toward the conversion action. This is not to say that long sales letter pages cannot be made better. There is definitely a lot of bloat to test and improve.

Avoid "Marketese"

The reality for most Internet surfers is that they are constantly subjected to a barrage of promotional messages and advertising. As a basic defense mechanism, they have learned to tune out most hype. Regardless of the method or device that you used to get visitors to your page, once they arrive you should stop screaming at them. You are no longer (for the moment) competing for their attention with other websites. So you need to change the focus from convincing them of your greatness to the task that they are trying to accomplish.

Your visitors detest *marketese*. Unfortunately, your landing page was probably written in this kind of incredibly vague yet over-the-top promotional style. It usually involves a lot of boasting and unsubstantiated claims. If your company is the "world's leading provider" of something, you are in good company. A recent search on Google turned up 297,000,000 matching results for this phrase. Your claims are probably not true, but even if they are, you can use different language to make your point.

Marketese may be (barely) acceptable in your press releases when you are trying to puff up your company and accomplishments. If you write in this over-the-top style, bloggers will ignore more of your releases, and social media audiences will likely refuse to share in social bookmarking or worse, demote your brand trust. But on your landing page, the consequences of using marketese are even more disastrous. Marketese requires work on the part of your visitor. It forces them to spend time separating the content from the fluff. It also results in much longer word counts (which, as we'll discuss later, also detract from conversions). You are missing an enormous opportunity by not creating a hype-free zone on your landing page.

How to Avoid Writing in "Marketese"

- Do not use any adjectives.
- Provide only objective information.
- Focus on the needs of your audience.

Your editorial tone and voice should have the following attributes:

Factual Writing factually will take a little work. It is difficult to stop making subjective statements. You may catch yourself lapsing into marketese at unexpected moments. But stick with it. You will be amazed at how much more effective your writing will be. Remember, your visitors are not looking to be entertained, and certainly not to be marketed to. They are there to deal with a specific need or problem that they have. The best kind of information you can give them is objective in nature.

Task-Oriented Task-oriented writing is focused on the roles, tasks, and AIDA steps (discussed in Chapter 3, "The Matrix—Moving People to Act") that are required to move your visitors through the conversion action. You should organize your text in the order that the visitor is likely to need it. For example, a big-ticket consumer product site might lay out the following high-level steps for the buying process: research, compare, customize, purchase. Once you have built The Matrix for your landing page, it should be clear where the gaps are.

Precise It is critical to be clear in web writing. The audience can be diverse and can bring a variety of cultural backgrounds to their interpretation of your language. Be careful about your exact choice of words. Never try to be funny or clever in a way that will not translate across regions or countries. Do not use puns, metaphors, idioms, or colloquial expressions.

This is doubly true for link text. Your visitors need to have a clear understanding of exactly what will happen when they take the action of clicking on something. Text links should describe the content on the target page. Unhelpful link labels such as "click here" are a wasted opportunity to focus the visitor's awareness on an important available option. Also, link text is used by search engines to help people find information.

Concise Become a word miser in addition to a page length slicer. Ask yourself, "How can I make this even shorter? Do I really need to communicate this at all?" Brevity has several advantages. It increases absorption and recall. It shortens the time that visitors spend reading—minimizing the likelihood of increased frustration and impatience. It supports the goals of inverted pyramid writing and the scannable text requirements described in the next section.

Simple Now that you're cutting page length and word count, the next bloat loss program candidate is syllables. Again, we take a standard from journalism, where the eighth-grade reading level is the expected target. You may want key landing pages to be written for an even lower grade level. However, most web copy, especially business-to-business copy, regularly exceeds much higher grade levels. You can check the Flesch–Kincaid readability level (a scale to assess reading grade level) directly in Microsoft Word's review tools.

The easiest way to reduce reading grade level in your content goes back to our key theme for this chapter: short. Keep the sentences short. This allows for distinct ideas in each line. Keep the words short. Shorter words tend to be more familiar, simpler, and easier to absorb.

Reducing a reading grade level does not mean dumbing down your content. It means writing intentionally to make reading easy as part of a task, not a leisure activity. It means writing for people who speak English as a second, third, or fourth language who might be completing a task on an English-only site.

Lower literacy groups are estimated to be as much as 30–40 percent of the online population. Your simplified word choices can result in vast improvement to the success of your landing page.

Format and Style

Since people don't read the Web, the format and style of your writing should support their opportunistic scanning behavior.

You should use the following guidelines for writing style:

- Write in fragments or short sentences.
- Turn paragraphs into bulleted lists. Limit lists to three to seven items (the limit of human short-term memory "chunking").
- Use ordinary language (avoid industry jargon and acronyms that are not widely understood).
- Use active voice and action verbs.
- Use descriptive link text (describing what will happen on the target page).

Also use the following guidelines for writing structure and mechanics:

- Use digits instead of words to write out numbers (e.g., "47" instead of "forty-seven")

- Highlight important, information-carrying words (do not highlight whole sentences; stick to two- or three-word phrases).

- Use clear, emphasized fonts to label headers and subheads.

- Do not use more than two indenting levels for lists or headings.

- Use supporting links to direct readers to secondary and "see also" cross-referenced information.

Usability Checks

You can undertake several activities that can improve the usability basics of your landing page.

Formal and Informal Testing

Usability testing allows you to test your design ideas on representative users of your website. It can be an effective means of uncovering disconnects between users' expectations and your designs. Usability testing companies can help you recruit appropriate subjects, conduct the tests, and deliver detailed findings.

Usability testing can often be done inexpensively and informally. Steve Krug's excellent book *Rocket Surgery Made Easy* (New Riders Press, 2010) is a readable and practical primer on the subject of informal testing. After running as few as three subjects through your mission-critical conversion task, you can often uncover significant issues with your current landing page. All you need for this kind of informal approach is a quiet room, a mock-up of your proposed design (possibly just hand-drawn on paper), and a clear task statement (of what you want your subjects to accomplish).

There are several available protocols for the tester to get information from the subjects. We have found that the simple "talking out loud" approach is often all you need. You can simply ask subjects to narrate their thoughts as they attempt to complete the task. In this protocol, the testers are silent and observe or take written notes. Most marketers are shocked when first watching subjects struggle with the seemingly simple assigned task. Because they have been so close to the design of the pages, they have a hard time putting themselves in the shoes of first-time visitors. After the initial shock has worn off, many marketers have a much higher degree of empathy for their audience and can see the landing page problems in a new light.

Best Practices Expert Reviews

You do not always have to conduct full-scale usability testing yourself. Hiring usability experts for a high-level review of your landing pages is often a terrific investment.

Usability experts have often seen hundreds of poor landing page designs and have learned to extract their subtle commonalities. They can quickly focus on potential problems without even conducting a usability test.

Besides their expertise, usability experts also bring an outside perspective and a mandate to uncover problems. Often organizations that would be reluctant to take input from their own staff will listen to the advice of an external expert conducting a landing page or website review. SiteTuners offers an inexpensive and hard-hitting interactive Express Review, which is recorded via online meeting software and can be shared with other members of your online marketing team for a quick and sober assessment of your current situation.

Visual Attention Prediction

If you are not visually aware of the intended call-to-action on a webpage, or if you are distracted from it by stronger visual stimuli, you will have a much lower likelihood of successfully completing the intended task. So the first screen for designing an effective landing page is to diagnose existing problems at a gross visual attention level in order to determine whether the call-to-action is clear.

Such insights into visual attention can be obtained by a variety of means. Which one you choose will depend on the time and resources that you have to devote to the project and level of accuracy you require. Here are three options:

Eye-Tracking Eye-tracking is particularly useful in detecting problems in the early stages of the decision-making process (awareness and interest). If most test subjects do not look at the desired part of the page, they are not even aware that the conversion action is possible. Eye-tracking allows you to record voluntary and involuntary gazing, fixation of attention, as well as corresponding voluntary body movements (such as scrolling or clicking). Such studies are an excellent tool for uncovering problems regarding page layout, visual presentation of information and images, and proper emphasis.

Mouse Tracking Mouse tracking uses the movement of the mouse as a proxy for visual attention. A Carnegie Mellon study found that some 85 percent of mouse "rests" correlated to site areas that the user notices. Since then, several tools, primarily aimed at small businesses, have launched as less expensive alternatives to eye-tracking. The data is collected via snippets of code placed on target pages and the subsequent recording of site visitor actions.

Software Simulation Computer algorithms for computational attention can predict areas of site attention for landing page components or entire pages. These systems base their calculations on models that include texture, shapes, contrast, movement, flicker, object recognition, font treatment, color use, the number of competing elements, and other items proven to influence attention. This type of modeling allows for visual attention checks before the page is finalized or published, and can be done without involving real people at all.

Mouse tracking and software simulation tools for visual attention prediction are discussed in more detail in Chapter 5, "Conversion Ninja Toolbox—Diagnosing Site Problems."

If you can diligently apply all the general principles in this chapter, you are well on your way to becoming a conversion rate improvement professional. In the next chapter, we will examine specific best practices for a number of situations.

Best Practices for Common Situations

In previous chapters you have learned how to uncover problems with your landing page and some optimization basics. But in case you haven't realized by now, landing page optimization isn't as easy as you might have thought at first.

In this chapter we will begin to give you some building blocks—some best practices for common situations—that you can apply on your webpages to give you a great kick-start in your optimization efforts.

Chapter Contents

Homepages

Information Architecture and Navigation

E-commerce Catalogs

Registration and Multiple-Step Flows

Direct Response Pages

Mobile Websites

Homepages

You have probably visited hundreds of different websites and seen some awful homepages. In one sense this is natural since the expectations placed on a homepage are many and often contradictory in nature. Unfortunately, visitors will judge your whole website by just the homepage.

The general guidelines in this section will help you to improve your homepage.

Focus on Clear Self-Selected Navigation

Unfortunately homepages often become dumping grounds for many stakeholders. Instead of replacing older content or features, new ones are simply added on to the existing content. This makes many homepages very long and full of competing content. As a result, visitors are often paralyzed and unable to decide what to click on. This indecision often prevents them from finding what they are really looking for.

In this sense, homepages often turn into "Turkish bazaars" where many vendors and hawkers compete for your attention and try to draw you in. Not everything currently on your homepage deserves to be there. You need to focus on only those elements that support the mission-critical activities described in Chapter 2, "Understanding Your Landing Pages." It may be a tough internal battle to clean up your homepage, but your visitors will certainly thank you for doing so.

The main purposes of any homepage are to act as a traffic director to get your visitors deeper into your site and to provide "trailheads" or "information scent" that gets them closer to content that is of interest to them. This is best accomplished by offering visitors a small set of choices that allows them to "raise their hand," self-identify, and get off the homepage.

To figure out which self-selected choices to offer to your visitors, it's best to put yourself in the shoes of your visitors and create different "use cases." These are common scenarios that represent a specific user class (role) combined with a specific intent (task) that they are trying to complete on that particular visit. Please review The Matrix in Chapter 3, "The Matrix—Moving People to Act," to identify key roles and tasks.

Once you have created a few use cases (typically 2–8 are enough to cover important uses of your website), you should prioritize visually, and decide how to group and arrange the content on the page.

Figure 8.1 shows the redesigned homepage for the Revit Architecture product center homepage on the Autodesk corporate website. This design was developed jointly between SiteTuners and the Autodesk internal optimization team, and the whole subwebsite was also redesigned to support the user-centered perspective.

Figure 8.1 Scenario-based navigation on the Autodesk Revit Architecture product center homepage

As you can see, the five gray boxes in the middle of the page clearly correspond to several common scenarios that visitors may want to complete, and they provide the information scent that visitors need to navigate deeper:

- Unfamiliar visitors who want to understand the product and its capabilities can focus on the "About Revit Architecture" box.

- Existing AutoCAD users (another popular design software package from Autodesk) who might be considering switching to Revit Architecture can focus on the "Revit Architecture vs. AutoCAD" box to understand the implications of the move.

- The financial buyers and upper management concerned with the full life-cycle cost of using the software can focus on the "Building the Business Case" box.

- Existing Revit Architecture users can investigate the "Already Using Revit?" box.
- Those interested in trying the product can focus on the "Free 30-Day Trial" box.

This design was tested against the original version of the homepage (which was not scenario-focused) and performed significantly better in terms of the percentage of free trial sign-ups over time. For additional discussion of e-commerce homepages, please see the "E-commerce Catalogs" section later in this chapter.

Restrict Use of Advertising

Banner ads (whether for outside parties or featured areas within your own site) are another common offender on homepages. The only reason you should have commercials or ads on your homepage is if you are a media/publisher website and rely on ads for a significant portion of your revenue. Even then you should limit the number on the homepage. Not only do these banners and ads distract and look ugly, but they often can help form a negative first impression of a website. Auto-playing sound within such advertising is irritating for the visitor, particularly when they don't know the source of the audio or how to stop it.

It's certainly no coincidence that more and more websites are realizing this negative correlation and at the very least are removing the leader board banner from their homepages. Review your homepage and make sure you remove or limit the number of ads you include. This will help build a better first impression and reduce your bounce rate.

Limit Unnecessary Words and Images

Visitors will be more comfortable on your homepage if you don't overwhelm them with too many words. Review the words you use. If any of them don't help the visitor get off the homepage or make a clear choice, remove the text. If you have the traffic to conduct a simple A/B split test, you'll see that the version with fewer words usually converts better. Remember, website visitors rarely read—they scan. See Chapter 7, "Conversion Improvement Basics" for additional discussion of copywriting and editorial tone.

In theory you could take the copy editing too far and be left with too few words to have effective remaining copy for SEO. In practice this is rarely a problem. Don't let SEO considerations paralyze you. The "on-page" factors that have to do with your actual words and page content are an increasingly small part of SEO rankings. The majority of the signals that search engine algorithms now pay attention to revolve around inbound links as well as social media signals of popularity.

You should review the use of photos on your homepage as carefully as you scrutinize the text. Don't use photos just because you think your website needs them as window dressing. Avoid using generic stock photography. Your visitors have an uncanny knack for noticing canned stock images. This recognition will devalue and cheapen a website in their minds. If you must use photographs, have some quality professional images created specifically for your purpose.

Information Architecture and Navigation

One of the key things a website has to do is provide its visitors with clear and easy ways to find content. The guidelines in this section will help you to improve navigation and information discovery.

Offer Multiple Navigation Methods

Complex websites may need to provide multiple ways to navigate because visitors look for products and information in many different ways. For example, some visitors make use of header navigation functionality, whereas others prefer to make use of internal search tools or guided wizards to find what they are looking for. So don't emphasize or rely on just one navigation method—you will be doing a disservice to your visitors.

Provide Internal Site Search Tools

If website visitors can't find what they are looking for by browsing, they often rely on using an internal search tool. Some jump straight into the internal search tool without even browsing first. Therefore, if you don't offer an internal search tool in a prominent place your website visitors may be leaving prematurely.

It's become a common best practice to place an internal search field in the top right of your website. You shouldn't confuse your visitors, however, by placing things in the top right that look like search boxes. In particular, don't put a newsletter opt-in field in that spot—users will often enter a search phrase there thinking it's an internal search, only to be annoyed to realize it's not. Additional places for the search box include the top of a left navigation column, and either the extreme left or right of your main horizontal navigation bar.

You can take your internal search box functionality to the next level by offering predictive search results in a drop-down menu. This gives visitors extra ideas for what to search for, and also makes it quicker for them to type their intended search phrase. Amazon does this with their internal search input box, as seen in Figure 8.2.

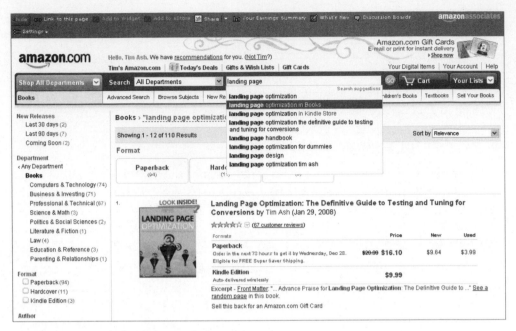

Figure 8.2 Predictive search suggestions on the Amazon site

Improve Your Navigation Menus

Header navigation menus and subnavigation menus are one of the most common ways of navigating through a website. There are many best practices you should adopt for these major navigation menus.

Use Standard Menu Locations on the Page

It's usually considered a best practice to have either top navigation (horizontally under your header), left navigation (in a dedicated vertical column), or a combination of both (with the top nav serving as the primary, and the left nav as the deeper secondary that may only appear when you are deeper in the site).

In addition to the main navigation used to describe your content, it is often common practice to have a discreet supporting nav bar in the upper-right corner of your header. It can include transactional and operational items such as login, shopping cart, customer support, or contact links.

If you have a shallow site (without deep menu subcategories), then either a top or left nav bar is effective. We recommend a top nav in such situations since it allows for a more expansive and open page design.

If you have a deeper navigation design, you must consider the following navigation layouts. Figure 8.3 shows an "accordion style" left-column-only navigation from an older version of the SiteTuners website.

Figure 8.3 Accordion-style left navigation column from the previous version of the SiteTuners' website

Such an approach has several advantages:

- It takes up much less space than a fully expanded menu with all choices shown at once.

- It doesn't overwhelm the visitor with too many choices.

- It helps the visitor understand where they are globally in relation to your website.

- It is persistent and does not rely on mouse hover-over.

Accordion navigation should not be used for more than three levels of menu nesting and should not be used when you already have very long menu or submenu lists (see the following section, "Limit the Number of Menu Items"). The disadvantage of the accordion style is that it permanently takes up the left column on every page.

Let's turn now to deeper sites with a horizontal top navigation. Here you have two options: multiple levels of tabbed submenus, and drop-down menus. As with accordion-style menus, we do not recommend using more than three levels of tabbed navigation at the top of the page.

A hybrid approach involves using tabbed horizontal top navigation for the first couple of menu layers, and then introducing a left navigation column for deeper pages. You can see an example of this on the current SiteTuners site interior page shown in Figure 8.4. The advantage of this approach is that it preserves the full width of the top-level pages and only uses the left column when necessary.

Figure 8.4 SiteTuners interior page with tabbed top-level navigation and left-side navigation

You can also use drop-down menus with top navigation. These come in two flavors: traditional drop-downs and mega drop-downs.

Traditional drop-downs have many problems. They include too many items (frequently requiring scrolling), appear and disappear unpredictably when the mouse is moved slightly, and are difficult to operate if they are not sized properly (especially when they include flyout "walking" submenus).

Mega drop-downs are characterized by the following:

- Large two-dimensional panels
- Divided into groups of navigation options
- Structured through the use of layout, type, or images
- Always visible and requiring no scrolling
- Are usually persistent (that is, they do not disappear until you click outside of their frame or explicitly dismiss them by clicking an icon in the upper right)

Web usability pioneer Jakob Nielsen has pointed out the following advantages of mega drop-downs for navigation:

Affordance Unlike traditional drop-down menus, which hide most of the available options, mega drop-downs show everything at a glance—making it much easier to compare and remember available choices (lowering reliance on short-term memory).

Grouping Traditional drop-downs make it difficult to indicate grouping or show hierarchy or other relationships.

Graphics Images can be used to change the emphasis within the drop-down and to direct visual attention. You can be more restrained and still accomplish a lot of visual attention–focusing simply by using different font treatments, separators, and background colors within the mega drop-down.

The Clinique website navigation is an example of the mega drop-down menu approach (see Figure 8.5).

Figure 8.5 Clinique top navigation with mega drop-down

The Diapers website shows how a mega drop-down can provide parallel navigation options within a category (see Figure 8.6). The expanded mega drop-down shows both the product subcategories and popular brands under the "Feeding & Nursing" area.

Figure 8.6 Diapers top navigation mega drop-down with subcategories and brands

Limit the Number of Menu Items

Another critical thing to consider is the number of elements in menus and submenus. Try to limit your website to fewer than 7 items in each of your main navigations and submenus, since that number is at the limit of short-term memory capacity. Order menu items by importance (unless alphabetical or some other order is particularly appropriate). Doing so will ensure that the most important or popular items are likely to be found more quickly.

Supporting items like Contact Us and Help should rarely reside on main navigation; they belong in the top-right corner of your website instead.

Simplify Your Navigation Labels

The exact wording used in your menu item labels needs to be clear to visitors. In particular you should avoid using jargon, technical speak, or words that aren't intuitive to your website visitors. Poor navigation wording is a fairly common website mistake that can easily be remedied with some careful consideration and replacement. Use plain language that is accessible to all people, and when in doubt err on the side of the simpler and more common choice.

Highlight Where the Visitor Currently Is in the Navigation

It's a best practice to indicate in the navigation menu where the user is in relation to the rest of the website. This is particularly important when a visitor arrives from a search engine deep within your website and doesn't know where they are in relation to the rest of your website. This is best achieved by background color and text treatment of the active navigation element (a slightly different visual look is a great way of indicating this). The same applies to any secondary subnavigation.

Offer Clear Ways to Get Support

If a visitor needs help at any time on your website, it's important for them to be able to find a way of getting it. Otherwise, they may get frustrated and leave your website.

At the very least you should prominently show your support phone number in the top right of your website or in the footer, next to a link to your support page. You may also offer web chat functionality, as visitors often appreciate being able to communicate with support directly online, rather than having to switch to another modality by picking up the phone. This option is particularly important for e-commerce shopping cart related pages, because many errors can occur here. In fact, a study by BoldChat found that 76 percent of visitors would initiate a web chat in response to issues they were encountering during the checkout process.

Ideally the web chat link should be placed in the top right of your website next to your support number, and you should only show this web chat support option if it's actually available at the time—it's frustrating for visitors to click on web chat only to find that due to nonwork hours it's not currently available.

Although web chat can be a useful tool, you shouldn't just spring a web chat window on a visitor when they first arrive on your website or because of a lack of activity by them for a short period of time. This is frustrating for visitors and can cause premature abandonment.

More Navigation Best Practices

Here are several other more traditional best practices you should offer on your website to help improve navigation and usability:

Breadcrumbs Breadcrumbs are another way of highlighting where you are in the overall navigation of a website and should appear in the topmost left portion of your main content area. They are displayed in a horizontal list of text links that terminates in a (nonclickable) label for the current page. See the top of the white content area in Figure 8.4 for an example. Breadcrumbs are particularly important for visitors who arrive deep within your website from a search engine. Breadcrumbs should not be emphasized and should be subtle (use fonts that are smaller than the page font and don't have any embellishments).

Sitemap You should create a well-organized sitemap and place a link to it in your website footer. This sitemap needs to list and break down each section and list all the pages found in each one (or show subsections if it's a very deep site or an e-commerce site). It is also an important requirement for good SEO practices.

Clickable Logo You should make your logo clickable on every page and have it return the user to the homepage after they have clicked it. It's usually best to have the logo in the top left of your website.

E-commerce Catalogs

An e-commerce catalog cannot be designed in a free-form way. We have certain expectations about how online catalogs function, and any significant deviation from that will just confuse the visitor (since they are bringing all of their past knowledge with e-commerce catalogs to bear).

In effect, an e-commerce website is a set of page templates types:

- Homepage
- Search Results and Product Listings
- Product Detail
- Shopping Cart
- Checkout Options
- Shipping Information

- Billing Information
- Review and Order Placement
- Order Confirmation

Applying best practices to each of these templates will give you a great foundation for optimizing your e-commerce website. So let's get started with examining the first one, homepage.

Homepage

We covered best practices for homepages in general earlier in the chapter, but it's important to realize there are a few other best practices that apply only to e-commerce homepages.

Restrict the Use of Promotions

One of the major causes of confusing and nonengaging e-commerce homepages is long lists of products or too many marketing promotions or banners. Most visitors will not be ready to buy or sign up for specific products after looking at just the homepage page.

The primary use of your homepage should be for category-level navigation. Most visitors will want to make a quick choice, get off the homepage, and get closer to their goal. Without a clear high-level map of their navigation options, people will be lost. See the B&H Photo homepage body (Figure 4.8 in Chapter 4, "Common Problems— The Seven Deadly Sins of Landing Page Design") for a best practices example of how to do this instead. The purpose of the content is to orient the visitor to the choices that are possible, and not to distract them with what are effectively poor guesses about what they might want or stuff that you currently want to "push" at them.

The top of the Lowes homepage (see Figure 8.7) features a giant promotional banner for last-minute pre-Christmas purchase in-store pickup.

Figure 8.7 Top of Lowes homepage showing promotional banner

Unfortunately the promotion does nothing to support an understanding of the available range of product categories, and the visitor is forced to use the small text nav bar at the bottom of the header.

Avoid Large Rotating Banners with Movement

Although large banners (that slide, fade, or otherwise visually transition among the frames of an ongoing slideshow) also appear on many other sites, they are endemic on e-commerce homepages.

Rotating banners are absolutely evil and should be removed immediately. Here is a short list of the many reasons to do so:

Large File Sizes Typically banners include several still images, animation, or video that result in larger files sizes compared to other page elements. Google in particular is on a mission to speed up the online experience because they have found that longer page load times will result in lower conversion rates and lower user satisfaction with the search experience (reflecting on them). As a result, Google has started to consider page load times in their search results algorithm.

Inconsistent Messaging and Look Often the individual frames of your slideshow will look very different. They will use wildly divergent messaging, visual imagery, and calls-to-action. Since they are so visually dominant on the page, the experience of your site radically and repeatedly changes within the span of a few seconds—creating a schizophrenic identity for your site.

Lack of Editorial Responsibility Rotating banners are a bad idea because you have basically abdicated your responsibility for curating and editing the content on your page. You have thrown up your hands and said, "I'm not sure what is important, so I am going to throw it all up against the wall and see what sticks." You need to prioritize importance of your content and edit or remove nonessential items. If something is truly important, it deserves permanent real estate on your page.

Wasted Time No one likes to wait. On the Web, people are especially impatient because they are in a highly activated information-seeking mode and because there is a world of infinite options available. By forcing the visitor to involuntarily sit through a series of commercials, you are forcing them to have a linear and out-of-control experience. This is the wrong metaphor for the Web. We will (barely) tolerate interruptive commercials when watching TV, but only because we have voluntarily locked ourselves into longer-timeframe and passive linear unfolding experiences. On the Web we are in control, and a 10–15 second slideshow is way outside what we are willing to sit still for. Instead of letting someone actively find what they are looking for, you are wasting their time.

Motion-Triggered Reassessment Motion in a scene triggers the reptilian portion of our brain (see Chapter 6, "Misunderstanding Your Visitors—Looking for Psychological Mismatches," for a more detailed discussion). This occurs at the level of automatic survival instinct and cannot be avoided. Frequent motion changes in a part of the page keep stealing the visitors' attention and make it difficult to visually prioritize or to consume any other content on the page.

Pushing Navigation Down As we discussed earlier, the primary purpose of your homepage should be to create a high-level map of the world for your visitors so they can understand the range of available products that you carry. The giant banner will take up all of the prime real estate on the homepage and push this navigation off the visible top of the page—sabotaging the page's primary purpose.

Just say "No" to large rotating banners on your e-commerce homepage.

Do Not Push Product-Level Items

Your homepage should focus on primary navigational choices for drilling into your main categories (for example, women's clothes, men clothes, and kids clothes for an apparel e-commerce website), with limited other categories being promoted. Do not try to show all of your subcategories on your homepage, as this is likely to overwhelm the visitor.

Many companies do not have the self-discipline to use their homepage primarily for navigation and try to push individual products on their homepage. The homepage of consumer electronics e-commerce website Newegg is an example of this (see Figure 8.8).

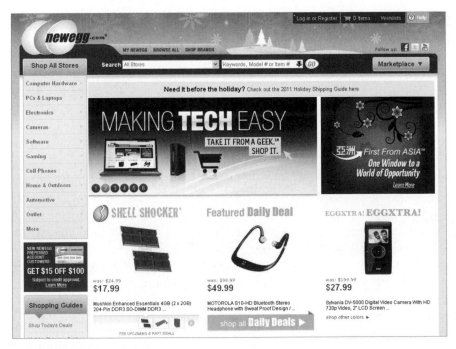

Figure 8.8 Newegg homepage

Below the annoying rotating banner (see previous section) are three featured Daily Deal items. Out of the huge inventory of available products, these represent nothing more than guesses at what the visitor might want, or desperate attempts to "move" certain items. The potential loss of customers is extremely high since the main navigation is relegated to small text items in the left column.

Search Results and Product Listings

E-commerce sites must provide a way for visitors to search for what they are looking for, either through advanced browsing capabilities or an internal search tool. In particular if you don't offer an internal search on every page in a consistent spot (usually in the top-right corner or at the top of the left navigation column), visitors are more than likely going to leave your website.

Once your visitor drills down to the appropriate subcategory on your site, it is time to show them a list of product-level items. These product listing pages are in many ways similar to search results pages and will be discussed later in this section.

Offer Advanced Sorting of Results

Depending on what the visitor has searched for on your website, they can be often inundated with search results to review. To make this easier on them, one of the most basic best practices that you should offer is a way of sorting the search results.

This sorting function is usually found just above the search results in the form of a drop-down menu or a row of links. Here are some sort options that you should consider using to optimize your website further (depending on what you are selling and the complexity of implementing):

- Relevance
- Price: Low to High
- Price: High to Low
- Highest Customer Rated
- Best Selling/Most Popular
- Newest
- Alphabetical or Reverse-Alphabetical (by name or brand)

Allow for Results Filtering

In addition to offering sorting options, you can help visitors by providing ways to filter results. Filtering should be contextual depending on what the user has searched for and should allow the user to drill deeper into particular subcategories, brands of products, or price ranges. For example, a shoe-related category browse or search results page should offer ways of filtering by shoe color, shoe type (dress shoes, casual shoes, boots, sandals, etc.) and shoe brand.

This filtering functionality is best offered in the left-hand column of search results and browse pages, as this has become the most common place to find this functionality and users will expect to see it there.

Offer Options to Customize Search Results Display

Presentation of the search results needs to be configurable to meet the user's exact needs. Some visitors prefer a grid view with fewer items per row, but more information for each item. Others prefer looking at more results in a grid format, with less information for each item. Still other users prefer looking at many results on one long list page so they can scan vertical columns. Target allows reconfiguring of product listing pages to accommodate a variety of browsing styles. Figure 8.9 shows a large-image grid view with some product detail.

Figure 8.10 shows a small image grid view optimized for visual scanning. This version includes much less text and product information.

Figure 8.11 shows a vertical list view optimized for linear scanning.

You may also want to consider adding rollover pop-up windows with additional product detail. This saves the visitor from having to click back and forth to the product detail pages that they are interested in.

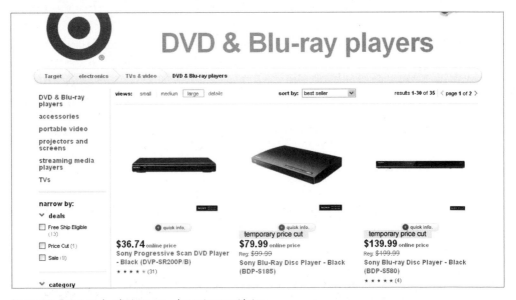

Figure 8.9 Target product listing page—larger-image grid view

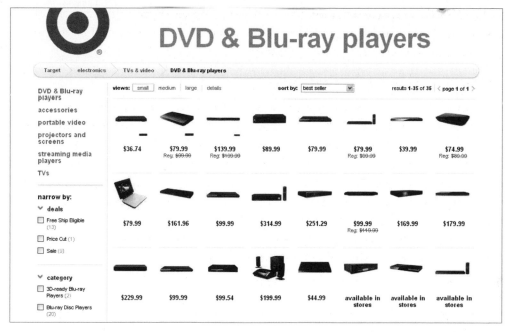

Figure 8.10 Target product listing page—small-image grid view

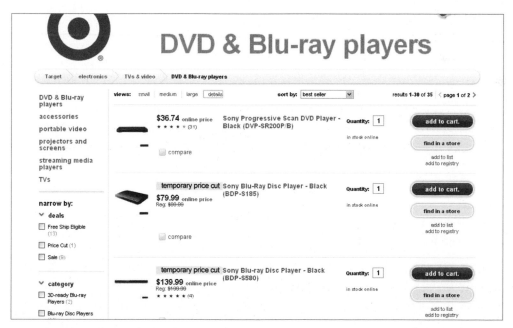

Figure 8.11 Target product listing page—vertical list view

Add Essential Information to Each Result

Depending on your display type (see the previous section), each of your individual search results should give the visitor just enough basic information (without overwhelming them) to enable them to decide which items to learn more about.

In addition to basic price, here are key elements that you should consider offering:

- Sales price
- Amount saved (as a percentage and total monetary savings)
- Average customer rating
- Stock details
- Whether free shipping is offered

Let Visitors Compare Results Easily

Another best practice is to allow visitors to compare search results easily. This is usually achieved by placing a check box next to each result with the word Compare next to it and having a Compare Items button at the bottom of the results. Ideally this functionality needs to work across multiple search results pages.

After the visitor clicks the Compare Items button, they need to be shown expanded details for just the results they checked. This is usually best represented in a column format to allow for easy comparison of key features.

Product Detail

There is huge variation on product detail pages, and many best practices seem to be routinely ignored. All too often you will see product pages with poor images, poor product descriptions, and poor calls-to-action. Use the following advice to optimize your product detail pages.

Use the Correct Layout and Visual Emphasis

Canon's Canadian e-store (conversion optimized by SiteTuners) shows many of the product detail page layout best practices (see Figure 8.12).

Important elements of layout include:

High-Contrast Body Area The page body should ideally be white, whereas all other parts of the page shell (header, navigation, supporting columns, and page sides) should be indicated with a different background shade.

Clear Page Headline A centered and large headline spans the whole page. No promotional banners or other visual clutter are above the headline.

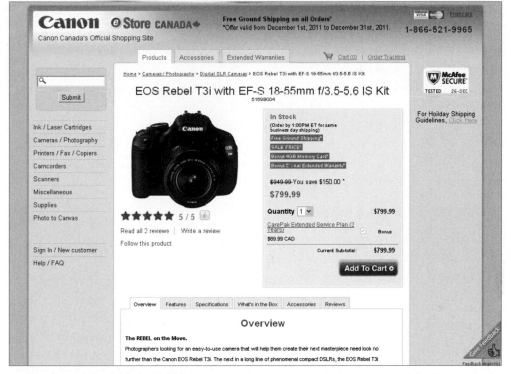

Figure 8.12 Canon Canada product detail page

Large Product Image Left placement of the product image is the standard. It should be professional quality and big enough to see important product details. Additional small thumbnail images can be displayed in a row immediately below this large image if necessary.

Action Block The area at the right of the body should be clearly delineated with a light background color rectangle and should include a single button with the primary call-to-action (usually Add To Cart). The action block should also include all important information such as in-stock status and customization (quantity, configuration, and options). The subtotal as configured should appear immediately next to or above the button.

Tabbed Supporting Information Below the image and action block you should have a tabbed area that includes supporting information such as a general description, reviews, accessories or related products, and detailed specifications). It is critical that the tab bar be visible above the fold; otherwise, this information will not be discoverable on the page without scrolling.

Provide Overview and Relevant Product Features

Great pictures (we'll talk more about these shortly) can speak a thousand words on a product page, but adequate product overview information and key features is just as essential.

Best practices on product pages involve prominently placing an overview that is a few sentences long (as on the open tab in the tab bar below the picture and main action block in Figure 8.12). The overview avoids going into too much technical detail and offers key product features, ideally in bullet point format to make it easier for the visitor to scan quickly. If long product overviews are necessary, it is best to provide them in a separate tab called Detailed Description.

Add Product Benefits, Not Just Features

Product detail pages are unfortunately not usually created from the viewpoint of the potential buyer, and the real needs of the prospect are often overlooked. A better way to improve product pages is to offer key product benefits in addition to the features—that is, how the user will benefit from purchasing this product or service.

Clearly State Your Return Policy

Visitors are far more likely to purchase online if they are offered ways to reduce the risk of the purchase not meeting their needs or standards. One great best practice to reduce this risk is to clearly state your return policy—particularly advantageous if you offer a free returns policy since this counteracts the risk of buying even further. Therefore you should clearly offer a link on product pages for the visitor to learn more about the return policy.

Upsell and Cross-Sell Related Items

You should help users who are browsing rather than looking for something specific. One of the best practices for doing this is to offer related and recommended products on your product pages, usually toward the end of the product details, or to bundle in additional related products.

Amazon does a great job of this. Rather than have a section called Recommended Items, they call this section Customers Who Bought This Item Also Bought (see Figure 8.13). This label is likely to mean more to the visitor than just Related Products or You Might Also Like. As shown at the top of Figure 8.13, Amazon also has a Frequently Bought Together area and suggests a bundle involving an additional item. Typically such bundling also involves a discount, but in the case of Amazon, the bundle price is the combined individual price of the two items. Simply surfacing this in-context association between the two items and displaying it to the user undoubtedly leads to higher average order value.

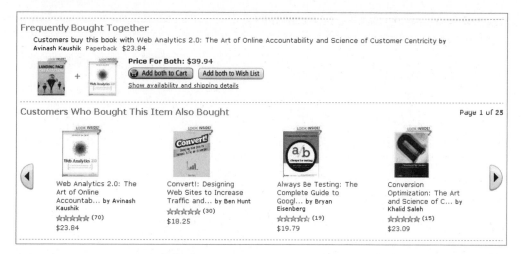

Figure 8.13 Amazon cross-sell and bundling

■ Let Visitors Experience Your Product with Images

Some of the best e-commerce websites have realized the importance of images on product pages. Images are particularly important because there is no tactile element when shopping online—the only way to experience the product is to look at it. Images are particularly important for e-commerce sites selling physical items (such as apparel, home furnishings, and consumer electronics). Additional images are less important for items that cannot be easily opened or fully experienced in a store setting (such as software, books, or wine).

Include as many images as possible, preferably from different angles, highlighting key details, and with the product in action if applicable.

Taking this a step further and building even more value for the visitor, some websites now offer both official product photos and user-submitted photos. We recommend curating and reviewing such submissions to make sure that they meet your quality standards and reflect well on your company and the product in question.

It is also important to allow visitors to interact with images, particularly by zooming in, panning, or rotating the images.

Allowing images to be zoomed is crucial. Large images can convey information that is important to the visitor. Take the highest possible resolution professional images yourself if they are not otherwise available.

How you display zoomed images is also important. Many sites simply let you zoom in on the main product image and then drag it to show different parts that are not visible. This leads to a "tunnel vision" view that does not effectively showcase the whole product.

An even worse idea is to automatically pop up a parallel magnified view when someone mouses over the main image. On the Hugo Boss website (see Figure 8.14) any mouse movement over the original image by the user automatically creates an enlarged zoomed hover-over area to the right of it.

Figure 8.14 Hugo Boss product detail page—image mouseover automatically triggering a zoom hover-over

This is an unexpected surprise for many visitors. The new image is also not that much bigger in scale, and is not particularly sharp. It does not offer a qualitatively different experience of the product.

Worst of all, when this type of approach to the image zooming is used, it covers the action block with the Add To Cart button. Figure 8.15 shows what was hidden under the zoom in Figure 8.14.

Our recommended best practice is for the user to actively (not accidentally) initiate the zoom. The image should then be displayed in a lightbox popover window that is as big as possible (showing the whole image). If additional images are available, forward and back arrows should be used to look at them from within the lightbox window.

If you have an item available in a number of different colors, patterns, or visual variations, you should show a swatch for each. When the swatch is selected, all of the images should be swapped out to show the item in the matching color.

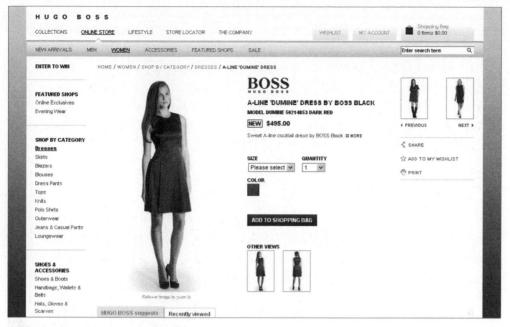

Figure 8.15 Hugo Boss product detail page—normal view

Optimize the Main Call-to-Action Button

The appearance and location of the Add To Cart button are critical elements of the product detail page. Poor choices for color, wording, or location can all significantly lower conversion rates. The following aspects of your button presentation should all be tested to optimize results.

The color of your button should make it stand out on the page. Ideally it should be the only element of that color inside the body of the page. It is not so much the particular color that is important, but rather its relationship to the rest of the page. Color association often plays an important role. Red is usually a negative or warning color that reduces conversions, with greens and oranges usually having the best results. However, it's recently been found that some usage of red on call-to-actions increases conversions, particularly in instances where an element of fear-based marketing is being used or red is a dominant color of the brand itself.

The size and style of the Add To Cart or call-to-action also has a big influence. Buttons usually work better than text links. Often larger buttons do better than smaller ones (up to a certain size).

Also, depending on what you are selling, to increase the percentage of visitors clicking your Add To Cart button, you should try testing different text variations. For example, if you are selling clothes or other accessories, you should try using Add To Bag instead.

As mentioned in the layout discussion at the beginning of this section, the button should be enclosed in a colored action block, and should appear in the lower-right corner of it.

Another best practice to increase the conversion of an Add To Cart button is to display transactional trust seals (and other safe shopping assurances) very close to it. This is one of the most important times that a visitor will need reassurances of their safety. However, make sure that the visual emphasis of these trust seals is appropriate and does not overwhelm the impact of the button.

Include Elements of "Social Proof"

One of the biggest influences on people when they are buying a product is the experience of others who have already done so. When this is presented on the product detail page in the context of shoppers considering the product, it can have a strong impact on conversion. Conversely, visitors are more likely to be wary of a product with no ratings, reviews, or other signs of popularity, and this wariness will decrease the likelihood of them purchasing it.

Amazon has always been the pioneer when it comes to customer review functionality and now dedicates much of the product detail page to this content, including an option for visitors to rate the usefulness of other user reviews, a breakdown of all the ratings, and sections to show the most recent and most helpful customer reviews. These features are shown in Figure 8.16.

Figure 8.16 Amazon user reviews

Online customer reviews have become so important that they have an impact on the offline "brick and mortar" world of retail stores. With the rise in mobile browsing, it is now increasingly common for retail store visitors to check out reviews of products online before buying them in the store they are in. Because customer reviews are so important, if there are no customer reviews for one of your products, you should encourage the addition of reviews by prominently using copy like Be The First To Review This on this page.

Another best practice that takes social proof one step further is to include easy ways to share via e-mail or on popular social networks. As you can see in Figure 8.17, Lands End has a dedicated portion of their page for social media and sharing located directly below the Add To Bag button.

Figure 8.17 Land's End sharing bar

Apple combines customer support and social proof by allowing users to submit and answer questions about the product. This is useful for prospective buyers who likely have similar questions.

Shopping Cart

Sometimes people add items to a shopping cart simply to see a product price, or as a convenient way to maintain a "wishlist" while they comparison-shop on other sites. However, for most people the shopping cart page is the gateway to the checkout process. Consider the following to optimize your cart experience.

Make It Clear When an Item Has Been Added

As soon as a visitor has added an item to the cart, it needs to be clearly stated at the top of the next page they are on, or they need to be taken directly to their cart. If you don't do this, visitors will get confused about whether the item has actually been added or not and may try adding it again—resulting in potential multiple orders of the same product and visitor frustration.

Even Amazon does a poor job of this. When you add something to the cart, the page refreshes and you see a list of other products. The only place they tell you that it has been added to your cart is in the right-hand column—which is a well-known "banner blindness" area that visitors commonly ignore.

On the other hand, Coldwater Creek uses a lightbox popover that confirms the addition of an item to their shopping cart and includes follow-up options (view the full bag, check out, or return to shopping). This popover, shown in Figure 8.18, avoids visitor confusion and gives the visitor clear options.

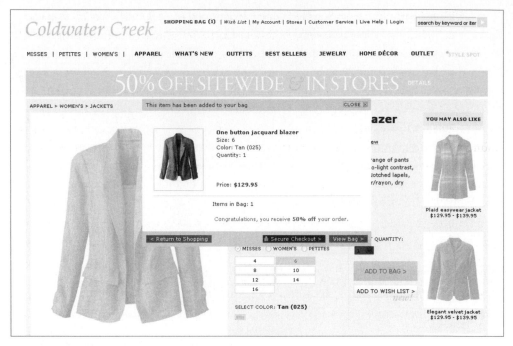

Figure 8.18 Coldwater Creek add-to-cart confirmation lightbox popover

Show the "As Delivered" Price as Soon As Possible

There should be no surprises in terms of shipping costs, taxes, or other charges for the visitor during the checkout process. Visitors should be armed with as much information as early as possible in the decision-making process—ideally on the shopping cart page.

You should include at least an estimate or basic calculator of the charges on the page.

It's important to make it obvious that users can change their shipping options, and many shopping cart pages allow you to change the shipping type on the very first step of the checkout process.

Allow Changing of Quantities

It may sound like a simple thing, but there are still far too many shopping carts that do a bad job of letting visitors remove or change quantities for items in their shopping cart.

Show Related Products

A prime place to upsell related products is after the visitor has added something to their shopping cart. When done in a way that helps the visitor, without overwhelming them, this approach can increase the number of products and services purchased in a single order.

This is best done with complementary items—for example, if a visitor has just added a cell phone to their shopping cart, it would be of value to suggest things like car chargers or phone cases to the bottom of the shopping cart. Good labels for a section like this might be "Don't Forget These Products" or "You Might Also Be Interested In."

State How Much Extra Is Needed to Qualify for Free Shipping

Many online marketers offer free shipping on their websites if the visitor purchases a minimum threshold amount. If you offer this type of promotion, indicate on the shopping cart page how much extra they need to add to their order to qualify for free shipping.

Place Trust Seals and Messaging Near Checkout Buttons

Visitor purchase anxiety will often be the highest just before beginning the checkout process, and doing as much as possible on this page to reduce this anxiety will increase the chances of a successful checkout.

A best practice for reducing visitor anxiety is to place trust-building security seals, like a VeriSign, McAfee, or buySAFE, near the checkout button on the checkout page. You can also build on this trust by placing messaging conveying that your order is safe and secure. As shown in Figure 8.19, ProFlowers does a great job of helping to reduce anxiety.

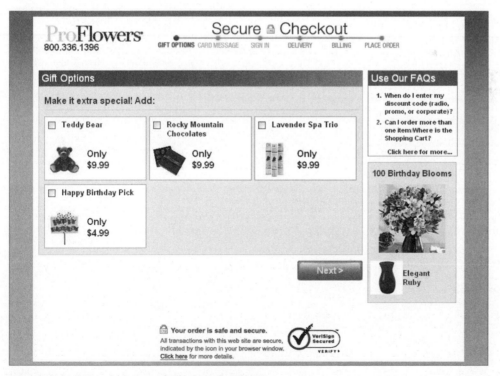

Figure 8.19 ProFlowers checkout trust seal and safe shopping text

Although they have determined that visitors only buy one item at a time and have technically done away with the notion of a cart page (indicated by their accurate use of the Order Now button text as a call-to-action on the preceding product detail page), they do include upsells (as discussed earlier) and place the VeriSign seal and Safe & Secure message below the Next button that leads to the checkout process.

Checkout Options

After a visitor decides to click the Check Out button, most sites will force the visitor to select their preferred tracking method. This usually includes the following options:

- Repeat customer required to log in
- New customer asked to create an account
- New customer able to check out without account creation

From the perspective of your company, it is ideal to know who the visitor is. If they return again, you would like to have them log in so that you can tie the current transaction to their whole payment history. That same reasoning is also in play when you ask a new customer to create an account. Some sites go as far as forcing registration and not allowing a guest checkout. This is not recommended.

From the perspective of your visitor, the account creation or login process is at best an unnecessary annoyance, or actually an impediment to their ability to buy. There is little value in creating an account. Having their information autofilled at some indefinite future point when they might again order from you is simply not that compelling. They can accomplish this just as easily (across all websites) by turning on the autofill features of their web browser software.

Another reason to create an account is the ability to see past history or check order status. Although that may be a benefit to frequent customers, it is not helpful for the vast majority of your customers. So you are trying to be helpful to a tiny handful of people while annoying all of your shoppers.

The decision (backed up by lots of testing across a number of e-commerce categories) is simple: You should give up your ability to perfectly track all transactions back to a specific person in exchange for higher conversion rates through your checkout. See additional discussion in the "Action" section of Chapter 3.

1-800-Flowers demonstrates our recommended best practice by offering the guest checkout option as the default, and a sign-in backup for registered users who desire it (see Figure 8.20).

1-800-Flowers subtly informs visitors that they can sign up for an account at a later point if they continue as a guest now. If in doubt about how to configure your checkout options, test moving your registration to a point later in the checkout process (but also monitor the impact of doing so on your ability to market to existing users, which relies on this registration information).

Figure 8.20 1-800-Flowers checkout with Continue As Guest default option

If you decide to have registered user checkout (like the vast majority of e-commerce websites), it's important to offer some best practices when registering. We'll cover this topic in its own section, "Registration & Multiple-Step Flows," later in this chapter, since this is pertinent for many types of websites.

Another best practice is to make sure the visitor knows that their login is secure. This can be done by using security-related language and security seals on the login page. Amazon accomplishes this by mentioning security-related text directly on their login button (shown in Figure 8.21).

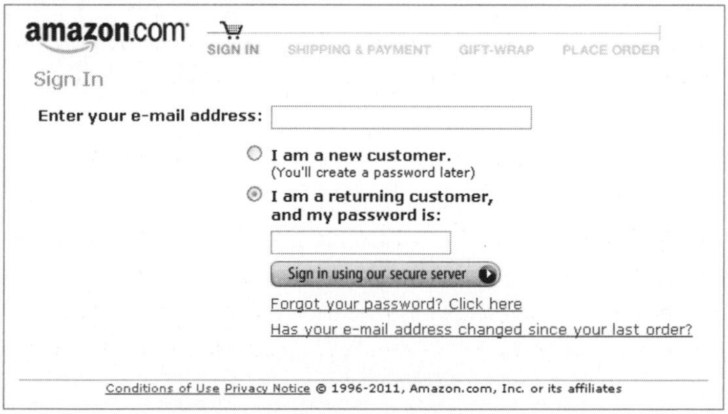

Figure 8.21 Amazon checkout options with trust language on the button

It's also important to offer to retrieve lost member name or password functionality at this step of the checkout process. If a user is not sure if they have an account, or don't remember it, they can easily check and retrieve their information.

Shipping Information

Not being up-front about shipping-related information such as costs and shipping times is a common problem found with e-commerce websites.

Allow Several Options for Shipping and Costs

A best practice to increase conversions is to let the visitor pick from a variety of shipping types and speeds. If they need to rush the order, they can pick a faster delivery method. If they don't care how long it takes, they can pick less expensive, standard delivery. You should also clearly state shipping prices, particularly useful for price-conscious shoppers.

Give Estimated Ship and Delivery Dates

To avoid potential disappointments regarding order delivery dates, it's a best practice to state estimated ship and delivery dates on this page for each type of shipping method available (placing it on the order review page may end up wasting the visitor's time).

Visitors find it particularly important to know this information around holiday periods, and not offering estimated delivery dates can be a reason for them to not order on your website.

Allow Copy to/from Billing Address

For those many visitors who have the same billing address as their shipping address, it's important to give an option to copy their information between shipping address and billing address. This saves the user time by not having to re-enter the same address. This option is usually offered by having a check box at the top of the address fields that says Same As Billing Address or Also Use For Billing Address.

Allow Ability to Store Addresses

Another great best practice to improve your shipping page is to allow users to save multiple shipping addresses for future use. This is especially useful for visitors who regularly ship to multiple addresses and don't want to keep having to retype the different addresses every time they check out.

Some e-commerce sites combine the shipping page with the billing details page, which we will now review.

Billing Information

Simple mistakes on the billing portion of a checkout process can doom your checkout conversion rates. This section provides best practices to use on your billing pages.

Simplify Field Entry/Error Handling

People are not very good at filling out long forms. The most important thing during the billing information step is how you handle the inevitable user errors. Do not make users fill out the whole form only to flag a number of problems with it when they submit. Ideally form-field validation should be done inline (as the form is being completed). When the focus is taken off a form field, the contents should be checked and the outcome shown—either with a small success indicator such as a green check mark, or via a specific error message indicating what is wrong.

Target does a particularly great job of this on their billing and shipping pages, with exact reasons for errors, and they even state reasons why certain fields are needed. See Figure 8.22 for an example of an improperly entered credit card number (with the error message icon and red bolded text immediately shown below it).

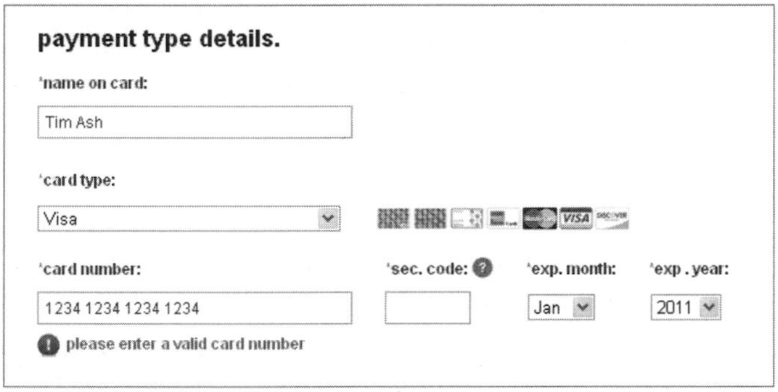

Figure 8.22 Target inline error validation

Allow for Alternative Payment Methods

Consumers now have more flexibility regarding product payments than ever before. Credit cards used to be the dominant way of paying for products online, but now usage of Bill Me Later or store-specific deferred payment options has increased considerably, as has the usage of PayPal and Google Checkout.

Add Tooltips for Credit Card Security Code

To verify physical possession of a credit card, many sites require a numeric code to be entered (which is only displayed on the back or front of the printed card). This code entry requirement often causes confusion and leads to many orders being abandoned or rejected.

We recommend putting a small question mark icon or a "What's This?" text link next to the security code input field. If the tip is clicked it should display a lightbox popover showing an example of the security code location on the payment card selected.

Review and Order Placement

You probably wouldn't sign a restaurant credit card receipt without first checking the cost and whether items matched what you ordered, so don't ask your visitors to place their order without a way of checking it first.

Confirm Sales Tax and Shipping Cost

If there are surprises in the total cost stemming from shipping or other additional fees, visitors will often abandon the checkout process. Your shopping cart page could only estimate these fees. As specific information becomes available (about shipping destination, method, or promotional codes applied), the total cost can change. Be very clear about the reasons for any changes.

Confirm Shipping Address

Mistakes can often occur regarding an incorrect shipping address, particularly with typos or using the wrong previously saved shipping address. The best way to reduce the risk of shipping errors is to clearly state the shipping address on the review page.

Clearly Show Real-Time Support Options

The Review and Place Order page is one of the most important places to show a clear support phone number or web chat option. Similar to the start of the checkout process, anxiety levels are likely to be high just before "pulling the trigger" and finalizing the purchase. Offering real-time support (phone, click-to-call, chat, or e-mail) here will help reduce anxiety, because the buyer knows that support is available, even if they don't need it at that moment.

Order Confirmation

Many online marketers will do their "happy dance" after the order placement because they have captured the visitor's revenue and completed the transaction. They pay little or no attention to the post order confirmation page. This is a lost opportunity since this page can have tremendous value. Remember, the visitor is already in a happy mood and has already opened their wallet, so at this point you should either reassure them, or try to extract additional value.

Confirm All Aspects of the Order

Every aspect of the order—the order number, the products and quantities that were ordered, breakdown of cost (including shipping and tax if applicable), the estimated ship date, and ideally, the estimated delivery date range—should be confirmed on this page.

Visitors will often want to print out this order confirmation page, so make this page printer-friendly. If you have already collected their contact e-mail, clearly state that a receipt has been sent to their address.

Send Automated E-mail Order Confirmation

Just in case a user needs to access their order details at a later point, it's best practice to also e-mail the confirmation details automatically to the purchaser. The e-mail should contain all the information about the order that the user would want to know. It is particularly important to offer e-mail confirmation if you don't have mandatory registration; without registration users will find it hard to track their orders.

Prominently Show Customer Support Options

Your user may still have some lingering hesitations or post-purchase remorse. Some of them may want to back out of the transaction. This tendency can be minimized as follows.

Begin with a positive title headline such as "Your Order Has Been Successfully Placed!" or "Thank You For Your Order!"

If a user isn't clear on anything regarding the order they just submitted, they will immediately look for support options to help address their concerns. Therefore it's a best practice to clearly state support options on this confirmation page, particularly the support phone number, chat, and e-mail address.

Ask for Account Registration

For many e-commerce sites that don't make it mandatory to register before purchasing, this page represents the ideal spot to ask for any additional information necessary to create an account and save their details for ease of use in the future.

Ask for Feedback

Asking for feedback about the online user experience can be very powerful. Visitors will often give you specific information that can be used to fine-tune your website. You can also ask for additional information such as "likelihood of recommending to others" or other subjects of interest to your online marketing department—for example, demographic or psychographic information. Keep these surveys short. In some cases you may want to incentivize people financially to take the survey.

Make It Easy to Share

Place prominent sharing options on the page, allowing people to announce that they have purchased a particular item (from you!) on common social networks. Amplify this effect by offering incentives for sharing.

Pass Them on to a Partner

You have done the hard work of getting someone to open their wallet. At this highly susceptible moment it has been shown that people are more open to other offers. In some cases if your business model supports this, you should consider passing the person on to a landing page for a specific partner company (or set of companies).

This will extract additional value if you get paid for the lead or even on a performance basis by the partner. In some situations (depending on the law in your country or jurisdiction), you may even be able to transfer the payment information in an encrypted format to the partner for a subsequent downstream purchase. Such "data pass" practices and their surrounding disclosure requirements can be complicated and stringent, so get guidance from your legal counsel before launching any kind of partner hand-off program that involves data pass.

Registration and Multiple-Step Flows

Getting personal details from a website visitor via a single or multipage form is the key conversion goal for many websites in business-to-consumer lead generation and business-to-business arenas. In many cases the ultimate conversion action can be months away, or may be completed via phone or some other offline method. But the beginning of the process requires some kind of nonpurchase form-fills.

Ideally, if your sign-up flow is long and involved, you should split apart the initial mandatory registration elements from the rest of the "nice to have" sign-up flow. For example, an initial account sign-up on a dating site can be short, and a detailed personal profile can be completed later. Let's first examine the registration page and the best practices you should employ there.

Registration Page

Many websites require users to register before obtaining information or making a purchase. Usually this is of benefit to the website marketers who run the website, as a visitor's behavior and e-mail address provides valuable insights to enhance marketing efforts to registered members. Registering often provides a benefit to the user too, though, as it allows the user to save their preferred shipping address or credit card details, as well as previous browsing or purchasing behavior.

Registration pages are particularly common for paid media sites and single-item e-commerce sites, and are usually limited to just one page, with minimal information needed from the visitor in order for them to register.

Clearly State Value and Benefits

A visitor should always know why they are being asked to register and what's in it for them (even if it may seem obvious to you), especially if they have arrived on this page unexpectedly. Do not just use a generic registration page—customize wording and imagery of this page depending on its context (what you know about the visitor's traffic source and intent).

An often-overlooked best practice on a registration page is to offer clear registration benefits—not just the features—to the visitor. This is an important part of the AIDA decision-making process that we discussed in Chapter 3 (benefits clearly help increase the "desire" aspects of AIDA). The benefits of registering can often be supplemental to the main reason why the user is being asked to register, so look for other reasons that may benefit a visitor downstream.

For example, if the visitor gets a free newsletter or coupons as a benefit of registering, state this clearly on the registration form, ideally in the form of bullet points.

If your website has a fee associated with registering, it's also a best practice to state risk-reducing aspects of the registration—for example, if you offer a free trial or a money-back guarantee.

Simplify Field Entry/Error Handling

As we mentioned earlier in this chapter (in the e-commerce billing page section), it's important to reduce the chances of a user not being able to complete a form due to poor error handling.

Remember to use inline validation as a best practice by highlighting errors as they occur (don't make users hit the submit button before discovering issues). When errors do occur, they should be highlighted using visual indicators (such as red arrows next to the field in question or a change in its background color). It's also a best practice to put an error message at the top of the page in bolded red font indicating that there are issues below, and also preferably next to the field that is causing the issue.

Inline validation also works very well for allowing visitors to create unique usernames without them having to first click the main submit button to check availability. The same applies to validating the format and strength of passwords. Most people will not read your small text requirements for password format and will be forced to re-enter the password unless you are validating inline.

Avoid Character-Recognition CAPTCHAs

A *CAPTCHA* is a means of automatically generating challenges that intend to:

- Provide a problem easy enough for all humans to solve
- Prevent standard automated software from filling out a form

With the increase in hacking and phishing, website marketers and owners have been forced to adopt such technical approaches to limit fake account creation spam by hackers, bots, or other automated means. The most common way of doing this is to ask the visitor to read a computer-generated set of words and type them in order to continue (see example in Figure 8.23).

Figure 8.23 Example of text-recognition CAPTCHA

Unfortunately, while this helps keep out bots and hackers, it also is keeping out many legitimate site visitors and is a source of frustration for many more. As automated character-recognition algorithms continue to evolve as a CAPTCHA countermeasure, the challenge words are becoming harder and harder to read, resulting in increasing work for the user and the more frequent frustration if the incorrect text is entered. Another form of simpler CAPTCHA requires posing a simple math question, such as "11 + 3 = ". This approach requires reasoning skills instead of advanced visual recognition. Both methods create unnecessary cognitive, visual, and motor "loads" on the user.

The bottom line is that you should avoid using CAPTCHA if at all possible. This may involve some discussions with your IT staff since they may be insisting on it as a spam defense. You may have to run a quick split test without the CAPTCHA to document the conversion decrease that it is causing (along with a calculation of the annualized revenue value that results from its use). Much more subtle (and noninvasive) means for detecting real human form-fills are available and should be used instead.

Limit Registration Fields to the Essentials

Like we have seen with the homepage, any time you place too much in front of a user, you will increase your chances of them prematurely abandoning your website. The same applies to your registration page. Having too many fields to complete is an all-too-common error that can easily be rectified.

The bottom line is to think of your visitor. Don't ask for information that seems too personal to the visitor, particularly if the information won't assist with your marketing efforts.

 Remember visitors hate spam. You should state on your registration page that you won't spam visitors or sell or rent their e-mail address.

Here are some examples of commonly found registration fields that can often be removed in order to help increase sign-up completion rates:

- Repeat e-mail address (users will often just cut and paste this from the first e-mail field anyway)
- Date of birth (unless needed for the Child Online Protection Act [COPA] or other age restrictions)
- Full address (unless needed to mail specific related items)
- Phone number (unless visitor has to schedule a callback)

Which fields to omit may vary depending on the exact context of your registration page. Ideally you should test removing all noncritical fields and look for the impact they have on your sign-up completion rates. This may involve a bit of a tussle between your sales department (which only wants fully completed and highly qualified leads), and marketing (which is trying to optimize the end-to-end lead-generation experience). Often the right answer is to develop fully qualified leads over some period of time by asking for progressively more information in exchange for higher value bribes (such as whitepapers or phone consultations).

You need to state clearly the reasons why specific (particularly personal or sensitive) information is needed. Many visitors are hesitant to register if they have to give their e-mail address, but if you place a tooltip or comment next to the field explaining the benefit to user (so you can send them a confirmation e-mail and regular updates, etc.), your form completion rates will be much higher.

Send Confirmation and Welcome E-mails with Recommended Next Steps

It's considered a best practice to automatically generate and send an e-mail to the visitor upon their registration, asking them to confirm their account. This e-mail should also welcome the user and provide next steps (particularly if they need to complete additional steps or additional information is needed).

Try Third-Party Website Registration Methods

It's becoming increasingly common to be able to use your favorite social network credentials to register with other websites. This can greatly simplify registration pages and greatly reduce barriers to registering. Facebook Connect is one of the more common tools to allow you to do this, in addition to using OpenID.net. With a click of a single button, all of the visitor's profile information can be pulled from another source without the need to ask for it again.

Registration pages are usually a single page, but sometimes a longer sign-up process is required. We will next examine the requirements of such multiple-step flows.

Multiple-Step Flows

Sign-up flows are usually longer versions of individual registration pages and are typically found where more in-depth details are needed before signing up is possible. Examples of this include online service websites like e-mail or analytics tools, social networking sites, and dating sites. Here are some best practices considerations when working with multiple-step page flows.

Tip the Risk-Reward Scales

In the mind of every website visitor, being asked to complete a task is similar to trying to balance a scale. On the one side are the benefits of doing so; on the other are the costs. Costs can be indirect, such as a waste of their time, the effort of filling out the form, or the opportunity cost of not searching for an alternative to what you offer.

Just because a visitor arrives on your sign-up page, don't presume that they understand the full benefits of your value proposition. One of the best ways to increase the chances of the visitor completing the sign-up form is to restate the benefits of signing up. Ideally, this should be done with bullet points to avoid overfilling the page and overwhelming the user with too much text. The best location for your list of benefits is the right-hand column on each of the pages within your sign-up flow.

On the flip side, you can minimize apparent risks of signing up. For example, if you offer a free trial or money-back guarantee, this is the perfect place to re-emphasize it. Badges and visual seals (such as a 100 percent money-back guarantee graphic) can quickly convey your message.

You should also be sure to include security seals and business approval seals on this page (like VeriSign and BBB seals, as discussed earlier). Presenting them at the head of the multipage flow will have the highest positive impact and influence on a visitor who is considering signing up.

Get the Essential Information First

To make sign-up flows less overwhelming, smart online marketers have tested and created versions of sign-up flows that split apart this flow into two parts. They get the most important information on the first page (just the bare information needed to register and sign up), and then put more in-depth sign-up parts onto the following pages. We suggest using e-mail enhancement tools such as the ones described in Chapter 5, "Conversion Ninja Toolbox—Diagnosing Site Problems," to increase your conversion rate. Of course without getting the e-mail address first, this becomes impossible.

Match.com is an example of getting the essentials onto a first page—in a sense signing visitors up (Figure 8.24).

Figure 8.24 Match.com's first sign-up page

All additional information for full personal profile setup is asked for on later pages, starting with the screen in Figure 8.25.

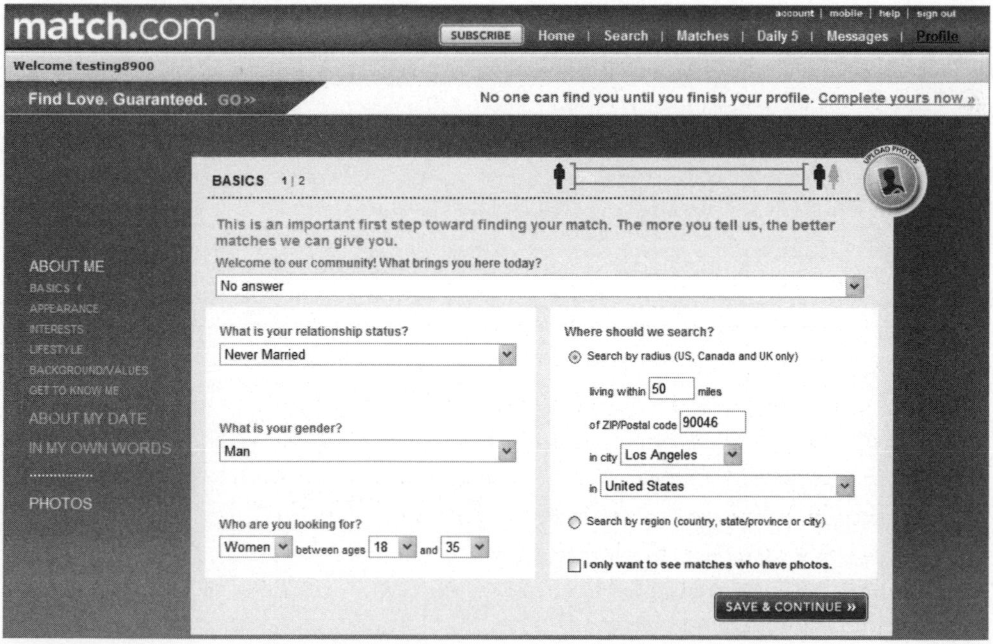

Figure 8.25 Match.com's first profile setup page

Experiment with Information Staging and the Number of Total Pages

Although you must eventually collect all the necessary information in order to complete the flow, there is quite a bit of latitude in how you stage and chunk the required data.

Staging refers to the order in which you ask for the information. By examining your form fill-out behavior (see "Visual Analysis Tools" in Chapter 5), you can determine which fields are most commonly left blank or take the longest time to complete. Consider asking for the "easy" information first, and only asking for the "difficult" items closer to the end of the process when the visitor has more personal effort ("skin in the game") already invested.

Similarly, you should experiment with the "chunking" of the information. The problem with many flows is that the information that appears on a single screen is not necessarily conceptually clean or unified. For example, the Esurance auto insurance quote screen in Figure 8.26 is titled "Primary Driver Information" and looks long and imposing. It asks for 10 fields and then requires a checkbox acknowledgment of the site's privacy policy.

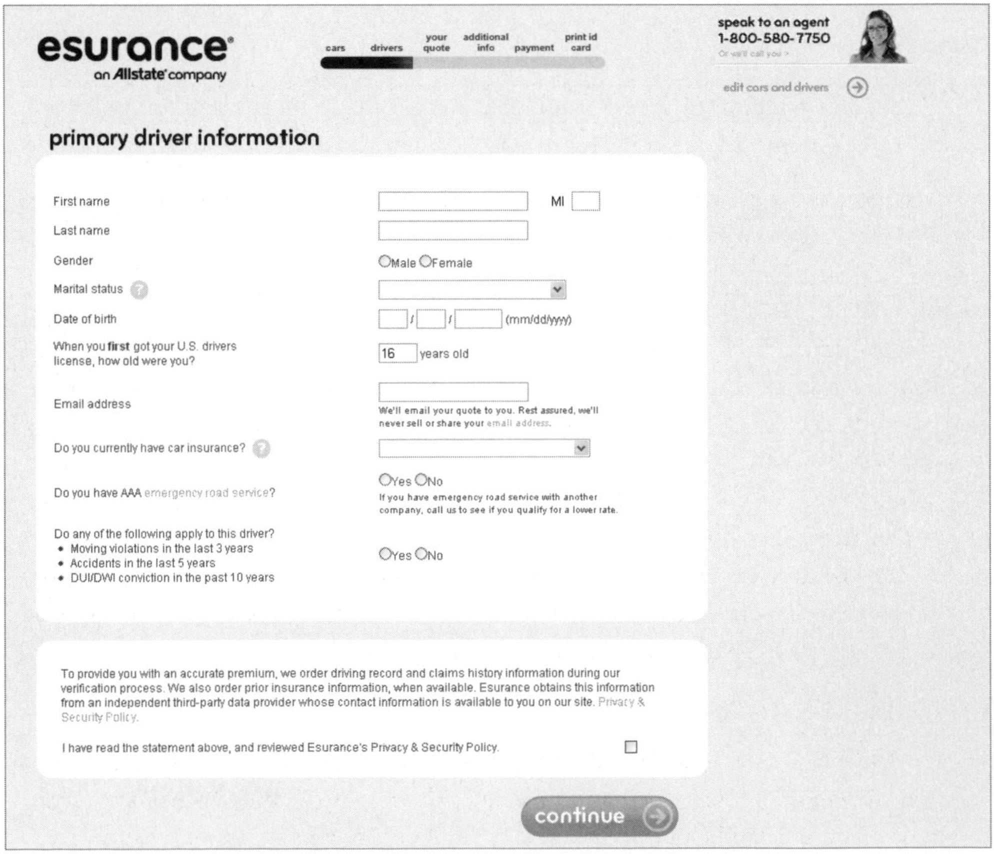

Figure 8.26 Esurance's primary driver information screen

This screen could just as easily be broken into two cleaner (and much less imposing pages) as follows:

Primary Driver Information

- First Name
- Last Name
- Gender
- Marital Status
- Date of Birth
- E-mail Address

Primary Driver History

- Age at which you first got a U.S. license
- Do you currently have car insurance?
- Do you have AAA emergency road service?
- Do any of the following apply (moving violations, accidents, DUI)?

As you can see, by reordering and splitting up the information you get a more compact page as well as a conceptually more atomic purpose and theme for the requested information. In the extreme, you should consider going to a conversational "wizard" with one or two questions per screen.

On the other hand, if you have a relatively small number of fields needed for your sign-up flow, you may want to consider combining the registration and sign-up into a single page. "One step sign-up" can also be compelling since the visitor knows exactly what will be expected of them at one glance.

Constant Contact (an e-mail service provider) uses a longer single form and breaks it up into conceptual groupings by using action blocks with subheading labels (see Figure 8.27).

The clear subheadings help explain why the details are needed. This page also uses another best practice described earlier: reiterating benefits to increase perceived value in the right-hand column.

This form could've just as easily been broken up into multiple pages. The bottom line is that there is no correct answer for form chunking or staging, and you must experiment to get the highest conversion rates.

Clearly Indicate Steps and Progress

Particularly when detailed information is needed across multiple pages, visitors like to know how much progress they are making in the sign-up flow and what steps are ahead of them. Much like in a shopping cart checkout, these progress indicators are usually shown at the top of the page either above the headline (breadcrumb style) or immediately below it.

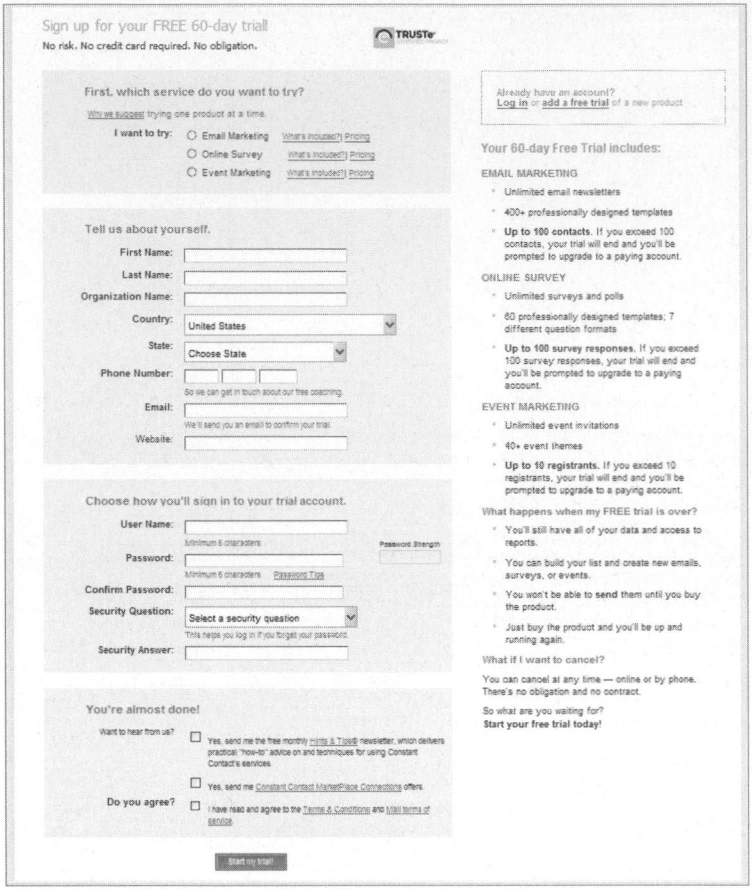

Figure 8.27 Constant Contact single page sign-up with multiple sections

Limit Sign-up Fields to the Essentials

Just as we noted above for registration pages, it's also a best practice to limit the number of fields on your multipage flow pages. Yes, your sales team wants as much qualifying information as they can get, but that doesn't mean you should ask for it. More fields certainly won't help your sign-up conversion rates. Here are some examples of fields in sign-up pages that can often be removed to increase conversion rates (hopefully with little impact on sales and marketing teams):

- What industry you are in
- Job title
- Marital status
- Household income
- Ethnicity

Remember that you can always get more information from the visitor at a later point after they have signed up. One way to do this is to ask additional one-off questions upon each future user login until your profile is complete. Such progressive disclosure strategies can be very powerful but may require implementation support from your IT department.

Direct Response Pages

Many stand-alone landing pages are designed specifically to elicit a direct response, usually signing up to a service or purchasing a product. These pages may be designed for traffic from a specific campaign or traffic source. For example, they can be used for a specific affiliate or for a paid search engine campaign. This allows the page to be tweaked to match the intent and messaging of the upstream originating traffic source.

Begin with a Compelling Page Headline

The success of a direct response page can sometimes be determined within seconds. If your page does not capture a visitor's attention and spike their curiosity almost immediately, it will fail.

A strong headline gives your visitors a reason to stay and digest more of the page content. The headline should ideally relate to solving a common need or be in a question format. Different variations should be tested to find the one with the highest positive impact on your conversion rate. You should also test increasing your headline font size and choice of color, as these aspects also play an important role in increasing conversions.

Understand the Page Fold and Avoid Scrolling

A visitor's time on your direct response page may be fleeting. The best way to ensure they see all the key information they need, complete with a compelling call-to-action, is to present this all on one fairly short page. Ideally, all of the key information should be presented above the page fold and not require the user to have to scroll vertically.

A long-form sales letter is an occasional exception to this rule. These long scrolling pages work particularly well for more expensive products and services where in-depth details are needed from a visitor in the decision-making process. Their power is primarily based on persuasive copywriting, with a powerful headline leading into sales copy that compels you to read further. So in a sense, as long as the headline is above the fold for such long-form pages, they are also meeting the general rule described earlier.

A great way to see what your page looks like above the fold for common browser types is to use Google's Browser Size tool (`http://browsersize.googlelabs.com`). In Figure 8.28, you can see what the UsedWatches.net website looks like when overlaid with the distribution of browser sizes.

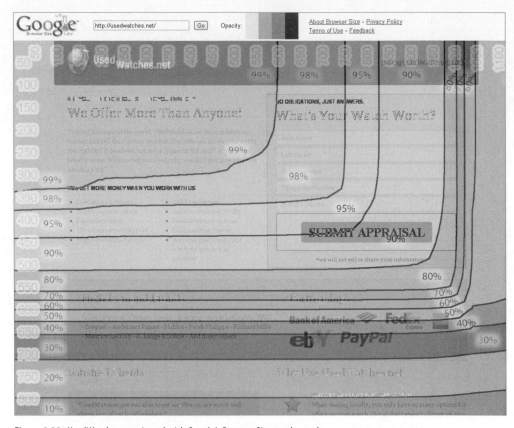

Figure 8.28 UsedWatches.net viewed with Google's Browser Size overlay tool

As you can see, the Submit Appraisal button would have been seen by over 90 percent of typical visitors. If it was moved a bit up and to the left-hand side of the page, this view rate can be increased to 95 or even 98 percent.

Remove Unnecessary Text and Images

As with other pages, you should remove clutter because this will help reduce friction for the visitor and help them to understand what you are you trying to sell.

Remove unnecessary images and streamline text. As we've said before, don't use canned photos just for the sake of having a photo. Eliminate dense blocks of text or convert them into shorter bullet points. If you are unsure of what to remove, try removing different items one at a time and run tests to see what improves your conversion rate.

Support the Headline with Key Benefits

Just below the main headline, you need to outline the key benefits and reasons that a visitor should consider purchasing the product or service. Use bullet points to convey this information. Keep the text to one line per bullet point, since doing so makes the text easier to read and scan. Try to limit these benefits and reasons to the most important ones (keep it to five or less)—too many bullet points will overwhelm the visitor.

It's also a best practice to have these bullet points shown above the page fold so the user can see them immediately without having to scroll. If it's likely that the visitor may need more information, you should place Learn More or See Details links that display this extra information in lightbox popovers without taking the visitor away from the page.

Make Use of a Supporting Trust Area

The main benefits and call-to-action should live in the main body of your direct response page, but it's important to offer a smaller supporting information block also. Users often look to this spot for additional information to help them with their decision.

Typically this supporting block contains additional elements to help influence and convert the visitor. This can include items like testimonials (both customer and outside experts) and client logos (for business-to-business pages). If you have a considerable user base, you should also state the number of clients. These all help build credibility of the product or service on your direct response page.

The supporting information block is often displayed as a dedicated right column on the page, but it can also be included as a horizontal row immediately below the main call-to-action block.

Make Use of Video and Audio

Remember that visitors don't read long blocks of text on webpages, but a user can process information much faster by listening or viewing videos. Consider creating and using audio or video segments that a user can click if they want to listen and learn more. See Chapter 7 for additional information on video best practices. Audio works particularly well with user testimonials—it helps build authenticity.

As a higher-risk tactic, you can even test autoplaying shorter, powerful sound bites to help increase conversion rates—just as long as you clearly show an option to turn off the sound or mute it.

Test Your Calls-to-Action

As we mentioned earlier in our discussion of e-commerce product pages, one of the things that has the most influence on your conversion rates is the call-to-action button or link. The same applies to direct response pages. Therefore, it's important to come up with variations of your call-to-action, including different text options and button styles, and perform A/B testing on them to find out which one converts the highest.

Remember that using distinctive colors for your call-to-action button usually will have a higher conversion rate. You should also try to avoid nondescript text like Order Now because this doesn't focus on any benefit to the user signing up or purchasing.

Split Up the Sign-up Process to Key Fields on the First Page

Just as we mentioned when discussing multiple-page flows earlier, splitting up the sign-up form is a great idea. In fact, it works even better on direct response pages. Ideally, the fewer sign-up fields on your page that have to be completed, the better. The initial page can be as simple as name and e-mail address, and the rest of the sign-up details can be collected on a longer, secondary sign-up page. This way, you receive key marketing information to contact the user again in case they decide to abandon your page midstream.

Mobile Websites

With the continued rise in popularity of mobile smartphones and tablets, a rapidly growing proportion of your visitors will look at your website in a nondesktop or laptop web browser format. Unfortunately, too many traditional websites don't display well on smaller screens and result in a horrible user experience.

This phenomenon isn't just limited to media and social network sites. Mobile-based e-commerce revenue is also growing at a rapid pace, so it's important to optimize e-commerce sites for mobile pages. A full description of mobile marketing is outside the scope of this book. We recommend *Mobile Marketing: Finding Your Customers No Matter Where They Are* (Pearson Education, 2010) by Cindy Krum for a detailed examination of this topic.

Create a Dedicated Mobile Version of Your Website

It is impossible to make your website look good and function well simultaneously for traditional and mobile audiences. Instead, you will need to create a different version for those visitors looking at your website on a mobile platform.

Luckily it's fairly easy for websites to technically detect mobile browsers. If a mobile browser is being used, the site can automatically display the mobile version.

Make Sure It Loads Quickly

The mobile site should be a "lite" version of your regular website, and in particular, it should be much less bandwidth-intensive to make up for the slower Internet connection speeds found on most mobile devices. Remember that mobile web browsing is often done under extreme time pressure, so any delays will be experienced as extremely frustrating by your visitors.

Although many websites will still look good on tablet-based mobile platforms because of their higher resolutions, they will also take much longer to load because of the lower connection bandwidth.

To reduce page download times for your mobile version, you need to ruthlessly eliminate anything that requires a large file download. Reducing the number of images in general is a best practice for creating mobile websites. You should also consider what a partially loaded page will look like. In general you should try to ensure that the core elements of the page appear first.

Optimize for Narrower Experiences

Mobile devices have very different capabilities ranging from processor speed, memory size, operating system, available applications and plug-ins, and most importantly screen resolutions. It is hard to predict what a mobile site experience will look like on a particular device.

However, one consideration should be paramount—do not make the user scroll horizontally. Vertical scrolling is okay. In general, you should also try to eliminate the need for manipulating what is currently on the screen (such as pinching or zooming).

Therefore, you should create single-column skinny pages on your mobile website that work in a much narrower resolution. Tickets.com is one of many websites that now adopts this best practice. Their traditional site, shown in Figure 8.29, uses a conventional three-column layout.

Figure 8.29 Traditional Tickets.com website with three-column layout

Their mobile site, shown in Figure 8.30, uses a simplified one-column format and larger clickable areas to facilitate usability.

Figure 8.30 Tickets.com mobile website on iPhone4

In general, you should stick to single-column lists and ruthlessly eliminate any nonactionable text. It is frustrating to try to interact with tiny form elements, buttons, or links on your site. Make sure that any controls or calls-to-action are large and easy to click on. This is especially important on touch-screen phones. If you have to enlarge the link text or make extra-large buttons, you should do that.

If your website is likely to be accessed frequently in a mobile setting, consider creating a dedicated mobile app version of frequently used tasks on your site. Dedicated apps are an increasingly popular way to access simpler forms of information and offer a richer user interface experience than most mobile websites.

To help users find content on such a narrow resolution, it's also a best practice to put a search box near the top of every page (as shown in Figure 8.30). This way, users don't have to browse to find products and can simply use text-based search.

Test for Many Devices

Unfortunately, just as there are many differing technologies for mobile platforms and devices, there are few standards for web development on mobile devices. Not only can browser resolution sizes impact how your site looks and works (as we just discussed), but the many different combinations of mobile browsers and mobile operating systems can potentially wreak just as much havoc on how your website looks and functions. Although some mobile CMSs claim that they allow a single development of your mobile web content to be seamlessly deployed to all devices, this is currently very far from reality.

Therefore, it's critical to conduct quality assurance on your website covering the most common combinations of mobile browsers, operating systems, and popular devices. High-end professional tools are becoming available for cross-device interactive testing, and simple free static preview tools like Mobilizer (`www.springbox.com/mobilizer/`) will continue to improve.

Optimize for Flash Issues

As of this writing, Adobe Flash still did not (quite intentionally) work on Apple devices (iPads and iPhones in particular). Flash is used on many traditional websites especially for complex or interactive functionality. There is a longer-term transition to an HTML5/CSS3–based experience that would mimic Flash functionality natively across all popular browsers, but this is not currently the case.

Therefore, you should consider re-creating Flash elements on your mobile website in technologies like DHMTL or JavaScript that will work with Apple-based mobile browsers. This is especially important to consider for Flash-based navigation elements or Flash-based value proposition elements on your site.

Don't Try to Do It All

Your mobile site should not re-create all of the functionality or depth of your traditional site. Remember that people in a mobile setting are in a hurry (even more than traditional web browsers are). They will not generally want to read a lot of text, or fill out an intricate and long series of forms. Only focus on the specific tasks that they may want to do while on the go.

Here are a few examples:

- Checking for the latest information (flight times or traffic alerts)
- Looking for nearby establishments
- Finding your physical location and hours of operation
- Getting an immediate problem resolved (click-to-call can be very powerful in this context)

Although it's critical to offer a mobile version of your website, it's also important to offer a link that allows the visitor to see the full traditional website if they want to. This is necessary because some users may want to access a feature that is not present on the mobile version, and they would be extremely frustrated if they kept getting redirected to the limited (and for their specific needs inadequate) mobile version.

In the next chapter we will provide you with a framework for identifying the most important elements of your site from a conversion improvement perspective.

The Strategy of
What to Test

9

There is no such thing as the right answer in landing page testing. So how do you decide what sorts of things to include in your landing page test? This chapter will provide guidelines for identifying promising test elements and cover testing themes that have consistently produced solid results.

CHAPTER CONTENTS
How to Think About Test Elements
Selecting Elements to Test
Testing Multiple-Page Flows
Timeless Testing Themes
Price Testing

How to Think About Test Elements

If you did your homework after reading the previous chapters, you should have come up with a long list of potential problems and concerns about your site. These issues probably ranged from tactical problems to fundamental mismatches between your visitor's goals and your landing page.

So how do you decide which ones are worthy of testing? The following filters will help you to separate the wheat from the chaff.

Breadth of Impact

The 80/20 Rule (the Pareto Principle) has been applied to a wide range of disciplines and observations. It predicts that a vital few (20 percent) are responsible for the vast majority (80 percent) of the results. If you apply this notion to landing page optimization, it follows that fixing a few fundamental problems will result in the greatest benefit-to-conversion rate. Conversely, it also implies that some of the elements that you decide to test will not affect conversion rate at all.

So how do you determine what is vital and what is trivial? In general this can be hard to do, but you can follow the guideline of looking for the widest potential impact.

Most Important Conversion Actions

In many cases, you will have more than one desired conversion action. You should concentrate on improving or emphasizing the action that results in the biggest financial rewards. For example, if you offer three different service levels, you probably know which ones your audience already prefers and their relative revenue value. By fixing or emphasizing the most popular one, you stand to gain the most. If your least popular plan only accounted for 1 percent of sales, even doubling its conversion rate would not have a dramatic impact on your overall revenues.

Biggest Possible Audience

Often companies have multiple landing pages for specific online marketing campaigns. You should examine which ones have the highest traffic levels and result in the highest number of conversions. Give first priority to the pages that are generating the most revenue, and cater what's displayed to their preferences.

Many companies only focus on obviously underperforming landing pages. Of course, shoring up your weaknesses is a valid approach to improving your business. However, you should not let it blind you to the opportunities hidden away in your best-performing pages. Just because they are generating a lot of revenue does not mean they are optimized or performing as well as they could be. By improving your top pages even more, you can usually unlock a lot of value.

Most Popular Paths Through Your Site

Web analytics software shows you the most popular paths (flows of traffic) through your site. Some of these packages even show you the reverse goal paths—the common sequences of pages that led the visitor to the conversion action.

Analyzing paths can be a somewhat complex business. You need to know where traffic lands on your site. In the case of main-site landing pages, the traffic may land on several types of pages on your site. For example, for an e-commerce catalog, you may have significant traffic hitting your homepage, category pages, brand pages, search results pages, and product detail pages. The mix will depend on your particular business.

Do not pay attention only to the size of the landing page traffic flows because not all traffic has equal value. For example, your homepage may have a high percentage of type-in traffic. This may mean that you have a strong brand and people are proactively seeking out your company, with a correspondingly higher likelihood of conversion. Or most of your homepage traffic may be from your successful SEO efforts. Unfortunately, the traffic may be coming primarily from generic keywords. In such cases, the large number of visitors may hide the fact that they are disinterested "tire kickers" who are much less likely to convert.

A lot of traffic (especially from paid campaigns) lands on pages that are deep within your site. This *deep linking* is intentional and is used to present the most relevant content possible. Deep linking is common in PPC campaigns, where the intent of searchers can be inferred from their keyword. Those who use generic keywords are sent to your homepage, whereas those showing more specific intent or knowledge about their needs are taken directly to particular information or to product detail pages. The conversion likelihood of the deep-linked traffic is usually significantly higher because of visitors' later position in the decision process, and the targeted information that they see on the landing page.

You can combine all these factors into a single metric for estimating the magnitude of the potential losses for each type of landing page within your site. Multiply the revenue per visitor for a particular type of landing page by the number of visitors who land on it. This will give you a revenue estimate for the traffic source. Multiply that number by the bounce rate (the percentage of visitors who immediately exit without viewing another page). This will give you a rough sense of the potential lost revenue. You can now rank your pages and focus on the ones with the largest lost revenues first.

Still, things can get a little more complicated. Sometimes a page can serve as both a landing page and as a link in the conversion path from other pages upstream of it. In such cases, the lost revenue calculation can be extended to include not only its bounce rate but also its abandonment (or drop-off) rate for traffic that is simply passing through it. But the basic idea is still the same—to estimate the value of the dollars draining out of your leaky conversion bucket.

Let's take a look at a specific example. Assume that you run a site for generating real estate agent buyer leads. You get paid a fixed amount for each visitor that you deliver to a local real estate agent's page. Your only traffic source is a national PPC campaign on popular search engines. You use a mix of general and specific keywords, such as "buying a house," "california home listings," or "san diego real estate."

Depending on the intent of the keyword, the traffic is landed on the homepage, a state-specific page, or a local community page. If searchers land on the national page, they must select a state page and then a particular local community page before taking the desired conversion action (clicking over to a local real estate agent's website). Similarly, those landing on state pages must first click on a local page, and then on the paid link.

The three types of pages have the following characteristics:

National page

    National Visitors (NV) = 1,000,000 per month (landing page)

    National Bounce Rate (NB) = 50% (for traffic landing on this page)

    National Revenue (NR) = $0.20 per visitor

State pages

    State Visitors (SV) = 500,000 per month (directly landing on it)

    State Bounce Rate (SB) = 40% (for traffic landing on this page)

    State Revenue (SR) = $0.30 per visitor

    State Abandonment Rate (SA) = 35% (for through traffic from the national page)

Local pages

    Local Visitors (LV) = 200,000 per month (directly landing on it)

    Local Bounce Rate (LB) = 35% (for traffic landing on this page)

    Local Revenue (LR) = $0.50 per visitor

    Local Abandonment Rate (LA) = 30% (for through traffic from the state page)

Based on these figures, we can calculate the potential lost revenues for each page:

National page

    $= NV \times NR \times NB$ (national bounce revenue loss)

    $= 1,000,000 \times \$0.20 \times 50\%$

    $= \$100,000$

State pages

    $= SV \times SR \times SB$ (state bounce revenue loss)

    $+ NV \times NR \times (1 - NB) \times SA$ (state abandonment revenue loss from national page visitors)

    $= 500,000 \times \$0.30 \times 40\%$

    $+ 1,000,000 \times \$0.20 \times (1 - 50\%) \times 35\%$

    $= \$95,000$

Local pages

= LV × LR × LB (local bounce revenue loss)

+ SV × SR × (1 − SB) × LA (local abandonment revenue loss from state page visitors)

+ NV × NR × (1 − NB) × (1 − SA) × LA (local abandonment revenue loss from national page visitors)

= 200,000 × $0.50 × 35%

+ 500,000 × $0.30 × (1 − 40%) × 30%

+ 1,000,000 × $0.2 × (1 − 50%) × (1 − 35%) × 30%

= $83,000

As you can see, the lost revenue of each page is surprisingly close, especially given the significant differences in direct traffic levels. Because the state and local pages act as conduits for upstream traffic, their value is enhanced significantly.

Remember, you will not be able to convert all your visitors under any circumstances. So the lost revenue calculation is an upper limit on the actual performance improvement and should serve only as a rough guide for prioritizing the pages to test first. See Chapter 14, "Developing Your Action Plan," for a detailed discussion of the economic value calculations for landing page testing.

Most Prominent Parts of the Page

All page elements are not created equal. A visitor's scanning behavior changes based on the specific task at hand. During e-commerce comparison shopping, visitors may inspect all items on a particular search results page with roughly equal attention until they find the right one. When reading articles or a column of search results, visitors will scan the material starting from the upper-left corner and focusing with decreasing attention on each new subheading or entry in the list.

But there are common general considerations. Eye-tracking and other behavioral studies have consistently shown that people pay great attention to the information near the upper-left corner of a page when they are trying to get oriented. They look for important content in the central portion of the visible page and typically ignore the upper-right and lower-left corners. Placing items above the fold is critical for the awareness stage of the decision process (since you can't click on a link that you do not even know exists). But there is some evidence to indicate that that the fold is not at the actual visible limit of the browser window. People start tuning out when they get about two-thirds of the way down the screen. In fact, many people would rather scroll something up into the middle of their screen to examine it than look down to the bottom of the page.

Granularity

The granularity of your test elements is the level of detail at which you will make changes to your design. At one extreme, you can use specific and fine localized variations (such as changing button colors or text font sizes). At the other extreme, you can create coarse and fundamental changes that join dozens of smaller individual design alternatives. It is not uncommon to completely redesign your whole landing page and test it head-to-head against your original.

In between is a continuum of possible scales at which you can test proposed changes. Sometimes these design alternatives can be nested within one another. For example, you may change the text of the call-to-action button on your form, change all of the text labels on the form input fields, or also change the size of the form and its position on the page.

The size of your test will be constrained by the traffic to your landing page and its data rate (the number of conversion actions per unit time). Changing the granularity of your tests allows you to include all or most of your important ideas while still fitting into a reasonable test size. For example, reducing search space size is done by combining several individual changes into a single larger variable for testing.

When a large visitor pool for a test size is available, it makes sense to get very granular on most of the changes that you are considering. With other testing methods or low data rates, you will be forced to consolidate your test size. At that point, you have to decide if you want to focus on granular changes or combining several of them into larger tuning elements.

The advantage of fine granularity changes is that they are quick and easy to implement. For example, you may want to consider different headlines for your page. It would not take long to come up with some reasonable alternatives, set up a test, and start collecting data. By continuously running back-to-back fine-granularity tests, you can often make significant conversion improvements. By their nature, these kinds of small incremental tests do not require a lot of work or emotional investment, and are ideal for this kind of champion-challenger continuous testing.

Wholesale page redesigns are sometimes the only option when you want to consider many potential changes but do not have the data rate or time to run a series of finer-granularity tests. Such redesigns are also the only way to deal with landing pages that have low coherency (see the "Coherency" section later in this chapter). The main drawback of whole-page redesigns is the time and effort that goes into creating them. Since you don't know if the new design will outperform the original, you are taking a gamble that your larger up-front investment will pay off. I have also heard online marketers argue that complete redesigns deny them so-called "learnings" about which individual elements contributed the most to the improved performance. This is based on the flawed assumption that the individual elements are completely independent of one another. In fact, they are often highly dependent on the context in which they are presented.

There is no inherent advantage to testing fine or coarse granularity changes. In a fine granularity test, changing a single headline from "Free Quote Request" to "Instant Quote" saw the form-fill conversion rate skyrocket by 58 percent. On the other end of the spectrum we have seen lifts of several hundred percent with coarse split testing of completely different whole-page designs.

Granularity does not have to be uniform among the elements that you are testing. You can devote more attention to key elements of the landing page like call-to-action button colors (complementing the rest of the page or contrasting), formats (a button only or a button with a text link under it), and text (several alternative variations). For less prominent parts of the page such as the footer, one test might contain several concurrent changes.

Sweep

Closely related to the granularity of a tuning element is the notion of sweep. Do your alternative testing element ideas represent radically different thinking? Or are they tame tweaks unlikely to produce significant changes in visitor behavior?

Tactical changes (such as strikingly provocative headlines) can be radical, whereas whole-page redesigns that merely change color-schemes can be considered tame. So sweep does not necessarily correspond to granularity.

> *Efficiency is doing things right; effectiveness is doing the right things.*
>
> —BUSINESS MANAGEMENT GURU PETER F. DRUCKER

You have a choice. You can continue to evolve your landing page within the current framework of its design, messaging, and intention. Or you can test radical revolutionary alternatives that can fail miserably or produce unexpected levels of breakthrough performance. There is no correct answer. The level of iconoclasm in your testing depends on your company's culture of risk tolerance and business objectives.

Coherency

Coherency is the harmonious consistency in the relation of all landing page parts to the whole. It is clear to most Internet surfers within a split second of clicking on a link whether the destination page has coherency.

Visitors respond to incoherent pages with a variety of gut reactions, and none of them are flattering. In the extreme, such pages can be experienced as tacky, cheesy, bewildering, or obnoxious. Unfortunately, you have probably seen hundreds of examples before.

Who you are screams so loudly in my face, I can't hear a word you are saying.

—RALPH WALDO EMERSON

Low-coherency landing pages affect visitors on an emotional level, and no amount of logic will convince them to stay. And that may be a pity, because the content may be relevant to their needs. But they can't get past the cognitive dissonance to even focus on the intended message. Incoherent and unprofessional pages also give most consumers a low confidence in the product.

Review the best practices in Chapter 8, "Best Practices for Common Situations," to make sure that everything works smoothly together. The visual design of the page is particularly important. This includes consistent color palettes; professional graphics in the same visual style; consistent font sizes, colors, and families; and the amount and layout of the writing.

The coherence of the landing page can also be related to the connection of the path a visitor took to arrive on the page. Say you've been using four sets of task labels to drive visitors in a coordinated campaign between PPC and ad retargeting, where the ad banner creative is rewritten based on that searchers' previous behavior. If you've provided this personalization to hone in on a prospect, how coherent would it be to start using internal-speak as soon as they actually click? Does the landing page carry the same brand signals as the previous banners (remember, neither has really been read yet)? For this component of coherence, see the "Connected" section later in this chapter.

Coherency means all of the supporting elements contribute to a unified whole. Because of this, coherency-related elements should often be grouped into a single unified look-and-feel element and tested as a unit that governs the visual experience of your landing pages. The need for high coherency is an excellent reason to consider whole-page redesigns (especially in low data rate environments). This allows you to fix all known visual problems in one shot. At large companies, details of good coherence might be captured in brand or visual design brief documents, and reflected in standard HTML or CSS coding libraries. At smaller companies, founding documents like marketing plans may be a good starting point for online coherence.

If fine-granularity elements are used, the tester can unwittingly decrease the coherency of the landing page. This happens in two primary ways: mixing and conflict.

Let's assume that all of the elements you decide to test on your original page have significant problems—that is, of course, the reason you chose them in the first place. You spend considerable time writing your test plan document and coming up with better alternatives for each of the original elements, and you succeed. Each of the new elements is *in isolation* indeed better than its original counterpart. In fact, when they are all collected together in a highly coherent new whole they become even more synergistic and powerful.

Unfortunately, if you are running a typical multivariate test, the new elements will be mixed and matched at random with other elements that were part of your original design. When this kind of mixing occurs, the new elements may actually suffer by their combination with poor-quality original elements (or vice versa). They will be judged not on their own merits, but by the company that they keep. In such cases the new elements will look worse than they really are. They may even seem worse than their original counterparts due to the fact that the mixing produced a wider range of quality differences on the page. In other words, the original design elements may have been mediocre, but they were all roughly equally mediocre. The introduction of a new element into this mix brought the quality difference into even sharper contrast, thus making the overall design seem worse.

Since all elements are shuffled randomly in the testing process, it is critical to consider in advance how nearby combinations of elements may appear, and to anticipate potential problems.

For example, let's assume that you have a landing page that includes a call-to-action button, long descriptive text, and a second call-to-action button with different text. Your test plan contains alternatives for the last two elements. In your brainstorming, you decide that since most people won't read the long descriptive text, the alternative is to remove it altogether (a reasonable variant to test). You also figure that having a consistent call-to-action is important for the strength of your messaging, and decide to use the same call-to-action copy on both buttons (also a reasonable course of action in isolation).

However, based on this multivariate test plan, a quarter of your audience will see a version of the page that includes two back-to-back copies of the first call-to-action button without any text. Most visitors will think that your landing page is broken or coded sloppily. In either case, they will probably have a negative reaction to it. So both the removal of the descriptive text and the repetition of the first call-to-action is a bad mix in the overall test. This example was fairly obvious, but this type of test design mistake is common among inexperienced testers.

Audience Segmentation

There are two different outlooks on whether to segment your audience for testing. One group insists that you should test for the winning combination of elements separately for each traffic source. The other suggests that you aggregate all your available acquisition traffic together for purposes of testing. Both are correct depending on the main focus of your testing:

Content and Offer Focus If you are primarily focused on tuning elements of your offer (such as price, promotions, or service levels), the traffic source can become important.

If you know something about the demographics and psychographics of your online campaigns, you may want to test different elements (such as sales copy or the way your incentive is framed) for each major traffic source. Similarly, if you are attracting visitors with diverse needs to specially themed landing pages, the page content should be tailored to the intended audience segment. It is important to note that you should still have a high enough data rate to test each segment. Depending on the scale of your traffic, it is possible that you will only be able to do this on your largest campaigns, or not at all.

Function and Usability Focus If your focus is on more functional and usability basics, there is probably little difference across your online channels. For example, fixing the clunky checkout process on your e-commerce site will positively impact all of your visitors. In such cases, it is best to combine all traffic so you can conduct larger or faster tests. In effect, you are tuning for the best possible performance across your most representative and realistic mix of traffic.

The two approaches can be combined. For example, let's assume that your visitors land on a large number of landing pages that all share a common structure. You can first tune across all traffic sources to fix your functional and usability issues with the page template and then tune the message and content of the pages for each specific audience.

If your ultimate conversion action may be in the future and the conversion decision is a complicated one, you also have to consider segmenting by the changing role of your visitors over time.

Web analytics attribution tools can help determine common paths visitors might be taking for a more expensive or high-commitment conversion. They might make multiple, short visits as they cautiously nibble at the content bait on your site. Subsequently there might be an AIDA role transition from a researcher (desire) to a purchaser (action). There is a fine balance between pushing them too fast and drawing them along too slowly. With these visitors, you'll also need to consider how, when, and where you are encouraging them to return to the site. So don't forget to test the "connective tissue" between visits (such as the content of your e-mail communication during this time).

Longevity

Another key consideration is the longevity of the elements that you are considering. The value of a landing page change depends on how well it will hold up into the future. Changes to time-sensitive promotions or special offers may cause a significant conversion improvement, but they will be short-lived. By contrast, changes that fix underlying problems will continue to provide benefits for the lifetime of the design.

You should test both types of elements, but even smaller improvements to elements with high longevity will deliver high conversions over time.

More transient elements need to be retested more frequently to make sure that they retain their effectiveness, or rotated to account for seasonal factors. Additional issues for testing highly seasonal elements are discussed in the "Not Accounting for Seasonality" section of Chapter 15, "Avoiding Real-World Pitfalls."

Baggage

Many of the ideas for possible tuning elements that you come up with in your brainstorming may be much better than the corresponding originals. However, some of them may have baggage. In other words, it may not be possible to test them through your efforts or those of your team alone. They may require resources or cooperation from others who may not be available to you for a number of reasons:

- **Turf** Elements that you may want to test are controlled and jealously guarded by others (such as your advertising agency, webmaster, brand managers, or IT). See Chapter 13, "Assembling Your Team and Getting Buy-in," for a detailed discussion of the various roles involved.

- **Skills** You don't have access to the outside experts needed to help create certain elements (such as usability reviewers or professional graphic designers).

- **Resources** A significant amount of money or staff time is required to implement the elements (such as web design, copywriting of new content, or programming).

- **Approval** The approval process to make certain changes is bureaucratic, time-consuming, and onerous (such as legal reviews).

- **Schedule** The creation of certain elements would introduce long delays (such as programming functional changes).

Such practical considerations should definitely be a part of your decision making. If you feel that you have plenty of other ideas that may yield significant conversion rate improvements, you may want to leave the baggage out of your current test plan. You can always include some of the elements you skipped in a follow-up test once you have established a track record of success. However, if the changes are important enough, you may want to push them through anyway, despite the political cost and effort involved.

Selecting Elements to Test

Not all things on your landing page matter. A few key changes to your page could result in the biggest conversion rate improvement. This implies that there are a large number of trivial changes that will not help at all. Since you don't know ahead of time which those are, you must resign yourself to the fact that not all of your testing ideas will pan out. In fact, some of your elements may already be great performers, and your proposed alternatives will actually drag down conversion rates during the test.

Here's one key thought to keep in mind: "Your mileage may vary." Do not automatically copy recent changes that your competitors have incorporated in their sites. They may not know what is best, or their audience may respond differently than yours. The only way to be sure is to test on your own audience. There have been classic cases where the market leader in an industry actually had a much worse site design than their smaller challenger. Testing allowed that challenger to take and hold the lead.

Landing page testing can be like emergency room triage—you have to prioritize the most critical issues first. Don't occupy yourself with unimportant matters and neglect priorities during a crisis. There is no point fixing some superficial problem when something more fundamental undermines its effectiveness.

You have to use your current landing page as a starting point. No one can tell you where your biggest deficiencies currently are. However, they usually fall into several closely related classes of problems, which we'll explore in this section.

Page Structure

Page structure is closely related to both coherency and emphasis. It defines how the real estate on your page is organized and used. By changing the sizes and positions of various page sections, you can also dramatically impact the emphasis that key areas receive.

If you have a number of similar landing pages for specific content topics, you may not have enough traffic on a particular one to conduct a landing page test. However, it is often possible to combine traffic from all of your pages and test the elements related to their common page structure.

Typical page structure testing elements include the following:

- Size and contents of page header
- Size and contents of page footer
- Size and location of page navigation
- Placement of trust symbols and credibility logos
- Separation of page shell and navigation from page content
- Size and location of forms or other calls-to-action
- Mirror images (swapping) of key page sections (such as a form located to the left of the text or to the right)
- Vertical stacking versus horizontal arrays of page sections
- Single versus multiple columns

The location of your navigation is closely tied to the number of columns on your page. In general, try to use vertical menus because horizontal menus take up more valuable vertical screen real estate. Since people do not like to read wide text blocks, vertical menus also enhance readability by making the page content narrower on wide-screen monitors.

Information Architecture

Information architecture basically creates an accurate mental map of how your site works, and how the visitor can interact with it.

Typical information architecture–related test elements include

- Self-selecting by role or by task
- Clear and distinct descriptive link text and choices
- Sensible and prominent page titles
- Breadcrumbs or orienting context ("you are here")
- Consistent placement of all page elements
- Navigation (organization of menu options)
- Number of available choices presented
- Alternative navigation methods
- Cross-linking to other key information
- Availability and format of on-site search
- Ability to avoid, minimize, reverse, or easily correct mistakes (such as on-page error checking or context-sensitive form fields)

Presentation

Presentation mainly has to do with the *format* in which you deliver your message. Although it is a close cousin of both page structure and emphasis, it has its own distinct flavor.

Typical presentation testing elements include

- Degree of detail (such as full text, or links to supporting information)
- Writing format (prose, length of text)
- Choice of input elements (such as radio buttons or pull-down lists)
- Action format (such as buttons, text links, or both)
- Editorial tone of your writing
- Use of alternative formats and modalities (such as charts, figures, audio clips, video, presentations, or demos)

Emphasis

Emphasis is about the *relative* importance that you place on something. Resist the temptation to pump up the volume on everything, since this just annoys, stuns, or distracts your visitor. Instead, try to selectively focus attention on the key elements on your page and de-emphasize everything else.

Typical emphasis testing elements include

- Amount of screen real estate devoted to an item
- Use and size of relevant images (such as specific product or believable people)
- Image captions
- Font sizes and font families (such as headline sizes)
- Font emphasis (such as italics, bolding, underlines, background colors, text colors, or capitalization)
- Background color blocks or background images
- Call-to-action button shapes, sizes, visual styles, and effects (such as beveling, borders, or drop shadows)
- Visual separators (such as horizontal rules)
- Use of whitespace and visual isolation to focus on important items
- Removal of distracting secondary information

Testing Multiple-Page Flows

We covered some best practices for multiple-page flows in Chapter 8. This section is designed to give you some additional perspective on testing them since multiple page flow testing presents its own unique challenges.

It is common in linear flows (such as registrations or checkouts) to ask for the least invasive and personal information first. By starting small, your visitors are drawn in smoothly and painlessly. By the time you ask for the bigger commitments (like credit card details), they already have a lot of investment in the process and are much more likely to continue.

A common testing element is the number of steps in the flow. In some cases (if you have fewer fields on your conversion form), you may want to squeeze all of the input onto one page. The conversion action can then be labeled something like "instant one-step." Another approach is to break up the process into multiple pages. Each page can then contain a small and nonthreatening micro-action that is easily completed by visitors on their way to the ultimate goal.

In general, flows should exhibit certain characteristics, which we'll cover in this section.

Systematic

The Matrix described earlier provides a framework of *who* needs to accomplish *what* on your site and makes sure that visitors have the *proper support* at every step along the way. When identifying problems with your current site, you should note any missing or incomplete parts of The Matrix for your campaign. Now is the time to rectify the situation.

Imagine that you are trying to get your visitors to cross a rickety rope bridge over a wide chasm. In terms of attention spans on the Web, you are requiring a significant commitment on the part of your visitors. If you do not put in place a series of solid and reasonably spaced planks, most people (except for a very determined few) will not make it across to the conversion goal on the other side. It's a tenuous path with the risks of too much space between planks or not enough planks.

You should consider testing changes to your site that will fill in the missing pieces. Sometimes doing so will require creating significant new content (such as wizards, demos, or videos), but often you will only need to reorganize content that already exists. Finally, you need to put the copy and labels in the language of your visitor (instead of your company).

Connected

Even if all of the cells in your Matrix have been properly filled in, this is not enough. There must be strong and obvious connections between adjacent steps to maintain or increase the visitor's momentum toward the conversion goal.

Researchers Peter Pirolli and Stuart Card at the Palo Alto Research Center (formerly known as Xerox PARC) have worked for many years on their *information foraging* theory. It describes how people hunt for information on the Web much like wild animals in search of their prey. They follow *information scent* to determine if they are getting closer to their goal. They will keep clicking on additional links if they feel that the scent is getting stronger. Otherwise, they might simply give up and start foraging somewhere else (your competitor's website, for example, or a search engine).

The information scent is conveyed by clues in the immediate environment, especially in links and the connections between pages. To enhance this information scent:

- Make in-content and navigation link text clear and objective.
- Describe exactly what visitors will see on the destination page.
- Match the title on the destination page with the inbound link text used.
- Do not use cute language, made-up words, or industry jargon in link text.
- Do not use generic link labels such as Click Here or Learn More.
- Restrict your link text to scannable short phrases (do not create links out of long sentences).
- Lead people to more specific information with each click (since they try to zero in on their goal).
- Provide feedback about visitors' current context and their position in the big picture.

Your visitors' process may have started somewhere other than on your site, unless they typed in your URL directly. In such cases, the landing page should match their expectations. If this consistency is lost, you may appear unreliable or worse, underhanded and spammy, to your visitor. Echo the search term (or inbound link text) on your page, or take visitors to the most relevant starting page possible. Unique steps might be needed to bring the varying ad, social media, and search messages to the central hub of a campaign. A visitor following a specific message should bypass all of the more generic information near the top of your site, and deep-link closer to their intended goal. Once the visitor gets to the site, the path to the goal must be evident and encourage the reader to progress at their own speed. Again, we rely on conventions to signal the progress they expect to see.

If you are using graphical buttons to advance visitors through a process, follow the language conventions listed earlier for button labels. In addition, consider augmenting your buttons with identical text links just below. Some people will overlook larger graphics but will respond to the humble text link. Get rid of nonessential buttons like the common form "Reset." If you absolutely *must* have more than one button, follow proper conventions (such as the button on the left should represent the primary desired action, with the others serving as exceptions). You can also use different button colors or sizes to indicate relative importance or to shift the visual focus.

Flexible

Unfortunately, even a well-connected and systematic Matrix is not enough. In reality, many of your visitors will not follow an orderly progression along the neat and well-marked little paths that you have laid out. They may jump around, they may back up, or they may leave and return much later (after forgetting most of their previous interactions with your site).

The Stranded Parachutist

Imagine that your website visitor is a parachutist who was blown off course in the middle of the night. He crash-lands and breaks through the roof of your house, and lands in the middle of a particular room. He is completely disoriented and knows nothing about his surroundings. There are several closed doors leading out of the room.

What have you done to prepare for these kinds of unexpected guests? Have you left enough clues and markers to quickly guide them to their goal with a minimum of confusion, disorientation, and frustration?

Many visitors will not even arrive at your front door. They will enter on pages deep within your site that were never designed as starting points for your conversion process (such as previously bookmarked pages, links in blogs, or from organic search results).

You can do several things to prepare for the random entry points and unpredictable visitor behavior:

- **Provide Context** It is important to provide consistent global navigation on your site. In addition, you should provide "you are here" information via breadcrumbs. Alternatively, you can include a map showing progress and the current step in a linear process. Provide cross-links to important pages in your conversion process from all deep-linked content pages that might serve as entry points into your site.

- **Allow Detours** Don't prevent visitors from wandering off the conversion path and looking around. Heavy-handed corralling could be reflected in bounce rates. Always let visitors back up or easily undo actions that they have recently taken. Include obvious cross-links to return them to various points in the conversion path.

- **Support Return Visits** Use cookies or other tracking methods to record your visitors' behavior. If they have previously filled in some information on a particular page, always save and repopulate it upon their return. If they asked for notification for a trial or whitepaper, return them to the closest category. If you normally collect information in a linear fashion, try to piece it together opportunistically instead. Sometimes the order in which it is entered is not important; as long as you end up with all of the required information by the end of the conversion action, you should not insist that it be collected in a predetermined particular sequence. Yes, this is a bit more of a pain from a programming standpoint, but it is your visitors who are buying your product, not your software developers.

Timeless Testing Themes

There are certain commonalities on what leads to consistent conversion improvements. These are not specific prescriptions, but rather promising areas and directions for your own testing explorations. Not surprisingly, all of the testing themes are directly related to the AIDA decision process stages described in Chapter 3, "The Matrix—Moving People to Act."

Less Is More

Although the general idea of uncluttering is powerful throughout the decision process, this testing theme has an especially powerful impact on improving visitor awareness. If visitors do not recognize quickly that you have something in which they might be interested, they will leave your site immediately. In Figure 9.1 you can see a web analytics report showing distribution of visit lengths to a site.

Length of Visit	Visits	Percentage of all visitors
0-10 seconds	758	55.65%
11-30 seconds	98	7.20%
31-60 seconds	108	7.93%
61-180 seconds	168	12.33%
181-600 seconds	134	9.84%
601-1,800 seconds	77	5.65%
1,801+ seconds	19	1.40%

Figure 9.1 Web analytics report on length of visit

The bars show an initial bump, and then a bell-curve shape with the peak at 61–180 seconds. This amount of time spent on a non-news site is impressive. However, the big bump at the top indicates that over 55 percent of visitors punched out within 10 seconds. They represent a significant lost opportunity.

Within this problem lies the potential for greater page focus and increasing the number of people who have meaningful interactions with your site.

Less is more applies to a whole range of test elements:

- Fewer and smaller graphics
- Shorter bulleted text
- Reduced number of choices and links

"Less Is More" is an exercise in editing: Instead of creating alternatives to the original page's elements, you should consider doing away with them altogether.

Cut until you can't stand it any more, and then cut some more. You will be surprised at how little content is needed on a well-designed landing page. Don't be afraid to try radically stripped-down alternative test elements. You can also consider the number of steps to a conversion instead of providing an overloaded content buffet. The assumption that a visitor is interested in sorting and self-selecting from larger volumes is a fallacy.

Case Study—RealAge.com

RealAge.com has developed a unique test that determines the biological age of your body based on how well you have maintained it. The whole business depends on the number of people who sign up for the free RealAge Test. RealAge had already tested a number of ideas to improve the efficiency of the sign-up process and thought that they were doing well because of their high (double-digit) conversion rate. Here is the original page. How could the conversion rate of the sign-up process improve even more?

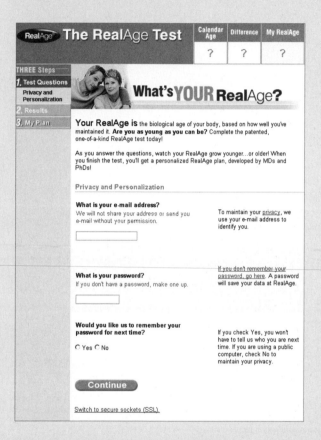

SiteTuners identified 12 variables that might improve performance, among them the page header, navigation bar, headlines, sales copy, call-to-action, graphics, and button format. For each variable, the original version was included in the test, along with one or more alternatives. The variables and values tested resulted in 552,960 unique recipes (versions of the page).

At the end of the test, the best alternative champion design was run head-to-head against the original baseline and showed a 40 percent lift in conversion rate. The bottom-line impact of this change on RealAge was significant. This is the champion design.

continues

If you compare the two pages, at first glance you might conclude that the two pages basically look the same.

However, upon careful inspection, you will note that many simplified page elements ended up in the final solution:

- A smaller and simpler header graphic
- Removal of the left navigation menu
- A shorter headline
- A different graphic (a calendar with question mark instead of the photo of a couple)
- Shorter lead-in sales copy
- Shorter question labels
- Removal of the question explanation text
- A single background color for questions (instead of alternating for each question)

In fact, the only added or expanded element that made it into the winning solution was the list of media mentions on the left side. This is no surprise since these brand logos function as credibility signals for the visitor.

Although the individual element changes are subtle, the combined effect of the simplified page is powerful. However, although only one original element ended up as part of the winning recipe, that does not mean all the alternative tuning element ideas were good. In fact, many variable values hurt performance during the test and were weeded out along the way. It takes a combination of good ideas and statistical testing to find the best answer.

Personalize It

Personalization builds desire and affinity for your particular solution. Customization can be a powerful conversion tool. Personalization can be tested using a wide array of available tactics. Here are some examples:

- Echo the searcher's keywords as the page title for your landing page (consider dynamic keyword insertion).

- Prepopulate your search box with the text of the keywords that visitors used to find your landing page.

- Present localized content by using geo-targeting information.

- Tailor the results for the context of use, whether it's an operating system (for example, Mac-compatible product versions for Mac users) or a device (mobile sites).

- Do not require people to log in if they have been there before.

- Allow common cross-system logins like Open ID or Facebook Connect.

- Fill in checkout information for returning e-commerce buyers.

- Customize content by visitor role once someone has self-selected.

- Retain audience segment information and continue to customize content for repeat visitors.

- Allow visitors to configure your product or service offering.

- Display deeper or richer content to those who have shown enough commitment (based on page views or time on your site).

- Show last-minute special offers or alternatives via exit pop-ups to visitors who are about to leave your site without converting.

- Follow up by phone or e-mail if someone abandons your registration process partway.

- Proactively initiate a live chat session if your visitor is clearly struggling with something on your site.

Some of these testing elements require the use of a content management system and multiple session tracking, or even tie-ins to your customer relationship management (CRM) or sales force automation (SFA) systems. New segmentation, targeting, and business trigger capabilities are also becoming increasingly common in web authoring tools. But even without these, many personalization tuning elements can be implemented with the use of simple cookies and information extracted from the visitor's browser environment settings.

Test the Offer

Ultimately, it is your offer that gets a visitor to act. However, when considering specific testing elements you have a lot of ways to influence someone:

- The primary offer
- The total solution surrounding the offer
- Headline
- Sales copy
- Images chosen
- Defaults
- Call-to-action text and graphical format
- Repetition of the call-to-action in multiple screen locations and formats
- Offer context (such as by bracketing the desired action in a bronze/silver/gold set of options or time constraints)
- Limited availability (such as deadlines or remaining inventory)
- Other potential concessions (such as training with a purchase or discounts for volume)

Pricing is also a vital part of the offer and will be discussed in more detail in the next section.

Soothe the Nerves

A common theme is how much work you're doing to push the visitor past hesitations and anxieties about nearly any action online. Even the term *download* brings anxieties about malware, install troubleshooting, or new technical learning challenges.

Demonstrating that lots of people, ideally friends or peers, value the site is one effective technique. Verifications of good standing and other signals of authority take the offer out of isolation. They infer trust by placing the website in the context of a larger reliable network. Showing the success of typical audience members further strengthens the visitor's resolve. For example, the nonprofit Kiva restricts donations to small amounts and then uses a goal completion icon to show how close a recipient is to a target amount, combining like-party lenders in a community.

These techniques are reflected on a landing page through

- User reviews
- Indicators of high standing in common social media platforms (MVP status, fans, or likes)
- Affiliations, awards, verifications, and other trust emblems

- Customer, client, or patient quotes of an experience favorable to the largest audience type
- People shots where the image subject shares traits of the common audience member

Price Testing

Technically, testing price is simply a component of the offer. But because of its powerful influence on purchase conversions, and other particular qualities, it deserves a separate closer look. It is difficult to price-test when discussing a whole portfolio of products in a large e-commerce catalog. This section describes a single-product purchase (or a single product with a single upsell).

The advantage of price testing on the Web is that you have several desirable conditions:

- Large numbers of new prospects who have not been exposed to your company before
- Ability to easily modify pricing displayed to a particular visitor
- Ability to hold all other factors constant
- End-to-end tracking and immediate recording of the sale

However, a host of possible issues make price testing potentially problematic even on the Web:

- Seasonality
- Changing supply-demand imbalances
- Product obsolescence
- Degree of commoditization
- Reactions of your competitors

Because of this shifting environment, it is important to regularly retest your price to detect any significant changes. Although we refer to product pricing in this section, the same applies to services pricing as well. True price testing is still something of a "Wild West" situation in practice. The following summary will give you a framework for how to approach it.

Qualitative Methods

There is a whole industry centered on pricing and profit optimization. Most companies in this field are consultants and have an array of qualitative methods to determine the correct price.

Some common approaches and considerations are

- Expert judgments
- Primary research
- Benchmarking
- Internal data analysis
- User or sales prospect focus groups
- Product lifecycle

Pricing consultants have radically different approaches. Some are more evidence based, whereas others prefer more intuitive "soft" considerations.

Quantitative Methods

At the end of the day, whatever pricing you come up with via qualitative approaches, you would still have to test the predicted best price point on your actual visitors. This section gives you an overview of common methods that can be used on your landing page.

Price Testing Basics

All of the website elements that we have discussed so far in this book have something in common: They are *discrete variables*. In other words, they involve distinct choices. Should you have a red button, a blue one, or a green one? Should you use your current page headline or a new one? Should you offer free shipping with product purchase or not?

Focusing only on discrete variables overlooks an important class of variables that can also dramatically improve conversion rates. *Continuous variables* can theoretically be set to an infinite number of different values. One of the most important continuous variables is the price of a product. Price can be varied over a wide range in one-cent increments. There is no way to properly guess the exact value that will give you the highest profits.

A typical price/profit curve for a single product looks like an inverted "U" shape (see Figure 9.2). At the lower end, your profits will be zero because you have no profit margin left. In other words, the price of the product equals your cost to produce and deliver it. At this point, it does not matter how many people buy—there is no profit to be made. At the higher end, your profits will also approach zero because the price will be too high and you will not have any customers.

Of course, the shape of the profit curve will vary widely depending on your specific situation. It may have a flat top and gentler fall-off at the shoulders. Setting the wrong price can have disastrous consequences for the success of your product or service. Your goal should be to set the price at (or near) the profit sweet spot at the top of the curve.

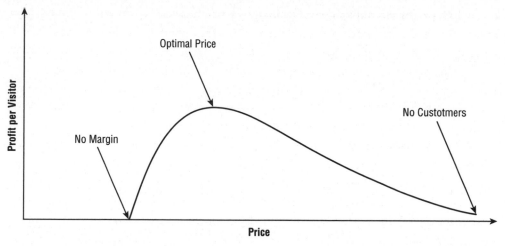

Figure 9.2 Typical profit curve as a function of product price

There are several common approaches to finding the right price, and we'll examine those next.

Spot Testing

Most companies treat price as a discrete variable. If you try to test price as a discrete variable (for example, you test three distinct prices—your current price, a specific lower price, and a specific higher price), you are only getting information about the *exact* prices you choose to test. You will know which one of the tested prices is best. But you will not know if *any* of them are at the best price for maximum profit. The only advantage to this approach is that it works with your landing page optimization tools and can be tested like all the other discrete variables. If your only alternative is not to test price at all, you should use spot testing—a little bit of something is better than a whole lot of nothing.

The situation is even more difficult with upsells. Because of the strong variable interactions between the base product and the upsell, it becomes difficult to test reasonable combinations of the base product price and the upsell price by using spot tests (see the "Price Elasticity Modeling" section later in this chapter for an alternative method).

Walking the Price Curve

As we mentioned earlier, the typical single product profit curve looks like an inverted "U" shape. Many companies conduct informal price testing by "walking" this curve. They change the price and measure the results. If it improves, they incrementally change the price again in the same direction (either raising it more or lowering it more depending on the circumstances). Eventually they will overshoot the top of the curve and experience a decline in profits. At that point they back up to the previous price and lock that in as their winner.

This approach has significant drawbacks. First, it can be time consuming. Depending on the size of the price change increment that you choose, you may have to run several back-to-back tests. The lost opportunity cost of being at suboptimal pricing for the length of these tests can be significant. Second, there is no clear way to decide on how to calculate your price change increment. Some companies use a fixed amount, whereas others use a percentage of the current price. Regardless of the approach, if you choose incorrectly, you will either require many tests (as mentioned earlier) or not find the top of the profit curve because your increment is too large. Third, pricing changes are done sequentially. Once a change is made, everyone sees the new price. Sequential sampling should be used as a last resort. You don't know what outside factors have impacted price across all of your tests.

Price Elasticity Modeling

It is possible to build a model of the predicted sales conversion rate as a function of price. Such price elasticity models are constructed using a variety of mathematical approaches, and they include different assumptions at their core. But the basic idea is the same. If you can predict what percentage of people will buy your product at a given price, and you know your costs at any price point, you should be able to calculate your profit per visitor for all prices.

It is possible that your current price is already close to the profit optimum, especially if the top of the profit curve is pretty flat across a wide range of prices. Since the model also predicts the conversion rate at a given price, you can consciously make the trade-off between higher market share and perceived exclusivity in such cases. In other words, you can choose a lower price and more customers, or a higher price and fewer customers while still maintaining a near-optimal profitability per visitor.

Price elasticity modeling also works for a product with a single upsell option. Within this configuration you need to determine the revenue-per-visitor optimal pricing for both the base product and the upsell. The upsell can be displayed in parallel (shown side by side on the same page) or serially (shown on a subsequent page once someone has decided to buy the base product).

Single-Product Price Elasticity Model

This example shows the original price and two bracket prices that are randomly presented to new visitors. If the profit maximum falls between the two bracket values, you can create a model for all of the intermediate prices. From this you can determine where the top of the profit curve lies. You then conduct a head-to-head test of the original price against predicted best to verify results.

This chart shows the results of a single-product price test.

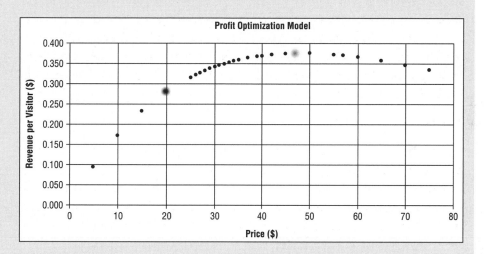

The original e-book product price was $20. Even though fewer units were sold at the profit optimum price of $47, it was actually 37 percent higher in terms of revenue (and profit) per visitor.

Parallel and serial presentations can result in radically different pricing models. Parallel presentations tend to show stronger influences between the base product and upsell since they appear near each other on the same page. Serial models are more independent, because the visitor has already decided to "open their wallet" for the base product, and is then presented with the upsell. As a result, it is best to independently find the best price settings for the parallel and serial models, and then pick the one that produces the highest profit per visitor.

Single Product with Upsell Price Elasticity Models

In this chart, the optimal pricing for the base product alone would have suggested a $36 price point.

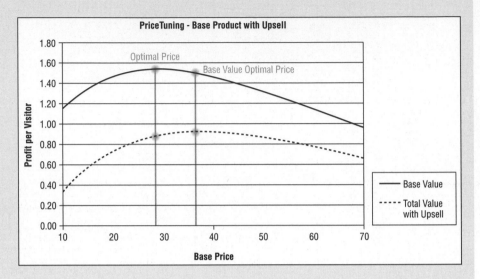

However, when you take the value of the upsell into account at different base prices, the best price point for the base product turns out to be $28. If left uncorrected, this mistake can cost the client approximately 5 cents in profit for every visitor (a large sum considering the traffic to their landing page).

Now that you have a framework for what to test, in the next part of the book we will focus on the mechanics of testing. This topic includes the math of testing, preparation of your content, and various testing methods.

The Mechanics of Testing

IV

Landing page testing is one of the most powerful techniques available in your conversion improvement arsenal. In this part of the book we will discuss some of the common questions relating to testing, how to best prepare your content for testing, and the actual testing methods.

Chapter 10   **Common Testing Questions**

Chapter 11   **Preparing for Testing**

Chapter 12   **Testing Methods**

Common Testing Questions

In the previous chapter you learned how to select elements for landing page tests. Our focus was on how to pick elements that would have the greatest impact on your landing page performance. We are sure that you can't wait to get started.

But how do you interpret the results of your tests? To understand the power and limitation of testing methods, you first need to grasp the basics of the underlying math.

CHAPTER CONTENTS

Lies, Damn Lies, and Statistics
Crash Course in Probability and Statistics
Have I Found Something Better?
How Sure Do I Need to Be?
How Much Better Is It?
How Long Should My Test Run?

Lies, Damn Lies, and Statistics

> *There are three kinds of numbers: lies, damned lies, and statistics.*
>
> —MARK TWAIN, quoting Benjamin Disraeli

The statistics branch of mathematics has a poor reputation among the public. Much of modern science and economics is based on it in a fundamental way. So is public policy. Since public policy is a matter of priorities and heated debate about the allocation of government budgets, statistics has gotten pulled into the fray to support or undermine various political positions. Unscrupulous or ignorant people have corrupted it for their own purposes.

While there is nothing wrong with statistics itself, there are many common misuses of it. In this section, we survey these misuses along with some implications for landing page tuning.

As additional background we recommend *Rival Hypotheses: Alternative Interpretations of Data Based Conclusions* (HarperCollins, 1979) by Schuyler W. Huck. The book describes one hundred social sciences experiments along with the possible experimental problems that may cast doubt on, or completely invalidate, the reported results.

Throwing Away Part of the Data

Statistical studies are based on a confidence level in the answer (commonly 95 percent). If you conduct a large number of experiments, even two identical effects can seem different based simply on a statistical streak. For example, if you flipped a coin five times you might be surprised to see it come up heads every time and might even suspect that it could be loaded. However, this is exactly the result that you would expect based simply on random chance about 3 percent of the time. So if this experiment was repeated one hundred times, a series of all-heads would be expected to come up about three times.

Unscrupulous people might rerun the experiment many times and report a single all-heads result as proof that the coin was loaded. By discarding the remaining experiments that did not support their desired conclusion, they are misrepresenting the results.

As you will see in Chapter 12, "Testing Methods," there are sometimes valid (or at least practical) reasons to hold out some of the data that you collect during a landing page test. But do not cherry-pick and only look for data that supports your conclusions.

Biased Samples

Statistics assumes that a random selection of test subjects was drawn from the population in question. However, samples can be biased by oversampling or undersampling from certain groups. In extreme cases, no representatives are drawn from a particular subset of the population.

For example, online or call-in polls are often skewed by definition. They represent self-selecting groups of people who are motivated enough to answer the polls. This usually implies that they have a strong opinion and want to express it. So these types of polls tend to produce more polarized results with a disproportionately large percentage of extreme views (at the expense of the more moderate outlook of the silent majority).

Let's take a look at some common types of sampling bias.

Traffic Filtering

In landing page testing, you generally want to get as wide a range of traffic sources as possible. That way, they are more likely to be representative of your visitor population as a whole. However, you generally want traffic sources that are recurring, controllable, and stable. If your traffic does not have these characteristics, it may be hard to tune. For this reason, you may want to remove unstable sources (such as some of your larger but highly variable affiliates or volatile social networking traffic) from your testing mix. You should also generally remove nonrecurring e-mail traffic.

Data Collection Method

Let's assume that you have picked appropriate filters for your traffic and are selecting the largest possible stable group among your population of visitors. If you have implemented your test properly, then each new visitor should be assigned at random to see one of the alternative versions of your landing page. However, even this sample may not be completely random because of technology considerations.

For example, many testing tools (see the Appendix, "Landing Page Testing Tools," for a partial list) require visitors to have JavaScript turned on in their web browser and to accept *first-party cookies* (small files left on the visitors' hard disks by the website in question, which contain information about their visit and can be used to customize and personalize their experience upon return visits). If a visitor does not meet these technical criteria, they are not included in the test and are simply shown the original landing page.

Based on current web usage statistics, these technical requirements disqualify fewer than 5 percent of Internet users. When your test is completed, you are forced to make some assumptions about how that 5 percent will react to your new page design. You assume that they will act like the other 95 percent that you are able to track. But this may not be true. Since they have JavaScript or first-party cookies turned off, they may represent a small, self-selecting group of people who are more cautious, technically savvy, or concerned with privacy. Such people may indeed behave differently than the rest of the population. As a practical matter, this does not change your recommendations very much. Since the missing 5 percent represents such a small segment, even a significant difference in their behavior will be overwhelmed by the much larger conversion rate improvements that you usually uncover among the sampled visitors. However, it is important to be aware of such technical sampling issues.

Sequential Testing

Another type of sampling bias can be introduced by sequential testing. For example, you may test your original design for a month, and then replace it with another one during the following month. It is hard to reach any conclusions after this kind of experiment. Any number of external factors may have changed between the two testing periods. For example, there may have been a holiday with common family vacations, some major breaking news that affected your industry, or a major public relations announcement. The point is you are comparing apples to oranges. In landing page testing you should always try to collect data from your original version and your tested alternatives in parallel. This will allow you to control for (or at least detect and factor in) any changes in the external environment. Only use sequential testing as a last resort.

Short Data Collection

Even if you run your tests by splitting the available traffic and showing different versions of your site design in parallel, you may still run into biased sampling issues related to short data collection periods. Experiments involving very high data collection rates may be especially prone to this.

For example, let's assume that you are testing two alternative versions of your page and are measuring clickthroughs to a particular target page as your conversion action. Because of the high traffic to your landing page, you collect about 10,000 conversion actions in the first hour of your test. This data shows you that one of your versions outperforms the other to a very high level of statistical confidence. Many people would conclude the test at this point and immediately install the best performer as the new landing page.

But what if we were to tell you that the data was collected in the middle of the night? You might correctly conclude that people visiting your site during the day are a different population, or at least that they behave differently then. The same is true of weekday (accessing the Internet from work) versus weekend (accessing the Internet from home) traffic. Regardless of your data rate, you should collect data for at least a one-week period (or multiple whole-week increments if your data rate is low). This will allow you to get rid of the short-term biases discussed earlier. Of course, this does not address the question of longer-term seasonality (which will be covered in more detail in the "Not Accounting for Seasonality" section of Chapter 15, "Avoiding Real-World Pitfalls").

Overgeneralization

Overgeneralization is the erroneous extension of your test conclusions to a setting where the original results no longer apply. For example, let's say that you set up an experiment to count the ants in your kitchen and tracked it for a full week during a record cold spell in the wintertime. Your finding was that there were no ants in the kitchen at all during the study period. However, it would probably be incorrect to assume that the same would hold true during a heat wave in the summer. Often the overgeneralization is not made by the original researcher, but rather by those who subsequently summarize or cite the results.

A common overgeneralization in landing page testing is to assume that traffic sources that were not part of your original test will behave in the same way as the tested population. For example, if you see a particular effect with your PPC traffic, you should not assume that it will hold up when you expose the new landing page to your in-house e-mail list.

Loaded Questions

The answers that people give in surveys can be manipulated to skew the results in a certain direction. This is done by asking the question in a certain way, or preceding it with information that will support the desired answer.

For example, imagine a survey that is polling about support for a salary raise for local firefighters. Depending on which side of the issue the pollster was on, you might imagine two different questions:

- Given the chronic neglect of city streets and the rising crime rate due to the understaffing of our police force, do you support a raise for our firefighters at this time?
- After considering the extraordinary risks that firefighters face every day to protect your family and property, do you support a raise for our firefighters at this time?

In normal surveying, loaded questions and the context for how the information is presented can be a problem. But in landing page testing, you stand this premise on its head. You *want* to create loaded landing page content. In fact, your whole goal is to see what your audience responds to best. A cynic might even say that landing page testing is the scientific and systematic discovery of the best audience manipulations available to you.

False Causality

> *Correlation does not imply causation.*
> —COMMON SCIENTIFIC SAYING

This saying does not use the word *imply* in its common sense (that is, to suggest). The scientific sense of *imply* (taken from formal logic) can be better translated as *require*. If reread this way it can be paraphrased as "because effects are related or occur together, one does not necessarily cause the other." There may be a third previously unrecognized lurking variable (also called a confounding variable, or confounding factor) that causes the other two.

For example, if we told you that the vast majority of car accidents occur within five miles of people's residence, you might be tempted to start taking the bus instead of driving. But it would be wrong to conclude that accidents are caused by the proximity to your home. There is a third confounding variable that could explain both: People do the vast majority of their driving close to home, and accidents are directly related to the time spent driving.

In landing page optimization, many people insist on extracting so-called "learnings" from their test results. Hindsight is used to rationalize why a particular landing page version had a higher conversion rate. For example, you may test two call-to-action buttons: orange and green. If the green one performs better, you may be tempted to conclude that your audience likes the color green more than orange. In fact, there may be another explanation: the contrast of the button color with the main color theme of the page. If your page was predominantly orange themed, the orange call-to-action button would seem muted and may get lost in a scene composed of similar colors. The green button may perform better not because of the actual color used but because the contrasting color sticks out and seems more prominent.

There may also be more subtle issues relating to other design changes that were also made at the same time. For example, the green button may have been a different size, or perhaps it used a different color for the call-to-action text. It may have been these look-and-feel factors rather than the button color that increased the propensity of people to act.

Trying to rationalize results after the test is a dangerous activity because it may cause you to inappropriately fixate on elements of your design that had nothing to do with the performance improvement. You should try to restrain yourself from engaging in this kind of after-the-fact myth construction.

Crash Course in Probability and Statistics

Let's go back to the roots of the statistics underlying landing page testing. Within the vast field of mathematics, we will guide you down to the specific subset that you will need to understand. Along the way, we will point out the specific relationship to landing page optimization. And since landing page testing is often a messy business, we will also flag where real-world considerations and issues deviate from the theoretical framework. This drill-down is a quick overview. You may need to do some additional background reading in the areas of probability and statistics.

Probability Theory

Probability theory is a branch of mathematics that deals with the description and analysis of random events. The key building blocks of this framework are as follows:

Random Variables A *random variable* is a quantity whose value is random or unpredictable, and to which you can assign a probability distribution function. The *probability distribution function* determines the set of possible values that can be assigned to the random variable, along with their likelihood. The total of all possible outcomes' likelihood must by definition equal one (that is, one of the possible outcomes must happen, and its value will be assigned to the random variable).

Let's use a fair gaming die as an example. The top face of the die can take on one of six possible outcomes (1, 2, 3, 4, 5, 6). The probability distribution function is uniform (there is an equal one-in-six chance of any value between 1 and 6 coming up). When you sum all of the possible probabilities, they add up to exactly one.

Stochastic Processes There are two kinds of processes considered in probability theory: deterministic and stochastic. A *deterministic process* will go along a set path depending on its starting conditions. In other words, if you know where it starts, you can exactly compute where it will end up at some point in the future.

A *stochastic process* (also called a random process) is more difficult to understand. You cannot tell exactly where it will end up, but you know (based on its probability distribution function) that certain outcomes are more likely. In the simplest case, a stochastic process can be described as a sequence of samples from random variables. If these samples can be associated with particular points in time, it is a *time series* (a series of data points that were measured at successive times).

In our die example, the stochastic process is the repeated roll of the die. Each roll will produce a random variable outcome (one of the six possible values), and successive rolls are independent of each other (what was rolled on the previous attempt has no influence on the likelihood of any particular number coming up on the next roll).

Events An *event* in probability theory is a set of all possible outcomes to which a probability is assigned (also called the sample set). In the simplest case, the set of possible outcomes is finite. Each of the basic possible outcomes is called an elementary event, but more complex events can be constructed by selecting larger groupings of elementary events (a proper subset of the sample space).

In our die example, the elementary events are individual possible values of a die roll. But you can also construct other events and assign the proper probabilities to them (for example, an even roll of the die—with a probability of one-half—or a roll with a value greater than 4—with a probability of one-third).

Probability Applied to Landing Page Testing

So how does all of this apply to landing page optimization?

The random variables are the visits to your site from the traffic sources that you have selected for the test. As we have already mentioned, the audience itself may be subject to sampling bias. The probability distribution function is pretty simple in most cases. You are counting whether or not the conversion happened as a result of the visit.

You are assuming that there is some underlying and fixed probability of the conversion happening, and that the only other possible outcome is that the conversion does not happen (that is, a visit is a Bernoulli random variable that can result in conversion, or not).

As an example, let's assume that the actual conversion rate for a landing page is 2 percent. So there is a small chance that the conversion will happen (2 percent), and a much larger chance that it will not (98 percent) for any particular visitor. As you can see, the sum of the two possible outcome probabilities, as required, exactly equals 1 (2% + 98% = 100%).

The stochastic process is the flow of visitors from the traffic sources used for the test. Key assumptions about the process are that the behavior of the visitors does not change over time and that the population from which visitors are drawn remains the same. Unfortunately, both of these assumptions are routinely violated to a greater or lesser extent in the real world. The behavior of visitors changes due to seasonal factors, or with changing sophistication and knowledge levels about your products or industry. The population itself changes based on your current marketing mix. Most businesses are constantly adjusting and tweaking their traffic sources (for example, by changing PPC bid prices and the resulting keyword mix that their audience arrives from). The result is that your time series, which is supposed to return a steady stream of yes or no answers (based on a fixed probability of a conversion), actually has a changing probability of conversion. In mathematical terms, your time series is *nonstationary* and changes its behavior over time.

The independence of the random variables in the stochastic process is also a critical theoretical requirement. However, the behavior on each visit is not necessarily independent. A person may come back to your landing page a number of times, and their current behavior would obviously be influenced by their previous visits. You might also have a bug or an overload condition where the actions of some users influence the actions that other users can take. For this reason it is best to use a fresh stream of visitors (with a minimal percentage of repeat visitors if possible) for your landing page test audience. Repeat visitors are by definition biased because they have voluntarily chosen to return to your site and are not seeing it for the first time at random. This is also a reason to avoid using landing page testing with an audience consisting of your in-house e-mail list. The people on the list are biased because they have self-selected to receive ongoing messages from you, and because they have already been exposed to previous communications.

The event itself can also be more complicated than the simple did-the-visitor-convert determination. In an e-commerce catalog, it is important to know not only whether a sale happened, but also its value. If you were to tune only for a higher conversion rate, you could achieve that by pushing low-margin and low-cost products that people are more likely to buy. But this would not necessarily result in the highest profits.

Some tests involve tuning for the highest possible revenue per visitor (or profit per visitor after considering the variable costs of the conversion action). For these kinds of situations, you need to consider real-valued random variables and their cumulative distribution functions. That discussion is more involved and is beyond the scope of this book.

Law of Large Numbers

The *law of large numbers* states that if a random variable with an underlying probability (p) is observed repeatedly during independent experiments, the ratio of the *observed* frequency of that event to the total number of experiments will converge to p.

Let's continue with our die rolling example. The law of large numbers guarantees that if you roll the die enough times, the percentage of sixes rolled will approach exactly ⅙ of the total number of rolls (that is, its expected percentage in the probability distribution function). An intuitive way of understanding this is that over the long run, any streaks of rolling non-sixes will eventually be counteracted by streaks of rolling extra sixes.

The exciting thing about this law is that it ties something that you can observe (the actual conversion percentage in our test) to the unknown underlying actual conversion rate of your landing page. It guarantees the stable long-term results of the random visitor events.

However, before you start celebrating, it is important to realize that this law is based on a *very* large number of samples and only guarantees that you will over the long term *eventually* come close to the actual conversion rate. In reality, your knowledge of the actual conversion rate will accumulate slowly.

Moreover, the law of large numbers does not guarantee that you will converge to the correct answer with a small amount of data. In fact, it almost guarantees that over a short period of time, your estimate of conversion rate will be incorrect. Short-term streaks can and do cause conversion rates to significantly deviate from the true value.

The best way to look at this situation is to keep in mind that collecting more data allows you to make increasingly more accurate estimates of the true underlying conversion rate. However, your estimate will always be subject to some error; moreover, you can know only approximate bounds on the size of this error.

The Normal Distribution

The *Gaussian*, or *normal*, distribution (also commonly called the *bell curve* because of its characteristic shape) occurs commonly in observations about science and nature. The exact shape and position of the bell curve is defined by two parameters: the position of its center point, and how wide it is. The bell curve can be tall and almost needle-like, or a wide low smudge (as shown in Figure 10.1).

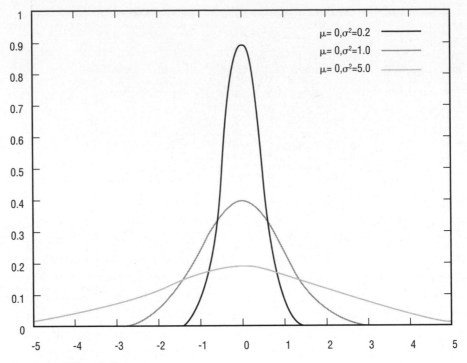

Figure 10.1 Different bell curve shapes

The shape and position of the curve are described by the following parameters.

Mean (μ) The *mean* is the sum of all of the random variables divided by the number of random variables observed. It also commonly called the "average" value.

Variance (σ^2) The *variance* shows how spread out or scattered the values are around the mean. If they are tightly clustered, then the variance is lower. If they are very spread out, then the variance is higher.

Standard Deviation (σ) A standard deviation is defined as the square root of the variance. It is often more useful than the variance itself since it is directly comparable to the underlying measurement.

The *unit* normal distribution is a special case of the more general Gaussian distribution. Basically, a particular Gaussian distribution can be standardized (by moving its mean to zero and magnifying or shrinking it so that it has a standard deviation equal to 1). Normalizing a particular bell curve allows you to easily compare its properties to those of other bell curves. The area contained under any normal distribution is always one by definition.

The 68-95-99.7 rule (also called the *empirical rule*) tells you that for a normal distribution almost all values lie within three standard deviations of the mean (see Figure 10.2).

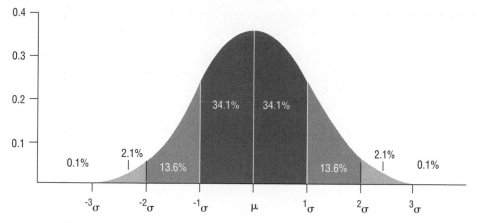

Figure 10.2 The normal distribution

About 68 percent of the values are within one standard deviation of the mean ($\mu \pm \sigma$). About 95 percent of the values are within two standard deviations of the mean ($\mu \pm 2\sigma$). About 99.7 percent of the values lie within three standard deviations of the mean ($\mu \pm 3\sigma$). For many scientific and engineering purposes, the 95 percent confidence limit is commonly used as the dividing line for making decisions. In other words, if your answer falls into the plus or minus two standard deviation band around a predicted value, it is considered to be consistent with the prediction.

The Central Limit Theorem

The *Central Limit Theorem* tells you that regardless of the distribution that the original random variables were drawn from, if that distribution has a finite variance, their average will tend to conform to the normal distribution. This is the case across a wide range of real processes, including data collection in landing page testing.

The Central Limit Theorem assures you that the conversion rate estimate that you observe for a particular landing page design will look like a normal distribution. This allows you to estimate the probable range of values for the actual underlying conversion rate. The more data you collect, the tighter your estimate will become.

Statistical Methods

One of the common questions answered by statistics is whether a relationship exists between some predictors (independent variables) and the response or resulting effects (the dependent variables). Often, your experiments can be arranged so that when you detect such a relationship, you can say that changes in the independent variables caused the changes in the dependent variables. There are two main types of statistical studies:

Experimental Studies In *experimental studies* you first take measurements of the environment that you are studying. You then change the environment in a preplanned way and see if the changes have resulted in a different outcome than before.

Landing page testing is a form of experimental study. The environment that you are changing is the design of your landing page. The outcome that you are measuring is typically the conversion rate. As we mentioned earlier, landing page testing and tuning is usually done in parallel, and not sequentially. This means that you should split your available traffic and randomly alternate the version of your landing page shown to each new visitor. A portion of your test traffic should always see the original version of the page. This approach will eliminate many of the problems with sequential testing.

Observational Studies Observational studies, by contrast, do not involve any manipulation or changes to the environment in question. You simply gather the data and then analyze it for any interesting correlations between your independent and dependent variables.

For example, you may be running PPC marketing programs on two different search engines. You collect data for a month on the total number of clicks from each campaign and the resulting number of conversions. You can then see if the conversion rate between the two traffic sources is truly different or possibly due to chance.

The basic steps of any scientific experiment are well known. We have summarized them next with notes on their applicability to landing page testing. Chapter 14, "Developing Your Action Plan," covers these steps and all of the other required landing page testing activities in more detail.

Plan the Research Determine the landing page to tune, your traffic sources for the test, and the traffic levels available. Understand and try to correct for or eliminate any sampling biases among your population.

Design the Experiment Create a written test plan that explicitly lays out the alternative landing page elements that you intend to test (your independent variables). Define the performance measurement that you will be trying to improve (typically the conversion rate for a key process on the landing page).

Collect the Data You will need to collect the number of visits or impressions for your test pages as well as the number and value of any conversions.

Summarize the Data Use descriptive statistics (see the next section) to summarize your findings. Hide unnecessary levels of detail.

Draw Conclusions Use inferential statistics (see the next section) to see what information can be gleaned from your data sample about the underlying population of visitors on your landing page. Normally this would involve statistical tests to see if any of your alternative landing page designs are better than the original.

Present the Results Document and present the results of your experiment. This can be a casual e-mail or a detailed formal report, depending on your circumstances and purpose.

Applied Statistics

Statistical theory (also known as *mathematical statistics*) is based on probability theory and mathematical analysis, and is used to understand the theoretical basis of statistics. Applied statistics falls into two basic types:

Descriptive Statistics *Descriptive statistics* is used to summarize or describe a collection of data. This can be done numerically or graphically. Basic numerical descriptions include the mean, median, mode, variance, and standard deviation. Graphical summaries include various kinds of graphs and charts.

Inferential Statistics *Inferential statistics* is used to reach conclusions that go beyond the specific data that you have collected. In effect, you are trying to infer the behavior of the larger process or population from which you drew your test sample. Examples of possible inferences include answers to yes-or-no questions (hypothesis testing), as well as other techniques like Analysis of Variance (ANOVA), regression analysis, and many other multivariate methods such as cluster analysis, multidimensional scaling, and factor analysis.

Both types of applied statistics are commonly used in landing page testing and tuning. Unfortunately, descriptive statistics are often viewed as a substitute for the proper inferential tests and are used to make decisions. Remember, descriptive statistics only summarize or describe the data that you have observed. They do not tell you anything about the meaning or implications of your observations. Proper hypothesis testing must be done to see if differences in your data are likely to be due to random chance or are truly significant.

Have I Found Something Better?

Landing page optimization is based on statistics, and statistics is based in turn on probability theory. Probability theory is concerned with the study of random events, but a lot of people might object that the behavior of your landing page visitors is not "random." Your visitors are not as simple as the roll of a die. They visit your landing page for a reason and act (or fail to act) based on their own internal motivations.

So what does probability mean in this context?

Let's conduct a little thought experiment. Imagine that we are about to flip a fair coin. It has the potential to be in one of two states (heads or tails). What would you estimate the probability of it coming up heads to be? Fifty percent, right? So would we.

Now imagine that we have flipped the coin and covered up the result after catching it. The process of flipping is now complete, and the coin has taken on one particular state. Now what would you estimate the probability of it coming up heads to be? Fifty percent again, right? We would agree because neither of us knows any more than before the coin was flipped.

Now imagine if we peeked at the coin without letting you see it. What would you estimate the probability of it coming up heads to be? Still 50 percent, right? How about us? We would no longer agree with you. Having seen the outcome of the flip event we would declare that the probability of coming up heads is either zero or 100 percent (depending on what we have seen).

How can two parties experience the same event and come to two different conclusions? Who is correct? The answer is—both of us. We are basing our answers on different available information. Not having seen the outcome of the flip, you must assume that the coin can still come up heads. In effect, for you the coin has not been flipped, but rather remains in a state of pre-flipped potential. We know more, so our answer is different. So probability can be viewed as simply taking the best guess given the available information. The more information you have, the more accurate your guess will become.

Let's look at this in the context of the simplest type of landing page optimization. Let's assume that you have a constant flow of visitors to your landing page from a steady and unchanging traffic source. You decide to test two versions of your page design, and split your traffic evenly and randomly between them.

In statistical terminology, you have two stochastic processes (experiences with your landing pages), with their own random variables (visitors drawn from the same population) and their own measurable binary events (either visitors convert or they do not). The true probability of conversion for each page is not known, but must be between zero and one. This true probability of conversion is what you normally call the conversion rate and you assume that it is fixed.

From the law of large numbers you know that as you sample a very large number of visitors, the measured conversion rate will approach the true probability of conversion. From the Central Limit Theorem you also know that the chances of the actual value falling within three standard deviations of your observed mean are very high (99.7 percent) and that the width of the normal distribution will continue to narrow (depending only on the amount of data that you have collected). Basically, measured conversion rates will wander within ever narrower ranges as they get closer and closer to their true respective conversion rates. By seeing the amount of overlap between the two bell curves representing the normal distributions of the conversion rate, you can determine the likelihood of one version of the page being better than the other.

One of the most common questions in inferential statistics is to see if two samples are really different or if they could have been drawn from the same underlying population as a result of random chance alone. You can compare the average performance between two groups by using a t-test computation. In landing page testing, this kind of analysis would allow you to compare the difference in conversion rate between two versions of your site design. Let's suppose that your new version had a higher conversion rate than the original. The t-test would tell you if this difference was likely due to random chance or if the two were actually different.

There is a whole family of related t-test formulas based on the circumstances. The appropriate one for head-to-head landing page optimization tests is the *unpaired one-tailed equal-variance t-test*. The test produces a single number as its output. The higher this number is, the higher the statistical certainty that the two outcomes being measured are truly different. It is very easy to compute and requires only basic spreadsheet formulas.

How Sure Do I Need to Be?

Online marketers often make the mistake of looking only at the descriptive statistics for their test and neglect to even do basic inferential statistics to see if their answers are due simply to random chance. They often do not have the knowledge or discipline to specify the desired confidence in their answer ahead of time, and to patiently collect enough data until that level of confidence is reached.

There are three common issues associated with lack of statistical confidence.

Collecting Insufficient Data

Early in an experiment when you have only collected a relatively small amount of data, the measured conversion rates may fluctuate wildly. If the first visitor for one of the page designs happens to convert, for instance, your measured conversion rate is 100 percent. It is tempting to draw conclusions during this early period, but doing so commonly leads to error. Just as you would not conclude a coin could never come up tails after seeing it come up heads just three times, you should not pick a page design before collecting enough data.

What many people forget is that there can (and should) be short-term streaks that significantly skew the conversion rates in low data situations. Remember, the laws of probability only guarantee the accuracy and stability of results for very large sample sizes. For smaller sample sizes, a lot of fuzz and uncertainty remain.

The way to deal with this is to decide on your desired confidence level ahead of time. How sure do you want to be in your answer—90, 95, 99 percent, even higher? Your level of certainty completely depends on your business goals and the consequences of being wrong. If a lot of money is involved, you should probably insist on higher confidence levels.

Let's consider the simplest example. You are trying to decide whether version A or B is best. You have split your traffic equally to test both options and have gotten 90 conversions on A and 100 conversions on B. Is B really better than A? Many people would answer yes, since 100 is obviously higher than 90. But the statistical reality is not so clear-cut.

Confidence in your answer can be expressed by means of a *Z-score*, which is easy to calculate in cases like this. The Z-score tells you how many standard deviations away from the observed mean your data is. In other words, it is the same as the number of standard deviations in the test's normal distribution. The Z-score therefore follows the 68-95-99.7 rule that we discussed earlier. Z=1 means that you are 67 percent sure of your answer, Z=2 means 95.28 percent sure, and Z=3 means 99.74 percent sure.

Pick an appropriate confidence level, and then wait to collect enough data to reach it.

Let's pick a 95 percent confidence level for our earlier example. This means that you want to be right 19 out of 20 times. So you will need to collect enough data to get a Z-score of 2 or more.

The calculation of the Z-score depends on the standard deviation (σ). For conversion rates that are less than 30 percent, this formula is fairly accurate:

$\sigma = \sqrt{(\text{Conversions})}$

In our example for B, the standard deviation would be calculated as follows:

$\sigma = \sqrt{(100)} = 10$

So you are 67 percent sure (Z=1) that the real value of B is between 90 and 110 (100 plus or minus 10). In other words, there is a one out of three chance that A is actually bigger than the lower end of the estimated range, and you may just be seeing a lucky streak for B.

Similarly, at your current data amounts, you are 95 percent sure (Z=2) that the real value of B is between 80 and 120 (100 plus or minus 20). So there is a good chance that the 90 conversions on A are actually better than the bottom end estimate of 80 for B.

Confidence levels are often illustrated with a graph. The *error bars* on the quantity being measured represent the range of possible values (the confidence interval) that would include results within the selected confidence level. Figure 10.3 shows 95 percent confidence error bars (represented by the dashed lines) for our example. As you can see, the bottom of B's error bars is higher than the top of A's error bars. This implies that A might actually be higher than B, despite B's current streak of good luck in the current sample.

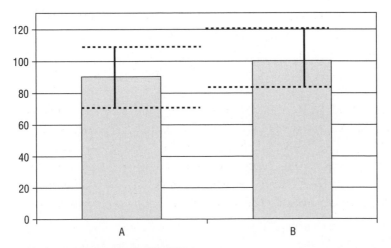

Figure 10.3 Confidence error bars (little data)

If you wanted to be 95 percent sure that B is better than A, you would need to collect much more data. In our example, this level of confidence would be reached when A had 1,350 conversions and B had 1,500 conversions. Note that even though the ratio between A and B remains the same, the standard deviations have gotten much smaller, thus raising the Z-score. As you can see from Figure 10.4, the confidence error bars have now "uncrossed," so you can be 95 percent confident that B actually is better than A.

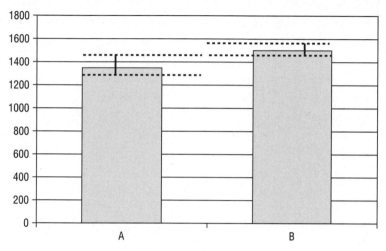

Figure 10.4 Confidence error bars (more data)

All of this may seem a little intimidating at first, but the math for these calculations can easily be programmed into a spreadsheet formula. After that, you just plug in the current test numbers and see if your desired confidence level has been reached yet. Believe us; this is preferable to making wrong decisions one-third of the time as you might have done in this section's example.

Confusing Significance with Importance

In the preceding section we discussed how people often want to believe that large effects are statistically significant when they do not have enough data to support such a conclusion. Because of their lack of statistical literacy, many people also make the converse mistake—they believe that just because they have found something statistically significant, it is also practically important.

The word *significant* in statistical terms means only that you have high enough confidence in your answer. It does not mean that the effect found in your test is large or important. If you collect a large enough data sample, even tiny differences can be found to be statistically significant. Most people would probably not get excited if the difference between two landing page versions on which they collected test data for a long time turned out to be extremely small (yet significant to the required confidence level).

Even if you reach a high level of statistical confidence, you may not have found an effect that is interesting in practical terms.

Understanding the Results

The *null hypothesis* in probability and statistics is the starting assumption that nothing other than random chance is operating to create the observed effect that you see in a particular set of data. Basically it assumes that the measured effects are the same across the independent conditions being tested. There are no differences or relationships between these independent variables and the dependent outcomes—equal until proven otherwise.

The null hypothesis is rejected if your data set is unlikely to have been produced by chance. The significance of the results is described by the confidence level that was defined by the test (as described by the acceptable error "alpha-level"). For example, it is harder to reject the null hypothesis at 99 percent confidence (alpha 0.01) than at 95 percent confidence (alpha 0.05).

Even if the null hypothesis is rejected at a certain confidence level, no alternative hypothesis is proven thereby. The only conclusion you can draw is that some effect is going on. But you do not know its cause. If the experiment was designed properly, the only things that changed were the experimental conditions. So it is logical to attribute a causal effect to them.

However, as we have already discussed, there are often subtle and gross sampling bias and test design errors in landing page optimization, and the documented effects can also be attributed to these. Under such conditions you can only strictly state that there is a high degree of correlation between the tested changes and the corresponding outcomes, but not true causality. Having said that, online marketing is an applied discipline that has to earn its keep, so don't let such considerations dissuade you from using statistics to run your tests. We just feel obliged to point out the specific deviations from the pure underlying math.

What if the null hypothesis is not rejected? This simply means that you did not find any statistically significant differences. That is not the same as stating that there was no difference. Remember, accepting the null hypothesis merely means that the observed differences *might* have been due simply to random chance, not that they *must* have been. Statistics cannot prove that there was no difference between two test conditions. The absence of evidence for a difference does not provide any evidence for the notion that no difference exists.

How Much Better Is It?

Internet marketing produces a detailed and quantifiable view of your online campaign activities. As we discussed earlier, most numbers produced fall under the general category of descriptive statistics. Descriptive statistics produces summaries and graphs of your data that can be used for making decisions. The descriptive information has to do with the value of a particular quantity as well as its variability (how scattered it is). Unfortunately, most people focus only on the measured average value and completely ignore the variability. This is a major problem that continues to persist because people confuse the precision of the observed effects (the ability to measure conversions during the test) with the precision of describing the underlying system (the ability to draw conclusions and make predictions about your landing page visitor population as a whole). You should not generally quote the observed improvement as a certainty. Even though you've observed an exactly computable conversion rate improvement percentage, you don't know what it really is for your visitor population as a whole.

Exact measurement of observable effects does not imply that you know anything about the underlying process.

By itself, the mean of an observed value can be misleading, especially at small sample sizes. The situation gets even murkier if you are trying to model two separate means (each with its own variance). The situation gets downright ugly if you are trying to compute a ratio of such numbers. Yet this is exactly what is required to estimate a percentage improvement between two landing page versions.

Figure 10.5 shows the results of an A-B split landing page test conducted by an online marketing educational publication.

Page Layout Optimization Micro-Test		
Metric	Page A	Page B
Unique Visitors	2478	2384
Orders	36	65
Conversion Rate	1.45%	2.73%

What You Need To UNDERSTAND: Conversion of Page B (one column) was 88% better than that of Page A (two columns).

Figure 10.5 Summary and conclusions from a published landing page test

Based on a sample size of 36 conversions for page A and 65 conversions for page B, you are told to conclude that the conversion rate improvement is 88 percent. Indeed, we would probably be happy with such a result. But let's take a closer look.

Let's assume that you want a 95 percent confidence in your answer. This corresponds to a Z-score of 2, meaning that the number must fall within two standard deviations of the observed mean. If you compute the 95 percent confidence interval numbers on the number of conversions for both landing pages, you will find the following:

Page A: 36 ± 12 (the interval from 24 to 48)

Page B: 65 ± 16 (the interval from 49 to 81)

Let's take a look at the best-case scenario:

Conversions: A = 24, B = 81

Conversion rates: A = 0.97%, B = 3.40%

Conversion rate improvement: 251%

Now let's take a look at the worst-case scenario:

Conversions: A = 48, B = 49

Conversion rates: A = 1.94%, B = 2.06%

Conversion rate improvement: 6.2%

There is some rationale for reporting the conversion rate improvement based on the ratio of the means. Since more of the mass of the normal distributions lies close to the mean, the actual numbers are more likely to be near it. However, this should not be used as a reason to abandon the use of error bars or confidence intervals. Both the 6.2 percent and 251 percent conversion rate improvements are within the realm of possibility based on the confidence level that you had selected. There is a huge range of possible outcomes simply because the sample size is so small.

 To focus only on the observed improvement and to report it as a certain quantity is problematic, especially for small sample sizes.

All online marketing educators are walking a fine line. We are trying to get at least a basic level of mathematical literacy across to our audiences. However, if the going gets too rough, many online marketers will just tune out and give up on the math altogether. We are somewhat torn. On the one hand, it is good to use some kind of statistical benchmarks. On the other hand, "a little knowledge is a dangerous thing" and can be easily misapplied during landing page optimization.

The bottom line is this: Take the time and care to properly collect and analyze your data. When faced with uncertain measurements (basically all of the time), display them with error bars or confidence ranges.

How Long Should My Test Run?

We are often asked how long a landing page optimization test should last. The answer depends on the following factors:

- The data rate (number of conversions per day)
- Size of improvements found (percentage improvement)
- Size of your test (number of alternative designs)
- The confidence in your answer (how sure you need to be)

We have already covered the last factor in the "How Sure Do I Need to Be?" section. Let's take a look at the other ones next.

Data Rate

The data rate describes how quickly you collect data during your test. Many people are familiar with common metrics of web traffic such as the number of page views or the number of unique visitors. The volume of traffic for landing page optimization tests is best measured in the number of conversion actions per day (and not the number of unique visitors).

Another way of thinking about this is that conversions are very scarce and are the limiting factor. Unique visitors are relatively plentiful and do not tell you anything by themselves. You are simply splitting them up randomly and showing them different versions of the landing page. Websites with low conversion rates require more visitors to reach valid statistical conclusions.

A significant portion of your testing bandwidth (typically 15–50 percent depending on your circumstances) should also be directed to the original or *control* version of your website. This allows you to compare the performance of alternative recipes against a known baseline, even if that baseline continues to move around due to seasonal factors.

Probabilistic tests yield results slowly and require a lot of conversions to find the best results. In Chapter 12, we will give some guidelines for minimum data rates that are appropriate for different tuning methods.

So what can you do if your data rate is too low and no additional traffic sources are available?

You can decrease the size of your test. As discussed in the previous chapter, this can be done by decreasing the granularity of your test elements. In the simplest case, you may have to run a simple head-to-head test of your original page and one alternative version. The coarsest possible level is to do a comprehensive redesign of your landing page (with all of your best alternative design ideas included in it).

Another strategy is to measure different conversion actions. Sometimes, more plentiful measurable actions occur *upstream* of your current one (on preceding pages earlier in the visitor's interactions with your site). Since there are more of them, these intermediate actions can be used to bulk up your data rate.

For example, your e-commerce catalog may have too few sales, and your shopping cart abandonment rate is 90 percent. This implies that you have 10 times as many shopping cart "puts" as sales. This allows you to tune the main catalog experience up to the point that a visitor puts an item in their cart. If you assume that the shopping cart abandonment rate does not change, you can assign 10 percent of the average sale value on your site to each shopping cart put. You can then run your test and count the more numerous puts as the conversion action.

Size of Improvements Found

If you managed to uncover a clearly superior version of your landing page, the performance improvement would quickly become apparent. Often, an initial round of changes will fix some of the obvious problems and improve performance significantly. This will leave you with more subtle improvements in subsequent tuning tests. The cumulative impact of several small improvements (in the 1–5 percent range) can still be very significant. However, it can take much longer to be able to validate these smaller effects to the desired confidence level. Since you do not know the size of the possible improvements ahead of time, the length of the time required for the tuning test may vary significantly.

Of course, the amount of data collected also influences whether the difference found is considered significant. Table 10.1 shows the size of effects that can be reliably identified (to a 95 percent confidence level) at various sample sizes.

▶ **Table 10.1** Size of improvements and sample sizes required to identify them at a 95 percent confidence level

Sample size	Size of improvement
100	20%
1,000	6.3%
10,000	2%
100,000	0.63%

As you can see, resolving small effects requires a lot more data.

You typically know your available data rate and need to decide on an acceptable length of data collection for your test. Let's assume that you have about 500 conversions per month and are willing to spend two months on data collection. As a rough guide based on Table 10.1, you will be able to identify 6.3 percent improvement effects in your head-to-head test. Any found improvements smaller than that will be deemed inconclusive.

Size of Your Test

The size of your test can be measured by the size of the search space that you are considering. The search space is the whole universe of alternative designs possible in your test. A simple head-to-head test has a search space size of 2 (the original, and the alternative landing page version that you are testing). If you are testing multiple elements on the page, you need to multiply together the number of alternative versions for each one. For example, if you are testing three headlines, four offers, and six button colors, then there are 72 possible versions ($3 \times 4 \times 6 = 72$) in your test. As you increase the total number of elements and the number of alternatives for each one, the possible number of versions grows very quickly (geometrically).

The amount of data required to reach conclusions scales with the size of your search space. As you will see in Chapter 12, many testing approaches cannot practically be used in tests beyond a few dozen total recipes because they would require too much time to reach a reasonable confidence level. Since you can control the size of your search space, it is usually scaled to your data rate and the testing method that you have chosen in order to complete in the allotted amount of time while still finding reasonable size effects.

In the next chapter, we will examine the various ways to prepare your content for testing.

Preparing for Testing

In theory, theory and practice are the same. In practice, they are not.

— Attributed to Albert Einstein

"Just test it!" is a great and often heard refrain— if it were only that easy.... In this chapter we will explore the complexities of managing the different versions of your test content and address common testing problems.

11

Chapter Contents

Overview of Content Management and Testing

Content Management Configurations

Common Testing Issues

Overview of Content Management and Testing

Let's look at the basic components necessary to run a landing page test.

Content Management System

The purpose of a content management system (CMS) is to manage all of the pieces of content that make up a website or landing page. These include HTML code, Cascading Style Sheets (CSS), images, videos, and site organization features such as menus. They range from simple one-person blogs to huge systems for enterprise publishing that support multiple users in various roles, workflows, content syndication, localization and multiple languages, and much more.

At the lower end are a number of free and open source tools. At the enterprise level, picking a system can easily involve millions of dollars in migration, setup, training, and ongoing support costs. Some companies choose to buy off-the-shelf commercially supported systems, whereas others have evolved their own proprietary CMSs to support specific web publishing or workflow requirements.

Often, proprietary "hooks" are created to dynamically pull in data from outside sources and display it on the website. Data can also be exported to various supporting systems such as customer resource management (CRM), data warehousing, or web analytics.

Special-purpose CMSs exist in the form of e-commerce shopping cart packages (for online catalogs), wikis and collaborative workspaces (for group projects and information sharing), blogs (for self-publishing), and many others.

It goes without saying that the CMS a company chooses will have major implications for the ease of use in creating, maintaining, and changing content. Some systems are brittle, and seemingly simple content changes can have unintended consequences that often ripple through the whole website. Such systems make it difficult to test since a huge amount of time is consumed in debugging and testing changes to make sure that no problems were created by their introduction. Other systems are forgiving and are created in a modern object-oriented fashion that allows for easy changes to both local and sitewide content.

Testing Server

A testing server is the software (or dedicated machine) that runs and manages your landing page test. Common responsibilities of testing servers are

- To decide which version of your content to display to a new visitor
- To keep track of returning visitors and display a consistent user experience to them across multiple visits
- To collect data on any resulting conversion actions and their value

- To make periodic algorithmic changes to the mix of content being shown
- To determine the best-performing version and announce a winner of the test along with some measures of statistical confidence in the strength of evidence found to support its conclusions

Some testing servers also have built-in content management systems. Others are strictly a "black box" for running the test. A detailed look at testing methods and their important features is presented in Chapter 12, "Testing Methods."

Web Server

A web server is an Internet-connected computer that listens to content requests and fulfills them. It can be thought of as a responsive switchboard that fetches required files and objects at the request of people on the other end of a web browser (which we describe next).

The web server has several common jobs:

- Responds to inbound request for various data objects and files
- Locates and returns requested resources as quickly as possible
- Signals when appropriate resources cannot be located
- Documents all activities in detailed logs

The web servers can be viewed as being closely tied to the servers housing the CMS for the website. In other words, the web servers will typically sit in front of the CMS server on the computer network and act as a switchboard and a traffic director to handle requests from the outside world.

For the purposes of the rest of the chapter, we will refer to the combined CMS plus the web server as simply the web server.

Web Browser

The web browser serves as the graphical and functional rendering engine that finally displays a requested web page on a device under the control of your web visitor. Most often this device is a personal computer. But increasingly web browsers are built into netbooks, tablets, smartphones, or in-store kiosks.

These are the common responsibilities of a web browser:

- Requests files and information from web servers (see the previous section)
- Communicates with the web servers until the appropriate resource has been received (since each requested file is typically sent in small pieces, they must be properly received and reassembled in the correct order)
- Combines several resources and interprets their internal structure and appropriate visual representation

- Renders and displays the resulting web page
- Maintains supporting information (cookies) from the originating website in order to provide a consistent experience to returning visitors

Browsers work on different operating systems, including various flavors of Microsoft Windows, Mac OS, Android, Linux, and many others. Because they rely on the speed and capabilities of the underlying device, web browsers have very different capabilities. Some support Adobe Flash, for example, whereas others (most notably products from Apple) don't. Processor speed, Internet connectivity speed, and screen resolution are also important underlying factors in the total browsing experience.

New features are being constantly vetted and introduced by various standards bodies, and they gradually make their way into the latest browser versions. For example, it is expected that HTML 5 will be incorporated into most leading browsers in the near future. However, there are plenty of people with older machines and browser versions out there "in the wild." This leads to incompatibilities and compromises, since not all browsers display information the same way. Properly constructed "pure" HTML code is rare, and all browsers attempt to fill in the gaps by interpreting the coder's intentions and trying to gracefully display their appropriate best guess at the answer. Some browsers are notoriously incompatible and out of touch with the mainstream practice. They often require custom coding on the part of the web designer to detect a specific browser version and work around its limitations and quirks.

Content Management Configurations

There are three main configurations possible when deciding on or configuring your testing infrastructure. The basic difference among them has to do with where content is created and stored for the test, and how the page is constructed.

The three configurations are:

- Client-side page rendering
- Server-side page rendering
- Intercept page rendering

Each of the approaches has its own advantages and disadvantages and will be discussed in more detail in the following sections.

Client-Side Page Rendering

In client-side page rendering, the burden of swapping in the correct content and building the page is handled by the web browser. The typical sequencing and data flows of a client-side landing page test are illustrated in Figure 11.1.

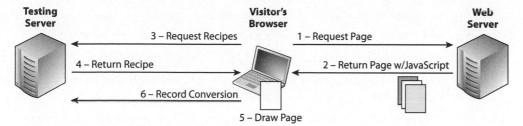

Figure 11.1 Client-side testing

Let's examine this flow in more detail:

1. The visitor's web browser requests a page from the web server.

2. The web server returns the requested page. This single page has all of the possible variants of the content embedded in it (or at least has the ability to reference them from somewhere else on the Web and pull them in later). In other words, the page is constructed with some internal JavaScript code "switches" inside of it. It can suppress or hide any unneeded versions later when the visual rendering of the page takes place.

3. The browser then calls out to the testing server and asks it which unique version of the page to show to the new visitor. If a repeat visit is occurring, then the same version as the one shown during the prior visit is shown again. This information is retrieved from a web browser cookie (usually a first-party cookie originating from the web server associated with the site and not blocked or disabled by most web surfers).

4. The testing server returns the *recipe*—a short code describing the exact version of the page to display.

5. The web browser executes the JavaScript code on the previously returned page and displays the appropriate configuration of the page.

6. If a conversion action subsequently happens, additional JavaScript on the post-conversion page "fires," notifying the testing server with the details of the conversion.

Many testing tools use client-side approaches similar to the one just described.

Pros

The advantage of the client-side approach is that no CMS is necessary to manage multiple versions of the content. Simple JavaScript "switches" are inserted into the page and can be retrofitted to nearly any static website or landing page.

Cons

There are several drawbacks to this approach:

- Extra JavaScript code needs to be added to the page just to enable the content swapping. Although this code is relatively lightweight in terms of the file size, it will still impact page download times.

- Redundant content is included in the page. There is some waste inherent in this approach since multiple versions of the content are imbedded in the page, yet only one of them will ultimately be shown. If the content being swapped out is small, this is not important. However, in many cases the content can be large, significantly impacting page download times.

- JavaScript is also difficult to use when dynamic page content is tested. Usually this content is created server-side, before the page is delivered by the web server to the web browser. So by the time the JavaScript on the page fires, any dynamic content is already in place and can no longer be manipulated or modified easily.

- It is difficult to test and run quality assurance on the extra JavaScript in your page. Often it can conflict with existing JavaScript. Script used for complex multivariate tests may require a high level of coding skill. Although an increasing number of the newer client-side tools claim to make this process easier with various "single tag on the page" approaches, they still require webmaster or IT involvement.

- This approach most commonly relies on JavaScript being turned on in the browser, and also the accepting of first-party or third-party cookies by the web visitor's browser. This is a pretty common situation. However, a small number of people will completely turn off JavaScript, disallow cookies, or regularly delete cookies. In practice, it is likely that a landing page test with this approach would lose 5–10 percent of the available traffic. Although this is not the end of the world (you simply want to know what *relative* advantage the winning page has, not the correct *absolute* number of visitors like in web analytics), it still makes it difficult to reconcile the test numbers with other measurements and tracking.

The Verdict

Client-side rendering allows visual page element selection and easier tagging and can be implemented without IT support in many cases. It is recommended for getting started with landing page testing unless you have an incompatible CMS that will not support the required JavaScript insertion.

Server-Side Page Rendering

In server-side page rendering, the burden of swapping in the correct content and building the page is handled by the web server (often in cooperation with the CMS). The typical sequencing and data flows of a landing page test are illustrated in Figure 11.2.

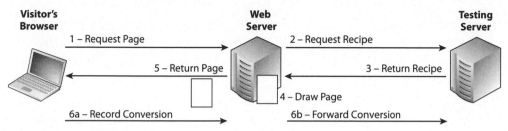

Figure 11.2 Server-side testing

Let's examine this flow in more detail:

1. The visitor's web browser requests a page from the web server.
2. The web server forwards the request to the testing server.
3. The testing server returns the recipe—a short code describing the exact version of the page to display to the web server.
4. The web server constructs the page.
5. The web server returns the requested page to the visitor's web browser.
6. If a conversion action subsequently happens, additional JavaScript on the post-conversion page "fires," notifying the web server with the details of the conversion.
7. The web server forwards any conversion information to the testing server.

Pros

There are several advantages of the server-side approach:

- Using server-side CMSs allows you to conduct visual page design and see a live preview of any page version.
- No IT or programming support is usually required, significantly lowering operational and organizational barriers to getting projects done quickly.
- You can test arbitrary changes to the page, including dynamic content and the use of rich media.

Cons

The biggest drawback for server-side systems is that they are usually self-contained. They do not "play well" with other CMSs or tools.

The Verdict

Server-side page rendering is ideal for testing stand-alone, well-contained landing pages or microsites.

Intercept Page Rendering

In intercept page rendering, the testing server serves as a barrier between the browser and the web server. It shields the web server from the reality of what is going on beyond its simple handling of page requests. In fact, it intentionally keeps the web server ignorant and creates new test content to send on to the web browser. The approach is based on fast recognition of a pattern on the page, and the immediate swap of it with another piece of content.

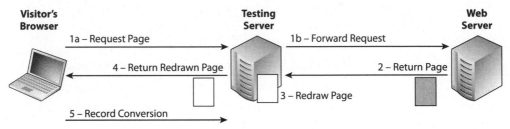

Figure 11.3 Intercept testing

Let's examine this flow in more detail:

1. The visitor's web browser requests a page from the testing server.

2. The testing server (which is masquerading as the web server to the outside world) forwards the request to the actual web server.

3. The web server returns a page to the testing server.

4. The testing server decides which version to show the visitor and constructs that page on the fly. In the process of doing this, it can arbitrarily swap out content as necessary to create the new page.

5. The testing server returns the redrawn newly created page to the visitor's web browser.

6. The visitor's web browser forwards any conversion information to the testing server.

Pros

There are several advantages of the intercept approach:

- No modifications are necessary to the original page that is produced by the web server. This means that the approach will work with any CMS. This is especially useful if you cannot get permission to change a certain part of the site and your CMS is rigid and difficult to work with.

- Little IT involvement is required.
- You can test changes and content substitutions of arbitrary format (including complex changes and the use of rich media).

Cons

There are a couple of drawbacks to the intercept approach:

- It requires DNS (domain name service) rerouting by your network administrator. In other words, the testing server acts as a barrier and a shield and pretends to be the web server to the outside world.
- This approach relies on sophisticated on-the-fly pattern matching in order to swap out content. Unless you are simply going to swap out static content, you will still need programming support. The programmer will simply be working for you inside of the marketing department and may no longer be in IT.

The Verdict

Intercept rendering is ideal for testing large sites and catalogs where making the changes on the actual site would be too difficult.

Common Testing Issues

Regardless of the page rendering approach that you choose, there are some general issues that impact all landing page tests.

Measuring and Counting

What exactly are you trying to optimize? This might seem like a simple question, but it deserves a second look. How you measure and record data during your test will have a profound impact on the results (and your test's validity).

Fixed Value vs. Variable Value

In many cases, your conversion actions all have the same estimated or actual revenue value (e.g., form-fills, downloads, registrations, or clickthroughs). For tests involving a single action with the same value, you can simply count the number of conversions, and use basic statistical tests (such as the t-test described in Chapter 10, "Common Testing Questions") to analyze the significance of your results.

However, if your conversion actions have a variable value, you must take this into account. For example, if you have an e-commerce catalog, you may sell items at widely varying prices. If your test variables have an effect on the average sales price, you must take this into account along with the conversion rate. If you do not, it is possible that any improvements in conversion rate might be diminished or actually canceled out by decreases in your average sales price. In such cases, you should measure the revenue per visitor. This will provide you with a normalized measure that takes into account the conversion rate and the average value of the transaction. By using revenue per visitor, you can determine whether a shift to a higher or lower average transaction value is actually a net benefit to your business.

Depending on your profit margin on different items (or categories of products), you may also have to consider the profit margin on each item. For example, it is easy to shift your product mix toward selling low margin or "loss leader" items in the hopes that your clients will eventually buy more from you (either during the same transaction or in subsequent ones). Such sales can increase your conversion rate, and even improve your overall sales—that is, they may increase your revenue per visitor. However, this may devastate your profitability.

In this case, use available information about the wholesale price of the individual product. You can then calculate the *gross margin contribution* by subtracting the cost of the product or service from the sales price. Although gross margin contribution is not technically your profit, it is closely related and we will use the two terms interchangeably. Instead of using revenue per visitor, you can use the more accurate profit per visitor measure for your test. If individual product margins are not available, you can often estimate them at the category level. For example, if you know that your cost of goods sold for a particular product category is 60 percent, you can assign a value corresponding to 40 percent of the sales revenue to the relevant transactions. If all of your product categories have similar profit margins, you can bypass this complexity and continue to record the simpler revenue per visitor.

Single Goal vs. Multiple Goals

If you have a single conversion goal, and it has a fixed value, you should be able to use simple counting as described earlier. If you have multiple conversion goals, you must use revenue per visitor (or profit per visitor) even if each type of conversion action has a fixed value.

For example, imagine that you run a lead-generation campaign. Visitors have the option of completing your online form (a $20 value), or calling your toll-free number and providing the same information over the telephone (a $40 value based on the higher conversion rate of this more motivated self-selecting audience segment). One of the variables that you are considering testing is the prominence of the toll-free number on the landing page. A smaller one will presumably lower the proportion of phone leads, whereas a more prominent one would increase it. To properly handle this trade-off, you should record each conversion action and its accompanying value for each landing page recipe. You can then use a revenue-per-visitor-based analysis to find the best recipe.

You also need to be clear about whether you are dealing with saturating goals versus accumulating goals. A *saturating goal* is one for which you receive no additional credit after it has been completed. For instance, in a lead-generation business, once the lead is generated and you get paid for it, you can't get credit for generating the same lead a second time even if the same person fills out the form again. Product sales is an example of an *accumulating goal*, where selling more product to the same person adds up additional revenues (and usually profit). These need to be handled differently.

Note that all of the metrics that you are trying to optimize are *normalized*. In other words, they are a ratio that divides one quantity by another. In all of our previous examples, the item that you normalize by has been the unique visitor—for example, conversion rate per visitor, revenue per visitor, and profit per visitor. In reality, things are more complicated. You will need to decide whether to normalize on a per-view, per-visit, or per-visitor basis. The correct choice is very important here. For most landing page optimization tests, it is appropriate to normalize per new visitor (per each first-time view), but this is not a given in all circumstances.

Maintaining Consistency

In most cases, you will want to maintain consistency of experience for visitors during their interaction with your test pages. For example, if you are testing the look and feel of a website, you would not want visitors to see an ever-changing presentation of the pages as they click around your site. A common way to stabilize your users' experience is to record the recipe that they were shown and store it in a cookie on their computer. The cookie should be a first-party cookie (originating from your website). The vast majority of people on the Internet currently allow such cookies. This will make it possible for you to present consistent information throughout their initial visit and during return visits.

Be aware that many people delete their cookies on a regular basis. If someone does this and then returns to your landing page, you may not know that they have been there before, and you may treat them like a new visitor, showing them a new re-randomized recipe instead of the same one that they originally saw. This is less of a problem with tests that have an immediate call-to-action. But it can be significant if you have a large "tail" of stragglers who convert long after their initial visit. The consequence of a significant percentage of delayed conversions is that you will be under-counting return visitors, and then counting them again as new visitors.

One solution is to use multiple methods for tracking and counting your visitors. But there are limitations to all Internet tracking approaches (as evidenced by the varying numbers produced by different web analytics software packages on the same website). You will never count all of your website visitors accurately. The requirements of landing page test tracking are generally not as stringent as those of web analytics.

As long as the sample that you collect is not too biased (due to classes of visitors that it underrepresents, or by the distortions created by your tracking and counting method), you should generally be okay. The main requirement is that you collect data consistently and compare apples to apples.

However, in some tests you may want to treat someone as a new visitor during every return visit. In those cases, reset their cookie and assign a new recipe to them. It is also possible to do this based on elapsed time between visits. For example, you may assume that if they have not converted within a day, they have forgotten about their previous experience and can be shown a new version of your page. Deliberately reusing your return visitors is sometimes done and often does not produce any negative effects. But be aware that it technically breaks the assumption of randomness required by the underlying statistical theory; the behavior of each visitor is supposed to be fresh, and not dependent on previous interactions with your landing page. As a general rule, we advise against this practice. There are simply too many real-world issues that already muddy the landing page testing waters without deliberately introducing additional sources of ambiguity.

Throttling

Throttling is the practice of adjusting the traffic data rate for your test as a whole (or for a portion of it). This is commonly done for three reasons: spreading out the pain, selectively focusing on certain parts of your search space, and reaching statistical significance faster.

Spreading Out the Pain

Some online marketers are worried that their conversion performance may get worse during their search for a better landing page. Many testers use affiliate traffic as part of their mix and do not want to alienate their affiliates by having them suddenly experience significantly lower conversion rates. It is also possible that few of the alternatives that you test will beat your original, especially in multivariate tests with large interactions.

If you are concerned about worse performance on your alternative recipes during the test, you can devote most of your bandwidth to the current baseline and reserve a bit for testing the new possibilities. This approach minimizes the risk of a sudden large drop in conversion rate.

For example, let's assume that the average value for the mix of recipes that you are about to test is 10 percent worse than your baseline performance. If you were to devote 20 percent of your traffic to the original, then your conversion rate during the test would drop by 8 percent:

Conversion rate = 20% × 1.00 + 80% × 0.90 = 0.92

If you devote 70 percent of the bandwidth to your original, then your conversion rate during the test would drop by only 3 percent:

Conversion rate = 70% × 1.00 + 30% × 0.90 = 0.97

There is, of course, a trade-off—your test would have to run approximately three times longer to collect the same amount of test data. This can be a problem if your data rate is already low and you run into seasonal effects during a prolonged test. If you do not see evidence of a significant drop in performance early in your test, you should reallocate more bandwidth to your alternative recipe mix.

Selective Focus

At SiteTuners, we normally devote significant data collection bandwidth to the baseline recipe (usually between 15 percent and 25 percent of the test traffic), because we want to have a good read on it. Since we are trying to beat the performance of the baseline, we want to accurately measure any fluctuations in it in order to adjust for outside factors in our test. If you simply devote a proportional amount of data collection to the baseline (inversely proportional to the size of your search space), your variance on the baseline data will be high, and you will have to wait longer to make decisions. The exception to this is in A-B split testing, where you will often (and should) devote 50 percent of available bandwidth to the baseline and alternative version.

You can also use selective focus as a kind of look-ahead—examining recipes that look promising by devoting more bandwidth to them on top of their usual allocation. This lets you get a better sense for whether a particular recipe is really better or is merely having a short-term run of good luck. However, be aware that uneven bandwidth invalidates many statistical analysis techniques commonly used in multivariate testing.

Reaching Significance Faster

Sometimes you may uncover large improvements over the performance of your baseline. If you are sampling at an equal data rate for all recipes (as measured in the number of visitor impressions), you will end up with more conversions on the best recipe. As you may recall from Chapter 10, the width of the error bars on the estimated conversion rate depends on the number of samples (conversions) that you have collected. The goal is to have the two bell curves "separate out" from each other. In other words, you want them to "un-overlap" as quickly as possible—until you have reached the desired statistical confidence level in your answer.

In Figure 11.4, you can see two conversion rate bell curves for versions *a* and *b* of a landing page. The observed average values (represented by the vertical lines) are different. The one for *b* is higher (to the right of the one for *a*). But the fact that we can calculate the exact observed average value for our data sample does not imply that we know what the true underlying mean is. One way to represent our uncertainty about the actual underlying mean is to represent it as a bell curve. The higher the bell curve is at a particular conversion rate value, the more likely it is that the actual mean also lies very near that value. In other words, the actual mean is most likely to be near the observed mean, and there is a rapidly decreasing chance that it lies further from the observed average value.

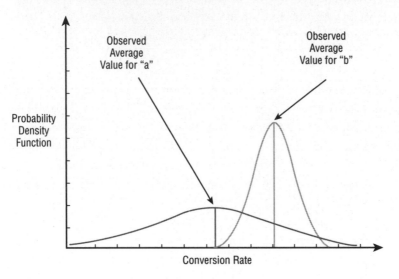

Figure 11.4 Two conversion rate bell curves for an A-B split test

The bell curve for *b* is narrower and taller than the one for *a* because *b* has had a higher number of conversions and we are more certain about the location of its actual mean. But the degree of overlap between the two bell curves is also high because the one for *a* has a wider "smudged" shape due to the lower number of observed conversions. Your confidence in the superiority of *b* depends on this degree of overlap, which in turn is mostly determined by the width of the wider *a* bell curve.

If *a* had a roughly equal number of conversions to *b*, its bell curve shape would also get taller and skinnier—minimizing the amount of overlap and giving you higher confidence in your answer. The quickest way to separate out the two curves from a statistical perspective is to have an exactly equal number of conversions for each recipe.

If you see a significantly higher percentage of conversions for a particular recipe in your test, you should reallocate your data collection bandwidth to equalize the number of conversions from each recipe. For example, let's assume that you are running a head-to-head test and version *b* is performing twice as well as the original version *a*. In this case, to make a decision as quickly as possible, you should give version *b* half as much traffic bandwidth as version *a*, so that the actual number of conversions is comparable. In other words, you should give *b* one-third of your total bandwidth and give *a* two-thirds. However, if your conversion rate difference is smaller than the 2-to-1 advantage in this example, you do not need to bother with throttling, since the length of required data collection will not change very much.

Audience Changes

Under ideal circumstances, your landing page is the only thing that changes during your test, so you can attribute causality to any conversion rate changes. You can say that making a certain landing page change resulted in the conversion improvement. In the real world, often other changes during your test can influence your results. These fall into two broad categories:

- Internal events
- External events

You should keep your data collection as clean as possible and try to prevent events that might bias your test. If you cannot, at least have some facilities for detecting significant changes. If you do detect anomalies, you can modify your subsequent analysis to mitigate or compensate for the effects. If that is not possible, you should rerun all or a portion of your data collection.

This section describes some of the things that you can do to avoid, or at least detect, this sort of problem.

Internal Events

Internal events are ones that are directly caused by actions taken within your online marketing program. As we previously mentioned, your overall goal should be to get as wide a cross section as possible of traffic sources, assuming that they are relatively stable, repeatable, and consistent.

Uneven or Flawed Sampling

Some traffic sources may result in uneven sampling. For example, many PPC search engines allow you to specify the exact timing for your campaign. This is okay as long as you subsequently apply your findings during the same time period but can be a problem if you overgeneralize the results.

For example, you may choose to buy PPC traffic only during the Monday through Friday workweek and turn off your program on the weekend. The resulting best landing page design from your test should only be used during the same time period. It should not be used during the weekend or evenings without additional testing, because you do not know how that untested audience would react to it.

More subtle sampling problems may occur when you offer a choice of different response mechanisms. For example, let's assume that you want your visitors to either buy online or call your toll-free number and order over the phone. You may test the removal of the toll-free number as one of your tuning elements. It is possible that by doing this you will significantly bias your sample. Visitors who are wary of conducting financial transactions online (such as older people or novice Internet users) will now be underrepresented.

If you use a toll-free number, it is usually available at the state or at the national level. This will preclude most international visitors from responding over the phone. Similar issues exist with chat, Flash, and any customized response mechanisms involving web browser plug-ins or downloaded software applications. Such response mechanisms will favor more technologically savvy visitors with advanced Internet technology, and undercount the cautious technology late adopters who do not have advanced capabilities in their web browser.

Biased Visitors

Bias can be introduced not only from the traffic source or method of sampling, but also from the interactions that a visitor has already had with your company or brand.

If someone has been to your website before, you must consider their whole history. They may have already transacted with you, or received a series of follow-up e-mails after a previous visit. In either case, they must be considered tainted. That is why we don't recommend using e-mail traffic for landing page testing unless you are exclusively tuning for this audience (and using well-respected direct marketing methods).

The basic problem with repeat visitors is that they may be making decisions based simply on familiarity. For example, let's assume that you have a horrible and user-unfriendly website and are testing an alternative design. First-time visitors may clearly favor the new design. But returning visitors may not. They are already familiar with the old design and have invested some time and mental effort in becoming familiar with it. Suddenly they are confronted with something different. This may cause them a moment of confusion as they reorient themselves and confirm that they landed in the right place. The anxiety produced by this discontinuity may be enough to wipe out any inherent advantages of the new design. In other words, the return visitor may experience an abrupt change in the page from their previous visit rather than consider the new page in isolation. In such cases it is often best to test with new visitors only and to accept the onetime performance drop due to returning visitors seeing different designs. This means you must take the short-term pain (a temporary drop in returning visitor performance) in order to realize the long-term gain (the improved performance of your new design as it applies to all future visitors from the same traffic source).

You will always have a certain proportion of repeat visitors when your landing page is your homepage or a permanent part of your website. With controllable traffic sources such as PPC or banner ads, you can aim where the traffic lands. This allows you to minimize the percentage of repeat visitors by using a specialized landing page just for that traffic source. If repeat visitors remain a significant part of your traffic mix, you may want to filter them out during your data collection (assuming that this still leaves you a high enough data rate for your test). Since many people intentionally delete their cookies or access the Web from multiple locations, you will never be able to detect or filter out all returning visitors. Just do the best that you can.

Technically, any prior exposure to your company constitutes a bias. A particular visitor may have seen or heard your offline marketing or advertising and will act differently than someone who has not, even if it is their first visit to your site. Even direct type-in traffic to your homepage should be considered suspect. Why would visitors type in your domain name directly? Obviously they must have heard about your company somewhere. Depending on the context in which your company was presented, they may have already formed some preconceived notions and may not consider your landing page design on its own merits.

Shifts in Traffic Mix

In most cases, you will combine a number of traffic sources for your test. The assumption behind the test is that this combined population of people behaves consistently, and that by testing you can find an alternative landing page design to which they will respond more favorably. So you have to be careful to not to change the composition of your audience during the test. Otherwise, you may tune for one population, and then try to apply the results to a different one.

Examples of changing traffic mix include the following:

- Increasing or decreasing spending significantly on a particular campaign (including turning on new traffic sources or deleting campaigns)
- Using automated bid management tools for PPC campaigns
- Significantly changing the mix of PPC keywords and positions that you are bidding on (even if the overall budget remains the same)
- Adding new high-traffic keywords to your PPC campaign
- Having search engines re-spider your site and increase your search results ranking for a popular keyword
- Negotiating a back link from a popular website

Of course, you cannot put all of your marketing activities on hold for the duration of your test, but try to make as few changes as possible during the data collection. If you introduce new traffic sources, you can usually filter them out and not use them for the test—that is, continue to show these visitors from new traffic sources your original landing page. If there are significant changes to your traffic mix, you may have to restart your test since your conclusions will be highly suspect, and you will want to properly tune for your new audience mix anyway.

External Events

External events happen as a result of changes outside of your online marketing program. Because of this, you usually do not have much control over them.

Seasonal external events are different depending on your industry. They may be long in duration and build up slowly (such as the fourth-quarter shopping season for many online merchants). Or they may be more abrupt and specific to your industry (such as the exact start date of deer hunting season for a rifle retailer).

If the external events are planned or foreseeable, you can schedule your test around them. If you are tuning for the best year-round behavior of your audience, you may choose to simply discard the data collected during any holidays or seasonal transitions during your test. This is also true during any significant major industry events or gatherings (such as planned conferences or expos). You can gather information about these types of events from industry press sources, and schedule your test accordingly.

Of course, you may want to tune specifically for a short time duration seasonal event because it represents a disproportionate percentage of the value to your business—for example, a flower site in the weeks leading up to Mother's Day.

Some external events are transient and nonrepeatable. These include

- Significant announcements from your company
- Major changes in your industry
- Media coverage of your company or industry

You must monitor relevant publications and news sources during the test period for events that may impact traffic levels, audience composition, or visitor behavior. If the external events are unforeseen, you may have to discard all your data for the affected time period.

Technology Changes

Sometimes the mechanisms for proper measurement and recording during your test can themselves impact the results. Some technological anomalies may be hard to detect, but many issues can be seen readily in your web analytics reports or server logs.

Examples include

- Page display times (based on web server load and Internet congestion)
- Broken landing pages (generating web server errors)
- Crippled landing pages (not displaying as you expect them to on all popular browsers)
- Upgrades to your web server, database, content management system, or web analytics software

Quality control after the implementation stage of your test is especially critical. You may be tempted to simply spot-check a few versions of your landing page in your browser, but this is not rigorous enough. There are often subtle and critical flaws that can only be found by disciplined quality control. For example, let's assume that your new landing page does not display properly for a web browser that has a 5 percent installed base among your visitors. During the test, this will show up as a 5 percent lower conversion rate (because people with that browser version cannot physically complete the transaction), and you may not even notice this drop in your reporting. However, since the page did not load properly, you are actually alienating all visitors with that browser. This has a consequence beyond your test—they may never return.

If possible, you should exhaustively check all possible versions of your landing pages on popular operating systems and web browsers and at common screen resolutions. Decide on an acceptable threshold for popularity of a particular technology—for example, all operating system versions with more than 1 percent installed base within your audience—and commit to testing with all versions above the threshold. This information is readily available in your web analytics reports.

In the next chapter we will look in detail at available testing methods, along with their advantages and limitations.

Testing Methods

If the only tool you have is a hammer, then every problem will start to look like a nail.

—Common saying

12

Each testing method has its own advantages, limitations, and hidden assumptions. The one that you choose will greatly influence the granularity of your test elements, the size of your test, the ability to uncover important variable interactions, and the quality of your results.

In this chapter we will introduce common testing terminology and test design issues. You will also learn how to choose the testing method that is right for your test.

Chapter Contents

Introduction to Testing Terminology
Overview of Testing Methods
A-B Split Testing
Multivariate Testing
Variable Interactions

Introduction to Testing Terminology

Before we discuss common testing methods, you need to understand some common concepts and definitions used in landing page testing. Members of the testing community refer to the same concepts but sometimes use different language to describe them. We will note such cases as appropriate, and will use the terminology interchangeably for the remainder of this book.

As we discussed in Chapter 10, "Common Testing Questions," the primary objective of landing page testing is to predict the behavior of your audience given the specific content on the landing page that they see. You will collect a limited sample of data during your test, summarize and describe it (using descriptive statistics), and predict how people from the same traffic sources will respond when interacting with the page (using inferential statistics). In other words, the ultimate goal is to find the best possible version of the landing page among all the variations you are testing.

Input and Output Variables

A landing page test has two basic components: a set of *input variables* (also called "independent variables") that you can control and manipulate, and one or more *output variables* (or "dependent variables") that you measure and observe. Note that what we mean by "independent variables" here is not the same as in the discussion of variable interactions at the end of this chapter. Independent variables as discussed here are simply the testing elements that you have chosen for your test, and which can be selected independently of the settings of the other variables. In other words, they are the "knobs" that you can fiddle with in this test.

Variable

The word *variable* (when used by itself) means a testing element that you have selected. As we mentioned in Chapter 9, "The Strategy of What to Test," variables can be of any granularity or coarseness. For example, a variable might be the headline of your landing page or a whole-page redesign. In multivariate testing, a variable is also commonly referred to as a factor.

In a multivariate test, you will have more than one variable. To distinguish among them we will use the following notation: a capital *V* followed by the number that you have assigned to a particular variable. For example, let's assume that you have a simple landing page with a headline, some sales copy test, and a call-to-action on a button. You might decide to test alternatives to each of these page elements and name them as follows:

V1 = Headline

V2 = Sales copy

V3 = Button text

V4 = Button color

Note that the variables do not necessarily define a unique physical location on the page. In fact, V3 (the button text) and V4 (the button color) actually occupy the same space. Nor do they have to be localized. For example, you can choose a variable to test a larger font size (for improved readability) versus an existing smaller one. In this case, the font size change would take effect throughout your whole landing page and would overlap with other variables (such as the actual text on the page) that you might also be testing.

Value

A value is a particular *state* that a variable can take on.

When traditional multivariate testing is used in other fields, variable values are often *continuous* (which means they can vary smoothly across a range). This allows you to predict the behavior at interpolated values of the variable (in between the places where you actually sample). For example, if you know that the power output of a car engine at 1000 RPM (revolutions per minute) is 100 horsepower, and at 2000 RPM is 200 horsepower, you can interpolate between these two values to estimate that the output should be 150 horsepower at 1500 RPM.

In landing page testing, variable values are almost always *discrete* (distinct from each other, and countable). For example, a button color might be green, blue, or red. We will number the possible choices by successive lowercase letters. By convention, the letter *a* represents the original version of the variable (as seen on your "baseline" original landing page). The letter is combined with the variable name to exactly specify the value of a particular variable. If V4 is our button color, an example assignment might look as follows:

V4*a* = green button (the original)

V4*b* = blue button

V4*c* = red button

Unlike continuous variables, measuring the effect of discrete variable values does not give us any information about the other possible values. Continuing our example from earlier, even if we had measured the average conversion rates with the green and blue buttons, we would not have any information about the performance of the red one.

Branching Factor

The total number of possible values for a discrete variable is called its *branching factor*. For discrete variables, the branching factor must be at least 2 (the original version and at least one alternative). As we will discuss later in this chapter, some experimental designs and testing methods additionally require that the branching factor be the same for all variables in the test.

In the button color example, V4 has a branching factor of 3 (because it can take on the values signified by *a*-green, *b*-blue, and *c*-red).

In traditional multivariate testing, the number of values for a variable is called the *level of the factor*. Each value is also called a *level* because historically it was drawn from continuous variables. For example, if your variable only has two values, they might be signified by "low" and "high" (or "–1" and "+1").

Recipe

A recipe is a unique combination of variable values in your test. It is a sequential listing of the specific values that each variable takes on in the specific version of the landing page.

For example, let's assume that you had set the following variable values from our previous example for a particular landing page in your test: V1*b*, V2*c*, V3*a*, V4*a*. The recipe could be abbreviated as *bcaa*.

Each recipe is unique. By convention, the recipe with all *a*'s (*aaaa* in the example above) is the original or *baseline* recipe to which all others will be compared.

Search Space Size

The number of unique recipes in your test is your *search space size*. It can generally be computed by multiplying together all of the branching factors of the variables in your test (for a possible exception to this rule, please see the next section, "Test Construction").

In our earlier example, let's assume that there are three headlines, four versions of the sales copy, four calls-to-action, and three button colors. BF stands for the branching factor for a particular variable.

Search space size

$$= BF_{V1} \times BF_{V2} \times BF_{V3} \times BF_{V4}$$

$$= 3 \times 4 \times 4 \times 3$$

$$= 144$$

This example is a small one. As you can see, if you have more variables, and higher branching factors for each one, the search space size will grow very rapidly. If the search space size is large, it can quickly exceed the practical limits of common testing methods such as A-B split, fractional factorial parametric, and full factorial parametric.

Test Construction

There are two primary types of multivariate test designs: unconstrained designs and constrained designs. Let's discuss these further.

Unconstrained Designs

Unconstrained design test variables can be created and displayed independently of each other on your landing page. For instance, if all variables can be displayed in separate locations on your landing page, they are usually unconstrained. Most basic landing page tests involve unconstrained designs.

This does not mean that there are no variable interactions (see the last section in this chapter) among variables in unconstrained designs. Some variables may indeed interact with each other. In our previous example, the call-to-action text on the button can obviously interact with the button color. Imagine that the button text says "Go." On a green button this makes sense. However, the same text displayed on the red button would be confusing since people commonly associate red with the word "stop." So you should look for possible interactions among all the possible variable value combinations of V3 and V4, but your choices of the exact wording of the alternative calls-to-action text can probably be considered independently of your choices about alternative button colors.

Constrained Designs

Constrained designs involve conditional rules for constructing certain recipes. In other words, some of the allowed values for a particular variable are *contingent* on the setting of others, or can exist only under certain conditions. Under such circumstances, take special care to properly define and structure your variables. You may also have to make sure that you sample appropriately during your test and do not accidentally create improper recipes for presentation to your visitors.

Let's consider a simple example. Assume that you have a two-page registration form. You want to test an alternative design for the second page, but you also want to consider a design where all of the form fields are moved onto the first page—that is, there's no need for a second page at all.

One possible test construction approach is as follows:

V1—first page contents

    a—original first page

    b—extended first page (containing all original first and second page fields)

V2—second page contents

    a—original second page

    b—alternative second page design

    c—no second page (all content moved to V1*b* first page)

Under this *unspecified constraint* approach, you will need to keep track of the fact that V1*b* and V1*c* can only appear together, and enforce it through rules that are external to the variable definition itself.

Another common solution is to flatten the constrained variables and create a single variable containing values for each allowable design:

V1—registration process

    a—original first and second pages

    b—original first page and alternative second page

    c—extended one page (containing all original first and second page fields)

As a more concrete example, imagine that you want to find the best position on your page for a transactional trustmark (such as TRUSTe, McAfee Secure, or buySAFE). The goal of the testing is to find the biggest conversion rate improvement possible due to adding the trustmark. You would do this by testing all possible visual logos (six for the purposes of our example) in multiple positions on the client's landing page (up to four). You test against the original landing page, which does not contain the trustmark.

Obviously, if the trustmark is not present on the landing page, the specific logo chosen and its position become meaningless. To run these tests, you can choose the *specified constraint* test construction approach. In other words, you reserve one variable specifically for the constrained condition and a placeholder variable value for it in all other appropriate variables:

V1—trustmark presence (branching factor = 2)

    a—no trustmark

    b—trustmark

V2—trustmark logo (branching factor = 7)

    a—no logo (placeholder for constraint in V1)

    b—red-horizontal logo

    c—red-vertical logo

    d—black-horizontal logo

    e—black-vertical logo

    f—white-horizontal logo

    g—white-vertical logo

V3—trustmark location (branching factor = 5)

    a—no location (placeholder for constraint in V1)

    b—location #1

    c—location #2

    d—location #3

    e—location #4

Based on the branching factors here, you might assume that this test has 70 distinct recipes ($2 \times 7 \times 5$). However, it only has 25. Besides the baseline recipe (specified by *aaa*), no other recipes are allowed to contain any *a*'s, so you'd calculate the total search space size as 1 (the *aaa* version) + 6×4.

Overview of Testing Methods

There are two key activities in landing page optimization:

- Deciding what to change and coming up with alternative landing page versions
- Verifying the impact of the changes on your audience

Choosing what elements to test and deciding on alternative versions is very important. If you do not test changes that have a significant impact on conversion, it does not matter how you verify the impact—there won't be any. At the same time, it is critical to understand the benefits and limitations of each testing method.

Several factors determine the testing method that you should use:

- The size of your search space
- Your available landing page traffic levels
- The desired level of confidence in the test outcome
- Whether you want to consider variable interactions

Some testing methods can only handle search spaces with a few total recipes, whereas others can routinely find the best answer out of millions of possible recipes. Simple testing methods can work with as few as 10 conversions per day (assuming that you are willing to wait months to collect enough data); others require higher minimum traffic levels. The desired statistical confidence level is completely up to you and depends on the severity of the consequences from making an incorrect decision. Typically values between 90 percent and 99 percent are chosen. Usually a lot more data will have to be collected in order to reach a higher confidence level. As we will discuss in the last section of this chapter, variable interactions play a huge part in online marketing experiments. Some testing methods do not consider them at all, but others identify them and take them into account in order to produce the best possible results.

The simplest testing method is A-B split testing, and it is a good starting point for getting your feet wet with landing page optimization. Multivariate testing is much more complicated and has several important complexities, twists, and considerations that can radically alter the end results—we do not recommend that you start there.

A-B Split Testing

The most basic testing method available is *A-B split testing*. The name comes from the fact that two versions of your landing page ("A" and "B") are tested. "Split testing" refers to the random assignment of new visitors to the version of the page that they see. In other words, the traffic is split and all versions are shown in parallel throughout the data collection period (usually in equal proportions). This is an important requirement. Parallel tests should always be conducted (as opposed to sequential ones). This allows you to control for as many outside factors as possible. The random assignment of new visitors to particular landing page designs is also critical, since randomness is the basis for the probability theory that underlies the statistical analysis of the results.

Usually version "A" is defined as your original control page, or baseline (commonly called the *champion* version). The other version is the alternative (commonly called the *challenger*). If the challenger proves to be better than the champion, the challenger replaces the champion after the test and becomes the new champion to beat in any subsequent tests.

In practice, you can often have more than two versions in a split test. For example, if you had one original and two alternative versions, you would have an A-B-C split test, and so on. However, split tests rarely have a branching factor higher than 10.

As we discussed in Chapter 9, the variable in your split test can be very granular or it can be a complete redesign of your landing page.

A-B Split Testing Advantages

Split tests have several advantages:

Ease of Test Design Unlike more complicated multivariate tests, split tests do not have to be carefully designed or balanced. You simply decide how many versions you want to test, and then split the available traffic evenly among them. No follow-up tests are required to verify the results—the best performer in the test is declared the winner.

Ease of Implementation Many software packages are available to support simple split tests. If you are testing granular test elements, you can design, set up your test, and be collecting data literally within a matter of minutes. This can be done in most cases without support from your IT department or others within the company. You may even be able to collect the data you need with your existing web analytics tools.

Ease of Analysis Only very simple statistical tests (as described in the previous chapter) are needed to determine the winner. Basically, all you have to do is compare the baseline version to each challenger to see if you have reached your desired confidence level.

Ease of Explanation No complicated analyses or charts are needed to present your results to others. You can simply declare that you are confident that a particular version is better than another. You can also give a likely range of percentage improvement (based on the amount of data you have collected and the width of the error bars).

Flexibility in Defining the Variable Values In whole-page split tests, you have complete flexibility in how different the proposed alternatives are. For example, in one alternative, you may simply choose to test a different headline. In another you may completely restructure everything about the page (layout, color scheme, sales copy, offer, and call-to-action). This ability to mix and match allows you to test a range of evolutionary and revolutionary alternatives in one test, without being constrained by the more granular definition of variables in a multivariate test.

Useful in Low Data Rate Tests If your landing page has only a few conversions per day, you simply cannot use more advanced testing methods. But with the proper selection of the test variable and alternative values, you can still achieve significant results in a split test. Improvements in the double or even triple digits are not uncommon.

A-B Split Testing Disadvantages

Split tests also have several drawbacks:

Limited Number of Recipes As we mentioned, the number of recipes in a typical split test is usually very small. If you did your homework properly, you probably came up with dozens of potential issues with your landing page and also constructed many alternative variations to test. However, because of the limited scope of split testing, you will be reduced to testing your ideas one at a time. You will also be forced to guess which ideas to test first (based on your intuition about which ones might make the most difference). In other testing methods, you may be able to test many of your key ideas at once and find all of the changes that improve your conversion rate in one test.

Does Not Consider Variable Interactions By definition, split tests consider only one variable at a time, so you cannot detect variable interactions (see the last section of this chapter). Furthermore, a series of split tests is not the same as a multivariate test with the same variables. Depending on the variable interactions, you may not be able to find the best-performing recipe at all. Whether you do depends on the order in which you conduct your split tests and the exact nature of the interactions.

For example, let's assume that you are testing two variables, each of which can take on two values. There are strong interactions between the two variables. The conversion rate for each recipe is as follows:

aa = 5%
ab = 2%
ba = 3%
bb = 7%

If you had conducted a multivariate test and collected data on each of the four recipes, you would have seen the superior performance of recipe *bb* and crowned it the winner.

However, this is not possible if you had simply done two back-to-back split tests (starting with V1 first). You would have tested recipe *aa* versus recipe *ba* (leaving V2 unchanged in its original V2*a* setting). Since *aa* would perform the best, you would conclude that V1 should be locked in as V1*a*. You would then test V2 in this context by conducting another split test between *aa* and *ab*. After this second test, you would come to the conclusion that V2 should be set to *a*. So the winning recipe would be determined to be *aa*. There is no way to sequentially get to the best answer in this example. This situation is actually quite common. The chances of being led astray from the best solution also increase as you continue to do more split tests over time.

No Way to Discover the Importance of Page Elements Often, you may choose very coarse variables for your split test. Because of the limited data rate, you are forced to make your best guess at testing elements that might improve performance. These elements may involve many simultaneous changes to your landing page. In the extreme case of a whole-page redesign, you may have changed dozens of details on the page in question and defined them as a single alternative recipe.

However, the same flexibility that allows you to do this *also* limits your ability to interpret the results and attribute credit for the conversion improvement to any particular change that you made. Was it the button color? Or was it the headline change? Or was it the different offer? You will never know. By squashing multiple changes into one variable value, you have confounded their effects and lost the ability to look at them separately.

As we mentioned earlier, this may not be such a huge issue, since many of the so-called "learnings" about the relative importance of variables are based on the spurious assumption that they are all independent. Furthermore, the best effects may be due to the specific variable *values* you have chosen, and not the *variable* itself. For example, a particular headline that you chose to test was very powerful. But this does not allow you to generalize about headlines being more important than the other variables tested.

In any case, you should avoid trying to interpret the results of your split test if the variable values involve changing multiple elements on the page.

Inefficient Data Collection As you will see in the next section, multivariate tests are often carefully constructed in order to get the most information from a smaller data sample. In effect, they allow you to more efficiently conduct multiple split tests simultaneously, and even to detect certain kinds of variable interactions. Conducting multiple split tests back-to-back is the most wasteful kind of data collection—none of the information from a previous test can be reused to draw conclusions about the other variables that you may want to test in the future.

Multivariate Testing

The purpose of *multivariate testing* is to simultaneously gather information about multiple variables and then conduct an analysis of the data to determine which recipe results in the best performance.

Multivariate testing approaches differ on two important dimensions:

- How the data is collected
- How the data is analyzed

The data can be collected in a *full factorial* or *fractional factorial* fashion (see the "Data Collection" section that follows). The subsequent analysis can be either *parametric* or *nonparametric* (see the "Data Analysis" section later in this chapter). Within parametric analysis there are also significant differences. Some forms of parametric analysis take complex variable interactions into account, and others do not.

We have presented data collection and data analysis as independent dimensions. In fact, they cannot always be separated. If you choose fractional factorial data collection and test design, you automatically lock yourself into a very restricted subset of parametric models—nonparametric analysis is impossible if you conduct fractional factorial data collection.

Data Collection

Full factorial experimental designs sample data across your whole search space—that is, each possible recipe in your test is sampled. If this is done properly, the subsequent analysis allows you to consider not only the main effects, but all variable interactions as well, including higher-order ones.

Technically, all fractional factorial designs fall under the *design of experiments (DOE)* umbrella. DOE is a systematic approach to getting the maximum amount of useful information about the process that you are studying while minimizing the amount of effort and data collection required.

By definition, fractional factorial experimental designs make simplifying assumptions about the possible form of the parametric model for subsequent analysis. For example, they may simply assume that there are no higher-order interactions at all (that the values of the corresponding coefficients in the model are zero). In the extreme case, they can assume that only the main effects matter and that there are no interactions of any kind (even lower-order ones).

One feature of DOE is that it allows you to explicitly define the interactions among the variables that you want to study and examine. This is in contrast to repeated A-B split testing of different variables (discussed earlier in this chapter), which may not find the best solution and depends heavily on the order in which you test the variables.

There is an inherent trade-off among various DOE test constructions. Full factorial parametric designs do not scale very well but get more complete information about the exact relationship among all main and interaction effects tested. Fractional factorial designs can scale to larger search spaces but make assumptions about the underlying process that may not be valid and may actually lead you astray.

Data Analysis

Parametric data analysis in landing page optimization builds a model of how the variables tested (the "independent variables") impact the conversion rate (the "dependent variable"). For each recipe in your search space, the model will produce a prediction of the expected conversion rate (or other optimization criterion of interest).

Unless you happened to have sampled data on the exact recipe predicted by the model as being the best, you do not really know if the prediction will hold up. That is why it is critical to run follow-up A-B split tests between the predicted best challenger recipe and the original baseline recipe for all parametric data analysis methods.

By contrast, nonparametric data analysis does not try to build a model based on the input variables. Nonparametric methods try to identify the best challenger recipe, but without being able to tell anything about *why* it is the best, or exactly how much better it is than your baseline.

The two approaches are unrelated and are answering different questions. They are both a recognition of the fundamental reality that only so much useful information can be extracted from your data collection sample. The only question is what you want to do with the data. You can try to create a general model of the output variable and try to describe it in terms of the input variables, or you can find the best individual recipe and not know why it is the best.

Parametric Analysis

After you collect your data, you can build a model that expresses how your dependent variable (the conversion rate) varies based on the settings of your independent variables (your testing elements and their specific values).

The models are made up of two types of components. *Main effects* describe the impact of an individual variable value on the results. In other words, they look at each variable in isolation and see how changing its value affects the results. *Interaction effects* consider combinations of variable values and how they influence each other when presented together. Interaction effects are possible among two or more variable values. For example, if you had five variables in your test, you could have interactions involving any subset of two, three, four, or five variable values. Interactions involving smaller numbers of variables are called lower order, and those involving many variables are called higher order.

As we mentioned earlier, variables are commonly referred to as factors in parametric multivariate testing terminology. Likewise, variable values are often referred to as levels. If a variable has a branching factor of two, the levels are often referred to as "high" and "low" (or are denoted by "+1" and "-1"). Similarly, three levels are often denoted by "+1", "0", and "–1."

Usually parametric multivariate testing uses the general mathematical class of *linear models* based on the analysis of variance (ANOVA). In other words, you are trying to predict the output variable by adding up the contributions of all of the possible main effects and interaction effects of the input variables. You start with the average value of your output variable in the test, and then add in the positive or negative impact of your input variables and their interactions.

Let's consider the simplest possible multivariate example. Assume that you are testing a new call-to-action button and are considering two colors (variable 1—blue, green) and two font styles (variable 2—Arial, Times Roman) for the text:

V1*a* = blue

V1*b* = green

V2*a* = Arial

V2*b* = Times Roman

You can create a model of the conversion rate that "fits" your data as well as possible and uses the average value, main effects, and all possible combinations of variable values (interactions). The coefficients (denoted by c's in front of each effect) indicate the magnitude of the contribution of each effect and can be either positive or negative. The full model to predict the conversion rate (CR) of any particular recipe would look like this:

$$CR = c_1 + c_2 \times V1a + c_3 \times V1b + c_4 \times V2a + c_5 \times V2b$$

$$+ c_6 \times V1a{:}V2a + c_7 \times V1a{:}V2b + c_8 \times V1b{:}V2a + c_9 \times V1b{:}V2b$$

c_1 represents the average value, c_2–c_5 are the main effects of the individual variables, and c_6–c_9 are the two-variable interaction effects (involving all four possible combinations of the two variables).

Let's assume that your experiment is slightly larger. You now add a third two-way variable to the test (designated by V3a and V3b). The full model with all interactions is shown here (the new terms resulting from the addition of the third variable are bolded):

$$CR = c_1 + c_2 \times V1a + c_3 \times V1b + c_4 \times V2a + c_5 \times V2b$$

$$+ c_6 \times \mathbf{V3a} + c_7 \times \mathbf{V3b}$$

$$+ c_8 \times V1a{:}V2a + c_9 \times V1a{:}V2b + c_8 \times V1b{:}V2a + c_9 \times V1b{:}V2b$$

$$+ c_{10} \times \mathbf{V1a{:}V3a} + c_{11} \times \mathbf{V1a{:}V3b} + c_{12} \times \mathbf{V1b{:}V3a} + c_{13} \times \mathbf{V1b{:}V3b}$$

$$+ c_{14} \times \mathbf{V2a{:}V3a} + c_{15} \times \mathbf{V2a{:}V3b} + c_{16} \times \mathbf{V2b{:}V3a} + c_{17} \times \mathbf{V2b{:}V3b}$$

$$+ c_{18} \times \mathbf{V1a{:}V2a{:}V3a} + c_{19} \times \mathbf{V1a{:}V2a{:}V3b}$$

$$+ c_{20} \times \text{V1a:V2b:V3a} + c_{21} \times \text{V1a:V2b:V3b}$$

$$+ c_{22} \times \text{V1b:V2a:V3a} + c_{23} \times \text{V1b:V2a:V3b}$$

$$+ c_{24} \times \text{V1b:V2b:V3a} + c_{25} \times \text{V1b:V2b:V3b}$$

As you can see, the number of coefficients that you must now estimate in the model has mushroomed from 9 to 25. For the first time, you see the presence of three-variable interaction effects.

These examples are among the smallest possible multivariate tests. As you can see, if you have a higher branching factor for each variable, or a larger number of variables, the number of coefficient terms in the model grows very quickly.

 With a large number of coefficient terms in a parametric model, it becomes impossible to accurately estimate each one.

Fractional factorial parametric approaches force you to choose the complexity of your model ahead of time. This means you must somehow decide in advance which main effects are important, and also which interactions will be included in the model. The simpler your model is, the fewer visitors will need to be sampled during data collection in order to accurately predict all of the coefficients.

Nonparametric Analysis

It is a practical impossibility to do the following three things simultaneously without a ridiculously large data rate:

1. Find the best-performing recipe (considering the impact of variable interactions)
2. Search a very large search space
3. Predict the performance of all recipes and explain why they perform as they do

Nonparametric approaches use a different mathematical foundation and starting assumptions to focus on items 1 and 2. They do not assume anything about the underlying model or even the presence or size of variable interactions.

Parametric approaches focus on item 3. So in effect, parametric versus nonparametric can be viewed as the inherent trade-off between being able to model and predict the performance of all recipes and being able to find the best single recipe quickly in a much larger search space.

Unfortunately, some companies in our field make ludicrous assertions to the contrary. They claim to be able to test a "virtually unlimited number of variations" of a landing page by using a modified fractional factorial DOE approach while still taking variable interactions into account, and be able to describe which individual values of the winning recipe contributed to its improved performance. Claims like this make everyone in our industry look bad.

Fractional Factorial Parametric Testing

As we mentioned earlier in this chapter, fractional factorial data collection cannot really be divorced from parametric data analysis. So we will refer to the combination of the two simply as "fractional factorial."

In theory, it is possible that every variable that you test has interactions with every specific value of every other variable. In practice, this is usually not the case. During your test, you may discover that many or even most of the elements that you have decided to include do not impact performance at all. They simply do not matter to your audience. It is also common that strong interactions between two variables exist but that higher-order interactions (among three or more variables) are insignificant. In such cases, the behavior of the output variable can be described by looking at the main effects and a few low-order interactions (involving two variables).

This basic idea arises as a consequence of three empirical principles commonly understood in the testing community.

Hierarchical Ordering Principle

Lower-order effects are more likely to be important than higher-order effects.

Effects of the same order are equally likely to be important.

The hierarchical ordering principle suggests that when resources are scarce (the data collection rate is low), priority should be given to estimating main effects and lower-order interactions.

Effect Sparsity Principle

The numbers of relatively important effects in a factorial experiment are small.

The effect sparsity principle is another formulation of the 80/20 rule. Only a few variables combine to produce the biggest effects, and all the rest will not matter nearly as much.

Effect Heredity Principle

In order for an interaction to be significant, at least one of its parent factors should be significant.

The effect heredity principle is another application of common sense. If a variable does not produce any big effects on its own—that is, it is benign or negligible—it is unlikely to do so when combined with something else. It may be that a big interaction effect is produced by variables that do not show the largest main effects, but at least one of the variables involved in an interaction will usually show some main effect.

The whole idea behind fractional factorial design is that you can collect data on a fraction of the recipes needed for an equivalent full factorial design and still maximize the model's predictive value.

Creating a proper fractional factorial design is beyond the scope of this book. The basic steps are as follows:

- Based on the generators of your design, you can determine the *defining relation*.
- The defining relation specifies the *alias structure*.
- A fractional factorial experiment is created from a full factorial experiment by using the chosen *alias structure*.

One common constraint on fractional factorial tests is that the branching factor is two for all variables. The methods for creating custom test designs outside of this constraint are complex. Many testers simply copy "standard" designs from statistical texts, and restrict themselves to a choice of variables and branching factors that fit the model.

Overview of Common Fractional Factorial Methods

Although there is some difference in common fractional factorial methods, their basic predictive power, required data sample size, and underlying assumptions are pretty similar. The main difference lies in the *shape* of the search spaces (as defined by the number of variables and their exact branching factors) that each can be used for. So if you are going to use any of the methods described next, you should base your decision on your familiarity with each and the number and branching factors of the variables in your test.

The sparsest fractional factorial approaches are

- Plackett-Burman
- Latin squares
- Taguchi method

All three of these fractional factorial methods suffer from the same fundamental issues. These problems are a direct consequence of their origins in manufacturing. Let's take a look at some of the characteristics of this original environment:

Expensive Prototypes The underlying assumption is that creating alternative recipes is difficult, time-consuming, or expensive. When applications involve physical processes, human medical trials, or manufacturing technology, this is indeed the case. So the goal is to minimize the required number of recipes (also called "prototypes" or "experimental treatments") in the experiment.

Small Test Sizes A direct consequence of the expensive prototypes is that you need to keep the number of elements that you test to an absolute minimum and focus only on the most critical variables.

No Interactions As another consequence of the expensive prototypes, you can only measure the main effects created by your variables. The small test size and expensive data collection force you to assume sparse fractional factorial models that cannot accurately estimate even two variable interactions.

High Yields In most cases, the process or outcome that you were measuring had a high probability of success.

Continuous Variables Many of the input variables involved in the tests were continuous (such as temperature or concentration of a certain chemical compound). Even though you had to pick specific levels of the variable for the test, you could often interpolate between them to estimate what would happen at nonsampled settings of the variable.

These approaches were transplanted to the online marketing arena (and landing page optimization in particular) because of their relative simplicity and familiarity. Unfortunately, the assumptions that accompanied them came along for the ride, even though they are not applicable to the new environment. Let's take a closer look at the reality of landing page testing:

Free Prototypes When you create a test plan, you define exactly which page elements to test and specify the alternative variable values for each. In most cases, the alternative test elements are easy to implement. They involve changes to the HTML structure of your page, text changes, and graphics.

Once this preliminary work has been done, you have the capability to create any of the recipes in your search space. In other words, the process of creating a different version of your page is completely automated. There is no incremental cost to showing any of the possible recipes to your next visitor. So there is no need to restrict yourself to showing only a small percentage of the possible recipes.

Huge Test Sizes If you critically reviewed your landing page, you were probably able to identify dozens of potential problems (large and small) with it. For each of your original test elements, you can probably come up with several alternatives that can reasonably be expected to produce better results and should be included in your test plan. If you did, your search space size would be in the millions (or even billions) of possible recipes. Unfortunately, multivariate testing is specifically designed for small test sizes. Most real-world tests involve search spaces of a few dozen total recipes.

Significant Interactions As discussed earlier, variable interactions play a huge role in landing page optimization. Some interactions are unexpected and are the result of the reduced coherency of the mix-and-match presentation of variables during a test. The effect may be something like Frankenstein's monster—stitched together from functional parts, but not resulting in a very appealing whole.

Other variable interactions are intentional. In fact, as an online marketer you should want to create interactions. You should look for page elements that work together and support each other in getting your visitor to act. These kinds of synergies are at the very heart of good marketing. Yet most fractional factorial designs assume that there are no interactions (or that they are very small).

Low Yields Some landing pages have double-digit conversion rates, but most pages have lower rates. Many e-commerce websites have conversion rates that are well below 1 percent. The limiting factor in the length of the data collection for these pages is the number of conversions (rather than the number of recipes sampled in the test).

Discrete Variables Most of the elements that you test on a landing page are discrete. They involve completely distinct choices that are unrelated to each other. For example, if you tested a particular headline for your page, you would not be able to predict the performance of an alternative headline.

By now, you have probably determined our preference for full factorial over fractional factorial data collection for landing page optimization if you are going to use parametric data analysis. There is no efficiency disadvantage to full factorial designs during the data collection stage and significant advantages during the analysis stage.

All three fractional factorial methods can only estimate the main effects in the model. In other words, they cannot capture all possible two-variable interactions (or any higher-order interactions). Some of them explicitly assume that there are no interactions. They use this radical assumption to dramatically lower the number of sampled recipes and amount of data required to estimate the main effects. An important additional requirement for all of these approaches is that the data collection is balanced across all possible values of a variable. For example, you cannot use throttling, or it may complicate or throw off your use of standard data analysis.

Let's assume that you want to collect data for each of the variable main effects in the examples that follow. You can construct a series of increasingly larger tests and see how few recipes you can get away with.

The simplest case is an A-B split test containing two recipes, *a* and *b*. You need to split your traffic 50/50 across *a* and *b*. So you need two recipes to measure the two values of variable V1. These two recipes represent your entire search space.

Now imagine that you have two variables, each with a branching factor of two. This results in four possible recipes: *aa*, *ab*, *ba*, and *bb*. You choose to sample only from recipes *aa*, and *bb* (still only two recipes, as in the previous example). Note that half of the data that you collect will involve V1a (from recipe *a*a), and half will involve V1b (from recipe *b*b). Similarly, half of your data will cover V2a (from recipe *a*a), and half will involve V2b (from recipe *b*b). As you can see, you have collected equal amounts of data on each main effect, and you did it by sampling only half of your total search space (two out of four recipes).

Let's extend our example to three variables, each with a branching factor of two. This results in eight possible recipes: *aaa, aab, aba, abb, baa, bab, bba,* and *bbb*. You choose to sample only from recipes *aaa* and *bbb* (still only two recipes). Note that half of the data that you collect will involve V1a (from recipe *aa*a), and half will involve V1b (from recipe *bb*b). Similarly, half of your data will cover V2a (from recipe *aaa*), and half will involve V2b (from recipe *bbb*). Half of your data will also cover V3a (from recipe *aa*a), and half will cover V3b (from recipe *bb*b). You have again collected equal amounts of data on each main effect, and have done it by sampling only a quarter of your total search space (two out of eight recipes).

Of course you cannot continue to sample just two recipes and still cover all main effects at larger test sizes. But by clever test construction, you can keep the number of unique recipes surprisingly small (especially when considered as a proportion of the total search space). If you think that the previous examples are a bit contrived and artificial, you are right.

Underlying the use of fractional factorial methods is the assumption that creating a test run is difficult or time-consuming—so you need to keep the number of recipes that you sample as low as possible. This may have been true in the manufacturing setting (such as retooling an assembly line to test for a change in production quality), but it is not true or necessary in landing page optimization. Internet technology allows you to easily create any recipe of your landing page test. The page is dynamically created on the fly for each new visitor. For practical data collection purposes, it does not matter how many unique recipes you have in your test.

For the assumption of expensive recipe construction, you pay a heavy price during data analysis. By sampling limited recipes, you destroy your ability to do a comprehensive analysis and find variable interactions later.

Fractional Factorial Advantages

The following advantages of fractional factorial parametric tests are only from the perspective of A-B split testing. They are *not* advantages when compared to full factorial methods (see the "Full Factorial Parametric Testing" and "Full Factorial Nonparametric Testing" sections later in this chapter).

Data Collection Efficiency   Instead of performing multiple A-B split tests, you can collect data simultaneously about several variables. As long as your data collection is properly balanced among all variable values, you can take different views (or "slices") of your sample to examine all variables in a single analysis.

Order Independence As discussed earlier, repeated A-B split tests may be unable to find the best solution depending on the order in which the tests are run. Since information about all variables is being gathered simultaneously in a fractional factorial test, the order problem is eliminated, and it becomes possible to find better solutions (although still not necessarily the best ones).

Fractional Factorial Disadvantages

Fractional factorial designs have several disadvantages:

Small Test Size Search spaces are very small (it is rare to see landing page tests with more than a few hundred recipes). Most online marketers want to run much larger tests.

Does Not Consider Variable Interactions The most common fractional factorial landing page testing approaches assume a model that is simple in order to capture important variable interactions. This can significantly skew the results and lead you to costly incorrect conclusions.

Piecewise Construction Errors Another common mistake is to take the winning values from each variable and combine them into a single recipe. This piecewise construction does not necessarily constitute the best-performing recipe.

Let's take a closer look at why this is the case. Assume that you have picked a 90 percent statistical confidence threshold for each variable in your test. In other words, you are 90 percent sure that the particular value for that variable is the best-performing one. If you had only one variable in your test, you would be wrong 10 percent of the time, and this might be acceptable to you.

But the likelihood of error grows quickly as you increase the number of variables in your test. For example, in a two-variable test your chances of finding the best recipe depend on you being correct about the best value for each variable independently of the other. This means that you must multiply together the probabilities of being right for each variable.

In our example, this would mean that your chances of finding the correct recipe are 81 percent (90% × 90%). So your error rate has increased from 10 percent for a single variable to 19 percent for two. By the time you get six variables in your test, you are only 53 percent certain of having found the best recipe. This is only slightly better than flipping a coin.

For this reason, it is critical to run a follow-up head-to-head test between your predicted best answer and your original baseline recipe. But what do you do if the predicted performance of your challenger does not measure up? If this is due to piecewise construction errors, you can raise your confidence threshold or lower the number of variables in your test. But the unexpectedly poor performance could also be due to huge interaction effects that you have failed to consider. The only way to find these is to rerun the test with a higher resolution design (preferably a full factorial one).

Highly Sensitive to Lucky Streaks In Data Multivariate test designs are sensitive to lucky streaks in your data. This is especially a problem if you are collecting very small data samples. For example, let's assume that you are testing a landing page that has a real underlying conversion rate of 1 percent. Within the first hundred visitors, it is almost equally likely that you would have zero, or two conversions. However, the estimates produced by your models would vary drastically in these two cases. The first model would take the data literally and conclude that the likelihood of conversion with this landing page is zero—that is, it will never produce a conversion. The second would conclude that your conversion rate is double its actual value. It is critical to collect a lot of data with multivariate testing models to reduce the problems associated with such possible small-sample distortions.

Requires You to Guess at Important Interactions All fractional factorial models require you to specify exactly what types of main effects and variable interactions are possible in your model. These assumptions must be built in ahead of time in order to simplify the complexity of the model and give you economy in terms of the number of recipes that must be sampled.

In the traditional testing, this might be possible since you know which *physical* processes can have an influence on each other. But in online marketing this is difficult. Unlike physical experiments (in manufacturing or pharmaceutical drug trials, for example), landing page optimization is trying to tease out the underlying *psychological* predispositions of people. Since everyone is different, it is impossible to accurately empathize with every member of your audience. You cannot take your own predispositions out of the experiment because you are the one choosing the elements to test. In such a setting, it is impossible to declare which specific interactions matter and which others don't.

Restrictive Test Design As previously discussed, there must be a certain pattern (in terms of the number of variables and their branching factors) in your test design. So you are forced to either stick with well-known "standard" designs from statistical textbooks or construct your own (with the help of statisticians).

Difficult Throttling If you throttle your data collection rates and do not devote equal bandwidth to each recipe in your test, your analysis will be invalid for all common fractional factorial designs.

Full Factorial Parametric Testing

A full factorial parametric test collects data on the response of every possible combination of variables (factors) and values (levels). In other words, it collects an equal amount of information about every possible recipe in your search space.

As we discussed earlier, in online marketing we *expect* strong variable interactions. In fact, we are doing everything that we can to create positive synergies among our testing elements.

> *We at Google are continually surprised by how common and strong variable interactions are in landing page tests.*
>
> —MIKE MYER, statistician, Google

Unlike fractional factorial data collection, full factorial data collection does not lock you into any restrictions during analysis. Full factorial parametric tests do not make assumptions about the underlying model. Analysis of your full factorial data can pinpoint your main effects as well as any interaction effects (lower order or higher order) present in your test.

One of the testing tools that always uses full factorial data collection is Google Website Optimizer (see the Appendix, "Landing Page Testing Tools"). We are glad that Google has chosen the full factorial data collection as their default. Even though the size of the search space is smaller than with comparable fractional factorial testing approaches, you can have a higher confidence in your answer if you run a complete analysis, including interactions. However, it is important to note that collecting data in a full factorial design does not mean that you have to subsequently analyze it to look for interactions. You may choose to look at main effects only. In fact, this is what the Google Website Optimizer currently does.

In a full factorial parametric test design, the baseline recipe would receive a fraction of the total traffic that is inversely proportional to the size of your search space. For example, if your search space is 64 recipes, the baseline would receive 1/64th of the total traffic. Since you are trying to beat the existing baseline, special attention should be accorded to it. You also need to be watching for external and internal changes to your traffic. This means that you want to get accurate conversion information about the baseline recipe even though you may not need to collect a large amount of data for *every* recipe. Because of this, we recommend a modification of the traditional full factorial parametric methodology. As a general rule of thumb, we suggest collecting 15–25 percent of your total data on the baseline recipe during a test. This allows you to get tighter error bars on the baseline recipe and reach statistical significance faster.

Full Factorial Parametric Advantages

There are three main advantages to full factorial parametric tests:

Availability of Information on Interactions If you use full factorial data collection coupled with a complete model, you can detect all important variable interactions. This is not the case with fractional factorial methods such as the Taguchi method, Plackett-Burman, or Latin squares.

Unrestricted Test Design You can choose any number of test variables and arbitrary branching factors for each one. This is in sharp contrast to the significant restrictions found in fractional factorial designs.

Better Estimation of Main Effects Even if you discard the interaction data and only build a model of the main effects, you will still be better off with a full factorial design. If there are interactions, your estimate of the main effects will be more accurate than with fractional factorial designs. This is due to the fact that you have collected data evenly across all recipes (all possible contexts and combinations) and are not relying on spot-sampling a small subset of your search space.

For example, imagine estimating the average elevation of the United States. Full factorial sampling could be compared to sampling on a grid with each measurement a mile apart. A fractional factorial design might be much sparser and might sample on a grid that spaces each measurement every hundred miles. The coarse sampling might overlook geographic features that are smaller than one hundred miles wide, and your elevation estimate might be significantly biased based on the exact position of the sampling grid points. This is much less likely to be a problem with the finer grid, since you would capture all significant features greater than a mile wide and could not go too far astray in your estimate.

Full Factorial Parametric Disadvantages

There are several disadvantages to full factorial parametric tests:

Very Small Test Size Because of the exponential growth of the number of model coefficients as you increase the number of variables (and/or their branching factors), full factorial design quickly hits its limits if you are planning to conduct an analysis of all possible interactions. Because of this, full factorial designs are rarely used in landing page optimization unless your search space is smaller. But remember, the search space size can remain as large as a comparable fractional factorial test if you are planning to only model main effects.

Complicated Analysis Although Google Website Optimizer and other full factorial testing tools are available, most of them will only report on the main effects within your test (the significance of the individual variable values). If you collect information about possible variable interactions to ensure that you have a more accurate answer, you will have to have a background in statistics to understand which interactions are meaningful.

May Not Consider Variable Interactions If you simply conduct a main effects analysis after collecting the data, you will not find variable interactions. In this situation you will also be subject to the piecewise construction errors that we discussed in the "Fractional Factorial Disadvantages" section earlier.

High Uncertainty at the Recipe Level One other slight drawback of the full factorial parametric approach is that the amount of data that you collect on each individual recipe is small, so you may have poor resolution (a lot of variance) at the recipe level. Because of this, you usually have to run a follow-up test to see if your predicted best answer holds up in the real world. Follow-up tests are also highly recommended (for different reasons) for all fractional factorial tests.

Full Factorial Nonparametric Testing

Nonparametric data analysis can be used with full factorial data collection. In fact, as we mentioned earlier, it *cannot* be used if you impose any restrictions on the recipes allowed during the data collection. To our knowledge, there is only one deployed and proven nonparametric approach currently being used for landing page optimization, and we will sketch out its unique features in a moment. We are confident that other nonparametric methods will be developed in the future to address the obvious limitations of parametric analysis in this setting.

Because of the significant limitations of the methods described earlier, SiteTuners spent over three years developing proprietary math specifically tailored to landing page testing. The result is their proprietary TuningEngine technology.

This approach overcomes the two main limitations common to parametric model building. It takes into account all important variable interactions among your input variables *and* it can scale to very large search space sizes.

What makes this possible is a completely different mathematical framework and approach to the landing page optimization problem. Parametric analysis relies on a model building approach. In other words, it tries to gather enough data to accurately estimate the importance of all variable values to the quantity being measured—that is, the conversion rate. Once the model is built, it is possible to estimate which variables contributed to the improved performance and how much they contributed.

By contrast, the TuningEngine asks which combination of variable values (the recipe) is the best-performing one. But it cannot determine which individual variables in the recipe contributed the most to the result. In other words, it cannot tell you *why* the winning recipe is the best.

The TuningEngine has given up the explanatory power in exchange for tangible considerations. Online marketing is a practical discipline grounded in financial and business considerations. Your goal should be to find the landing page that makes you the most money as quickly as possible (preferably among many possible alternatives). Explaining why the winning recipe is the best is a secondary academic consideration. Once you have found the best-performing recipe, you can easily run a follow-up head-to-head test against the original to quantify the estimated amount of improvement.

Full Factorial Nonparametric Advantages

The TuningEngine has several advantages over parametric approaches:

Considers Variable Interactions As we mentioned, the TuningEngine takes variable interactions into account. Although full factorial parametric designs also do this, they are limited in search space size. Most fractional factorial designs ignore important and prevalent variable interactions altogether.

Handles Huge Test Sizes The TuningEngine can handle very large search spaces. SiteTuners routinely run tests involving millions or tens of millions of possible recipes. This scale is several orders of magnitude larger than what can be done with multivariate tests (using the same data rate). Unlike fractional factorial methods, the TuningEngine does not just collect data on a few dozen recipes at a time. It covers the whole search space (data collection is not extremely sparse and can take variable interactions into account).

Requires No Experimental Design Most fractional factorial designs require you to have a specific construction. This means you may only have a certain number of variables, and their branching factors must also conform to the specifics of the test design matrix being used. This often forces online marketers to limit or change their test plan in order to fit these requirements.

The TuningEngine does not place any constraints on your test design. You simply specify the variables that you want to test along with as many alternative values for each one as you would like. The branching factor for each variable can be different. This is also an advantage for full factorial parametric designs.

Allows Simple Analysis The final phase of a TuningEngine test is a simple A-B split test. The significance of the results is easy to understand (using a single statistical test).

Full Factorial Nonparametric Disadvantages

The TuningEngine has three main disadvantages.

Requires Higher Data Rates As a rule of thumb, the TuningEngine requires at least one hundred conversions per day to produce results in a reasonable timeframe. This is higher than the minimums recommended for A-B split tests or small parametric multivariate tests. If you cannot meet the minimum requirement, you may simply have no other option than to use A-B split or small-scale parametric multivariate testing.

Cannot Tell You Why the Best Landing Page Works As we discussed earlier, the TuningEngine cannot tell you why the winning recipe is the best. In other words, you cannot decompose the results into the contributions of the individual variables. However, this is not as much of a drawback as it first seems. Since variable interactions are prevalent in landing page optimization, any intuition about individual variables is frequently lost anyway. The value of the winning recipe lies in the *combination* of its variable values. So decomposing it into main effects is often a misleading exercise in fantasy.

Proprietary Technology Since the TuningEngine is proprietary, the only way to access it is through SiteTuners, with all of the sole-source dependencies that this creates.

Variable Interactions

What is a *variable interaction*? Simply put, it is when the setting for one variable in your test positively or negatively influences the setting of another variable. If they have no effect on each other, they are said to be *independent*. In a *positive interaction*, two (or more) variables create a synergistic effect (yielding results that are greater than the sum of the parts). In a *negative interaction*, two (or more) variables undercut each other and cancel out some of the individual effects.

> ### The Drunk Who Lost His Car Keys
>
> A policeman on patrol noticed a man on all fours crawling around under a streetlamp in the middle of the night. After stopping to take a closer look, the policeman quickly determined that the man was very drunk.
>
> "What are you doing, mister?" he asked.
>
> The drunk looked up at him bleary eyed and replied, "Looking for my car keys—I can't seem to find them."
>
> "Where did you lose them?" the policeman asked.
>
> The drunk scratched his head for a few moments, and then said, "Over there" as he pointed to the end of a completely dark alley several hundred yards away.
>
> "So why are you looking under this streetlamp?" asked the confused officer.
>
> "Because the light is better here," replied the drunk.

You need to step back and take a critical look at the testing method you are about to use and its implications for finding interactions. Are parametric multivariate testing methods powerful? Sure. But don't let that blind you to one of their glaring defects—most common multivariate techniques do not take variable interactions into account.

Like the drunk looking for his car keys, they are usually looking only at the main effects of your individual test variables because that is where "the light is better," and not because it is where the best solution lies. As a result, you may indeed find a *better* page than your original baseline, but you will be leaving money on the table because you will not find the *best* page.

An Illustrative Example

Let's look at a simple example. Assume that you are an auto dealer who sells both Ferraris and Volvos. Your goal is to sell cars and you want to test two different headlines and two different accompanying pictures. So there are a total of four possible versions based on your two variables.

If you believe that there are no interactions, you must also believe that there is a "best" headline regardless of the accompanying picture and that there is a "best" picture regardless of the headline used.

This is not always the case. Each variable can depend on the *context* in which it is seen. Figure 12.1 shows a strong *positive* interaction (connecting the speed and power in the picture with the word "fast" in the headline).

Figure 12.1 Example ad: Picture A, Headline A

Although the headline remains the same, Figure 12.2 shows a strongly *negative* interaction once it is paired with a different picture (making you think about the consequences of fast driving—"speed kills").

Figure 12.2 Example ad: Picture B, Headline A

Figure 12.3 shows a mildly positive interaction (supporting the notion that you can go fast and still be safe).

Figure 12.3 Example ad: Picture A, Headline B

Yet the same headline can be paired with what was previously thought to be a negative picture and produce different results. Figure 12.4 shows a positive interaction (playing on the fear of accidents and highlighting Volvo's longstanding safety record).

Figure 12.4 Example ad: Picture B, Headline B

So it's not the picture, and it's not the headline that determines the performance of the ad. It is their particular combination.

A Real-World Example

Obviously the example in the section above was created to dramatically demonstrate the presence of strong interactions, but this is not simply a theoretical consideration.

Variable interactions are common and significant in landing page optimization testing. This should not be a surprise to anyone, since online marketers are intentionally trying to create landing pages that are greater than the sum of their parts. You should be looking for synergies among all your page elements and trying to eliminate combinations of variable values that work at cross-purposes and undermine your desired outcome.

SiteTuners' client SF Video conducted a test of their PPC landing page. The purpose of the test was to capture leads for its DVD duplication and replication services. The page consisted of a lead form on the left, and a number of client logos on the right (to enhance credibility).

SiteTuners chose to test the following two page variables:

- Headline of the form input section
- Number of SF Video client logos

The form-headline variable took on two possible values:

- "Free Quote Request" (the original)
- "Instant Quote"

The number-of-logos variable also took on two possible values:

- 36 (the original)
- 6

The resulting test had a total of four possible recipes ("combinations" in the terminology of Google Website Optimizer, the landing page testing tool with which this test was conducted).

The original page is shown in Figure 12.5 with the "Free Quote Request" lead-form headline and 36 client logos.

Combination 1 is show in Figure 12.6 with the "Instant Quote" lead-form headline and 36 client logos.

Combination 2 is show in Figure 12.7 with the "Free Quote Request" lead-form headline and 6 client logos.

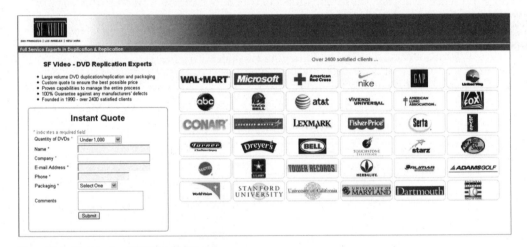

Figure 12.5 "Original" SF Video landing page

Figure 12.6 "Combination 1" SF Video landing page

Figure 12.7 "Combination 2" SF Video landing page

Combination 3 is shown in Figure 12.8 with the "Instant Quote" lead-form headline and 6 client logos.

Figure 12.8 "Combination 3" SF Video landing page

The results of the test were interesting (see the Google Website Optimizer main effects report in Figure 12.9). If you had only looked at the main effects (contributions of the individual variables), you would have concluded that the new headline was the best (96.6 percent confidence) and that the original client logo layout was superior (93.5 percent confidence).

Sort By:	Relevance Rating	Order Created			Download:			Print	Preview
Relevance Rating [?]	Variation	Estimated Conversion Rate Range [?]		Chance to Beat Orig. [?]	Chance to Beat All [?]	Observed Improvement [?]	Conversions / Visitors [?]
Heading 2 / 5	Original	2.72% ± 0.4%		—	3.39%	—	74 / 2724
	Instant Quote	3.58% ± 0.5%		96.5%	96.6%	31.9%	96 / 2679
Images 1 / 5	Original	3.51% ± 0.5%		—	93.5%	—	95 / 2710
	6 Images	2.78% ± 0.4%		6.55%	6.45%	-20.6%	75 / 2693

Figure 12.9 Test results—main effects

But this does not tell the whole story. A closer look (see the recipe-level report in Figure 12.10) reveals that changing the headline and leaving the client logos unchanged had a significant and large impact on the conversion rate. However, there were no big changes in conversion rate with *either* headline in the presence of the new client logo layout.

The SF Video experimental design was very simple—in fact you can't have a simpler multivariate test construction than a 2 × 2 configuration. Why did the headline have a large impact in the presence of the original client logo layout, whereas it had none in the presence of the new one? Who knows? The point is that surprisingly large interactions can exist even in such small multivariate test designs.

Combination	Estimated Conversion Rate Range [?]	Chance to Beat Orig. [?]	Chance to Beat All [?]	Observed Improvement [?]	Conversions / Visitors [?]
Original	2.73% ± 0.6%	—	0.96%	—	38 / 1393
Combination 1	4.33% ± 0.7%	98.7%	96.3%	58.7%	57 / 1317
Combination 3	2.86% ± 0.6%	58.4%	1.85%	4.97%	39 / 1362
Combination 2	2.70% ± 0.6%	48.5%	0.91%	-0.85%	36 / 1331

Figure 12.10 Test results—recipe-level

In online marketing, you *want* interactions. You want the picture to reinforce the headline, and the sales copy, and the offer, and the call-to-action. Similarly, you want to detect any parts of the landing page that are working at cross-purposes and undercutting the performance of other page elements. Your goal should be to find the best-performing recipe as embodied by a specific *group* of landing page variable values.

Obviously for online marketing, pretending that there can't be any interactions is an absurd assumption. Strong interaction effects (often involving more than two variables) definitely exist, and in SiteTuners' experience are fairly common. So while you may be able to get some positive results by ignoring interactions, you will not be getting the *best* results.

So where can you look for interactions? In general, there is no way to guarantee that any subset of your testing elements does not interact. However, you should consider elements that are in physical proximity or that are otherwise confounded with each other. For example, let's assume that you are testing a form and have chosen to test the call-to-action button color and text. Although these may seem independent, that is not the case. They both combine to create the specific presentation of the call-to-action, and you should test for possible interactions.

Similarly, if you are testing different headlines followed by different sales copy, you should expect interactions. The headline is supposed to draw the visitor into reading further. If a disconnect exists between the headline and the following text, you can expect negative interactions. If they reinforce each other, you should expect positive synergies. So far we have primarily focused on interactions between two test elements. In fact, there are often strong interactions among several variables on a landing page.

As we have already discussed in the "Full Factorial Parametric Testing" section earlier, full factorial data collection does allow you to later examine variable interactions. However, you need to be clear about full factorial *data collection* versus subsequent full factorial *data analysis*. They are independent of each other. Currently the Google Website Optimizer is the only widely used parametric multivariate testing tool that requires you to collect data for a full factorial design, but the reporting and analysis still only looks at the main effects. In theory, you can export the complete data and conduct a more complicated analysis, but this is not supported natively in the tool.

So the dirty little secret is out. If you still choose to ignore variable interactions, you have no one but yourself to blame for suboptimal results. The bottom line is this: If you do not have the minimum data rate to use nonparametric testing methods like the TuningEngine (which can handle large test sizes *and* considers variable interactions), you should at least use full factorial data collection coupled with a proper subsequent analysis that estimates variable interactions. Identifying interactions can be a complicated business. You may have to learn some additional statistics or bring in outside experts to help you design the test and analyze your results, but this is the only way to consistently get the biggest possible benefits from your high-value multivariate tests.

Don't Ignore Variable Interactions

- Interactions exist and can be very strong.
- If you ignore them, you will not get the best possible results.
- A-B splits and fractional factorial parametric testing generally assume that variable interactions do not exist.

Congratulations, you have made it through the most mathematical part of the book! This chapter also concludes Part IV, "The Mechanics of Testing." In "Part V: Organization and Planning," we will focus on practical issues related to getting your test program off the ground. These final chapters will cover getting buy-in and pulling together the right resources, developing your action plan, and avoiding common pitfalls.

Organization and Planning

You have learned a lot in the earlier parts of the book about what landing pages are, how to identify problems with them, ideas for fixing those problems, and the details of landing page testing.

The focus now shifts to the nuts and bolts of getting things done within your company. The skill sets required to get the best results from your testing program are diverse and will require talent from across your organization. You will need to work with a wide range of people whose perspectives and motivations may be different from your own. Once you have gathered the right resources, you will have to create the appropriate action plan and watch out for common testing program pitfalls that can derail all of your work.

Part V consists of the following chapters:

Chapter 13   **Assembling Your Team and Getting Buy-in**

Chapter 14   **Developing Your Action Plan**

Chapter 15   **Avoiding Real-World Pitfalls**

V

Assembling Your Team and Getting Buy-in

After all is said and done, more is said than done.

—AESOP

13

In this chapter, you will learn about the common roles required to create a successful testing program. Each role brings its own expertise, biases, and needs that must be addressed. You will learn how to bring the necessary people together and move them toward supporting you in your efforts.

CHAPTER CONTENTS

The Usual Suspects

Little Company, Big Company

The Company Politics of Tuning

Strategies for Getting Started

Insource or Outsource?

The Blind Men and the Elephant

by John Godfrey Saxe (1816–1887)

It was six men of Indostan, to learning much inclined,
who went to see the elephant (Though all of them were blind),
that each by observation, might satisfy his mind.

The first approached the elephant, and, happening to fall,
against his broad and sturdy side, at once began to bawl:
"God bless me! but the elephant, is nothing but a wall!"

The second feeling of the tusk, cried: "Ho! what have we here,
so very round and smooth and sharp? To me 'tis mighty clear,
this wonder of an elephant, is very like a spear!"

The third approached the animal, and, happening to take,
the squirming trunk within his hands, thus boldly up and spake:
"I see the elephant is very like a snake!"

The fourth reached out his eager hand, and felt about the knee:
"What most this wondrous beast is like, is mighty plain," quoth he;
"'Tis clear enough the elephant is very like a tree."

The fifth, who chanced to touch the ear, Said; "E'en the blindest man
can tell what this resembles most; Deny the fact who can,
This marvel of an elephant, is very like a fan!"

The sixth no sooner had begun, about the beast to grope,
than, seizing on the swinging tail, that fell within his scope,
"I see," quoth he, "the elephant is very like a rope!"

And so these men of Indostan, disputed loud and long,
each in his own opinion, exceeding stiff and strong,
Though each was partly in the right, and all were in the wrong!

So, oft in theologic wars, the disputants, I ween,
tread on in utter ignorance, of what each other mean,
and prate about the elephant, not one of them has seen!

The Usual Suspects

Your testing program can move forward and still fail. If it does, it will likely happen as a result of a "death by a thousand cuts." Your original test ideas will be reviewed, tweaked, overruled, and co-opted by many others along the way. Every minor change seems innocent enough on its own, but as the fine layers of changes are added on top of one another, you can end up with a locked grasp on the same basic errors.

But you have no choice because you need the cooperation of many people. You have to bear the ultimate responsibility for wrangling and herding them roughly in the desired direction. So your skills as a diplomat and persuader will be very important.

> *A camel is a horse designed by a committee.*
>
> —SIR ALEC ISSIGONIS (DESIGNER OF THE MINI CAR)

The "usual suspects" roles described here are commonly needed for a successful landing page optimization program. Depending on the scope of your program, not all of them may be applicable to you or your organization. If your company or department is small, several of these roles may be assigned to a single person. In fact, many of them may be you. If that is the case, use extra caution to take yourself and your predispositions into account. See additional discussion in the "Little Company, Big Company" section later in this chapter. Each role in this section has an associated scope of responsibilities or expertise. There are also typical skills and training required. Each role also has a specific overlap and brings up common issues that repeatedly come up in tests involving each role.

Remember to pay particular attention when you get to the sections describing your own role or roles. Read them with the additional perspective of understanding how others may view your responsibilities, biases, and working style. Don't become a stumbling block to your own program by ignoring your role in it.

User Experience Designer

User experience (or UX) is an interdisciplinary field that examines how users interact with a particular system, object, or device. This includes how they view it, learn about its capabilities, and use it in the real world. With landing page optimization, this concerns the navigation, content, and function of a landing page.

Skills and Training UX professionals will likely come with a design, content, or interaction background. In advanced programs, the UX role might arrive from the specialized disciplines of human factors, user-centered design, human computer interaction, information architecture, interface design, visual design, or usability testing. In some cases, UX people may be drawn from within your software development team, where they currently may design user interfaces. If no one at the company has these skills, it is possible to hire consultants on a project basis. An experienced UX designer with broad experience often provides critical insights into which elements to test.

Specific Overlap UX designers are usually given a wide scope of responsibilities. Because usability is a huge factor in conversion rate improvement, they are usually heavily involved in development of the written test plan (helping to determine the elements to be tested, along with the specific alternatives for each element to be considered). UX experts can also readily construct The Matrix (see Chapter 3, "The Matrix—Moving People to Act"). They can define roles, tasks, and AIDA decision process steps for your business and help you identify gaps. They are also experienced at matching important business objectives to the needs of users.

Common Issues UX practitioners are often generalists. They may have been involved in the design of many websites on a variety of topics. For this reason, it is important to team them with a subject matter expert. Without the support of someone knowledgeable in your industry or business, UX practitioners may miss important aspects of your audience, conversion process, or business goals.

UX people are usually good at the functional and architectural aspects of your design (that is, common usability issues that are likely to affect all of your visitors). They are usually weaker on the content issues, such as text copy, marketing message, and graphical design.

UX practitioners tend to believe that good design procedures and small-scale usability testing (involving a few representative test subjects) result in a high-performance and coherent design. However, they need to understand that you are not asking them to come up with a single perfect design. Their ideas may be used piecemeal as part of your test. It is often tremendously liberating for them to be allowed to come up with some brainstormed ideas to include in a test plan and not have ultimate responsibility for selecting the perfect one (which is done by the visitors to the test page instead).

The best landing page version will be found statistically through a larger audience, not through qualitative review or small group inputs. While UX practitioners generally support testing, the methods of evaluating landing page tests here are very different from the tests UX teams usually control. Because of this departure, their involvement should usually be confined to helping decide what to test and not how to analyze the results.

Product Manager

Product managers are typically responsible for all aspects of developing and marketing a particular product or service. They may also have profit and loss responsibility that makes them accountable for the performance of the product as a whole. Product managers have operational day-to-day responsibility for the product team, although they may draw on staff members from other departments as needed. They often represent the subject matter expertise group.

Skills and Training Product managers can come from a wide variety of backgrounds, including technical, management, and finance. Their main roles are to manage and facilitate. They are usually effective at putting together cross-disciplinary teams of people. Product managers make sure that the product features are responding to competitive marketplace needs and that the marketing is effective.

Specific Overlap At a minimum, product managers will have to approve any landing page project related to their product. Often they will be the person leading or managing the effort.

They may be needed to secure the help of any project-based people outside of your normal team. Product managers also help push through any approvals required from other departments.

Common Issues If your product manager is already behind your landing page optimization project, then you have a valuable ally. If that's not the case, you may have a hard time getting enough of your product manager's sustained attention to make it happen. Product managers typically wear too many hats and are overextended. Since their role is to herd others, they are also commonly interrupt-driven and easily distracted.

Product managers are also often in the "if it ain't broke, don't fix it" mode. If the landing page in question already drives significant revenue or value, you may have a difficult time lobbying for a test. The product manager may be preoccupied with other problems, and may not understand the financial opportunity presented by improving the conversion rate. This may especially be the case if the landing page testing effort requires the product manager to take on significant extra work to coordinate the project.

Webmaster

The webmaster, content manager, or web producer is responsible for the care and maintenance of your website. They maintain the content, control the site organization, and administer the filenaming conventions—for example, for page names and graphical images. The webmasters make sure that the site does not have any broken links, missing content, browser or device compatibility issues, or improper form handling. They also create and review the web analytics reports for the site.

Skills and Training Webmasters commonly come from a programming or technical background (operational focus), or from a creative or copywriting background (content focus).

Specific Overlap The webmasters will most likely need to approve (or at least be aware of) the changes that you propose to make to the site. They will need to provide you with the original page elements and help you upload the new test versions of all pages and graphics.

They will most probably oversee and be involved in the quality assurance (QA) and testing of all new page elements. Depending on your tuning technology, webmasters may need to tag all web pages on the site with additional JavaScript and tracking information. They may also be involved in the cutover from your QA environment to the live data collection. Webmasters may also track and monitor your data collection through web analytics software.

Common Issues Some webmasters are very territorial about exactly how and when changes happen on their site. This mind-set can often get in the way of testing, because you are perceived as violating their turf and creating extra work for them. In extreme situations, this can result in stonewalling or even outright denial of access to certain parts of the site.

You will need the help of your webmaster to download and upload content to the staging area of your web server—that is, one where you can test changes without affecting the live website. Ideally you should have the ability to transfer files to and from the staging server yourself. Most webmasters will be concerned about granting direct access (ostensibly for security reasons) to anyone whose familiarity with their systems is untested. They might insist on doing much of the production work themselves. Unfortunately, during quality assurance testing numerous uploads may be required to get rid of all known bugs and problems with your test implementation. If your webmaster is uncooperative or busy, this can drag out your implementation schedule considerably.

Webmasters are also in charge of policing the style guides and naming conventions for the site. They can be very particular about filenaming conventions and coding standards. This can hold up testing if not addressed ahead of time.

Because webmasters are often involved in the testing (and may even be in charge of it), it is always a good idea to get their active cooperation. The best way to do this is to arm yourself with information ahead of time, follow procedures, and communicate clearly throughout. Ask for design guidelines, style sheets, procedures, systems training, and coding conventions. Address exactly what content changes will be tested in your written test plan. This should include the names and locations of all files and content involved.

System Administrator

Your system administrators keep your server network running and operational. They are responsible for Internet connectivity, the load and demand on your web servers, keeping software up to date, backing up your data, and computer security.

Skills and Training System administrators usually come from technical backgrounds. They are often detail oriented and keep track of a large number of operational and procedural details.

Specific Overlap System administrators will be involved in the following ways in your test:

- Moving from the staging to the live environment
- Rerouting traffic for the test
- Reviewing the proposed testing technology and implementation requirements
- Certifying that personal or private customer data is not disclosed during testing
- Ensuring that network security is not compromised by the testing
- Assuring that server loads and web page loading times are not significantly affected by the test

Common Issues Since choosing a particular tuning technology or testing company partner involves technical elements, system administrators will typically want to get involved. They will vet the underlying technology and project implementation procedures in a lot of detail to understand the impact that it will have on their domain. In some cases, they have veto power over choosing certain kinds of tuning technology approaches.

Part of the system administrator's concern has to do with control over the hosting and presentation of the alternative tuning elements during the test. Some testing technologies rely on outside hosting of site elements on the web servers of the testing company. This is often strongly resisted by system administrators, because they cannot guarantee the security or response times of another company's web servers. Other technical approaches allow all tuning elements to be hosted on the company's web servers. This is much more likely to put the system administrator's mind at ease.

System administrators are also concerned about security and data integrity. They want to make sure that your testing method does not introduce any new vulnerability. This includes inadvertent disclosure of private customer data (such as e-commerce credit card information or personal contact information). These issues are usually easily addressed if you review the proposed technical approach in detail with system administrators, or arrange for them to talk directly with the technical staff of the testing technology company that you are considering using.

Graphic Designer

The graphic designer is responsible for creating all graphical elements of your landing page and its overall visual "look."

Skills and Training Typically, graphic designers will have an artistic background in the visual arts, including drawing, painting, film, animation, and photography. They may also have had additional training specifically in web design and related graphics, production graphic design for business, photo editing, animation, video authoring, and web design software packages.

Specific Overlap It is likely that you will need the involvement of a graphic designer for your landing page testing. They can create individual graphical elements such as pictures, buttons, navigation menus, and rollover images. Some of these changes are simple, such as changing button text or background colors. Other changes may involve a complete redesign of your landing page and its layout.

Graphic designers may also be needed if your test plan calls for special interactive content, such as comparison shopping guides, product demonstrations, and software wizards.

Common Issues Graphic designers usually have an artistic bent. This can mean that they are more concerned with self-expression than with business goals. In their creative bent, they often try to work on fun projects or turn routine assignments into artistic outlets. They also welcome opportunities to build their artistic portfolio.

Unfortunately, these tendencies can be at odds with the goals of landing page testing. Internet visitors often respond best to stark landing pages on which visual distractions are kept to a minimum. You must keep tight control over your graphic designers. Use the yardstick of "is it absolutely necessary?" to determine if design elements should be included or emphasized. In fact, it is often a good idea to test the complete removal of existing graphical elements. The graphic designer will likely not be the biggest fan of these tests.

The same applies to the use of more subtle color treatments. Bold ones may look more "interesting" to you or to other decision makers, but plain ones are often less distracting to the visitor. Something that draws visual attention to anything other than your primary call-to-action should be questioned. Instruct your graphic designers to create emphasis on key elements by toning down the surrounding page, rather than by making them even bolder to compete with other graphical elements.

An alternative approach is to allow one "artistic" option for some test plan variables. Who knows, it may even end up being part of the best-performing recipe. This, after all, is the whole point of testing.

Copywriter

Copywriters are responsible for the text content of your website.

Skills and Training Copywriters come from a variety of backgrounds. Most have formal education in writing and composition. Still others are experts in their subject matter area and have been asked to write specific content or articles for the website for that reason, regardless of their writing experience.

Specific Overlap Many of the elements that you may want to tune involve copywriting: headlines, body text, sales copy, the call-to-action, the naming of navigation links, button text, figure captions, and text embedded in graphics.

Common Issues Copywriters are often generalists. They may need the support of your marketing staff, subject matter experts, or product manager to make sure that your main messaging points and technical features are being presented effectively from the perspective of your intended audience.

Copywriters may write for a variety of corporate materials, including informational articles, technical writing, and print collateral. When writing for the Web, they tend to carry over the same editorial style, instead of using the best practices described in Chapter 7, "Conversion Improvement Basics." In fact, effective landing page copy often goes against the grain of traditional expositional writing and grammar.

Marketing Manager

The marketing managers are responsible for the marketing of your product or service. They formulate the marketing plan and oversee its execution.

Skills and Training Marketing managers often come from an advertising, communications, finance, or creative background. Depending on the size of your company, they may be generalists who are responsible for everything, or specialists who are only in charge of web promotion. If your advertising mix includes offline components, they may be responsible for making sure that a consistent view of your product exists across all channels.

Specific Overlap As part of your test plan development, marketing managers can often provide a lot of excellent input. This includes marketing intelligence about competitors and your product's positioning in your industry. They can communicate with the copywriter to ensure that specific marketing messages are included in your sales copy and headlines.

Marketing managers can also help you understand larger business goals and the potential impact of your landing page test on your business partners, customer service, and offline channels.

Common Issues Marketing managers should understand the full scope of your promotional and traffic acquisition activities. It is important to communicate to them and to product marketing the key requirements for your test traffic. The marketing manager can help you to identify the largest subset of your traffic that is recurring, controllable, and stable.

Marketing managers often control the marketing plan. They can tell you about the timing of external events (such as tradeshows and industry-specific seasonal changes). In addition, marketing managers can tell you in advance about any major public relations or product announcements. You must work closely with them to make sure that your proposed data collection period does not fall during these periods; otherwise, your data may be skewed or irreparably tainted.

Programmer

Programmers are responsible for the functional (as opposed to the strictly visual) aspects of your website.

Skills and Training The background of programmers is diverse. There are few acknowledged accreditations in the industry. Many excellent programmers are self-taught. The speed of technology changes requires programmers to become lifelong learners or face the prospect of skill obsolescence. Some programmers are focused on the presentation of information to the end user and are adept at scripting languages that make up the *front end*—the visual portion of the software application with which the visitor interacts. Others concentrate on the representation, storage, and manipulation of the underlying data that make up the *back end*—they focus on databases and algorithms.

Specific Overlap Any functional changes to your landing page or website may potentially require programming support:

- Mouse rollover behavior
- Reconfiguration of form elements based on visitor actions
- Capturing of additional information (changes to the database)
- Business rules and logic
- Changes in the flow through your pages
- Reorganization of the area where you collect data (and the order in which you collect it)
- Processing any new web-based forms

Common Issues Programmers tend to think in functional terms. If a certain capability is technically possible, they will not usually try to optimize or improve the user experience. Technical people often have little or no regard for (or even conscious awareness of) presentation issues such as messaging, visual design, or good usability. They are often very bright and can get through even challenging and complicated user experiences, and wrongly assume that others are equally capable and willing.

The result is that landing page changes touched by programmers are often unappealing to your visitors (with the consequence of lower conversion rates). So you must be specific in your quality control and testing about the details surrounding any changes that the programmers make. This includes background colors, fonts and font sizes, form field order and layout, text labels, and error messages and handling.

The best solution is to have detailed specifications for the required functional changes. Include wireframes or mock-ups of the proposed designs. You should also spend some time sensitizing the programmers to the subtleties of good design and emphasizing its importance.

On the other hand, programmers are often receptive to empirical real-world data. If you can show them that a design option performs better than an alternative, they are likely to be enthusiastic about finding more options like the successful one.

Quality Assurance Tester

The quality assurance (QA) tester ensures that all proposed changes to your website function properly before being released as part of your live site.

Skills and Training Most QA positions are not full-time. They are typically project based—for example, part of a complete website redesign process. Consequently, QA staff have a variety of backgrounds and may spend the majority of their time in other roles, such as webmaster, graphic designer, copywriter, programmer, or marketing assistant.

Specific Overlap QA should always be involved in the tuning process after the test plan has been implemented (and before the changes are moved to your live site prior to the commencement of data collection). Once problems are uncovered, they are sent back to the implementation team for rework.

Common Issues It is important that the person assigned to perform QA is not the same person who oversaw the implementation of the test. Otherwise, there is a clear conflict of interest and a tendency to shortchange the QA testing process.

Your landing page optimization should be based on a formal written test plan document that defines the specific elements and values to be tested. As soon as the test plan is completed, you should independently create a QA plan to go with it. The QA plan should note all important design and technical constraints for the proposed test. The QA tester should use this plan to make sure that all variable values are independently tested and that all key combinations of variables are also considered (see Chapter 14, "Developing Your Action Plan," for additional details).

QA testers are supposed to be detail oriented. In fact, this is a requirement for the role. However, some people take things a bit too far. They refuse to sign off on any deviations from the original test plan that are even a little bit out of compliance. At this point you must often make a judgment call about whether the discrepancies are likely to significantly affect the outcome of the test. You may have to overrule the QA tester and accept the current state of the implementation.

Little Company, Big Company

Several roles might be combined in the work of a single person in a smaller organization. At larger companies, there can be an even greater degree of specialization in each role than indicated earlier. Additional large company capabilities might be added. This can include business intelligence, customer acquisition, web analytics, and similar teams that can provide much deeper insight into traffic and customer segments of interest.

Regardless of size, the company's business model will influence web resourcing. For example, an online retailer that saves operating costs by increasing direct web sales might have a larger web team than a larger company whose website's purpose is brand awareness only.

Little Company

The differences between a small company and a large company can vary widely depending on the characteristics of the business. Despite the sweeping generalizations, there are still some consistent themes based on company size. Small companies will likely have a smaller web team with different skills, and with more hats worn by a single person. However, they tend to have more flexibility and can adapt to changes more quickly.

Skills and Training At a small company, the core competency of the business will have a stark impact on the skill level of the team. A small startup with an innovative web focus might have its choice of web-savvy candidates. A small insurance company with a low-priority e-commerce arm might end up with a team that's not as skilled in as many areas. In all likelihood, the company will be entirely satisfied with that skill level based on their needs and sophistication.

Small companies will likely have generalists with strong project management skills. With fewer resources, they often juggle so many hats that they are left strapped for time to keep up with ongoing trends. They may have one particular area of expertise and work with a vendor to manage other areas.

Common Overlaps The overlaps in smaller businesses tend to be separated along the lines of content overlaps and technical overlaps, or between types of work. For example, a small or medium-sized e-commerce company may focus online marketing on the store arm and a generalized content role on the corporate side, with a technical layer supporting both sides.

Some messaging-centric roles may not be built until mid-size growth is reached. Content, UI, design, and marketing roles may be combined with vendor support whenever a larger project is funded. Web product management or marketing might be the only main online functional group, though the job description itself for a smaller company's online marketer or web product manager might have a similar scope. Brand managers, website production, editors, and deeper specializations may not be built until even further into business expansion.

On the technical side, several roles might be similarly combined. Webmaster, system administrator, web analytics, and QA lead might all answer to the same name (or indeed be one person). Often, UI and design roles are consolidated even at mid-size companies. However, at a small company, design may be one aspect of the technical role because of the reliance on front-end coders for the site build.

Common Issues and Testing Implications Smaller businesses tend to have less documentation and less formality. They may also not have the depth of audience profiling, established reference points like formal documentation, and internalized best practices guidelines that you might find as an organization matures.

There is likely less formality around the financial process as well. Though there might be approval levels required for budget to be released, there will likely not be as many layers of signoff. In addition to faster approval, planning will likely be less restrictive. Projects can be initiated very quickly. Incremental budgets, however, tend to come in tight discretionary chunks.

For a testing program, these differences have clear implications in terms of the relationships to develop with the messaging or technical role. A smaller organization that commonly relies on vendors for key projects would be comfortable with a decision to outsource landing page optimization. The pros and cons of this decision are examined in detail later in this chapter.

Big Company

As with small companies, the amount of specialization in a large company will depend on the fundamentals of the business. However, the size of the company will have vast implications on the variety of specialized roles that might exist. In addition, there may be expansions into regional and global roles that repeat the same skills with a geographic overlay.

Skills and Training The degree of specialization required in an enterprise tends to create a small tribe of skilled specialists. Since they are able to focus very narrowly, they will often have a better academic understanding of web best practices. Because of this they may be more likely to "know it all" and not be inclined to test or revisit their assumptions.

Common Overlaps For large companies, there is often a dedicated team for each role described in this book. Because of the degree of specialization, it's sometimes harder to distinguish roles and responsibilities in the similar roles. This is especially true if a role (like web marketing manager) is repeated for geography, language, or business specialization. Instead of an absence of skills, the volume of qualified staff with related objectives—improve the ROI of an online store or deliver more visitors for brand awareness—means politics and hierarchy are as important as the role overlaps themselves.

Because socialization (educating and getting consensus) is critical to move programs forward in a larger company, the time devoted to this function can be significant. The cultural difference of a company that requires cordoned "swimlanes" versus one that expects cross-functional collaboration can also have as much of an impact on a testing program as the difference in roles.

Common Issues and Testing Implications The formality of a larger company budget process can mean that while larger amounts might be available, they must be scheduled out far in advance. Lower-level managers may have authority to sign off for smaller amounts, but any flexibility to spend would be based on someone else's budget miscalculation.

Larger companies also have extensive barriers set up by procedural gatekeepers. For example, it's more likely that a legal department will need to review all web activities and online copy at an enterprise. They also may require more legal copy on each type of page, which means more content to de-emphasize in the design's content hierarchy. Regulatory compliance, while a process step throughout some industries, can be more formalized in terms of language use and require longer throughput timeframes in a larger group.

Businesses with multiple distribution channels, alliances, and partnership agreements may also have legal or business development restrictions so that the fundamental sales model is not threatened by highlights on direct promotions or changes in advertised pricing. This limits the degree of price and promotion testing in an optimization program.

In general, a larger organization will have a slower path to testing and reaction. They likely have greater financial resources, so it could be worthwhile to invest in a long-term testing program once an outsourced series of tests proves the concept's profitability.

The Company Politics of Tuning

You need the active cooperation of all the usual suspects to pull off the project. Although there are common difficulties with some of the required team roles, there are ways of mitigating these issues.

But there is another class of constituencies within your company that is also critical. Each of these groups has a goal of empire building at worst, self-perpetuation and reputation building at best. Members of these groups often achieve their goals through noncooperation (by restricting or blocking the initiatives of others). Departmental silos and territorialism are often the biggest obstacles to successful landing page optimization. Unlike the usual suspects (whose active cooperation you may need), these people have the power to withhold permission. Remember, it only takes one "no" from any of these group leaders to stop your landing page optimization program in its tracks.

Brand Guardians

The brand guardians within your company can include elements of advertising, PR, marketing communications, product development, and product management. These functions can be augmented by external ad agencies, media buyers, or PR firms. Tangible embodiments of your brand include your logo and acceptable logo use, website style guides, messaging points, and color choices.

A brand can be one of the most powerful assets that a company possesses. It can serve as a shortcut to decision making when it's well regarded by a prospect. Many companies spend huge sums of money promoting and building their brands for this reason. They also vigilantly guard against distortions or miscommunications of their competitive positioning and messaging points.

There is a danger of a brand becoming fossilized. As the brand becomes increasingly powerful, it takes on a life of its own. The stronger the momentum of the brand, the more difficult it is to make significant changes to it. For better or worse, this is not an issue for many online companies that are contemplating landing page optimization. Chances are your brand is not that well known (at least to the new visitors who arrive on your landing page as a result of your traffic-acquisition efforts).

> *A foolish consistency is the hobgoblin of little minds, adored by little statesmen and philosophers and divines.*
>
> —Ralph Waldo Emerson

One of the biggest concerns of brand guardians is the lack of consistent messaging. Because of this, brand guardians are often insistent that the key messaging point must be repeated across all media outlets and marketing channels without variation. Although this is generally a worthwhile aspiration, remember that the goal of landing page optimization is to find a landing page that your audience responds to best.

As a part of this, you are trying to find the right message and the best presentation of it. So brand guardians' insistence on messaging orthodoxy can often shut down the testing of even the slightest change to tone, style, language, or approach to sales copy or headlines. If one of your alternative messages draws a better response, it means that it resonated better with your target audience. The winning element can in fact become part of your new and improved messaging.

Brand guardians must understand that landing page testing can be an excellent way to conduct market research and understand the changing needs of the target audience. They must not simply insist on the endless (and sometimes mindless) repetition of the current approach. The original messaging and presentation may very well beat out any of the tested alternatives. But at the core of testing philosophy lies the possibility that you may not have the optimal solution, and that you may find better performance through the testing of alternatives.

IT Staff

The gulf between marketing and IT within a company can be wide. The mind-sets of the two groups of people are fundamentally different. IT tries to keep marketers from sabotaging their systems, whereas marketers rarely understand the level of effort that goes into different system choices.

IT staff members are often legitimately busy and overwhelmed. Since their support is often requested (or demanded) by many people in the company, they have developed a multilayered defensive strategy. Even if they do not directly refuse a request for assistance, they can effectively block progress by a series of escalating responses. Common tactics include the following:

Technical Feasibility Determinations If IT staff does not want to work on a project, they will examine the proposed underlying technology and declare it unfit for some reason. They might insist that it cannot be effectively or securely integrated with existing technologies or systems. In landing page optimization, this approach is commonly used to disqualify the tuning technology. Since the reasons for the objection are often highly technical, few marketers can muster the necessary ammunition to counteract it.

Most testing companies have come up with noninvasive approaches to testing. The only underlying technologies required are JavaScript and the setting of first-party cookies (allowed by the vast majority of Internet users). With many approaches, the alternative tuning elements can remain in the client's original web server environment. Uptime levels, site speed, and response times (collectively referred to as "availability") can also be guaranteed or effectively addressed.

Operational Policies Most landing page optimization projects do not require a lot of IT support time, but they often involve a number of small interrupt-driven tasks. IT has the power to bring the project to a virtual standstill by insisting that detailed, time-consuming, and labor-intensive systems be used to interact with their staff. There are many names for these systems, including "change requests," "trouble tickets," and "issue tracking." Even more troublesome, these tasks can be bunched into a backlog for infrequent dev releases on a schedule dictated by IT's whim, budget allocation, or business priority. Their use is appropriate for larger projects (so component tasks will not be overlooked), but they can be overkill when the required changes can be addressed within a few minutes by the IT staffer. In such cases, a small request for help can be tied up for days or weeks in the system without resolution. If this happens repeatedly, it can throw off a landing page project by many weeks.

Common ways to proceed in the face of IT's delaying tactics include the following:

Work on a landing page outside of IT control. It is often difficult to get permission to change parts of a company's main website. However, many marketing programs use stand-alone landing pages or microsites that are not connected to the main site. In many cases, such landing pages have significant inbound traffic and are controlled by the marketing department. Since you can control many of the traffic sources for the landing page test, you can redirect their traffic to anywhere you would like.

Get a project-based support commitment. You can often get a specific IT staff member assigned to you for the duration of your project. As long as you can guarantee that the individual will be used at only a small percentage of the person's total time availability and for a short duration, you can often get IT approval. These kinds of arrangements transfer the person nominally to your team (or have that person remain under joint jurisdiction). This allows you to bypass many of the IT procedural requirements and have the IT staffer complete your tasks with minimal delay.

Prioritize projects based on financial impact. If you properly lay out the financial case for your landing page test, you may be able to show the potential for a large profit impact on the company. In many cases, IT projects are prioritized based partially on this criterion. By focusing on the financial impact, you may be able to reprioritize your project to the head of the IT queue.

C-whims

"C"-level officers in your company are often driven leaders. They include not only the Chief Executive Officer (CEO), Chief Operating Officer (COO), Chief Marketing Officer (CMO), Chief Technical Officer (CTO), and Chief Financial Officer (CFO), but also the top vice presidential levels. They are different in their roles and responsibilities but share the authority to fire you (or at least make your life miserable).

Many can effectively delegate responsibilities to subordinates. Others can't. We have seen a surprisingly high level of meddling in landing page testing by senior executives who should be several levels removed from the operational testing.

Landing page testing is often the target of their attention for the following reasons:

High Visibility Landing pages are exposed to the public and seen by huge numbers of your company's potential prospects.

Large Potential Profit Impact If you consider the money trail, testing has by far the largest profit impact of any online marketing activity.

The Fun of Testing Brainstorming gets the creative juices flowing and provides a forum to guess how your audience might respond.

Unfortunately, just because C-level executives can get involved in landing page optimization does not mean that they should. Their opinions are based on gut feelings that are philosophically the polar opposite of large-scale statistical sampling of your audience's actual behavior. And these opinions carry disproportional weight in the decision-making process. Web analytics evangelist Avinash Kaushik and author of *Web Analytics 2.0: The Art of Online Accountability and Science of Customer Centricity* (Sybex, 2009) refers to such decisions as "HiPPO"—highest paid person's opinions.

Instead of fighting the input of your executives head on, try to actually accommodate it by testing their suggestions (along with your own original ideas, of course). If their ideas do not prove to be the best (as is often the case), you can point to the numbers and quantify the financial impact of the different versions. In other words, if you can show a big financial win, whose ideas prevailed will become much less important.

Strategies for Getting Started

A testing program has to be established, and then it becomes an ongoing or periodic activity in the online marketing department. The success of the first project is critical for establishing the long-term momentum for subsequent engagements. There are a number of strategies that you can pursue as you get started.

Start Small

A common way to start your testing program is with a small test. Once you have demonstrated your ability to pull off a complete end-to-end landing page experiment, you should have enough support to continue. The key to this approach is to appear non-threatening and not ask for a lot of help.

Components of a small test may include the following:

Unimportant Landing Page Do not try to fix your home page or highest-traffic landing pages first. Such efforts may be actively resisted before you have proven yourself. Pick a secondary landing page that has a reasonable amount of traffic (perhaps from a single online marketing campaign).

Small Diversion of Traffic If you have only one landing page, you can still conduct your test by diverting a small percentage of the traffic to testing alternatives. This will guarantee that even if your tested alternatives underperform the current baseline, the overall drop in conversion rate will be small.

Simple Page Changes If you make simple changes such as headlines, sales copy, and call-to-action buttons, you will not need a lot of outside support to create your alternative tuning elements. You can also make such changes in a short amount of time.

Basic Test Structure Use A-B split testing (either on a granular or coarse level) for the test. The data analysis is simple—there are no complex variable interactions or complex design matrices to worry about.

Low-Cost Testing Platform Several low-cost tools are available for running basic A-B split and multivariate tests. Many of them are hosted on the Internet and do not even require installation. See the Appendix, "Landing Page Testing Tools," for additional details.

But remember, your test must still produce results that are meaningful. This means your data rate must be high enough to complete the test in a reasonable period of time, and the financial impact (or at least the percentage of improvement in the conversion rate) must be significant. Don't run your test if the data rate will be too low, or if the proposed test elements are unlikely to produce conversion improvements on the landing page.

Stay Below the Radar

> *It's easier to ask forgiveness than it is to get permission.*
> —Rear Admiral Grace Murray "Amazing Grace" Hopper

Another option for running your first test is to do it out of public view. Sneak it into your normal activities. This can be done by diverting a portion of your existing budget to testing activities. You and your testing team can also run tests "off the clock" in addition to your normal activities.

Many online marketing programs run on a cost-per-acquisition (CPA) basis. If you bring in a reasonable volume of leads or sales at the target cost per acquisition, people will not care exactly how you do it. In this environment you can spend some of your media dollars on testing and still hit your volume numbers by squeezing more conversions out of the lower ad spend. Once you have a case study pointing to a real success, you can go into the open and get additional budget specifically for testing.

Sneak It Through Your Affiliate Program

You can also consider testing as a part of your affiliate program. Since improved landing pages increase lead volume without changing the affiliate's payout structure, they have a "force multiplier" effect on all of your current and future affiliates. You can legitimately funnel off some of your affiliate program management budget to the landing page optimization effort.

One way to bypass the need for budget approval is to roll your testing into your performance-based affiliate payouts. Once some success has been demonstrated on affiliate landing pages, you can spread out and migrate to other areas like PPC landing pages.

Make the Financial Case

Most top managers are receptive to financial arguments. They understand that there are two basic ways to improve profits: increase revenues and lower costs. They like and appreciate staff who also speak the language of money and understand their contribution to the company's financial success.

Take the time to dig up financial information that allows you to estimate the lifetime value of the conversion action. Build your own financial model once you understand the revenue and variable cost percentage for your landing page. Remember to use conservative assumptions and estimates to make your business case stronger and more defensible.

Your project may be the most financially promising marketing initiative available to the company. Once you get high-level executive buy-in based on the financial case for the project, you should have the political support to move it along and get the active cooperation of other team members.

Build a Coalition

If you are convinced that your landing page optimization program will be ongoing and successful, you can try to build the required commitment and support inside your company from the very beginning. This task will involve significant effort and emotional commitment to rally support for your project and address or neutralize key sources of opposition to it. Coalition building may produce the most durable results, but it is also the hardest and most time-consuming approach that you can choose. For the fastest results, it's best to start with one of the other approaches and do coalition-building activities in parallel on an ongoing basis.

Insource or Outsource?

Should you outsource your testing program or "insource" it by doing everything in-house?

> *Consultants are people who borrow your watch and tell you what time it is, and then walk off with the watch.*
>
> —Robert Townsend, Author of *Up the Organization*

Do consultants add any real value?

> *Working definition of insanity—doing the same thing over and over again and expecting a different result.*
>
> —Common quote

Can you make any real progress with your landing page optimization program given your current internal team and culture?

The decision to insource or outsource your landing page testing project is complicated and depends on many factors:

Core Competency Focus Some companies consider online marketing in general, and landing page optimization in particular, as functions that are not part of their core competency. They focus instead on product differentiation, manufacturing, distribution, or service fulfillment as the basis for their long-term competitive advantage. They view Internet marketing as a volatile and rapidly changing activity that is best left to specialist companies whose sole mission it is to stay on top of this chaotic environment and deliver the best results.

Other companies view online marketing as their primary revenue-generating activity and the gateway to rapidly growing markets. They are committed to building the required team in-house, and consider a landing page optimization capability to be strategic to their success. Such companies typically spend considerable resources recruiting, training, and motivating key employees. They create systems and processes to monitor and continually improve the way that they carry out testing projects. They view any experience gained during the building of their program and team as a source of lasting competitive advantage, and relish the sense of control that this gives them over their revenue-generating activities.

There is no right answer here. This is simply a matter of determining how your organization defines its main focus. If your company feels strongly one way or the other, the decision to insource or outsource will often be made on the core competency issue alone.

Learning Curve and Lost Opportunity Costs As you can appreciate from the scope of this book, landing page optimization is a complex activity that draws on expert skills from a wide range of disciplines. It is unlikely that you already have all of the required skill sets in-house. You can hire people with the necessary skills, or train your staff members to acquire them (either formally or through on-the-job experience). Either way, there is a significant direct cost to acquiring the necessary skills.

There are also four often-overlooked indirect costs to the insourcing decision:

- If you retrain existing staff members, you've made a choice between their previous scope of work and the testing program.
- People with the skill sets in this discipline remain in short supply and may jump to other companies for better pay after you invest in them.
- Their initially low experience level will produce suboptimal results, and this lack of expertise can cost you in terms of lost potential revenues.
- Riding the learning curve takes time, so your improved landing page may become operational some months later than it otherwise might have. The opportunity cost of this delay can be large.

Availability of Appropriate Outsourcing Partners Landing page optimization touches mission-critical parts of your company. If your landing page test is mishandled or the tuning elements that are chosen actually decrease conversion rates, you can see the results directly in your business performance. So a high level of trust is required if you are going to outsource this function.

Outsourcing also requires a good cultural fit with your prospective partner. This includes an alignment at the business values level. It also requires organizations that operate at the same pace and frequency of communication as your company.

The way that your website is engineered or the specific site elements that you want to test may require you to use specialized technology. As a general rule, free tools or Internet-hosted application service provider (ASP) testing solutions are simpler and have fewer capabilities than some of the advanced testing platforms developed by full-service testing companies. If your tests are relatively simple and your underlying site technology is straightforward, you have many more choices. If you have special needs, you may have to outsource to one of the few firms that can accommodate your technical requirements.

Testing companies may have their own requirements to consider you as a potential client (besides your ability to afford their services). If you have a bureaucratic company that requires reviews by several gatekeepers, testing companies may not want to work with you. Most testing companies also have minimum requirements for data rates on the landing pages that you are tuning.

If you cannot find a partner that is in alignment with you on these issues, you may have no choice but to go it alone.

Perspective   Thinking outside the box is difficult if you work in it. Your experience in your industry, company, and department conspire to straightjacket you with invisible assumptions. It is hard to throw away all of your biases and beliefs and come up with truly original approaches to testing. Your current landing page may loom like a huge case of writer's block and prevent you from seeking any radical change. It probably already represents your best thinking, or at least the baseline of your cross-team agreement.

When you outsource, you will bring fresh minds to your testing program. The people at the testing company are experts in testing. But they are not knowledgeable about your specific industry and business. This allows them to bring a "beginner's mind" to the problem at hand. They may ask silly and naïve questions, or question assumptions that you hold as sacrosanct. They may also break your fixation with sales copy and messaging and focus on more fundamental usability issues that you did not even know your landing page had.

Capacity and Schedule   Can you dedicate full-time staff to move your project along or will they be distracted and pulled in too many directions? If you do not have someone on your team whose primary responsibility is the success of your testing program (as opposed to being in charge of testing along with several other higher priorities), you probably will not achieve the best possible results.

If you know that you will be building a robust, ongoing program, it makes sense to build or hire the resources in-house. But if there are gaps and lulls in your activity and commitment, this may be a lot of wear-and-tear and wasted effort. Project-based outsourcing has several advantages from this perspective: a larger dedicated team, significant prior experience, better systems and processes to deploy tests faster, experience with complex implementations, working knowledge of powerful testing tools, and an awareness of common mistakes in analyzing test data.

Affordability and Payment Methods   Your current team should be working on highest-impact activities that contribute the most to your company's success. Given their skill set and other company responsibilities, this may not be landing page optimization.

Even if you consider the burdened staff time and other carrying costs, outsourcing may be more expensive over the length of the actual test. But you also have to keep in mind the cost of keeping your in-house capability around and idling between tests. This can be even more expensive in the long term—especially considering the stop/start momentum required to reactivate the team for each test. Your choice will also depend on the ongoing cadence of your testing program.

Guidelines for Insourcing

As discussed earlier, there are no universal qualities that a good outsourcing partner has to have. It depends on the fit between the two parties.

However, if you decide to insource, there are some general principles and characteristics that you should try to build into your optimization team:

Strategic Perspective The team should be able to prioritize and initiate projects (with review from higher levels of your marketing organization). It should be focused on maximum financial impact company-wide and subject each test to a minimum economic impact threshold. Test prioritization should consider the economic value of the pages (see Chapter 14), the amount of potential upside opportunity (based on how broken or dysfunctional the current pages are), and the work and effort required to implement the test.

Capable and Complete The team should be self-contained with dedicated team members who are not distracted by other job duties. It must be complete and able to carry out projects from end to end. Of course this implies some level of redundancy with the rest of your company, and that is okay. The team should be cross-trained to spread conversion knowledge among members. This also helps to avoid narrowly focused specialist posturing and turf conflicts, which can undermine group cohesion. The team must also be solely accountable for the overall long-term results of the program. This does not mean that every landing page test will be a winner. You have to allow for a high degree of experimentation and realize that some individual tests may not result in improvements.

Minor Impact on Others The team will be dropping in to improve specific landing pages or parts of your website. You will probably have staff whose job it is to maintain and improve ("farm") these pages on an ongoing basis. It must be very clear that the optimization team will only *borrow and then return* the pages "owned" by others. The pages should be "frozen" (and their content not changed) only for the duration of the test and with as much advance notice as practically possible.

You should also be very clear that outside of any slated tests, innovation is encouraged by the people in the farming role. They do not need to check in with the optimization team, and are not subject to any restrictions to changes that they are contemplating. Such changes should simply be deployed and their impact measured via web analytics (via a before-and-after snapshot and not by parallel landing page testing).

Flexible and Fast The team should develop and follow a well-defined process for running tests. This should include a specific input process to solicit ideas from the page's stakeholders, and defined touch points for reporting ongoing progress. However, this does not mean that people outside of the team can second-guess or look over your shoulder. Their ideas are welcome—especially when defining problems and brainstorming solutions—but the ultimate responsibility for what ends up in the test plan and how the project is run rests inside the team.

You should also work to decouple the speed of the testing program as much as possible from normal software release and staging cycles. The machinery and processes that are used to maintain an operational site are not necessarily appropriate for the high-speed and experimental nature of landing page testing. If you are bogged down by other departments (such as IT), your testing program will not be able to produce results quickly enough. This also applies to the industrial-strength requirements of your live site (such as the need to create localized translated versions for larger international sites). For a test these constraints can be relaxed and you can take some shortcuts (such as running a test on English-speaking traffic only). Of course after any successful test, the winning site changes need to be implemented and permanently rolled out to the site. They are then subject to all of the normal procedural constraints.

Transparent and Enabling The team should publish its test priorities and estimated schedules with as much lead time as possible. Advance notice of test data collection start dates and estimated durations should be provided. Since the duration of the data collection is dependent on many factors, it should generally not be a fixed time and should be provided as an estimate only (see Chapter 10, "Common Testing Questions," for additional discussion). After each test you should publicly document the test results and their financial impact. Do not hesitate to document tests that were not successful. This is a normal part of a testing program and not something to be ashamed of. Often what-not-to-do can be a powerful teacher as well. You should create and maintain a storehouse of the learnings and best practices that you develop.

Continuously Learning and Improving Landing page optimization is a fast-moving field that requires expertise in a variety of fields. Your team should be continuously looking to improve its skills and capabilities. You can try to hire experienced people, but there are not too many of them out there. So you should always work to upgrade the skills of your team members.

In addition to the obvious (free online webinars and reading blogs), you should consider a more formal and ongoing knowledge acquisition program. This includes certification courses, attendance at industry events like Conversion Conference chaired by this book's co-author Tim Ash (see a coupon on the last page of this book for a special discount on upcoming Conversion Conference events), and reading the latest literature on the subject.

If your team is just now being formed, or is not complete and fully capable, you should also consider bringing in outside trainers or coaches to help you develop this capability. SiteTuners offers a knowledge transfer practice that includes in-person presentations and workshops with customized agendas, remote webinars, and a longer-term strategic mentoring program with the company's principals to bring your team up to speed as quickly as possible.

Once you have assembled your team and built internal company support, it is time to get to work. In the next chapter we will cover the specific action-plan steps required to execute your landing page optimization program.

Developing Your
Action Plan

He who fails to plan, plans to fail.

—Proverb

All of the preceding chapters in this book have, in a sense, been a preparation for this one. You now have a comprehensive understanding of the main issues surrounding landing page optimization. But all of this knowledge will do you no good if you do not apply it. This chapter will give you a step-by-step framework for developing your landing page optimization action plan.

14

Chapter Contents

Before You Begin
Understand Your Business Objectives
What Is the Lifetime Value of the Conversion Action?
Assemble Your Team
Determine Your Landing Pages and Traffic Sources
Decide What Constitutes Success
Uncover Problems and Decide What to Test
Select an Appropriate Tuning Method
Implement and Conduct QA
Collect the Data
Analyze the Results and Verify Improvement

Before You Begin

As you prepare your plan, start by reviewing your company's overall business priorities and the goals of your online marketing programs. This framework guides action plan development and identifies constraints or potential issues early in the process. The simplified sample questionnaire in the sidebar "Resource: Preliminary Questionnaire" can help you understand the big picture before you start your test. If you do not know the answers to some of these questions, you may want to gather them from the appropriate sources in your company.

Resource: Preliminary Questionnaire

Marketing and External Factors

- Are there any seasonal traffic spikes or bumps in your industry?
- Are you planning to launch any significant marketing or PR campaigns?
- Are you planning to introduce any new products?
- Are you planning to significantly change the functionality or pricing of existing products?
- Who are your three biggest online direct competitors?
- What are your main differentiators and positioning points against your competitors?

Site Performance and Traffic Levels

- What traffic source(s) will be used for the test?
- How many conversion actions per day do they represent?
- What site elements have you tested in the past? What were the results?
- What site elements would you be interested in testing? Why?
- Do you have any service-level or response time guidelines for your web servers?

Site Appearance and Functionality

- Do you have a formal creative brief for your logo and/or site?
- Are there any technical requirements for your site (screen resolution, plug-ins)?
- Are any portions of your site design or organization "off-limits" for testing and may not be changed?
- Do you have access to the original graphical files that make up your site (such as Photoshop or Flash)?
- What kinds of technologies and languages make up your site (operating system, scripting languages, content management system, and databases)?
- Do you have "staging" web servers for implementing and reviewing the modified web pages?

Use the contents of the simplified questionnaire as a starting point. You may want to create a more detailed or modified set of questions to suit your particular needs and environment.

Understand Your Business Objectives

You must begin with a solid understanding of your business objectives and know how your landing page or website supports them.

What drives your business? Is it sales, subscriptions, memberships, leads, downloads, e-mail sign-ups, or advertising and page views? What portion of your business marketing intersects with the Web? Is all of it conducted online? Are key parts influenced by offline marketing, or do they require subsequent phone or in-person follow-up? You may not have control over the whole process and may be a single step in the value chain. Your goal should be to make your piece as powerful and efficient as possible.

You may be tactically focused on hitting your cost-per-action (CPA) numbers or growing your volume by a certain percentage. But you may not have a good sense of your contribution to the company as a whole. Dig for financial information. Go as high up the financial management ladder as necessary to get the numbers that you need. Your managers will likely appreciate your newfound interest in the company's bottom line. In fact, you may be speaking their language for the first time.

You must build a model of the lifetime value (LTV) of your conversion action (see the next section for more details). If you base your program simply on the revenue from the initial transaction, you may severely underestimate the true worth of your marketing activities in general and the value of landing page conversion improvement in particular. After you have calculated the LTV, take seasonal factors into account and calculate the annualized revenue run rate of your conversion activities.

It is also critical to properly understand your variable cost percentage. This is different from the standard accounting definition and is not directly related to your current profit margin. For the purposes of landing page optimization, all of your in-house media buying (including banner ads and PPC traffic) are a fixed cost and should not be included in this number. Read "The Financial Impact of Conversion Rate Improvement" section later in this chapter to learn how to calculate the revenue and variable cost percentage for your specific business type.

The data that you ask for may not be readily available. You may be the first person to request it. It is okay to use estimates or averages when appropriate financial reports are not available. You should also be conservative when dealing with ranges and always err on the side of caution. Once you have the raw numbers, you may still have to make additional assumptions. Again, try to be conservative. In most cases you will find that even your most cautious scenarios still represent significant potential improvement to your company's bottom line.

What Is the Lifetime Value of the Conversion Action?

The *lifetime value* (*LTV*) of a conversion action is the total financial benefit that your company will receive from your relationship with the visitor over the course of the current interaction and all future interactions. In some cases, this is easy to calculate; in other cases it is very difficult.

The easiest cases are when the conversion action is your ultimate goal and its value does not change after the action occurs. For example, if you sell a onetime-use or durable product and the client is unlikely to buy another one from you (such as aluminum siding with a lifetime warranty), the LTV of the conversion action is your profit margin on that sale.

For most businesses, many factors need to be taken into account to properly understand the LTV of your relationship:

Length of Relationship How long will your relationship last on average? How many future transactions does this represent?

Repeat Buyer Rate Are you more focused on hunting for new prospects or tending to existing clients? What is your ratio of repeat to new buyers? What percentage of new clients will become repeat buyers?

Value of Repeat Sales What is the average value of a repeat customer? What additional products do you use to cross-sell or upsell to existing clients?

Economies of Scale Are there significant economies of scale that you can achieve by raising your sales to a certain level? Can you negotiate better terms with suppliers once you hit certain volume breakpoints?

Changing Product/Service Mix Do follow-on services involve more profitable reduced service levels? Are potential product upsells at a higher margin than the original purchases?

Referral Business How likely are the clients to refer additional business? What is the value of a referral?

The Financial Impact of Conversion Rate Improvement

The total financial benefit of an improved conversion rate depends greatly on your business model and margins. The increases in sales revenue or the increased conversion rate are only an indirect measurement of it.

SiteTuners has developed a simple model for determining the potential financial impact of a landing page optimization test. The profit impact is based on three quantities. Although the definitions that follow may not strictly match traditional accounting practices, they allow you to quickly establish the potential profit impact of your conversion test and focus your energies on the correct landing pages:

Revenue (R) Revenue is the annualized run rate of the full LTV of the conversion actions on the landing page in question, and it comes from the traffic sources being considered for the test.

The annualized run rate is used to remove the strong seasonal effects of many industries. LTV allows you to see the true future revenue stream as opposed to focusing only on the initial conversion transaction. It is important to take into account only the revenue that is generated through the landing pages and traffic sources that you are considering for the test. Do not include revenues that pass through other pages or that result from other traffic sources.

For example, let's assume that the immediate conversion action is a $20 sale, that an average initial sale leads to additional revenue of $30 over the course of your three-year ongoing relationship with the typical client, that 10,000 clients per year convert through your pay-per-click campaign, and that all of the traffic is directed to the landing page in question. The revenue in this case would be ($20 + $30) × 10,000, or $500,000.

Variable Cost Percentage (VCP) Variable cost percentage (VCP) is the total of variable costs on an incremental sale as a percentage of revenue (as defined previously).

Include your cost of goods sold (COGS), affiliate commissions, customer service, shipping, credit card charges, return and allowances, front-line staff salaries (sales, product production, service delivery, and customer service), and other variable costs as a percentage of the total revenue.

Do not include your fixed costs such as rent, utilities, administrative expenses, and non-front-line salaries.

Do not include current online media spending because this will remain unchanged even if your conversion rate improves. Normally this would be considered a variable expense. But your online marketing media buys are in effect part of fixed costs because they are not required to produce an incremental conversion action. The action is happening because of the improved efficiency of your landing page—not because of additional media spending required to produce it.

Also note that VCP is not directly related to your current profit margins (for example, if your profit margins are 10 percent this does not mean that your VCP is 90 percent). This is because your current fixed costs are also being included in calculating your overall profit margin. Since these costs will not change as you add incremental sales or conversion actions, they are not included. Only costs directly associated with the incremental conversion action should be included.

If we continue our earlier example, let's assume that the cost of the product and upsells over three years is $15, and the credit card fees and customer service cost another $5. The VCP would be [($15 + $5) × 10,000] ÷ $500,000, or 40%.

Conversion Improvement Percentage (CIP) The conversion improvement percentage (CIP) is the percentage improvement of the measurement criteria of the new (challenger) landing page versus the original (baseline) landing page.

The measurement criterion is the appropriate one for your test and depends on your conversion action. It can include average time spent on site (for educational goals), number of page views (for advertising supported websites), or revenue per visitor (for e-commerce).

Of course, it is impossible to precisely calculate the impact of your landing page optimization ahead of time. But if you use a wide range of possible improvement percentages, you can get a sense of the possible financial impact and the appropriate resources to apply to the effort.

Let's assume that in our example we expect at least a 20 percent potential improvement in revenue per visitor over our original landing page. Our CIP would then be 0.2.

> ### Conversion Rate Profit Impact Formula
>
> Profit Increase = R × CIP × (1 − VCP)

To conclude our earlier example, the estimated minimum profit increase would be $500,000 × 0.2 × (1 − 0.4), or $60,000.

Why are fixed costs not included in the SiteTuners financial model? The simple answer is that the fixed costs get canceled out when you subtract the profitability of your improved landing page from the profitability of your original. Since you only care about the *net* impact of the conversion test, it is not important to accurately calculate (or even include) the fixed costs in the financial model.

Each business has its own unique particularities, which may make constructing the financial model more difficult. Don't be paralyzed by your inability to create a perfect model. Some of the data that you need may not be tracked or easily reportable within your organization. Or you may simply not have access to it, or have the clout or resources to have it properly compiled.

Nevertheless, online marketing is a numbers game, so the closer you get to a correct model, the more strongly you will be able to make the financial case for conversion testing and tuning. Just remember that your goal is not to create a super-detailed and accurate model that would pass an accounting audit. You only need to understand the high-level economics of your business well enough to determine the value and impact of conversion testing. So get the best numbers that you can and make conservative assumptions about the missing information—but definitely build a financial model.

To help you find a way to come up with some numbers, we're providing the following examples for common types of businesses.

The numeric example scenarios are for illustrative purposes only. Although they may not exactly match your specific situation, they should provide enough guidance for you to develop your own model. The parenthetical abbreviations are not commonly used in accounting. They are simply shorthand used in the illustrative calculations and formulas. The computations are calculated and derived in different ways to fit the available information for each example business.

Purchase of Consumer Product

There are two main types of *business-to-consumer* (B2C) e-commerce websites: direct-to-consumer or retailer catalog. Some companies use the Internet to bypass the normal distribution channels and sell their specific narrow product line directly to consumers. Other companies try to compete with traditional retailers by carrying a wide inventory of available products from all leading manufacturers in their online catalog. In many cases, such aggregators never even take physical possession of inventory and rely on the manufacturer or distributor to drop-ship directly to the consumer.

Possible issues for e-commerce sites include the following:

In-Store Sales Many online retailers are not Internet "pure plays." They started as a physical store and decided to add a website. Because of the extensive information available on websites, many people will research the product on the Internet and then buy it at the retail store location. In some consumer product categories, such crossover sales dwarf the online component and are inaccurately attributed simply to in-store sales. Market research is available for a number of industries documenting the amount of crossover. In the absence of specific numbers for your business, you can use such industry research as your starting point.

Another tactic for accurately tracking in-store sales is to provide an incentive on your website (such as a special promotion or coupon code) that can be entered at the physical store point of sale. However, you will probably be underestimating the crossover since many people will not bother with your special offer. This is similar to coupon clipping in the newspaper—even though the coupon is available to everyone, only a fraction of households receiving the paper will take advantage of it. Of course, the value of the incentive will affect its participation rate, but most businesses cannot afford to offer huge discounts just to be able to track offline sales that originated online.

Print Catalog Sales Many businesses will mail catalogs to lists of prospects. This can create the reverse of the problem we just discussed—catalog sales may be falsely attributed to direct online sales and inflate the effectiveness of the website. This is especially true when catalogs are regularly mailed to a large base of existing clients who are frequent repeat customers. Even though most catalogs include special incentives for ordering online, the revenue of the catalog sales will probably still be understated. One way to estimate this effect is to document the size of any online sales spikes following each catalog mail drop. If you can estimate the increased web sales compared to a similar period without a catalog drop, you can use this factor to lower your online sales estimates accordingly.

Phone Sales If a significant portion of your sales come over the phone, it is very important to track this accurately. By assigning a separate toll-free number to each inbound traffic acquisition campaign, you can ensure that this happens. Do not use a single number for all channels and campaigns because you will improperly attribute sales to direct call-ins. There are limitations to this approach if you want to maintain a high degree of granularity in your tracking. For example, it would be difficult to track every keyword in your PPC campaign since you might potentially have to assign a unique number to each one.

Example Scenario: Purchase of Consumer Product

You run an online catalog selling consumer electronics. You do not have a physical store location or print catalog. Your sales revenues are on an annualized run-rate of $5 million. Your wholesale costs average 65 percent of retail price, and the customer pays for the shipping (which is not included in the revenue number). Credit card fees and refunds average 4 percent of your sales. Your average initial online sale is $85. Some 40 percent of your business comes from repeat purchases, which average $120 per sale.

You run an SEO campaign for your website in-house, and outsource your PPC management to an agency with a budget of $500,000 per year including media costs and agency fees. Some 20 percent of your sales are closed over the phone by your staff. The salaries of your phone sales and support people are $120,000 per year. Affiliates represent 35 percent of your sales and you pay 10 percent of the initial sale amount as the commission. You are interested in tuning the checkout process of your website to reduce your shopping cart abandonment rate.

Revenue (R)

$5,000,000 (annual revenue)

× 80% (since 20% are phone sales)

= $4,000,000

Since only the checkout process is being tuned, phone sales do not count. They must be considered as a parallel sales channel that is not affected by changes to your online checkout process (most people will not even see the checkout process if they call you to complete the sale). If pages further upstream of the checkout (such as your website home page) were to be conversion tuned, then the impact on phone sales should be tracked and the phone sales revenues and associated costs included in the model.

Average revenue per initial sale (ARIS)

$85 (average initial sale amount)

× 60% (percentage of initial sales)

= $51

Average revenue per repeat sale (ARRS)

$120 (average repeat sale amount)

× 40% (percentage of repeat sales)

= $48

Average revenue per sale (ARPS)

= ARIS + ARRS

= $51 + $48

= $99

continues

Example Scenario: Purchase of Consumer Product *(Continued)*

Cost of goods sold (COGS)

$99 (average revenue per sale)

× 65% (average wholesale cost percentage)

= $64.35

Credit card charges (CC)

$99 (average revenue per sale)

× 4% (average credit card fees)

= $3.96

Variable cost of affiliate sales (VCAS)

$51 (commissionable revenue—initial sale only)

× 10% (avg. affiliate commission rate)

× 35% (percentage of sales due to affiliates) = $1.79

Variable cost percentage (VCP)

= (COGS + CC + VCAS) ÷ ARPS

= ($64.35 + $3.96 + $1.79) ÷ $99

= 70.80%

Third-Party Lead Generation

If you run a lead-generation website, it is typical that you would be paid a fixed dollar amount for each lead. If the leads are exclusive—that is, they are not resold to multiple buyers—the LTV is the dollar amount of the lead. If the leads are nonexclusive, the LTV depends on the number of times that an average lead is resold.

Possible issues include the following:

Different Values for Specific Regions Some leads (such as from specific states) are more valuable than others. Use a blended average based on the mix of leads that you are currently selling. Some locations do not allow or support the use of leads at all. You can determine a percentage of leads that go to waste in this manner and use it in your calculation of lead value.

Capped Number of Leads Some buyers may not be able to handle additional leads past a certain number. Incremental leads past such a cutoff point may have a reduced value (if other buyers still exist for them) or none at all. You can build the cap into your economic formula.

Returned Leads Many lead buyers reserve the option of determining whether a lead is valid (after attempting to contact the person and qualifying them). Buyers typically get credit in full for such bad leads.

Example Scenario: Third-Party Lead Generation

You run a nonexclusive lead site for life insurance. You spend $240,000 per year to run your own PPC campaign, which generates 40 percent of your form-fills. The other 60 percent come from your affiliate program. You pay a flat $15 per lead for valid affiliate leads that are sold at least once. Your site averages 140 form-fills per day. Some 20 percent of your leads are from states where you are not allowed to sell them, or have no buyers. The average lead is worth $25 and is resold once an additional 30 percent of the time. Some 10 percent of leads are returned as unusable or bogus by buyers.

Revenue (R)

140 form-fills per day × 365 days (annual form-fills)

× 80% (since 20% are unsellable)

× 90% (since 10% are returned)

× $25 (average lead value)

× 130% (since a lead is resold 30% of the time)

= $1,195,740

Average revenue per sale (ARPS)

$25 (average lead value)

× 130% (resold an additional 30% of the time)

= $32.50

Variable cost of affiliate leads (VCAL)

$15 (avg. affiliate commission)

× 60% (affiliate leads as a percentage of the total)

= $9

Variable cost of nonaffiliate leads (VCNL)

= $0 (your PPC costs are considered fixed)

Variable cost percentage (VCP)

= (VCAL + VCNL) ÷ ARPS

= ($9 + $0) ÷ $32.50

= 27.69%

Subscriptions

Subscriptions can apply to both services and products. Consumers agree to be billed on a regular basis during the term of the subscription agreement. Often the term only includes the initial sale and can be "canceled at any time" in the future. The value of a subscription lies in extending its term. Typically there is a drop-off in customers each time a billing event occurs as more and more customers cancel their subscriptions. Subscription businesses that do not add a lot of real value are in a constant race to replenish the ranks of their customers before existing ones cancel.

Example Scenario: Subscriptions

You sell a unique "natural" weight loss pill (manufactured under contract) through a dedicated website. You offer a free 30-day trial of the product (for a $7 shipping and handling fee billed to the client's credit card). Some 40 percent of trials become paid customers who will purchase an additional three months' worth of product after the initial trial. Each monthly supply sells for $30, including shipping and handling. The cost of the pills is $4 for a month, and the shipping and handling adds another $4. One hundred new clients per day sign up for the trial. Half of your sales come from affiliates to whom you pay $20 for each new customer. An additional 25 percent of sales come from your PPC campaign, on which you spend $120,000 per year. The remaining 25 percent come through direct type-in of your URL by people who have heard of your product name.

Revenue from trials (RFT)

100 free trials per day × 365 days (annual trials)

× $7 (revenue from a trial)

= $255,500

Revenue from sales (RFS)

100 free trials per day × 365 days (annual trials)

× 40% (trial-to-sale "closing" percentage)

× $90 (revenue from average 3-month sale)

= $1,314,000

Revenue (R) = RFT + RFS

= $255,500 + $1,314,000

= $1,569,500

Unit cost (UC)

$4 (cost of pills)

+ $4 (cost of shipping and handling)

= $8

continues

Example Scenario: Subscriptions *(Continued)*

Trials units (TU)

100 free trials per day × 365 days (annual trials)

= 36,500

Paid units (PU)

100 free trials per day × 365 days (annual trials)

× 40% (trial-to-sale "closing" percentage)

× 3 (average number of paid refills)

= 43,800

Cost of product (CP)

$= UC \times (TU + PU)$

$= \$8 \times (36,500 + 43,800)$

$= \$642,400$

Affiliate cost (AC)

36,500 (trials units shipped)

× \$20 (affiliate payout per trial)

× 50% (percentage of affiliate sales)

= \$365,000

Variable cost percentage (VCP)

$= (CP + AC) \div R$

$= (\$642,400 + \$365,000) \div \$1,569,500$

$= 64.18\%$

In this example, there is an actual financial loss on the free trial (when considering the product, shipping, and affiliate costs). This results in negative short-term cash flow for the business until the money is recouped in subsequent months from refill clients.

Intermediate Conversion Actions

In many cases, the ultimate desired conversion action may occur months or even years after the initial visitor contact with your website. To complicate matters further, there may be several intermediate actions following the initial contact. This is typical of many high-ticket business-to-business sales. In such cases, the website serves as a tool for educating the prospect early in the sales cycle and identifying who they are.

To properly track such activities, you will probably need some way to note the whole history of an interaction with your company by an outside visitor. This may require having some sort of *sales force automation* (*SFA*) or *customer relationship management* (*CRM*) software.

Most of the time, as an online marketer you will not have all of the information required to make decisions. Perhaps the data can only be periodically compiled for you by other people at the company. This is the riskiest type of conversion action to value. You must make a series of assumptions to arrive at the value of the most upstream conversion action available. This is also your most frequent and least-delayed conversion action. Of course, these assumptions should be conservative. In addition, they must be verified once real data starts flowing in.

But this is confounded by three additional issues. First, the time lag between initial contact and downstream intermediate conversions can be significant, and you must wait until properly "aged" data is available. For example, if someone downloads a whitepaper, they may read it immediately but may not sign up for a pilot study of your product until the next fiscal year's budget has been approved and funded. Second, the number of ultimate conversion actions may be very small, making it hard to determine an accurate conversion rate. Third, the value of each sale can also vary dramatically, making it difficult to estimate the revenue per sale accurately.

Example Scenario: Intermediate Conversion Actions

Your company sells a complicated suite of special-purpose computers and custom software applications aimed specifically at managing human resources for large state and federal government departments. The sales amount depends on the size of the installation and the specific modules that the customer orders. It can range from $100,000 to $10,000,000. The product is sophisticated and requires a lot of education before a prospect understands the full benefits of your solution and how it differs from those of your competitors.

Ten thousand visitors per year to your website will give you their contact information to get an informational whitepaper about human resource management systems like the one you sell. All of the website traffic originates from a PPC campaign costing $20,000 per month.

After downloading the whitepaper, visitors start receiving ongoing informational e-mails that cover developments in your industry and encourage them to contact a sales representative. Some 8 to 10 percent of people on your e-mail list will eventually contact a sales person. Some 20 to 25 percent of sales contacts will lead to free trials. About 15 to 20 percent of free trials will continue on to become paid sales.

Your CFO cannot give you accurate variable cost percentages, but instead provides you with the following information based on last year's annual report. Your sales salaries and bonuses equal 10 percent of your revenue. Customer service is approximately 25 percent of revenues. Hardware and the cost of configuring your systems is 20 percent of revenues.

continues

Example Scenario: Intermediate Conversion Actions *(Continued)*

Value per download (VPD)

$250,000 (your estimate of average sale amount)

× 15% (low end of trial-to-sale conversions)

× 20% (low end of contact-to-trial conversions)

× 8% (low end of whitepaper-to-contact conversions)

= $600

Revenue (R)

10,000 (number of whitepapers per year)

× $600 (value per download)

= $6,000,000

Variable cost percentage (VCP)

10% (sales salaries and commissions)

+ 25% (customer service)

+ 20% (hardware and system cost)

= 55%

Assemble Your Team

You need to diplomatically rally all important contributors and gatekeepers around your cause. These will likely be the key roles mentioned as the usual suspects in Chapter 13, "Assembling Your Team and Getting Buy-in." Always understand every stakeholder's concerns, limitations, and biases. Show them why it is in their best interests to help you and how the project will make them look good.

If this is your first landing page test, then review "Strategies for Getting Started" in Chapter 13. Pick the approach that is most appropriate for your company and political environment. Since you have prepared the financial model to describe the impact of your proposed test, you should try to get the buy-in of the highest management levels that you can. If they have blessed it, it should be much easier to secure the cooperation of the needed team.

Of course, not everyone is likely to fall into line. In some cases the best that you can hope for is to neutralize active opposition. Another strategy would be to bypass potential sources of conflict or trouble altogether, if possible (this will likely depend on the scope of the test). Once the results are proven, they won't want to be left out of the conversation again.

Assembling your team is not a one-shot roll call—the cast of characters will change throughout your project. It is an ongoing process. The composition of your team will vary dramatically depending on the scope of your proposed test. If you test a very minor page change, such as an alternative headline or image, you may be able to handle the tests yourself with self-service landing page testing software tools. At the other extreme, you may be considering redesigning your whole site and re-architecting your conversion process in fundamental ways. This might involve changes to your branding, information architecture, content management or publishing system(s), or back-end databases. You may need the active participation of UI, graphic designers, copywriters, programmers, product managers, and/or various agencies.

In addition, you may have to deal with a complicated IT environment involving network administrators, webmasters, and QA testers. This may require intricate and formal code or file upload, separate staging areas, and elaborate quality control procedures before your test changes are approved.

There are many political dimensions to your landing page testing. Some of the design elements that you may wish to test come with significant baggage. This may be in the form of control and turf, skill sets needed, availability and cost of resources, or a long and difficult approval process. Regardless of the specific issues surrounding the design element, you will have to decide whether it is worth your time, reputation, and effort to fight for its inclusion in the test.

It may be appropriate for you to outsource your entire project to a full-service usability or landing page testing company. This is largely dependent on the skill sets you already have in-house, as well as people's availability during the proposed testing period. Sometimes you may need specialized technology that is not available from landing page testing software packages. See the sidebar "Resource: Assembling the Team" for additional details.

Resource: Assembling the Team

Resources and Procedures

- Which roles can you and your immediate team fill?
    - User experience and interface design
    - Product manager
    - Webmaster
    - System administrator
    - Graphic designer
    - Copywriter

continues

- Marketing manager

- Programmer

- QA tester (should not be you unless this is your only role)

- Which of the above roles can other members of your company fill?

- Identify specific people and the approximate level-of-effort (in total hours) that may be required for all the roles in the preceding two questions.

- Who will have the primary responsibility for each of the following steps in the process?

  - Overall test project

  - Identification of landing page problems

  - Brainstorming of testing features

  - Drafting of test plan

  - Reviewing and approving of the test plan

  - Approval of the budget and allocation of staff resources

  - Implementation

  - Quality assurance

  - Move from "staging" to "live" environment

  - Data collection

  - Analysis

  - Presentation of results

  - Migration plan for new elements (if test is successful)

  - Expiration of alternate page

- Are there any reviews of your test required by the following entities?

  - Brand/style (logos, style sheets, colors, messaging)

  - IT (testing technology, uploading of files, policies)

  - Legal/compliance (legal requirements, disclaimers)

  - Product manager (copywriting, offer, call-to-action)

Determine Your Landing Pages and Traffic Sources

After you have determined your business goals, you should be able to identify the mission-critical parts of your website that lead to the desired conversion action or actions. Review the appropriate sections of Chapter 2, "Understanding Your Landing Pages."

Remember, unless a page or website section directly supports the completion of the conversion action, it is probably not mission critical.

Determine the type of landing page that you have: main site, microsite, or stand-alone. Each type has different implications for what can and cannot be tested. For example, if you are modifying the header and navigation structure of a page that is part of your main site, you will have to carry the changes over to the rest of the site. By contrast, you can often make arbitrary and radical changes to a stand-alone landing page that is used to convert visitors from a specific online traffic acquisition campaign.

Before the test begins, determine what subset of your audience you will be tuning for. Sometimes this may be traffic from all available sources. By choosing the widest possible cross section of your audience, you have the opportunity to improve average conversion performance for everyone significantly. At other times you may want to segment for specific online campaigns. This is especially important when the traffic sources represent diverse kinds of people with significant differences in their propensity to convert.

You may also want to "geo-target" and segment your audience by their location or preferred language. Device and operating system are other primary segmenting tactics. Time-of-day or day-of-week filtering is also common. For example, you may want to test which landing page design is preferred by your weekend versus weekday visitors, or your workday versus evening visitors.

Regardless of the filtering or segmentation that you have chosen, it is important to make sure that you have enough traffic from each source. Do not run separate landing page tests for traffic sources that do not meet the minimum data rate requirements of the tuning method that you have chosen. Review the appropriate sections on tuning in Chapter 12, "Testing Methods."

You should carefully consider the traffic sources that you use and make sure that they are from recurring sources, are controllable, and are stable. You should generally try to avoid spiky sources such as e-mail drops to in-house lists. Unless you are tuning specifically for repeat visitors, try to get your test traffic from fresh sources of visitors who are uncontaminated by prior exposure to your company brand, website, or offers.

Once you have picked your traffic sources, do not make the mistake of overgeneralizing the results of your test. Remember, even if you have no significant problems with data collection, audience bias, or analysis of the data, the advantage of your winning page is only predicted to hold up for your *original traffic source mix*. Do not start showing the new version of your landing page to audiences that were not part of your test. If you must use the same page for everyone, at least run a head-to-head test on the held-out traffic sources (the ones not in your original test) to make sure that the new page does not result in lower conversion rates for this new audience.

Landing Pages

If multiple landing pages are included in the proposed test, answer the questions in this section for each one.

- What is the landing page?

- Is the landing page a stand-alone page, part of a microsite, or part of your company's main site?

- What is the conversion page (on which the conversion action happens)?

- What is the confirmation page (the page displayed immediately after the conversion page)?

- What intermediate sequence of pages must be traversed between the landing page and the conversion page?

- Are the pages static, or are portions created dynamically on the fly?

- What other components are needed for the proper construction and display of the pages (such as files, database, cookies)?

- Do you have access to all components of the page (such as original graphics files from which the page images were created)?

Traffic Sources

- Do you have a web analytics package installed?

- What are the traffic sources that you will use for the test?

- How many conversion actions per day do they represent?

- What tuning methods will be possible at this data rate?

- Are the traffic sources steady or sporadic?

- Can you filter out any undesirable sources (such as e-mail drops to in-house lists)?

- Can you filter out any visits from your own company or agents (such as call centers or customer service staff)?

Decide What Constitutes Success

At this point, you should already understand your business goals and the lifetime value of your desired conversion actions. From this, you can determine what you will measure in your test. The simplest measure is conversion rate. For many environments this will work well. However, if you have multiple conversion goals or multiple items for sale in an e-commerce setting, you may have to calculate and measure either conversion revenue or gross margin contribution. The math required to analyze this kind of data is much more complicated than the simple counting involved in conversion rate optimization.

Delayed conversions need to be taken into account. Depending on your specific audience and conversion action characteristics, a significant portion of your visitors may convert after a long period of delay. If this is the case, you may have to take this into account and "age" your data appropriately before making decisions.

Another key decision you will have to make is how confident you need to be in your answer. Remember, statistical confidence only tells you the *likelihood* that the new version of your landing page is better than the original. It does not tell you exactly *by how much* it might be better. If your landing page represents the lifeblood of your business and significant economic value runs through it, be conservative and accept only a tiny chance of being wrong.

However, if you are aggressively testing and time is of the essence, you should accept lower confidence levels. As described in the previous chapters on tuning, three major factors determine the length of your test: your data rate, the size of the effects that you find, and the confidence level that you choose. You have no direct control over the first two factors once the test starts, but by setting your confidence level lower, you can often significantly decrease the length of the data collection period.

Another way to look at this trade-off is that you may have to collect data for a much longer time to reliably find improvement effects of a certain size. If you have a fixed amount of time to collect data, perhaps due to seasonal factors or business deadlines, you will have to accept the fact that you will be unable to find effects of a certain size, and may have to hope that some big improvement will be found during the test. If the threshold for detectable improvements is very high, you will have to resign yourself to the very real possibility that you may have inconclusive test results.

Resource: Defining Success

Conversion Action

- Do you have a single conversion action or multiple ones?
- If you have a single conversion action, does it always have the same value?
- If its value differs, can an average value be estimated?
- Decide on your conversion criterion (what will you be optimizing):
  - Conversion rate—For single conversion actions with identical values or a steady average value

continues

- Revenue per visitor—For e-commerce catalogs with similar profit margins on all products, or multiple conversion goals with different values

- Profit per visitor—For e-commerce catalogs with substantially different profit margins on products or product categories, or for price tuning

Confidence Level

- Does a significant percentage of your company's value pass through the landing page(s) to be tested?

- Are you planning a single test or an ongoing campaign of testing?

- Is a significant part of your test traffic from affiliates or performance-based business partnerships?

- Is your conversion action immediate or delayed? If delayed, what is the delay required for 90–95 percent of visitors to eventually convert?

- Is your data rate high or low?

- Decide on your confidence level:

  - Low (90–95 percent)—If you plan to conduct multiple tests, have lower data rates, or have little performance-based traffic

  - High (95–99 percent +)—If you have high data rates, significant business value flowing through the landing page, or have a lot of performance-based test traffic

- Decide on how much bandwidth to devote to the baseline recipe:

  - Low (15–25 percent devoted to baseline recipe)—If you have a high data rate, a multivariate test, and little performance-based test traffic

  - Medium (50–60 percent devoted to baseline recipe)—If you are running an A-B split test (use the higher end of the medium range if you have significant performance-based test traffic)

  - High (75–90 percent devoted to baseline recipe)—If you have a conservative company management culture, a high percentage of performance-based test traffic, or are planning to test radical alternatives to your landing page design or content

Uncover Problems and Decide What to Test

The unflinching courage and clinical detachment with which you examine the existing landing page problems will in large part determine the success of your optimization program.

Look for all of the common landing page deadly sins from Chapter 4, "Common Problems—The Seven Deadly Sins of Landing Page Design." Use all of the applicable tactics and tools from Chapter 5, "Conversion Ninja Toolbox—Diagnosing Site Problems," to dissect your site. Try not to censor yourself or your information sources. This is brainstorming with no right or wrong answers. Simply record any issues dispassionately, regardless of how trivial or fundamental they may appear to be.

Once you have collected all of the raw data from this process, classify the issues into broad groups of themes. Group your findings under the broad categories of best practices covered in Chapter 9, "The Strategy of What to Test." Does anything jump out at you? Typically you will see that your problems cluster in areas such as page structure and emphasis, too much disorganization or clutter, unclear calls-to-action, verbose writing, or improper editorial style.

Now that you have listed and categorized all of the problems with your landing page, it is time to prioritize them. Think about the severity of the negative impact of your landing page problems, and the corresponding amount of improvement if the issue is fixed. Consider the breadth of your problems. Prioritize those that are standing in the way of completing the conversion action, affect the largest segments of your audience, and are prominently featured on your page.

The combination of your data rate and the length of time that you have allotted for your data collection will be another important factor in deciding how you define your tuning elements. If your data rate is low, and you want the test to complete in a reasonable amount of time, you will have to combine or "chunk" multiple design changes into coarser test elements. In the extreme case you may decide to completely redesign your whole landing page and include all of your desired design changes at once. If you have a high data rate and are using an advanced tuning method, you may be able to get very granular in the definition of your tuning elements.

Try to test elements that will have a long-term and consistent impact on your business. Unless your business peaks around a specific season or holiday period, avoid testing seasonal content or promotions. Once the appropriate season has passed, they will lose their relevance and impact completely. Consider the "Timeless Testing Themes" section in Chapter 9. After you have decided exactly what to test, document your specifications in a written test plan. The formality and level of detail of your test plan depends on the scope of your test and the involvement of other people in the project. If you have a small team, the test plan can be informal. If you are doing a simple A-B split test on very granular text elements (such as a page headline), you may not even need a written plan.

However, many tests are much more complicated. They involve multiple variables, which often depend on one another. The test implementation may require changes to website navigation, page flow, form contents, or back-end data storage and processing. In such cases the test plan needs to be very formal and detailed because it will serve as the implementation blueprint for your user interface specialists, graphics designers, programmers, and network administrators. The more people involved in your test, the more details you will need in your test plan.

Resource: Test Plan Overview

The test plan should have enough detail to clearly communicate the desired tuning elements to the implementation teams. A typical test plan will contain the following sections.

Overview

The overview is an executive summary that allows someone to understand the purpose of your test without reading the rest of the plan. Typical information includes:

Description of the Big Picture How the landing page supports the goals of the business, what constitutes a conversion action, and how its value is defined.

Landing Page(s) Chosen Include URLs and screenshots of the "before" pages.

Traffic Sources A description of the traffic sources chosen, approximate aggregate number of conversions per day, and notes about seasonality and stability of the traffic.

Constraints Describe any marketing, branding, technical, implementation, and schedule constraints. Discuss any page or site elements or pages that must not be modified during the test.

Variables and Values To facilitate communication among the test team members, it is helpful to visually block out the tuning element locations on the page and overlay them with descriptive names as reference labels. Note the number of variables in the test, the number of possible values (branching factor) for each variable, and the total number of unique recipes (search space size).

You should clearly define what specific page elements you are going to test, along with all possible variable values (including the original and any alternative versions).

Actions and Value Define the set of conversion actions that are possible in your test. For each action, define the value. For equal-value conversions, the value does not matter. But if you sell a variety of products, or have multiple conversion actions, you must use revenue or profit margin as the metric.

Implementation and QA Notes As you will see later in this chapter, you will also need to prepare an implementation plan and a QA plan. In this section of the test plan, you identify and flag any potential issues that will impact these areas.

Select an Appropriate Tuning Method

The tuning method that you choose will depend on several factors. Your choice of tuning method will influence your choice of available tools. This, in turn, can influence whether you choose to run the test in-house or outsource it. Factors you'll want to consider include the following:

Size Use the right tool for the right job. If your test plan involves only one variable, you can do an A-B split test. If it involves a small number of variables (with a search space of a few dozen total recipes), you can use some variation of parametric fractional factorial or full factorial multivariate testing. If your search space consists of millions of possible recipes, you will have to use proprietary advanced nonparametric full factorial methods.

Cost Software for conducting and tracking landing page optimization tests comes in three general varieties: free tools, paid tools, and packaged paid tools with services. Free tools include the Google Website Optimizer (described in detail in the Appendix, "Landing Page Testing Tools"). Basic free tools are built into a growing number of web analytics software packages. Paid tools are available from stand-alone testing tool software companies or can be unbundled from landing page testing companies. In some cases, you must buy full testing engagement services from landing page testing companies to get access to their tools and technology.

Technology The sophistication of landing page optimization tools varies widely. The most advanced tools are available from dedicated landing page optimization testing companies. Basic tools can handle A-B split tests involving a single landing page. More advanced capabilities will be required for multivariate testing, segmentation of visitors by traffic source, segmentation by physical location, segmentation by time-of-day or day-of-week, nested variables (one contained physically inside another), and the need to implement business rules (changes to your website functionality or appearance based on the visitor's history of interactions with your site). If you have a high-traffic website, you will also have to take into account the consequences of testing on your server response times and load balance across your network of servers. You may require a service-level agreement (SLA) with your testing company to ensure proper performance of your website during the test. An SLA guarantees certain minimum levels of uptime or specific maximum response times.

In-house vs. Outsource You will have to make a decision about conducting your test in-house or outsourcing all or a portion of it. If you outsource, you are locked into the tools and tuning methods available from the testing company that you have chosen. You may choose to outsource only the construction of the test plan and the subsequent analysis of the data, and handle the implementation and data collection yourself with the help of testing software. This is appropriate if you have the usability expertise, graphics, and programming support to handle the implementation. The statistics behind the test construction and interpretation of results can be handled by outside experts.

The sidebar "Resource: Selecting a Tuning Method and Outsourcing" guides you through the decision process.

Resource: Selecting a Tuning Method and Outsourcing

Appropriate Tuning Method

- What is your data rate (measured in conversion actions per day)?

- Are you planning to test complete landing page redesigns or granular elements?

- What is the number of variables in your test?

- What is the search space size of your test?

- Do you expect significant variable interactions among the tuning elements that you have chosen?

- Do you want to run one test or multiple tests on the same page?

- Consider A-B split testing if:

  - The data rate is greater than 10 conversions per day.

  - The search space is less than 10 recipes.

  - You are testing a whole page redesign.

  - You are testing a single granular variable (such as a headline).

  - You are planning only a single test.

- Consider fractional factorial multivariate testing if:

  - The data rate is greater than 50 conversions per day.

  - The search space is 10–100 recipes.

  - You are planning to test multiple page variables.

  - You are willing to ignore variable interactions and find only main effects.

  - You are planning to conduct multiple tests.

  - You want to explain and estimate main effects.

- Consider full factorial parametric multivariate testing if:

  - The data rate is greater than 50 conversions per day.

  - The search space is 10–100 recipes.

  - You are planning to test multiple page variables.

continues

Resource: Selecting a Tuning Method and Outsourcing *(Continued)*

- You want to consider variable interactions (if you conduct a full analysis of your data and don't build a main effects model only).

- You are planning to conduct multiple tests.

- Consider nonparametric full factorial methods if:

  - The data rate is greater than 100 conversions per day.

  - The search space is 1,000,000+ recipes.

  - You are planning to test over a dozen page variables.

  - You want to consider variable interactions.

  - You want to run one large-scale test (not a series of smaller ones) and get your answer.

  - You do not need to understand why the winning recipe performs better.

Outsourcing Considerations

- Is landing page optimization going to be a core competency of your company?

- Do you have anyone in the company whose *primary* responsibility is the successful completion of the test (in other words, who will "own it")?

- Do you have all necessary staff in place to execute your program? If not, which roles are missing?

- How long will it take you to find, hire, and train the required staff? What is the estimated cost of these activities?

- Do you have enough ongoing work to keep the new staff productively occupied? If not, what is their ongoing burdened salary "carrying cost"?

- How long will it take to assemble the complete team?

- Based on your business case, what is the range of lost-opportunity costs involved in waiting this long to start your testing program?

- Can your planned testing tool or technology implement all of the tuning elements that you may want to test?

- Do you have special technical requirements or constraints (such as software, content management systems, or dynamic content generation) that are incompatible with the use of certain landing page testing tools?

Implement and Conduct QA

As soon as your test plan is completed, start developing two additional documents: the *implementation plan* and the *QA plan*. The teams responsible for implementation and

QA should not be the same, but it is okay for the same person (or group of people) to write the two plans.

Implementation

The implementation of your test can be a complicated undertaking and require significant coordination. The sidebar "Resource: Implementation Plan Overview" gives you the perspective needed to tailor the plan to your specific situation.

Resource: Implementation Plan Overview

Team and Shared Resources

List the names, contact information, and scope of responsibility for every member of the implementation team.

List the access procedures and login information for any databases, staging areas, or file uploading directories that will be used for the implementation. If security and compartmentalization are an issue, you may choose to disseminate the appropriate information directly to specific team members.

Content List

Describe the list of content and files that are affected by the test. This should include the landing pages, any downstream pages that will be changed, graphics, supporting multimedia, programming code, as well as the postconversion confirmation page that will be displayed (your conversion tracking code will typically be inserted into this confirmation page). If you are proposing changes to the page structure or shell, contain them within include files or Cascading Style Sheets (CSS). Otherwise, you have to manually change each page in the site in order to maintain a consistent look and feel. If portions of your site are dynamically generated, you will need to include any necessary programming code, database changes, and business rules. If portions of your landing pages are stored in a content management system or database, clearly identify exactly which pieces will be touched by the test.

For each file, graphic, or code element, include the filename (or location) and a description. Use a specific naming convention for all required content. Often this is related to the variable number and value in question. For example, assume you had two variables in your test: two call-to-action button colors, and two different text treatments for the button text. This would result in four distinct buttons defined by the specific values of the two variables: V1aV2a, V1aV2b, V1bV2a, and V1bV2b. If you use this kind of naming convention, it is easy to tell at a glance to which variable and value (or combination of variables and values) the content is related.

continues

> ## Resource: Implementation Plan Overview *(Continued)*
>
> ## Task List
>
> Based on the content list, develop a detailed task list of the specific content and functional changes that you will need to implement. Broadly speaking, these changes fall into the following categories:
>
> **Text Content** Headlines, sales copy, or new site content
>
> **Page Structure and Layout** HTML, CSS, JavaScript, or other scripting code
>
> **Graphics and Multimedia** Images, animations, video
>
> **Functional or Page-Flow Changes** Programming, form processing, changes to data gathering or storage
>
> **Operational** Changes outside of the website itself, procedures, staff training
>
> For each task, assign a team member and schedule. Try to take into account any dependencies among people working on the implementation. Sometimes relatively small tasks can hold up important parts of the implementation if they are not attended to. Track the progress of the implementation via the task list. Add new items as follow-on tasks or "problem tickets" until all known issues with the implementation have been resolved. Also include some aspect of version control in your content naming convention. This will allow you to track changes and be able to quickly identify previous versions or iterations of your content.

Quality Assurance

Once the implementation is completed, the QA process can start. A launch page is the gateway to examining any version of the landing page that we want to see. By selecting the exact settings for the value of any variable in the test, you can create any recipe in your test. Such preview functionality is available in most landing page testing tools.

If your test is small scale (fewer than a couple of dozen total recipes), you may be able to exhaustively check all recipes and make sure that they were implemented properly. As the number of recipes grows, this quickly becomes impractical. A properly constructed QA plan can help to overcome this problem and make testing manageable. See the sidebar "Resource: QA Plan Overview" to understand how to approach QA plans.

Maintain a "problem ticket" or known issues list. This is similar to the bug-fix process that is used in software development prior to a new release. Classify or rank your unresolved issues by severity and work down your list in order. Once your issues get small enough, you may just decide that they will not materially change the outcome of your test and you can proceed without addressing them. In such cases, you always have the option of correcting them after the test if they are part of the winning recipe.

Resource: QA Plan Overview

Consider these kinds of review and factors:

Piecewise Review

The simplest kind of testing to conduct is element by element. You cycle through every variable value in your test plan to make sure that it looks and functions as expected. Even in large tests (with search space sizes in the millions of recipes), the total number of variable values is still manageable (typically no more than a couple of dozen).

Interaction Review

Piecewise review only looks at each variable value in isolation. However, you need to consider some of your variable values in the context of other variable values. Explicitly call out the important dependencies among your chosen tuning elements.

For example, imagine if one variable defines the button color and has five distinct values, and another one defines the button text and also has five distinct values—that means you have 10 total piecewise elements to consider. But in reality, there are 25 separate buttons that need to be created, and each one must be reviewed individually.

Note that the "interactions" that we are referring to here are not the variable interactions discussed earlier. They are visual or functional interactions among your variable values. As a result, you can identify them ahead of time and include them in your QA plan.

Constraints and Dependencies

You may have variable values that are dependent or contingent on the existence of another variable value. Depending on how you have chosen to define your variables and values, make sure that these constraints have been properly enforced. For example, if you add or delete steps in your conversion process, you must make sure that there are no disconnected parts or features of your site (that can't be reached through available links and navigation), nor any "orphaned" content or excess code/functionality.

Coherency Review

Even if you have conducted all of these QA steps, you may still have problems with coherency. Don't miss the forest for the trees. Even if everything was properly implemented, the end result may look odd because of unexpected juxtapositions. For example, if you remove a page element completely, you should examine the effect on the surrounding elements that now butt up against each other. Subtler coherency issues involve changes in emphasis and visual balance. For example, if you replace a short test description with a longer block of text, the main visual focus of the page can change because more of the screen real estate is now devoted to the text. If the coherency issues are severe enough, consider changing the test plan to address them.

Collect the Data

Collecting data during the test is a two-part activity. First, you must properly prepare for data collection. Then, you must closely monitor the data collection process.

Preparing for Data Collection

Preparing for data collection is a critical activity and involves the following steps:

Tracking Test to make sure all campaign tracking is coming across in your web analytics tool and has not been messed up by your test code and content changes. Such problems are especially common if you are changing flow through the site or renaming pages. Look for sudden drops in traffic from particular campaigns or referring websites. Uncover any breakdown in tracking by troubleshooting the issue.

If you have alternative contact methods such as toll-free numbers, you may have to temporarily set up multiple numbers (one per unique recipe in your test) in order to properly track and attribute activity.

Traffic Filtering Implement any required traffic filters. If certain traffic sources are not meant to be a part of your test, the affected visitors should still see the original version of your site. Filters can be implemented by routing traffic to the original or alternative page, or by displaying different content within the same page depending on passed-in parameters on the inbound URL.

Procedural Changes Some tests may require changes to company procedures or training, or the addition of extra staff. If your company is currently running at full capacity, identify the critical bottlenecks ahead of time and put in contingency plans. This will prepare you to quickly respond if the conversion rate during the test increases substantially. This may require keeping extra inventory on hand or training contract workers as extra surge capacity. If you are changing the method, amount, or sequence of the data that you collect online, brief all affected staff and departments ahead of time. For example, if you remove some fields from an online form, instruct your call center staff to collect the missing information on their subsequent follow-up calls.

Scheduling You must determine your approximate data collection period ahead of time. Ideally you would like a long window that is not affected by seasonal issues, significant business plan changes, or outside events. If it is impossible to avoid short-term disturbances in your data collection (for example, due to industry tradeshows or holidays), plan for them, and decide what you will do with the data from those time periods. You can choose to leave the data in your sample unaltered, try to compensate for the bias introduced, or discard it altogether.

You may decide to leave your data collection period somewhat open-ended. This is appropriate since you do not know the size of the effects that you will find ahead of time, and may choose to simply wait until you have reached a high statistical confidence in your answer. Conversely, if your data collection period is fixed, you should be able to calculate the size of effects that you will be able to identify. If the size of effects that you can resolve is large, the test elements you have chosen are more likely to produce inconclusive results.

Cutover to "Live"   Your implementation and QA should be done on a separate copy of your landing page in a *staging environment*. Before you start data collection, move all appropriate files, code, and data structures to the live environment. The live environment may be different from the staging environment, so this move can introduce additional instabilities and problems. It is best to make your cutover outside of your peak business hours, and you should have your network administrator, webmaster, and programmers standing by during this process.

It may be impossible to test some elements of your new landing page without being live. For example, you may not be able to test your e-commerce checkout process because it is only hooked up to your live site and is difficult to duplicate in your staging environment. Make sure that you run end-to-end tests (and back out any resulting data or transactions).

Your QA process is unlikely to have caught all issues during staging. Your cutover problems can range from severe—say your conversion process is broken and the conversion action cannot be completed—to mild—perhaps some small percentage of visitors may experience a nonstandard presentation of your landing pages under unlikely circumstances. You must have contingency plans in place to quickly back out and reverse your changes and restore the live site to its original state.

Monitoring Data Collection

Once your actual data collection has started, make sure that everything is going according to plan. Typical monitoring activities include the following:

Check Data Recording   Make sure that impressions and conversions are being recorded across all recipes in your test. Make sure that no corrupted or incomplete data is ending up in your tracking.

Check Data Rates   Verify that the expected number of visitors is being recorded based on the traffic sources that you are using for the test. Very low traffic numbers may indicate that your filters are too restrictive or are not working properly. Very high traffic numbers may indicate that you have not filtered out all undesirable traffic sources. Cross-check your data rates against other web analytics tools you may have in place, or examine their recording at the origin (for example, in the PPC account, affiliate tracking software, or ad network where the traffic originates).

Watch for any anomalies in the data rate. These may indicate unexpected external events. They may also alert you to the presence of sporadic or spiky traffic sources that you neglected to filter out.

Check Conversion Rates Make sure that the conversion rate being recorded for your baseline recipe is comparable to historic figures. Very low or very high conversion rates may be a sign of improper counting or recording. However, you should not worry if the conversion rate is on the low side initially, since delayed conversions are often a significant part of the total and will not happen until the data has been "aged" by the passage of time. Check the conversion rates of other recipes in your test.

Correct for Sampling Bias Even if your data rate is high and you quickly reach statistical confidence in your answer, continue to collect data across all appropriate time periods. As a general rule, correct for time-of-day and day-of-week effects by collecting data in one-week increments.

The sidebar "Resource: Data Collection" gives you a checklist to conduct proper monitoring.

Resource: Data Collection

- Verify that test end-to-end conversions are being properly recorded and tracked.

- Verify that traffic levels are appropriate for the traffic sources you have chosen (cross-check against your web analytics software).

- After collecting enough data, verify that there is at least one conversion for each recipe that you are sampling (this guarantees that a particular recipe is not broken).

- Verify that the conversion rate on your baseline is reasonable. Remember that it may be low at first because of delayed conversions.

- Verify that you have collected data long enough to correct for time-of-day or day-of-week biases (even if you had previously reached your desired level of statistical confidence).

- Note any traffic or conversion rate spikes that might indicate seasonal patterns or external news events (along with a changing audience composition).

Analyze the Results and Verify Improvement

How you analyze your data depends on the exact elements in the test plan and their constraints, the conversion actions and their respective values, the tuning method, and the specific landing page testing software chosen. In the simplest case, an A-B split test can be stopped when statistical confidence has been reached via a simple spreadsheet calculation. If you have a complicated multivariate test and are examining variable interactions, you may need the assistance of an outside statistician to properly interpret the results.

If your test proves inconclusive, you have three options:

- Abandon your test if the reasonable data collection window has passed.

- Start another test with different test elements.

- Continue to collect more data until the desired confidence level has been reached. Remember that this may happen rather slowly since your ability to resolve an effect does not depend directly on the number of conversions, but rather on the square root of it.

Even if your test finds significant improvements, you may still have work ahead of you. One of the assumptions behind the landing page statistics is that the behavior of the audience does not change over time. In reality, this is not the case. Nothing remains the same forever. You may launch additional customer acquisition programs and change your audience mix. Seasonal issues may encroach after the completion of the test. Your audience's sophistication and familiarity with your company or industry can also change, affecting the perceived value of your offer. New competitors may enter the fray, or functional substitutes may appear that begin to supersede your product or service.

You can't assume that performance improvement observed in your test will hold up over time. This is especially true if the tuning elements that you have chosen are short-lived or transient (such as changing the offer or running a seasonal promotion). Basic usability improvements should have a much longer shelf life. The best way to protect yourself against such changes is to continue to run your original version at a low level (say 5 to 10 percent of the total traffic) even after your test completes. It is likely that your baseline will continue to underperform the winning challenger recipe. However, you may want to hedge and give up a bit of the possible improvement as an insurance policy against downside risk. The sidebar "Resource: Data Analysis" makes sure that you do not overlook anything in your analysis.

Resource: Data Analysis

- Have you reached your desired statistical confidence level?

- If not, should you continue the test?

- Have you eliminated any questionable data collection periods or spikes from your data?

- Have you considered variable interactions of just main effects?

- Have you run a follow-up A-B split test involving your winner and the original baseline recipe?

- Is your program relatively stable in terms of traffic volumes and conversion rates? If not, what percentage of your ongoing traffic should you dedicate to the losing recipe?

By now you should be able to develop an effective action plan. In the final chapter, you'll learn how to avoid some common pitfalls that can undermine your work.

Avoiding Real-World Pitfalls

15

No battle plan survives contact with the enemy.

—HELMUTH VON MOLTKE (1800–1891), Prussian
Army Chief of Staff

How do you reconcile the need for planning with this quote? They seem contradictory, yet both are true. This chapter is about the real world. After all the planning is over, you still have to sidestep many pitfalls to complete a successful landing page test.

Many of the pitfalls reviewed here are cautionary tales that consistently trip up even experienced testers. All the planning in the world will not save you. Neither will being really smart. Most of the topics described here can only be learned through painful and costly direct experience. This chapter can help you learn from other people's mistakes.

CHAPTER CONTENTS

Ignoring Your Baseline
Collecting Insufficient Data
Not Accounting for Seasonality
Assuming That Testing Has No Costs
Not Factoring In Delayed Conversions
Becoming Paralyzed by Search Engine Considerations
Failing to Act

Ignoring Your Baseline

During a split test conducted by SiteTuners, the company saw performance improve on the challenger recipe from a 4.63 percent conversion rate in week one to 5.03 percent during week two. Normally you would be happy to see this kind of increase in conversion during your data collection period. But was it really a good thing?

On closer inspection, it turned out that the original baseline recipe had a conversion rate of 3.59 percent during week one and 6.18 percent in week two. In other words, during week one, our challenger recipe had a *29 percent advantage* over the baseline. During week two it was actually *19 percent worse*!

What had changed? Week two was a holiday week. Presumably the composition of the audience had changed. So while the new audience preferred the challenger a bit more than the old audience, they also preferred the baseline by an even higher margin over the old audience. SiteTuners would have never found this out if they had not looked at the baseline performance.

Do not get distracted by changes in your conversion rate during your test. Your conversion rate may fluctuate for a number of reasons, including not collecting enough data and seasonal factors, both discussed in a moment. The purpose of your test is not to get the absolute highest conversion rate on your challenger recipe during your data collection period. What is important is whether you are beating your baseline.

To do this, you must collect enough data to have a good read on the performance of your baseline recipe. If you simply assign a proportional amount of data to it (as is commonly done in full factorial multivariate testing data collection), you will require a lot more time to zero in on its true performance. You should typically devote a minimum 15–25 percent of the available traffic to the baseline recipe during multivariate tests. However, for certain parametric multivariate testing approaches, disproportionate data collection on the baseline recipe may invalidate the subsequent analysis (which assumes that the data collection design is balanced).

Don't Ignore the Baseline Recipe

- Collect enough data to know how the baseline performs.
- Measure improvements relative to the baseline.

Collecting Insufficient Data

One of the advantages of online marketing in general (and landing page optimization in particular) is the ability to measure everything. All online marketing campaigns and programs should be run "by the numbers." The difficult part is in knowing *which* numbers to use and *when*.

Many online marketers like to watch the pot boil. Like stock market day traders, they get hooked on the action and make frequent changes to their programs. Some even use automated tools, such as PPC bid management, to make decisions more frequently than is humanly possible. This goes back to the adrenal rush of the lizard brain looking for prey; we're pouncing for data checks instead. There is nothing inherently wrong with automated tools or frequent changes per se, but each change must be made after collecting an appropriate amount of data. Unfortunately, this is often not the case in practice.

Let's consider the dangers of small sample sizes. Let's assume that you have had four visitors to your e-commerce website. One of the visitors has bought something. So what is your conversion rate of visitors to sales? If you answered 25 percent (one sale out of four visitors), you are probably way off. Most e-commerce sites we have seen range from 1 to 5 percent. Unless your product is unique, indispensable, and available for sale only from your site, the 25 percent conversion rate is highly unlikely. Similarly, if you had no sales after the first four visits, you would probably be wrong to conclude that your conversion rate was really zero and that you would *never* get a sale. This example may seem a bit extreme, but too many landing page tests are decided with inappropriately small data samples. As we mentioned earlier, your sample size is expressed in the number of conversion actions, and not in the number of unique visitors.

Once you start the data collection in your test, resist the temptation to monitor the results frequently, especially early in the test. Otherwise, you run the risk of getting on an emotional roller coaster caused by the early streaks in the data. One moment you may be euphoric about excellent results, and the next you may be despondent as the indicated improvement vanishes like a mirage. So pick a statistical confidence level in your answer and wait until you have collected enough data to reach it. You need to have the self-discipline not to even look at the early results.

Remember, the law of large numbers tells us that our measured conversion rate average will eventually stabilize at the actual value. But it does not tell us exactly how long this will take. It is possible to have large deviations from the actual mean early in the data collection. Even if you are confident in the fact that your new landing page converts better than the original, you still do not have a clear indication of exactly how much better it is if you haven't collected enough data. Do not simply use the observed difference in lift as your reported answer. Always present it with the correct error bars (also called "confidence intervals").

Collect Enough Data

- Don't monitor test results frequently, especially early.
- Collect enough data to reach your desired confidence level.
- Always present data with error bars.

Not Accounting for Seasonality

Remember that it is a big mistake to conduct sequential testing. In other words, you should never run one version of your landing page design *followed* by another one. Too many outside influences can cloud or invalidate your results. The reason that you should collect data in parallel (by randomly splitting your traffic among the alternative recipes in your test) is to account for as many of these outside factors as possible.

However, even if you properly conduct data collection in parallel, you may still run into obvious or subtle seasonality issues. Underlying all landing page testing is the statistical framework that calls for an *unchanging visitor population* that *behaves consistently* over time. Unfortunately, neither of these prerequisites is likely to be strictly true in practice. Your audience mix changes as you modify your marketing activities, or as your competitors change theirs. The same population of visitors may start to change their behavior over time as they gain more familiarity with your product, company, or industry.

Very spiky seasonality may significantly complicate a test. Sometimes your goal is to specifically tune for such a short-term seasonal period. Or you may want to filter out any short-term holiday impacts and treat them as anomalies as you try to tune for "normal" visitor behavior during the rest of the year.

Make Peace with Seasonality Issues

- Choose recurring, controllable, and stable traffic sources.
- Don't change your marketing mix during the data collection.
- Plan data collection around any major product or company announcements.
- Average across obvious sampling biases (day-of-week, time-of-day).
- Schedule around any known seasonal trends or important industry events.
- Remove or mitigate data from unexpected external events.
- Continue ongoing low-level data collection on the original recipe even after the test is completed.

Assuming That Testing Has No Costs

Many people opine that landing page testing is a silver bullet. You pick some page elements to test, collect your data, and all of a sudden you have a better-performing landing page. In fact, not all of your test plan ideas are going to improve your conversion rate. Unfortunately, you don't know ahead of time which of your variable values will be successful. If you did, you would not need testing in the first place.

A certain kind of mental reframing is required as part of the proper perspective:

Each landing page test has a cost. You will have to expend time and effort to set up the test, monitor data collection, and analyze the results. Even if your test is successful, you still have to consider work that you could have been engaged in instead of testing and the lost opportunity cost. In other words, if you have bigger opportunities for making an impact on your program's profitability, attend to those first.

A particular test may not yield any positive results. It is possible that the tuning elements you have selected will not create any noticeable conversion improvement. A few may actually make things worse and lower your conversion rate. At the end of the test, your original baseline recipe for the landing page may still remain the champion and will have bested all challengers. This is not a problem. You cannot base your testing program on the outcome of a single test. You will guess wrong a significant percentage of the time when selecting alternative variable values to test. But this should not deter you from trying. Testing is an ongoing activity, and until you have completely exhausted all of your meaningful ideas, keep trying.

However, it is likely that you will see a law of diminishing returns if you continue to tune the same page over and over. Chances are you will get your biggest gains during your early tests, because at that point your landing page is in its worst shape and your ideas are many. During subsequent tests, you will probably be tinkering with smaller refinements that are not as likely to produce dramatic conversion improvements. So you have to soberly evaluate whether another test on the same page is warranted.

Performance may drop during a test but still lead to positive results. It is possible that the mix of alternative recipes you are testing will perform worse than the baseline recipe. Often some of your variable values are worse than their baseline counterparts while others are better, creating a sampled blend of recipes that has lower overall conversion. As a result, you will see an often significant drop in revenues early in your test. Don't panic or abort your test. Have the self-discipline to collect data with high statistical confidence.

If some variable values or recipes continue to underperform, you can eliminate them from the mix that you are testing. Eventually after several experiments, you should be able to cut out all of the poor performers and focus on what is working the best. This may get you into positive territory (where your final challenger recipes perform better than the original baseline).

In one particular series of landing page tests run by SiteTuners, the mix of all possible recipes initially performed *19 percent poorer* than the baseline (see Figure 15.1). Had the test ended at this point, the baseline would have remained the king of the hill.

However, over several additional test runs and successively better-performing recipes, a challenger recipe was found that performed *27 percent better* than the baseline in the final head-to-head test.

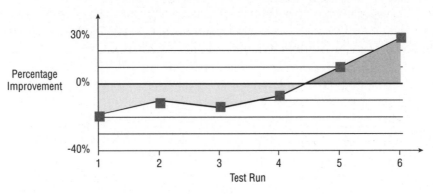

Figure 15.1 Average conversion rate improvement vs. baseline

However, all is not rosy simply because of the positive outcome. The shaded portion of the graph below the "0%" line is proportional to the lost revenues during the data collection period, and the shaded portion above that line constitutes extra revenues collected during the test as a result of improved performance. As you can see, the lost revenues are greater than the extra revenue, indicating that there was a net loss of revenue during the test. Since the new and improved landing page will presumably continue to outperform the original for a long time, the company will eventually recoup the difference and gain extra revenue.

> ### There's No Free Lunch
>
> You must be willing to suffer short-term pain during landing page testing in order to attain the long-term gain of improved performance and higher conversions.

Not Factoring In Delayed Conversions

Carefully consider delayed conversions in your data collection and subsequent analysis. A delayed conversion happens when a visitor acts only after a noticeable delay or on a subsequent return visit to your landing page. Such delays can range from hours to many months.

Depending on your audience and landing page, you may have a low percentage of delayed conversions. This is usually the case when the landing page is stand-alone and single purpose. The required conversion action is usually nonthreatening and does not involve payment or the disclosure of a lot of personal information.

For example, imagine that you run a lead-generation company in the financial services industry. You sell the contact information from people who download your free retirement planning guide to local financial planners around the country. The visitors arrive from PPC campaigns on major search engines. The traffic lands on a standalone page that offers the guide in exchange for the visitor's name, e-mail, and contact phone number. In such a situation you would expect the number of delayed conversions to be low. There is not a lot of information on the landing page—nothing to ponder or digest. It is basically an impulse decision to get the guide. If visitors decide not to get it, they are unlikely to type in the same keyword and click on your ad again. Since there is no other way to find your landing page, this is a one-shot attempt to get the conversion.

Figure 15.2 shows the conversion delay graph for a lead-generation SiteTuners client. The graph is on a logarithmic scale—that is, the horizontal axis displays the conversion delay time in orders of magnitude and not linearly. As you can see from the graph, most conversions have happened by the two-hour mark indicated by the "elbow." After that, you get a small stream of stragglers. But these do not change the end result significantly. Even after a thousand hours of delay (about six weeks), the stragglers constitute only 5 percent of total conversions. Even on a logarithmic graph, the conversion rate after the elbow stays pretty flat.

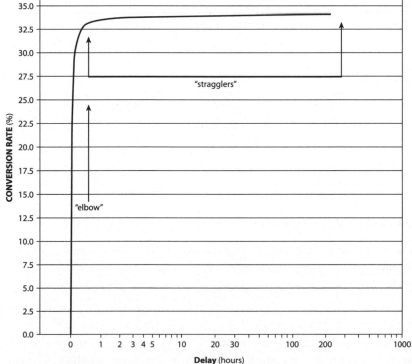

Figure 15.2 Conversion delay graph for a lead-generation landing page

By contrast, there are situations where stragglers constitute a significant percentage of the total conversions. This is most likely to happen when the conversion action is significant or requires an online purchase. There is growing evidence that online consumers are getting more comfortable looking for information on the Internet. One of the implications for e-commerce is that the conversion delay (from first landing page visit to the sale) continues to grow. Internet users are comfortable comparison shopping and researching before committing to the transaction.

Figure 15.3 shows the conversion delay graph for a typical e-commerce catalog. The traffic sources are from a mix of PPC, SEO, and type-in traffic. There is a possibility that someone will bookmark the catalog page. Repeat customers are also a significant part of the traffic mix. Notice that the elbow is not quite as pronounced as in the lead-generation example. The percentage of stragglers is also greater (as indicated by the higher slope of the graph past the elbow point). In fact, stragglers in this example constitute a full 15 percent of total conversions. So if you would have measured the conversion rate after one hour, you could expect it to drift up by almost 20 percent over the following few weeks.

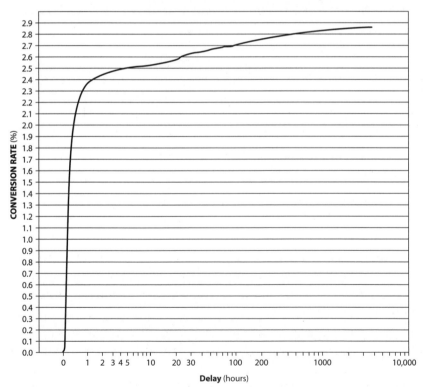

Figure 15.3 Conversion delay graph for an e-commerce catalog

Understand Your Stragglers

The important implication for landing page testing is that you have to understand the behavior of your stragglers and compare apples to apples. This can be done in one of two ways:

Ignore the stragglers. If your percentage of stragglers is low, you could measure at the elbow point on the graph. In other words, you can disregard all the conversions that happen after a certain maximum delay time (which corresponds to the elbow for your particular landing page). Since the percentage of stragglers is small, this does not change your results significantly and allows you to nearly instantly compare the newest results to those from previous data collection periods.

"Age" your data. Age your data from the most recent data collection period to make sure that you are comparing properly against past periods. As you can see on the graph in Figure 15.3 (as displayed on the logarithmic delay time scale), the conversion rate increase will usually begin to flatten out at some point. So you should wait the appropriate amount of time before looking at the conversion rate. Exactly where to make this cutoff is a judgment call. As a rough guideline, we recommend the point at which you reach 95 percent of the final conversion rate. Usually this time period is between a few days and a few weeks.

Consider Delayed Conversions

- Understand the behavior of your "stragglers."
- Compare properly aged results only.

Case Study: Power Options

Power Options (www.poweropt.com) sells access to their advanced stock option research database on a subscription basis. Clients can research 250,000+ tradable options and use the patented software to find the best possible trades.

The company offers an unrestricted 14-day trial without requiring any credit card information. After the trial is completed, some people continue with the service on a paid basis. This landing page test goal was to increase the percentage of visitors who signed up for the free trial.

The original free trial sign-up process involved landing on an information-rich page (shown in Figure 15.4). The page had a lot of details about stock option trading, Power Options, and related subjects.

A couple of the graphics on the landing page were links to the follow-on page, which allowed you to register for the free trial (see Figure 15.5). The registration page also had a lot of text as well as thumbnail screenshots of some sample software reports.

Power Options had a low data rate on the landing page in question, so a "coarse granularity" approach (see Chapter 9, "The Strategy of What to Test") and an A-B split test were used. In other words, all ideas were combined into a single best-practices redesign instead of tinkering with a specific landing page element.

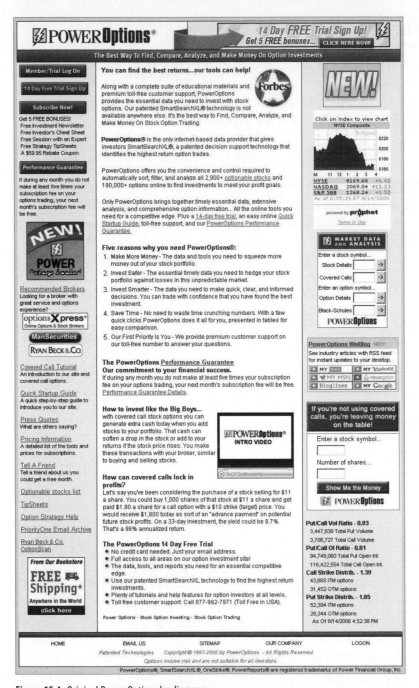

Figure 15.4 Original Power Options landing page

In the proposed redesign (see Figure 15.6), the two-page process became a single page. Among the most striking changes was a radical simplification of the page. The focus shifted to a simple description of the free trial offer, removing all supporting descriptions of stock option trading and the software.

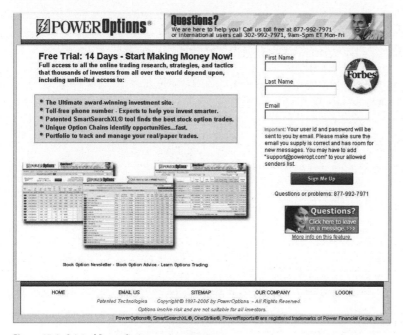

Figure 15.5 Original Power Options registration page

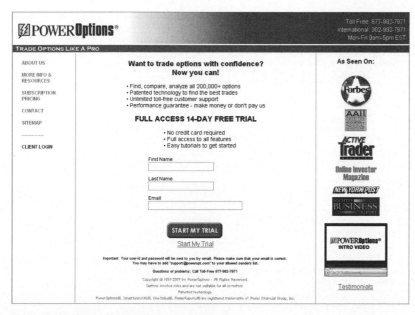

Figure 15.6 Redesigned Power Options registration process

There was a lot of pushback to the proposed alternative landing page, including that this kind of radical simplification would not work with their target audience's sophistication and interest in research. However, was including such detail worth the risk of complicating a page where people might otherwise take the low-risk step of starting a free trial?

Did the information-rich original page instill loyalty and provide value to visitors? Or did it serve to scare away prospects with its voluminous text, complicated page layout, and unclear call-to-action?

As it turns out, both sides were right—to a degree. Although the redesigned challenger version of the page ended up having much higher conversion rate to free trials, the baseline registration process instilled more loyalty and resulted in significantly higher delayed conversions among the stragglers. See the conversion delay graph in Figure 15.7.

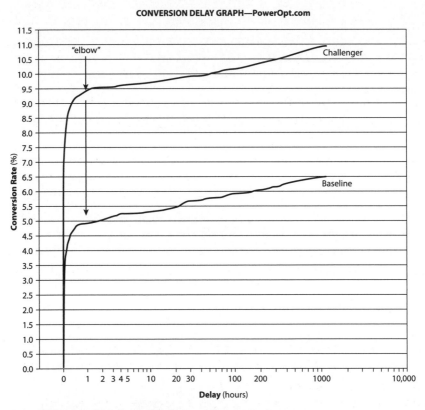

Figure 15.7 Conversion delay graph for the Power Options A-B split test

Usually we see a clear elbow and then delayed conversions trickling in. Sometimes the slope of the delayed conversion "tail" is proportional to the height of the elbow (when displayed on a logarithmic scale like Figure 15.7). The percentage of delayed conversions is the same for all tested versions of the landing page. But this is not always the case.

In the graph in Figure 15.7, our challenger version had an elbow at 9.5 percent and an 11 percent final conversion rate (an increase of 16 percent). The original baseline version of the site had an elbow at 5 percent and eventually peaked at 6.5 percent (an increase of 30 percent). So the original baseline had a higher percentage of delayed conversions but a lower overall conversion rate at the end of the day.

Tracking the actions of the stragglers was critical to predicting the percentage improvement accurately. If we had measured at the elbow point (one-hour delay), we would have predicted a 90 percent improvement (9.5 percent divided by 5.0 percent). Once we aged the data, we saw the more accurate 70 percent figure (11.0 percent divided by 6.5 percent). This was very close to the actual 75 percent observed revenue-per-visitor increase after the free trial was completed. Our subsequent analysis showed that the original version influenced a higher percentage of committed visitors to return later, and closed some of the performance gap against our simplified challenger over time.

If you observe different straggler behavior among the landing page versions that you are testing, you must age your data before analyzing the results.

Becoming Paralyzed by Search Engine Considerations

Often a significant portion of the traffic to a landing page comes from SEO. There are some important considerations about search engines as they pertain to landing page testing.

SEO is a very tricky business. There is an ongoing race between the search engines and people who are trying to understand them and optimize where their content appears. The stakes are pretty high. If you can dial in the right set of features and practices, you may be able to get significant traffic to your landing pages without a direct per-visitor cost. Of course, long-term SEO success requires a significant ongoing commitment of resources and time, so it is not "free" traffic.

The following SEO concerns often come up in our testing: fear, technical issues, and cloaking.

Fear

If you receive significant SEO traffic to parts of your site, you may be scared of testing changes to your current design. Many online marketers are afraid of changing even the smallest details for fear of losing their top ranking.

This fear is unnecessary for two reasons. First, the search engines regularly change their ranking algorithms. So keeping your site the same is not a guarantee of ranking stability. In fact, content updates are a factor in improving search engine rankings. Second, many of the main contributors to your high ranking are off-page factors that have nothing to do with the text, design, or appearance of your page. Such factors include age of your domain discovery (including how long it has been active), brand authority, the number and quality of inbound links to your page from other respected websites in your industry, and the relevance of your content to the searcher's specific query. In addition, a landing page test might provide the opportunity for SEO improvement in design and code factors.

On-page factors should not represent enough of an unmitigated threat to deter you from testing. As long as you follow basic SEO best practices, there's nothing to fear. You should not make radical changes that virtually cloak your page to search engines (at least as compared to competitor sites), such as creating your landing page completely in Flash or Ajax technology, removing all of the text from the page by putting it into include files, or changing all text to corresponding graphics. If an SEO expert participates in your test planning, it's likely that they can work with a variety of the 200-plus algorithm factors to counter any unexpected fluctuations in the search visibility of your page.

Technical Issues

Some online marketers are concerned that adding the required testing code and scripts to their landing pages will create technical problems that will get them disqualified from the search engine results. This concern is baseless.

Search engine spiders ignore most programming code and basically look at the text of the page (along with hyperlinks). Most testing software uses JavaScript code to alter the contents of the page based on the contents of a first-party cookie on the Web visitor's browser. This happens *client-side*.

In other words, the changes happen after the web server has created the page and handed it off to the web browser software. Since the spider does not know how to interpret the JavaScript code and does not accept cookies (which are used to control the behavior of the test page), it cannot possibly know what page a human visitor would see. As a result, the spider always sees the same page as it was before the data collection for the landing page test was started.

Cloaking

Another myth web teams use to reject conversion tuning is that they will be accused of *cloaking* by Google and be penalized by search engines, losing all rank and related search traffic.

Cloaking is the practice of showing different content to the search engine spiders and to actual human visitors to your page. Cloaking has the intention of deceiving the spiders and changing the page's ranking in the search results, particularly for a topic where there is no real content relevance but a high opportunity to drive visitors. In extreme cases this can be used as a bait-and-switch tactic to spam searchers. If these types of results were served too frequently, it would ultimately result in loss of trust in the search engine, not the anonymous link switching party.

At the same time, search engines support the goal of testing to determine appeals to your visitors and ultimately optimize the searcher's experience.

Google has a clear policy on cloaking as it applies to intention and landing page testing (this policy may be changed in the future, so please check directly with Google on their latest pronouncements). Ethical landing page testing is not considered cloaking. Follow these general guidelines:

- Keep your alternative versions on the same theme and topic as the original page.
- Remove testing code and install your new champion version of the landing page(s) as soon as the test is completed.
- Always show your original version as part of your recipe mix during data collection.

However, there is also a more subtle and fundamental online marketing issue underlying the cloaking discussion: Search is based on text, and many visitors are guided to conversion by design elements that Google cannot evaluate mathematically. What the spiders need to rank your page well is not always what your audience emotionally prefers.

Studies have shown repeatedly that Internet visitors don't "read" when they look at web pages. Stripped-down, stark versions of pages work best. All of the clutter and detail is often removed so that visitors can focus on their task with minimal distractions. This does not always jive with journalism's inverted pyramid and the concise content hierarchy that Google prefers. As online marketing evolves, there must be a balance of design to appeal to visitors with bias to copy or to visual elements.

Don't Use Decent SEO Rankings as an Excuse

All major SEO-related issues can be addressed if the testing process is handled properly.

PPC

Since you are paying for PPC traffic, you have the right to land it anywhere you want (within the editorial guidelines of the search engine). PPC is basically an auction model that tries to maximize the revenue per visitor for the search engine by considering the maximum bid amount that you are willing to pay and the clickthrough rate (CTR) when deciding where to place your ad in the search results.

Because of these characteristics you might think that PPC would be immune from search engine issues. However, Google has introduced the notion of a landing page quality score as part of its ranking algorithm. A poor score can cause your keyword to have a prohibitively high bid to appear at all in the search results. Because landing pages are often specifically designed for short-term PPC campaigns, they cannot be measured by the same standards as stable long-term pages on your website. In this case, on-page factors become more important.

In theory, this can mean that your conversion rate improves through testing, but the resulting page causes your quality score to get worse. The net result would be that you would see diminished PPC traffic to your new and improved page. In practice, this should not be a concern. Remember that from the standpoint of search engines, the whole point of landing page testing (and the very existence of Google Website Optimizer) is to increase the conversion rate. This improved landing page performance should translate into higher PPC prices paid by the most efficient advertisers. Google will not choose to cripple their main cash flow machine. In fact, they are proactively working to encourage landing page testing.

Failing to Act

It all comes down to this: As you are reading the last few words of this book, you have a choice to make. Hopefully you have learned something useful about landing page optimization. But your knowledge may remain in the realm of intellectual concepts only. If you do nothing, you will not improve your conversion rate.

You must *act* to produce any results. This does not have to be some giant undertaking. Start small. Take baby steps. Change or test something very simple. Even if you do not have a good outcome, you will learn something. And you will build the excitement and psychological momentum needed for your landing page optimization program to succeed in the longer term.

Start Optimizing Immediately

A little bit of something is better than a whole lot of nothing.

Now close this book, and start optimizing.
Best wishes and higher conversions!

Landing Page
Testing Tools

Landing page testing can be the key to the success of any website. As you've gleaned from this book, by far the most important part of testing is deciding what to test. Many companies mistakenly focus on the testing tools and technology first. They have a significant weakness when it comes to developing a testing strategy, creating effective landing page test plans, properly collecting data, and interpreting test results. We suggest that you first review the contents of Chapter 14, "Developing Your Action Plan," and only then select the proper testing tool company.

The field of testing tools continues to evolve rapidly. This appendix is an overview of some currently available tools. Most of the companies listed also offer some level of professional services for testing support. The list is not meant to be exhaustive, nor is it meant to be an endorsement of any company or its products and services. For up-to-date information, please visit ConversionNinjaToolbox.com.

Enterprise Tools

The following list of testing tool companies focuses on the large business and enterprise space. They all offer capable tools that are designed for large-scale deployment and often feature robust integration with web analytics, business intelligence, and other related technological platforms. Because of the complexities of the tools, a professional services division within each company also offers setup and ongoing support, including the ability to implement tests end to end.

Adobe Test & Target

If you are looking for a tool with a long history in the field, Test & Target (originally Offermatica) has been around for a long time. It was acquired by Omniture, and in addition to landing page testing the feature set expanded to include behavioral targeting. Omniture was in turn acquired by Adobe.

Test & Target is also one of the most versatile tools and has a comprehensive feature set, complete with full integration with Adobe Site Catalyst (an analytics tool), which is useful for doing additional analysis of test results. They have also recently upgraded their tool feature set to make it more suitable for websites other than e-commerce.

Although it has a strong feature set, along with that comes a considerable cost in terms of setup, learning curve, and licensing. The pricing model is partially based on the number of "server calls"—the more traffic your website gets, the more expensive it can be to run tests. If you leave elements of Test & Target variables up permanently after your test (to continue to serve up dynamic content), you will incur ongoing fees for these page views. This can be cost prohibitive for all but the largest companies.

Autonomy Optimost

For those looking for the most powerful and robust testing tool, Autonomy Optimost certainly fits the bill. This company evolved from the earliest testing tool company (Optimost), and was subsequently purchased by Interwoven, which was in turn purchased by enterprise information management company Autonomy. As of this writing, HP has acquired a controlling stake in Autonomy.

Particularly advantageous are its real-time proactive segmentation and targeting tools, and also its advanced test analytic tools. Both of these features, along with its solid website testing consulting services, enable clients to get value out of their testing initiatives.

The downside of having such a rich feature set is that the tool comes with sizable costs, which makes it suitable only for enterprise companies with considerable website testing budgets.

SiteSpect

SiteSpect offers a unique approach for implementation of their testing tools. Most testing tools allow the content to be manipulated either in the web browser (client-side) or on the server before the page is served up (server-side). SiteSpect uses the "intercept" approach discussed in Chapter 11, "Preparing for Testing." Its content swap happens on an intermediate server that is inserted ahead of the web server and content management system (CMS). When a web page is requested, the SiteSpect server dynamically picks out the appropriate portions of the content to replace and swaps them out on the fly before passing the content on to the web browser. This approach allows the CMS to remain undisturbed and unaware that the landing page test is going on.

Although significant custom code often still needs to be written to implement this custom swapping, landing page testing can be moved to the marketing department—without any support required from IT or the webmaster. This solution is particularly attractive to larger companies with brittle or complex CMSs that cannot be touched for technical or political reasons.

Maxymiser

Another website testing company is Maxymiser. The company is based in the United Kingdom and has a strong client base in Europe. Their tools compete with those of the more traditional players like Test & Target and Optimost. They have a professional services organization and can help with all aspects of testing, from test plan creation to implementation.

Maxymiser differentiates their tools by offering real-time website personalization, adapting your website to help make each visitor's experience a more useful one. They also support mobile testing.

Maxymiser's robust testing toolset is better suited to mid- to large-sized businesses that can afford their relatively expensive testing fees and professional services.

LiveBall

i-on interactive has been working on its LiveBall landing page platform for a number of years. The tool includes a CMS, testing platform, and basic web analytics.

Unlike many of the other testing solutions, LiveBall cannot be overlaid on an existing website. All of the pages must be created inside the tool. Therefore, it is not suited for testing on existing corporate websites and is designed for stand-alone landing pages, page flows, or microsites. If your testing focus is on self-contained experiences that can be implemented in LiveBall, then this is a good choice. If you also have to get another tool for testing on your main corporate website, the nontrivial cost of LiveBall tools and support services should be considered as only a part of your total testing support costs.

Free or Inexpensive Tools

The following tools are good for getting your landing page optimization program started. The learning curve associated with deploying your first test is short, and many of the tools are designed for a nontechnical online marketing user. The tools range from free to inexpensive but offer limited customer support for resolving potentially complex issues. All of them can be used quickly and repeatedly to get successful tests deployed.

Google Website Optimizer

Google loves to create free self-service tools and applications. In 2007 it shook up the landing page testing marketplace when it rolled out its free Google Website Optimizer (GWO) platform. This put landing page testing capabilities into the hands of even the smallest companies.

GWO has some functional limitations alongside some nice features. The tool allows you to automatically eliminate test variables as they prove themselves to be underperformers during data collection. In other words, it can automatically zero in on the best-performing version in the test and stop displaying content that is not working as well. A major drawback is that the testing math only supports countable goals with the identical value. That means it cannot optimize for variable value goals (such as assigning the revenue from the sale to an e-commerce transaction, or having multiple goals with different values in the same test). Its feature set is being updated slowly, and there are some unofficial hacks that help make up for some of the tool's shortcomings.

The GWO tool was originally based on tracking code developed for Google Analytics (Urchin). For a while it became an independent entity within Google, but it has been rolled back into the Google Analytics codebase. If you need help with test implementation or customization, Google does not offer any consulting support directly. Support is available on a paid basis from a large and international group of Google Analytics Authorized Consultants (GAACs).

Because of its price point, it is a reasonable tool to get your testing feet wet with, and it is fairly easy for technical or nontechnical people to set up and deploy. You will need to add some JavaScript to each page you want to test and upload your content variations into the tool.

Visual Website Optimizer

Visual Website Optimizer also aims at the basic testing market. The tool itself isn't hugely powerful, although it has slightly more options than Google Website Optimizer. For example, Visual Website Optimizer has the ability to test multiple conversions at once and provides heatmap tools, but its real strong point is the ease with which you can set up tests and tag your pages.

Using its WYSIWYG (what you see is what you get) editor on your pages, you set up the whole test and need to add only one tag to your pages. After doing this, you can also easily switch or create additional things to test without touching your page again. Along with its relatively low costs, Visual Website Optimizer makes it easy for inexperienced testers, or testers who have limited IT knowledge or capabilities, to begin a testing program.

Unbounce

Unbounce, another testing contender aimed at the lower end of the testing market, offers a slightly different angle for their testing tools than most other testing companies.

Unbounce's main selling point is that they specialize in allowing users to create landing pages from a gallery of their high-performing templates—meaning that you don't have to start from scratch and can learn from their gallery's landing page best practices. They then go a step further and host and run the test for you—meaning that you never need to touch a piece of code to perform a test. However, this does mean you may not have as much flexibility as if you were testing one of your own pages outside the tool.

Unbounce is fairly cheap and is particularly suited to lead-generation websites that need to test and optimize their lead-generation forms.

Optimizely

Optimizely is similar to Visual Website Optimizer in that it specializes in allowing the tester to create their tests using a WYSIWYG editor on their actual pages. Optimizely also makes it easy to implement the test by adding a single snippet of code to the page. You then control the test and content variations directly from the tool interface.

This tool is quickly gaining a lot of respect and trust in the industry, particularly from small to medium-sized companies that lack the budget or IT resources needed for larger-scale tests.

Glossary

A

A-B split testing The simplest form of landing page testing. A new visitor to the page is randomly shown either the original version ("A") or an alternative version ("B").

above the fold The portion of a web page that is seen without vertical or horizontal scrolling in a web browser window.

affiliate In online marketing, a company or individual that voluntarily chooses to promote the products or services of another company. Affiliates are paid based only on measurable and trackable tangible actions that result from their promotional activities.

affiliate program A performance-based marketing program set up by a company. Affiliates join the program and are compensated based solely on their performance. Typical payment methods include a percentage of sales revenue generated or a fixed amount per specified action on the company's website (see *affiliate*).

B

back end The portion of a website or web application (including the underlying database) that does not directly interact with the end user.

back links A hypertext link from another website to a page on your site. A sufficient number of properly constructed back links from reputable websites can increase your position on search engine results pages (see *search engine results pages [SERPs]*).

banner ads Rectangular graphical ads of various dimensions that appear on a website. Banner ads may contain animation or other interactive features. Normally the website owner does not have control over the content or color scheme used in a particular banner ad shown on their site.

banner blindness The tendency of website visitors to ignore and tune out banner ads.

baseline The original version of your landing page that is used as the benchmark against which other design variations are measured. Also called the "champion" or "control."

blacklist A list of "junk" e-mail addresses from which an e-mail program will not accept messages. Blacklisting is one form of spam filtering.

bounce rate The percentage of visitors who land on a web page and immediately exit without visiting any other pages linked from it.

breadcrumbs A type of web page navigation that shows the trail of pages that a visitor passed through to arrive at the current page.

brochure ware Websites that are static in nature and provide high-level descriptive information only, lacking any interactive features.

business-to-business (B2B) Refers to vertical industries or businesses whose clients are also businesses (rather than retail consumers).

business-to-consumer (B2C) Refers to vertical industries or businesses whose clients are consumers or the retail buying public (rather than other businesses).

C

Central Limit Theorem An axiom of probability theory that states that regardless of the original distribution of a random variable (such as conversion rate), its average will conform to a normal "bell curve" distribution (see *random variable*).

challenger A new version of your landing page that you are testing against your current "champion" version (contrast with *baseline*).

champion See *baseline*.

clickstream analysis A capability of web analytics software to display and represent popular sequences of pages that visitors navigate on a website.

clickthrough rate (CTR) The percentage of web page viewers who click on a particular link. CTR is often applied to the percentage of Internet users who click on a PPC advertisement and land on the advertiser's landing page.

client-side Programming functionality that takes place in the visitor's web browser software after the page has been loaded. Many landing page testing changes are implemented via client-side technologies.

cloaking The practice of showing different content to search engine spiders and human visitors to a web page for the purposes of manipulating the ranking of the page in search engine results (see *search engine results pages [SERPs]*).

continuous variables Variables, such as temperature or pressure, that can take on a range of numerical values (contrast with *discrete variables*).

control See *baseline*.

conversion action A desired measurable action on a landing page performed by an Internet visitor. Examples include clickthroughs to another page, form-fills, downloads, or product purchases.

conversion rate The percentage of landing page visitors who take the desired conversion action.

conversion rate optimization (CRO) The process of improving a landing page or website to improve its efficiency. Synonym for *landing page optimization (LPO)*.

cookies A small informational file stored by the web browser software on an Internet user's PC that records information about current or past visits to a particular website.

cost per click (CPC) The dollar cost to be paid by an advertiser for each clickthrough on an advertisement that is placed on a third-party website, or for each visit delivered by a third-party to the advertiser's landing page.

cost per thousand impressions (CPM) The dollar cost to be paid by an advertiser for each thousand appearances of an advertisement on a particular web page or set of websites.

customer relationship management (CRM) This type of software is used to track the whole history of a company's interactions with a particular person across multiple channels, including the Internet, telephone, mail, and in-store visits.

D

deep link A hyperlink to a web page with very specific information. Such a page may reside deep within a website, several links removed from the homepage (see *deep linking*).

deep linking   In PPC campaigns, the practice of landing traffic on the most relevant landing page possible within a website (see *deep link*).

descriptive statistics   A branch of applied statistics that is used to describe and summarize attributes of the data collected in an experiment. Typical descriptions include the mean (or average), median, variance, and standard deviation of the data.

design of experiments (DOE)   A discipline for multivariate testing and optimization that includes fractional factorial data collection and parametric data analysis. Examples include Taguchi method, Plackett-Burman, and Latin squares (see also *fractional factorial*).

discrete variables   Variables that can take on a set of distinct, enumerated values (contrast with *continuous variables*).

E

error bars   An indication of the uncertainly regarding the true value of a sampled quantity. Error bars can be represented graphically or expressed as a numeric plus-or-minus range around the average or mean observed value.

event   In probability theory, an event is the set of all possible outcomes to which a probability is assigned. In landing page testing, the event is commonly defined as the possibility of converting or not converting.

experimental studies   A statistical method in which you observe a control condition and then modify the environment in a preplanned way to see if the modification resulted in an observable change in the desired outcome.

F

first-party cookies   Cookies set by the particular Internet domain or website that an Internet user is visiting (see *cookies*).

fractional factorial   A subset of DOE multivariate testing that seeks to cut down on the proportion of recipes sampled from the total search space in order to extract the most useful information from the smallest number of recipes. Fractional factorial methods, such as the Taguchi method, make simplifying assumptions about the underlying model and often ignore variable interactions (see *design of experiments [DOE]*, *full factorial*, *main effects*, and *variable interactions*).

frames   A method of designing web pages in HTML by which information is pulled from a number of distinct sources and constructed in a collage-like fashion into the final page.

front end   The portion of a website or web application that interacts directly with and is seen by the visitor. Often used interchangeably with the term *user interface*.

full factorial   A subset of multivariate testing data collection that samples data evenly across all recipes in the search space. Allows for the most complicated and accurate models during subsequent data analysis by taking variable interactions into account (contrast with *fractional factorial*).

G

Gaussian distribution   A data distribution also known as a bell curve.

gross margin contribution   In accounting, the dollar amount that a purchase adds to the gross margin after subtracting all variable costs. Gross margin for websites is often used instead of profit for optimization (and is often referred to as profit) since the design of the website rarely has any impact on the difference between gross margin and profit. This book follows this convention and makes little distinction between profit and gross margin.

I

inferential statistics The branch of applied statistics used to predict or model the behavior of an underlying system based on an observed test sample.

information foraging theory A branch of applied computer science that describes the behavior of people when faced with a lot of available information in their search for a specific solution to a current need.

information scent The extent to which a person's attention can be kept on a particular task or desired outcome based on the visual cues such as text or links placed on web pages (see also *information foraging theory*).

input variables The variables in a landing page test that are assumed to have an impact on the conversion rate or other optimization criterion. Also called *independent variables*.

interruption marketing Marketing in which visitors must be interrupted in the course of their normal activities. Examples include billboards, television commercials, and web banner ads (contrast with *permission marketing*).

inverted pyramid A website copywriting style in which important information is put at the beginning of the page and summarized, and detailed information is provided lower on the page or accessed via related links.

K

keywords A word or phrase typed in by Internet searchers. A portfolio of keywords related to a particular topic or industry is commonly used as the basis for constructing PPC campaigns (see also *pay-per-click [PPC]*).

L

landing page The first page that a visitor lands on as a result of a traffic acquisition activity. The landing page can be a stand-alone page, a part of a special-purpose microsite, or a page on the company's main website.

landing page optimization (LPO) The process of improving a landing page or website to improve its efficiency. Synonym for *conversion rate optimization (CRO)*.

Latin squares A fractional factorial multivariate testing method (see *fractional factorial*, *design of experiments [DOE]*).

launch page A web page used in landing page testing quality assurance to display any possible recipe in the test (see also *recipe*).

lifetime value (LTV) The full economic value resulting from a particular conversion action as measured over the whole lifetime of that visitor's relationship with a company.

Likert scale A surveying response scale that measures affinity or agreement. Most commonly used with five response levels (strongly agree, agree, neither agree nor disagree, disagree, strongly disagree).

linear models A class of mathematical models that adds and subtracts the effects of all input variables and their combinations to estimate the corresponding value of the output variable.

list fatigue In e-mail marketing, when the response of a list to an offer or call-to-action declines after repeated mailings.

M

main effects The effects of individually changing the values of single variables in a multivariate data sample. If a model only measures main effects, it assumes that there are no variable interactions (see also *variable interactions*).

managing by exception A management principle that focuses on problems or deviations from normal behavior as measured by a set of performance indicators.

marketese A copywriting style that embellishes the effects or benefits of a product or service in an attempt to make it appear more attractive to the target audience. Frequently uses superlatives and adjectives.

mean The sum of all measured variable outcomes divided by the number of outcomes. Commonly called the average value.

microsite A special-purpose, small website that is designed to maximize conversion rates for an online marketing campaign or traffic source.

multivariate testing A type of landing page testing in which multiple elements on the page can be mixed and matched and changed independently of each other (contrast with *A-B split testing*; see also *design of experiments [DOE]*).

Myers-Briggs Type Indicator (MBTI) A framework for describing behavioral styles based on cognitive predispositions.

N

negative interactions During multivariate testing data analysis, when the effect of two or more input variables combines to produce a noticeably worse outcome than would be predicted by the settings of the individual variables alone (see also *variable interactions, input variables*; contrast with *positive interactions*).

nonparametric A type of multivariate testing data analysis that tries to identify the best-performing recipe in the landing page search space without building a model involving the input variables (contrast with *parametric*).

normal distribution See *Gaussian distribution*.

null hypothesis In statistical testing, the assumption that there is no difference in outcome based on changes to the tested input variables. If there is a significant observed effect, statistical tests will be able to *reject* the null hypothesis. Some advanced statistical techniques do not make use of a null hypothesis.

O

organic A type of search engine traffic that originates from nonpaid search results, often as a result of search engine optimization (see also *search engine optimization [SEO]*).

output variables The measured quantities that are optimized in a landing page optimization experiment. The goal is to find out how modifying the input variables changes the output variables. Typical output variables include conversion rate, revenue per visitor, and profit per visitor. Also called "dependent variables."

P

parametric A type of multivariate testing data analysis that attempts to build a model based on the input variables and their combinations to predict the corresponding value of the output variables (see also *input variables*, *output variables*; contrast with *nonparametric*).

pay-per-click (PPC) An advertising business model in which the advertiser pays a fixed or live-auction-based price for each visitor delivered to its website or landing page (see also *cost-per-click*).

permission marketing Any marketing activity that is voluntarily accepted by a member of your target audience. Permission marketing must be anticipated, personal, and relevant (contrast with *interruption marketing*).

persona A detailed profile of a hypothetical person representing an important class of visitors to your site. The persona allows you to empathize with them and understand their needs. Often used as the basis for constructing a relevant and effective conversion experience.

positive interactions During multivariate testing data analysis, when the effect of two or more input variables combines to produce a noticeably better outcome than would be predicted by the settings of the individual variables alone (see also *variable interactions, input variables*; contrast with *negative interactions*).

probability distribution function (PDF) In probability theory, the probability distribution function describes the set of possible outcomes for an event along with their likelihood. Also called a "probability density function" (see also *event*).

probability theory A branch of mathematics that deals with the description and analysis of random events. Probability theory is the underlying machinery of statistics.

promo code Abbreviation for "promotional code," which allows the person presenting the code to get discounts or special deals not available to the general public.

Q

quality assurance (QA) In landing page optimization, the function of testing alternative landing page designs to ensure that they have been properly implemented.

R

random variable In probability theory, an event drawn from a larger population of events that has a defined probability of occurrence and corresponding value. In landing page testing, the random variable is the item that you repeatedly sample (typically the conversion response value of a new visitor to your landing page design).

rate card Indicates current pricing for promotional advertising. Rate cards are commonly expressed in cost per thousand impressions (see *cost per thousand impressions [CPM]*) or cost per click (see *cost per click [CPC]*).

recipe A unique combination of values for all of the variables in a multivariate test. Defines a unique version of the landing page being tested.

resolution The size of the improvements that can be reliably found in a landing page test with a certain number of total conversions sampled. The larger the data sample, the smaller the effects that can be resolved.

run of network Distribution of an online advertisement across the whole network of available websites for a particular advertising network.

S

sales force automation (SFA) A type of software that allows you to track all important interactions with potential sales prospects and clients.

saturated main effect A type of parametric model that only considers main effects and thus assumes that variable interactions do not exist (see also *main effects*, *variable interactions*).

search engine optimization (SEO) The process for trying to get your website to appear as high as possible in the search results for relevant keywords.

search engine results pages (SERPs) The pages that are displayed by a search engine in response to a keyword(s) typed in by the searcher.

search engine spiders Automated computer programs that are the part of search engines that retrieve and index web pages for later retrieval in response to queries.

search space size The total number of distinct recipes possible in a landing page test (see also *recipe*).

server-side Program code and scripts for constructing a web page that execute on the web server before the file is transferred to the web browser for display (contrast with *client-side*).

service-level agreement (SLA) Guarantees of a certain level of responsiveness and availability for an online service. SLAs are typically expressed in the maximum amount of time it can take to access the data, the percentage of time that the website should be operational, and a maximum response time for complaints or service requests.

signal-to-noise ratio (SNR) The strength of a particular observed effect expressed as a ratio to the background noise associated with measurements of the effect.

staging environment A parallel implementation for a website or landing page that is used for testing new features or quality assurance before the content is moved to the live or operational environment. A staging environment should be as similar to the production environment as possible.

stochastic process In probability theory, a set of random events drawn from the related underlying distributions (see also *time series*, *event*).

T

Taguchi method A specific type of fractional factorial design of experiments (DOE) approach commonly used in manufacturing optimization and sometimes applied to landing page optimization (see also *fractional factorial*, *design of experiments [DOE]*).

third-party cookies Cookies left by websites other than the one that the Internet browser is visiting. These kinds of cookies are commonly used for tracking advertising campaigns and are often turned off by web surfers (see also *cookies*; contrast with *first-party cookies*).

throttling The practice of restricting the percentage of available traffic that is allocated to certain recipes in a landing page optimization test or restricting the percentage of traffic that is allocated to the test in general.

Throttling can decrease the impact of testing poor design alternatives, but it makes the test take longer because data accumulates more slowly.

thumbnail image A small product image that is used on e-commerce website pages to show a large number of products. Larger images are subsequently displayed on the product detail pages.

time series A stochastic process with time-based sampling (see *stochastic process*).

U

Universal Resource Locator (URL) A method for describing specific content (such as a web page) that is available on the Internet.

user-centered design A philosophy and practice that considers the needs and background of the intended user of an object or interface as central to the design process.

user experience (UX) A series of specific user interactions with a website that form a larger user experience.

V

value The specific assignment for a variable in a landing page test (see also *variable*). Also called a "level" or "variation." The number of distinct values for a particular variable is called the "branching factor."

variable A specific landing page tuning element or page section that is part of a landing page test. Also sometimes called a "factor" in statistical testing (see also *value*).

variable interactions Variable interactions are said to occur when the effect of a variable value depends on the values of one or more other variables. In other words, the context in which something is seen will have an effect on its impact. Most fractional factorial approaches assume that there are no variable interactions. Many landing page tests have very strong variable interactions (see also *positive interactions*, *negative interactions*).

variance The square of the sampling noise during a statistical experiment. As the sample size increases, the variance decreases. The standard deviation is the square root of the variance.

W

web analytics Software for analyzing and tracking the behavior of visitors to a website.

whitelist A set of e-mail addresses from which an e-mail program will always accept messages, regardless of whether the messages fail other spam-filtering criteria.

Z

Z-score A statistical measure of the difference between two quantities. The larger the Z-score, the less likely the two quantities are to have been drawn from the same population.

Index

Note to the Reader: Throughout this index **boldfaced** page numbers indicate primary discussions of a topic. *Italicized* page numbers indicate illustrations.

A

A-B split testing, 299, *299*, **331–332**
  advantages, **332–333**
  baselines, 317
  conversion rate curves, 317, *318*
  disadvantages, **333–334**
ability in Fogg Behavior Model, 159
"above the fold" considerations, 134, *134*
accessibility issues, **189–191**
accordion style menus, 206–207, *207*
accounts
  requesting, 233
  requiring, 228
  support for, **31–32**
accumulating goals, 315
acquisition activities, 10
  offline, **13–14**
  online, **10–13**, *11–12*
action blocks
  product detail, **219**
  well-defined, 70
action factors in AIDA decision process, **53–54**
  brand strength, **54–55**
  total solution, **55–56**
  transacting, **56–61**, *57–58, 60*
  unnecessary tasks, **56–59**, *57–58*
action plan development, **387**
  business objectives, **389**
  data collection, **416–418**
  implementation plans, **412–414**
  landing page selection, **403–405**
  preliminaries, **388–389**
  QA plans, **414–415**
  results analysis, **418–419**
  success criteria, **405–407**
  team building, **401–403**
  test area selection, **407–409**
  traffic source selection, **403–405**
  tuning method selection, **410–412**
activity funnel, **8–9**, *8*
addresses, customer, **230**, 232
Adorama homepage, **73–74**, *74*
advanced segments based on visitor behavior, **123–124**, *124*
advertising, **30–31**
  banner. *See* banner ads
  page layout, 175
  restricting, **204**
  traditional, 14
Aesop, 361
affiliate programs
  description, **11–12**
  in testing, 380
affinity
  for accessibility, 190
  vs. alienation, **162**
  creating, 105

  personalization for, 271
  raising, 98
affordability factor in insourcing vs. outsourcing, **383**
affordance, 189, 208
aging data, 429
AIDA model
  action stage. *See* action factors in AIDA decision process
  awareness stage, **40–42**, *42*
  desire stage. *See* desire stage in AIDA model
  interest stage, **43–45**, *44–45*
  overview, **39–40**
Alessandra, Tony, 142, 156
alias structure in parametric testing, 340
alienation vs. affinity, **162**
alpha-levels in null hypotheses, 298
alternatives
  payment methods, 231
  transaction mechanisms, 95
Amazon site
  checkout options, **229**, *229*
  homepage, 22, *23*
  Loop11 tool, 138, *138*
  search suggestions, 205, *206*
  upsell and cross-sell related items, 220, *221*
  user reviews, 225, *225*
amygdala, 149
analysis
  A-B split testing, 332
  in action plans, **418–419**
  multivariate testing, **336–339**
  nonparametric. *See* nonparametric analysis
  parametric analysis, **335–336**
    characteristics, **336–338**
    full factorial, **346–348**
analysis of variance (ANOVA), 293, 337
Andersson, Axel, 160
animation
  avoiding, **186**
  as distraction, 78
anticipated marketing, 41
anticipation in Fogg Behavior Model, 159
anxiety vs. trust, **161**
appearance
  in action plans, **388**
  as trust issue, **93–95**, *94*
applied statistics, **293**
appreciating visitors, 46
approval process for test elements, 261
archipallium brain, 149
Armani Exchange site, 183, *183*
Artisans temperament, *155*
assurances, transactional, **95–98**, *96–97*

AttentionWizard
  focus service, **129–131**, *129–130*
  heat maps
    1-800-flowers.com, **70–72**, *71–72*
    CREDO Mobile, 107, *107, 109*, *109*
auction sites, 30
audience and visitors, **141**
  in baselines, 422
  brains, **148–151**
  cultural differences, **165–168**, *167*
  demographics
    analyzing, **124–125**, *125*
    traffic sources, **145–148**, *147*
    web analytics, **144–145**
  empathy, 142
  information about, **143–144**
  learning modalities, **151–152**
  overview, **6–8**
  personality types, **152–153**
    Keirsey-Bates, **155–156**, *155*
    Myers-Briggs Type Indicator, **153–154**
    Platinum Rule, **156–157**
  persuasion frameworks, **157–158**
    Fogg Behavior Model, **158–160**, *158*
    key principles, **162–165**
    unbalancing scales, **160–162**
  segments
    advanced, **123–124**, *124*
    content and offer focus, **259–260**
    function and usability focus, **260**
    landing page tests, 404
    traffic sources, **145–148**, *147*
    web analytics, **144–145**
  in testing, 252, **319–322**
  variability, **145–147**, *147*
audio in direct response pages, 245
auditory learning modality, 151
authority in persuasion, 165
Autodesk corporate site, 202, *203*
automated e-mail order confirmation, **233**
availability, 189
average page depth, **116**
awards, 101
awareness stage in AIDA model, **40–42**, *42*

B

B&H homepage, **74–75**, *75*, 212
back end programmers, 370
background color, **76–78**, *77*
baggage in test elements, **261**

bandwidth for control version, 301
banner ads, **81**
    decline of, 11
    page layout, 175
    restricting, **204**
    rotating, **213–214**
basal brain, 149
baselines
    ignoring, **422**
    recipes, 328
Bates, Marilyn, 155
Beckwith, Harry, 54
behavioral targeting, 8
bell curves, **289–291**, *290–291*
Bernoulli random variables, 288
Best Buy site, 58, *58*
best practices, **201**
    direct response pages, **243–246**, *244*
    e-commerce catalogs. *See*
        e-commerce catalogs
    expert reviews, **197–198**
    homepages, **202–205**, *203*
    information architecture and
        navigation, **205–211**,
        206–209
    mobile sites, **246–250**, *247–248*
    multiple-step flows, **238–243**,
        239–240, 242
    registration, **234–237**, *236*
biased samples, **282–284**, 418
biased visitors, **320–321**
bidding sites, 30
big companies, **373–374**
billing information, **230–231**, *231*
Bingham McCutchen LLP homepage,
    177, *178*
"Blind Men and the Elephant", 362
blogs, **13**
    conversion actions, 29, 33
    for retention, **16**
Bly, Robert W., 193
body copy, **193**
    brevity, **194**
    format and style, **196–197**
    inverted pyramid structure,
        193–194
    marketese, **194–196**
BoldChat study, 210
bounce rates, 33
Brain Rules (Medina), 152
brain stem, 149
*Brainfluence: 100 Ways to Persuade
    and Convince Consumers with
    Neuromarketing* (Dooley), 150
brains, **148–149**
    combined, **150–151**
    limbic system, **149–150**
    neocortex, **150**
    reptilian, **149**
branching factor, **327–328**
brand awareness, 14
brand guardians, **375–376**
brand-related sites, 29
brand strength factor, **54–55**
branding in conversion actions, 33
breadcrumbs, 211
breadth of impact filters, **252**
    audience size, 252
    conversion actions, 252
    paths through site, **253–255**
    prominent page parts, 255
Briggs, Katherine Cook, 153
broken promises, **83–85**, *83–84*

Browser Size overlay tool, 243, *244*
browsers, 39, **307–308**
business case building, **390**
business model, **28–30**
business objectives, **389**
business-to-consumer (B2C)
    e-commerce sites, 393
buttons
    call-to-action, **223–224**
        CREDO Mobile, 107, *107*
        hot spots, 73, *73*
    graphics, 266
    page shell design, **191–192**
buy-in, **362–363**
    company politics. *See* company
        politics
    insourcing vs. outsourcing,
        380–386
    management, 401
    strategies, **378–380**
    teams. *See* teams
buying guides, 47
*Buyology: Truth and Lies About Why
    We Buy* (Lindstrom), 150

C

C-level officers, **377–378**
Cabrillo Yacht Sales homepage, 94, *94*
call-in polls, 283
call-to-action buttons, **223–224**
    CREDO Mobile, 107, *107*
    hot spots, 73, *73*
calls-to-action
    testing, **245–246**
    unclear, **66–72**, *67–69, 71–72*
canned reports, 145
Canon Canada site
    category page, 23, *24*
    product detail, 218, *219*
Canyon Tours homepage, 86, *86*
capable teams factor in insource
    testing, 384
capacity factor in insourcing vs.
    outsourcing, **383**
capped number of leads, 396
CAPTCHAs, **235–236**, *236*
Card, Stuart, 265
Carlin, George, 112
case studies
    CREDO Mobile, **106–109**,
        106–109
    Power Options, **429–433**, *430–432*
    RealAge.com, **269–270**, *269–270*
catalog sales, 394
catalogs
    e-commerce. *See* e-commerce
        catalogs
    print, 14
categoriness, 75
category pages, 23, *24*
causality and correlation, **285–286**
centered fixed-width designs, **176–182**,
    178–182
Central Limit Theorem, **291**
cerebellum, 149
cerebral cortex, 150
cerebrum, 150
certainty in statistics, **295–298**,
    296–297
certification sites, 30
Chak, Andrew, 39

challengers in A-B split testing, 332
champions in A-B split testing, 332
changes
    audience, **319–322**
    client-side, 434
    content, 8
    data collection, **416**
    frequent, 423
    technology, **322–323**
checkout options, **228–229**, *229*
checkout pages, 25, *26*
cheesy sites, 174
chief officers, **377–378**
choices
    excessive, **73–75**, *73, 75*
    unnecessary, 42, *42*
chunking information, 240
Cialdini, Robert, 102, **162–165**
CIP (conversion improvement
    percentage), **392–393**
clarity
    vs. confusion, **161–162**
    first impressions, **95**
Clark, Brian, 193
clear self-selected navigation,
    202–204, *203*
click-overlay heat maps, 34
click-through rate (CTR), **435**
clickable logos, 211
ClickTale site, 34, **127–128**, *128*
clickthroughs, 33
client referrals, 14
client-side changes and search
    engines, 434
client-side page rendering,
    308–310, *309*
Clinique site, 209, *209*
cloaking issues, **434–435**
clutter
    eliminating, **42**
    graphics, 76
    testing, 118, *119*, 268
    visual, 106, 108
Clutter Test, 118, *119*
CMS (content management
    system), 306
coalition building, 380
cognitive styles, **152–153**
    Keirsey-Bates, **155–156**, *155*
    Myers-Briggs Type Indicator,
        153–154
    Platinum Rule, **156–157**
coherency
    in design, **257–259**
    page layout, 174
    in QA plans, 415
Coldwater Creek site, 225, *226*
collaborative authoring sites, 13
collection. *See* data collection
collectivist societies, 166
color
    background, **76–78**, *77*
    cultural differences, 167
    page shell design, **186**
commenting support, 31
commitment in persuasion, **163–164**
common buy-in issues
    big companies, **374**
    copywriters, 369
    graphic designers, 368
    little companies, 373
    marketing managers, **369–370**
    product managers, 365

programmers, 370–371
quality assurance testers, **371–372**
system administrators, **367**
user experience professionals,
363–364
webmasters, **366**
community in conversion actions, 33
company politics, 375
brand guardians, 375–376
C-level officers, 377–378
IT staff, 376–377
testing, 402
comparisons
charts, 47
desire stage, 49–50
search results, 218
Compass of Pleasure (Linden), 149
Compete tool, 135
competitive analysis tools,
135–136, *135*
complete teams in insource testing, 384
concise body copy, **196**
conclusions in statistical methods, 292
Confetti reports, 126–127, *127*
confidence levels, **282**
null hypotheses, 298
sample size, 295–298, *296–297*
selecting, **407**
confirming
order information, 232–234
registration pages, **237**
shipping addresses, 232
confounding variables, **285–286**
confusion vs. clarity, **161–162**
connections in page flows, 265–266
consensus of peers, 101–105, *103–105*
consistency, 83
banner ads, 213
in branding messages, **376**
foolish, 375
in persuasion, **163–164**
in testing, 315–316
Constant Contact site, 241, *242*
constrained designs, 329–331
consumer e-tail company roles, 37
Consumer Reports site, 84–85, *84*
content
audience segmentation, 259–260
changes, 8
lists, 413–414
mission critical. *See* mission critical
content
presentations. *See* presentations
separation from page shell,
176, *177*
Content Drilldown reports, 116
content management
configurations, 308
client-side page rendering,
308–310, *309*
intercept page rendering,
312–313, *312*
server-side page rendering,
311–312, *311*
content management system
(CMS), **306**
context
flexible page flows, **267**
in research, 49
variable interactions. *See* variable
interactions
contingent variables, 329
continuity, 83

continuous variables
description, 327
fractional factorial parametric
testing, 341
price testing, **274**
contrast, 191
control by visitors, 47
control version in testing, 301
controllable traffic, 148
conversion activities and rates, 15
breadth of impact filters, **252**
business model, 28–30
data collection, **418**
delayed, **426–429**, *427–428*
improvement, **171**
usability checks, **197–199**
visual presentation. *See* visual
presentation
web usability overview,
172–173
writing for web, 192–197
micro-conversions, 33–34
multiple, 32–33
myths, 17–18, *18*
overview, **14–15**
types, 30–34
as weak link, **9–10**, *9*
Conversion Conference page, 11, *12*
conversion improvement percentage
(CIP), **392–393**
conversion point goals, 116, *117*
Conversion Report, 128, *128*
Conversion Suite, 127
cookies
client-side page rendering, 310
flexible page flows, 267
and measuring consistency, 315
requiring, 283
copying addresses, 230
copywriters, 368–369
*Copywriter's Handbook: A Step-by-
Step Guide to Writing Copy That
Sells* (Bly), 193
core competency focus in insourcing vs.
outsourcing, 381
coregistration, 59
correlation vs. causation, 285
cost factors
shipping, 230
testing, **424–426**, *426*
tuning method selection, **410**
counting issues, 313–319, *318*
Covey, Stephen R., 19
CrazyEgg tool, 34, 126–127, *126–127*
credibility issues. *See* trust
credit card security codes, **231**
CREDO Mobile case study, **106–109**,
106–109
CRM (customer relationship
management) systems, 145
intermediate conversion actions,
399
in testing, 272
cross-sells, 58, 220, *221*
CrossBrowserTesting tool, 133–134
CTR (click-through rate), **435**
Cultural Database, 168
cultural differences, 165–168, *167*
customer relationship management
(CRM) systems, 145
intermediate conversion
actions, 399
in testing, 272

customer support
conversion actions, 33
options, **233**
customers, 39
customizing desire stage, **52–53**, *52*

D

data collection
A-B split testing, 334
checklist, **418**
fractional factorial analysis, 343
monitoring, **417–418**
multivariate testing, 335–336
pitfalls, 422–423
preparing for, **416–417**
statistical methods, 292
insufficient, **295–297**, *296–297*
sampling, 283–284
data mining, 145
data rates
A-B split testing, 333
data collection, 417–418
full factorial non-parametric
testing, 349–350
for tests, 301
data recording activities, 417
data security, 98
dating service roles, 37
deadly sins. *See* seven deadly
design sins
debt negotiation sites, 91–92, *91–92*
decision-making process in AIDA
model
action. *See* action factors in AIDA
decision process
awareness stage, 40–42, *42*
desire stage. *See* desire stage in
AIDA model
interest stage, 43–45, *44–45*
overview, 39–40
dedicated test servers, 306–307
defining relations, 340
delayed conversions, 406, **426–429**,
427–428
delivery
estimated dates, 230
forms, 97–98
Delta Airline homepage, 44–45, *45*
demographics
analyzing, 124–125, *125*
traffic sources, 145–148, *147*
web analytics, 144–145
demonstrations, 48
dependencies in QA plans, **415**
dependent variables, 291, 326
Desco Software homepage, 67
descriptive statistics, **293**, 298–299
design in statistical methods, 292
design of experiments (DOE) umbrella,
335–336
design sins. *See* seven deadly design sins
designs for tuning methods
constrained, 329–331
unconstrained, 329
desire stage in AIDA model, 45–47, *46*
comparisons, 49–50
customizing, **52–53**, *52*
details, 50–51
research activity, 47–49, *48*
socializing, **51–52**

details
    desire stage, 50–51
    e-commerce catalog products, 218–225, *219*, *221–225*
deterministic processes, 287
detours in multiple-page flows, 267
Diapers site, 209, *209*
direct/bookmark traffic, **118–119**, *119*
direct marketing, 14
direct response pages, **243**
    calls-to-action, **245–246**
    headlines, **243–245**
    page fold, **243–244**, *244*
    sign-up process, **246**
    supporting trust areas, **245**
    text and images, **244**
    video and audio, **245**
direct-to-consumer sites, 393
director style in Platinum Rule, 156–157
discrete variables
    description, 327
    fractional factorial parametric testing, 342
    price testing, 274
Disraeli, Benjamin, 282
disruptions, 58–59
distractions, visual. *See* visual distractions
diversion of traffic, 379
DOE (design of experiments) umbrella, 335–336
Don't Make Me Think: A Common Sense Approach to Web Usability (Krug), 95, 173
Dooley, Roger, 150
download support, 31
drop-down menus, 207–208
Drucker, Peter F., 10, 257
dynamic content
    client-side page rendering, 310
    web analytics, 145

E

e-commerce catalogs, **211–212**
    billing information, **230–231**, *231*
    checkout options, **228–229**, *229*
    homepages, **212–215**, *212*, *214*
    order confirmation, **232–234**
    product detail, **218–225**, *219*, *221–225*
    review and order placement, **232**
    search results and product listings, **215–218**, *216–217*
    shipping information, **230**
    shopping carts, **225–228**, *226–227*
e-commerce sites
    conversion activities, 28, 32
    conversion delay graph, 428, *428*
    LTV conversion actions, 393–396
e-mail
    enhancement tools, **139–140**
    in-house mailing lists, 12
    order confirmation, 233
    registration pages, 237
    for retention, 16
    third-party lists, **12–13**
economies of scale, 391
educational saving plan provider roles, 37
educational sites, 30

Effect Heredity Principle, 339
Effect Sparsity Principle, 339
efficiency vs. effectiveness, 257
80/20 rule, 4, 252
Einstein, Albert, 305
elasticity price modeling, 275–276, 277
elements, test. *See* tests and testing
embedded video, 187
embellishments, visual, **78**
Emerson, Ralph Waldo, 258, 375
emotions
    color effects, 186
    limbic system, 149–150
empathy, **142**
emphasis
    on new customers, *58*
    testing, **263–264**
empirical rule, 290
endorsements, 101
entry pages
    with high bounce rates, **115–116**, *115*
    pop-ups, **81–82**, *82*
equal-variance t-tests, 295
error bars, **296–297**, *296–297*
error handling
    billing information, **231**, *231*
    registration pages, **235**
essential visitor information, **238–239**, *239*
estimated ship and delivery dates, 230
Esurance site, 240–241, *240*
etiquette in information requests, **87–92**, *89–92*
evaluators, 39
events
    industry, 14
    internal, **319–321**
    in probability theory, 287
exit pop-ups, 82
exit rates, 33
expectations
    buttons, 191
    meeting, **83–85**, *83–84*
expensive prototypes, **340–341**
experimental design
    full factorial non-parametric testing, 349
    statistical methods, **291–292**
experts
    reviews by, **197–198**
    for trust, **98–101**, *99–100*
external events, 322
external factors in action plans, 388
extroverts in MBTI, 154
eye-tracking studies, 155, *155*, 198

F

Facebook Connect tool, 237
facilitators in Fogg Behavior Model, 159
factual body copy, 195
false causality, 285–286
fast teams for insource testing, **384–385**
fault tolerance, 189
FBM (Fogg Behavior Model), 158–160, *158*
fear of changing pages, **433–434**
feedback, 131, 189
    Kampyle, **131–132**, *132*

loaded questions in, 285
    requesting, **233**
    SurveyMonkey, 131
    UserVoice, **132–133**
    Velaro, **133**
feelers in MBTI, 154
field entry in registration pages, **235–237**
filters
    data collection, **416**
    sampling, **283**
    search results, **215–216**
    test elements, **252–255**
financial arguments, **380**
financial impact
    conversion rate improvement, **391–393**
    prioritizing projects based on, 377
first-party cookies, 283, 310, 315
fixed values in testing, **313–314**
fixed-width designs, **176–182**, *178–182*
Flash issues, 249
flawed sampling, **319–320**
Flesch-Lincaid readability level, 196
flexibility
    A-B split testing, 333
    page flows, **266–267**
    search options, 49
flexible teams for insource testing, **384–385**
flourishes, visual, **78**
flows
    multiple-page, **264–267**
    multiple-step. *See* multiple-step flows
    visualization, 116, *117*
focus in testing, **317**
focus on negative, **113**
Fogg, BJ, 158
Fogg Behavior Model (FBM), 158–160, *158*
fonts, 167, **190**
foolish consistency, 375
forced registration, 56–58, *57*
Form Field Test criteria, 91
form-fill rates, 31
formal testing, 197
formats
    body copy, **196–197**
    buttons, 191
    testing, **263**
forms, simplifying, **87–92**, *89–92*
4Q tool, 131
fractional factorial design, 335–336
    characteristics, 335
    effects in, 338
    parametric, **339–340**
        advantages, **343–344**
        disadvantages, **344–345**
        overview, **340–343**
frames, 176
Franti, Michael, 141
free prototypes, **341**
free shipping, 227
freemium subscriptions, 32
front end programmers, 370
full factorial design, 335
    characteristics, 335–336
    effects in, 347
    nonparametric, **348–349**
        advantages, 349
        disadvantages, 349–350

parametric
advantages, **347**
disadvantages, **347–348**
overview, **346**
function focus in audience
segmentation, **259–260**
funnels
analysis, 33
goal, 116

G

game content, 13
garish text, 78
Gaussian distribution, **289–291**,
290–291
Gears of War 3 Xbox site, 183, *184*
geo-targeting, 404
Germany, McDonald's homepage in,
166–167, *167*
GlobalMaxer testing platform, 168
goals
conversion points, **116**, *117*
funnels, 116
in testing, **314–315**
goals report, 116, *117*
Godin, Seth, 15–16, 40–41, 88
Golden Rule, 142
Google Analytics
flow visualization, 116, *117*
goals reports, 116, *117*
Map Overlay reports, 124, *125*
paid keyword reports, 121, *121*
search engine issues, **434–436**
SEO traffic, 120, *120*
Top Landing Pages reports, 115,
115
top SEO pages reports, 115, *115*
traffic sources reports, **117–118**, *118*
Google Browser Size overlay tool,
243, *244*
Google Website Optimizer, **346**
granularity in testing, **256–257**
graphic designers, **367–368**
graphics. *See also* images
buttons, 266
clutter, 76
cultural differences, 167
guidelines, **185–186**
limiting, **205**
navigation, 209
gratuitous graphics clutter, 76
greedy marketer syndrome, 46
gross margin contribution, 314
grouping, 208
guarantees, 95, 98
Guardians temperament, 155

H

Hacker, Bob, 160
Hall, Edward T., 166
halo effect, 99
headlines
direct response pages, 70, **243–245**
guidelines, **193**, 218
healthcare system sites, 88
HearingPlanet form, **88–90**, *89–90*
Heatmap Suite, 127
heatmaps
1-800-flowers, **70–72**, *71–72*

AttentionWizard, **129–131**, *129–130*
click-overlay, 34
CREDO Mobile, 107, *107*, 109, *109*
mouse movement, 126, *126*
Helmet City search results page, 26, *27*
hero shots, 72–73
Hierarchical Ordering Principle, 339
high bounce rates, **115–116**, *115*
high context cultures, 166
high-contrast pages, 218
high-quality images, 185
high traffic page testing, 252
High vs. Low Context theory, 166
highest paid person's opinions
(HiPPOs), 7, 378
hippocampus, 149
Hitwise tool, **136**
Hofstede, Geert, 166
homepages, 20, 212
advertising, **204**
banner ads, **213–214**
cultural differences, **166–167**, *167*
mission critical content, 22, *23*
photos, **205**
product-level items, **214–215**, *214*
promotions, **212–213**, *212*
self-selected navigation,
202–204, *203*
words on, **204**
Hopper, Grace Murray, 379
horizontal top navigation, 207
hot spot areas, 72
"how" question about visitors, **144**
how-to guides, 47
Huck, Schuyler W., 282
Hugo Boss site, 222, *222–223*
hyperlinks, 190
hypothalamus, 149

I

Idealists temperament, 155
ignoring baselines, **422**
images. *See also* graphics
direct response pages, **244**
high-quality, 185
limiting, **205**
product detail, 219, **221–222**,
222–223
impact of insource testing
programs, **384**
implementation of A-B split testing, 332
implementation plans, **412–414**
importance vs. significance, **297–298**
improvement
conversion. *See* conversion
activities and rates
in insource testing, **385**
size, **302**
verifying, **418–419**
in-house mailing lists, **12**
in-house resources and procedures,
404–405
in-house vs. outsource decisions,
410–411
in-store sales, **394**
inaction, 436
independent variables
in causation, 291
interactions, 350
requirement, 288
in testing, 326

individualist societies, 166–167
industry tradeshows and events, 14
inferential statistics, **293**
Influence: The Psychology of
Persuasion (Cialdini), 162
informal testing, **197**
information architecture, **189**
guidelines, **205–211**, *206–209*
testing, 263
information foraging theory, 265
information gathering in MBTI, 154
information pages, 24, *25*
information processing in MBTI, 154
information requests, excessive, **87–92**,
89–92
information scent, 265
information staging, **240–241**, *240*
Innovate Media homepage, 187, *188*
input variables, 326
insource testing programs
guidelines, **384–386**
vs. outsource, **380–383**
insufficient data collection, **295–297**,
296–297
InsWeb site, 60, *60*
interaction review in QA plans, 415
interactions, variable. *See* variable
interactions
interactive game content, **13**
intercept page rendering, **312–313**, *312*
interest stage in AIDA model, **43–45**,
44–45
intermediate conversion actions,
399–401
internal events, **319–321**
internal site search
results pages, **26–27**, *27*
tools, 205, *206*
interruption advertising, 41
introductory offers, 95
introverts in MBTI, 154
intuitives in MBTI, 154
inverse color schemes, 186
inverted pyramid structure, **193–194**
Iron Systems homepage, 87, *87*
Issigonis, Alec, 363
IT staff, **376–377**

J

J. Crew homepage, 176, *177*
Japan, McDonald's homepage in,
166–167, *167*
JavaScript, 309–310
JoggingStroller.com site, 53
judgers in MBTI, 154
Juicy Couture product detail page,
24, *25*
Jung, Carl, 153
justification, 190

K

Kampyle tool, **131–132**, *132*
Kaushik, Avinash, 378
Keirsey, David, 155
Keirsey Temperament Sorter, 155
key activities
acquisition, **10–14**, *11–12*
conversions, **9–10**, *9*, **14–15**

overview, 8–9, *8*
retention, 15–17
key principles of persuasion, 162–165
keyword reports, 120–121, *120–121*
kinesthetic learning modality, 151
known issues lists, 414
Krug, Steve, *95*, 173, 197
Krum, Cindy, 246

L

labels
    buttons, **192**
    menus, **210**
landing pages
    overview, 4–6
    types, 20–21
Lands End site, 225, *225*
laptop configurator, 52, *52*
large numbers, law of, **289**, 423
last-minute up-sells, 58
Latin squares approach, 340
Law & Order homepage, 175, *175*
law of large numbers, **289**, 423
layout for product detail, 218–219, *219*
lead generation
    conversion actions, 28, 33
    conversion delay graphs,
        427–428, 428
    third-party, 396–397
lead paragraphs, 194
LeadSpend tool, 139
learning curves for insourcing vs.
    outsourcing, 381–382
learning in insource testing, 385
learning modalities, 151–152
LegalSteroids site, 45, *46*
legibility, 190
Lehrer, Tom, 3
length of relationship factor, 390
level of branching factors, 328
Lewis, Elias St. Elmo, 39
lifestyle orientation in MBTI, 154
lifetime value (LTV) of conversion
    actions, 390
    financial impact, 391–393
    intermediate conversion actions,
        399–401
    purchase of consumer product,
        393–396
    subscriptions, 398–399
    third-party lead generation,
        396–397
lightbox popovers, 187, *188*, 225, *226*
likeness, **105**
liking in persuasion, 164–165
limbic system, 149–150
Linden, David, 149
Lindgaard, Gitte, 174
Lindstrom, Marin, 150
line length, 191
linear models, 337
list fatigue, 13
little companies, 372–373
load speed for mobile sites, 246–247
loaded questions, 285
localization cultural differences,
    165–168, *167*
logos
    benefits, 100–101
    clickable, 211

long-tail concept, 73
longevity of test elements, 260–261
Loop11 tool, 137–139, *138*
low context cultures, 166–167
low-cost testing platforms, 379
low-key testing, 379–380
Lowes homepage, 212–213, *212*
loyalty programs for retention, 17
LTV. *See* lifetime value (LTV) of
    conversion actions

M

MacLean, Paul, 148–150
mailing lists, 12
main effects in parametric testing,
    336, 347
main site landing pages, 20
main traffic sources, 117–118, *118*
managing by exception, 113
Map Overlay reports, 124, *125*
maps
    heat. *See* heatmaps
    sitemaps, 211
Marine, Larry, 142
marketese, 194–196
marketing factors in action plans, 388
marketing managers, 369–370
marquee clients, 101
Match.com site, 238, *239*
mathematical statistics, 293
matrix, 35
    decision-making process. *See*
        AIDA model
    overview, 36
    roles, 36–38
    tasks, 38–39
"Maybes" visitors, 17–18, *18*
Mayer, Richard, 152
McDonald's homepages, 166–167, *167*
means in normal distribution, 290
measuring issues, 313–319, *318*
    consistency, 315–316
    fixed vs. variable values, 313–314
    single goal vs. multiple goals,
        314–315
    throttling, 316–319, *318*
media conversion actions, 33
media coverage activities, 14
media mentions, 101
media-related sites, 28–29
Medina, John, 152
menus
    highlighting, 210
    labels, 210
    limiting items, 210
    standard locations, 206–209,
        207–209
    for support, 210–211
messaging in branding, 376
micro conversions, 15, 33–34
microsite landing pages, 20–21
mid-brain, 149
minimal data entry requirements, 58
mission critical content, 22
    category pages, 23, *24*
    checkout and sign-up pages,
        25, *26*
    homepages, 22, *23*
    internal site search results pages,
        26–27, *27*

non mission-critical pages, 27–28
product and information pages,
    24, *25*
top organic search entry pages,
    22–23
top pages reports, 114, *114*
*Mobile Marketing: Finding Your
    Customers No Matter Where
    They Are* (Krum), 246
mobile sites, 246
    CREDO Mobile case study,
        106–109, *106–109*
    dedicated versions, 246
    Flash issues, 249
    limitations, 249–250
    load speeds, 246–247
    optimizing, 247–248, *247–248*
    testing, 249
monitoring data collection, 417–418
monochronic societies, 166–167
moods, color for, 186
motion, banner ads with, 213–214
motivation in Fogg Behavior
    Model, 159
mouse movements
    ClickTale, 127–128, *128*
    heatmaps, 126, *126*
    tracking, 198
Mouse Tracking Suite, 127
movement, banner ads with, 213–214
Mozilla download statistics page,
    103, *103*
muffin top headers, 180
multiple conversion actions, 32–33
multiple goals, 314–315
multiple-page flows, 264–267
multiple-step flows, 238
    essential information, 238–239,
        239
    information staging, 240–241, *240*
    progress indicators, 241
    risk-reward scales, 238
    sign-up fields, 242–243
multivariate tests, 326–327, 335
    constructing, 328–331
    data analysis, 336–339
    data collection, 335–336
    fractional factorial design. *See*
        fractional factorial design
    full factorial nonparametric,
        348–350
    full factorial parametric, 346–348
Myer, Mike, 346
Myers, Isabel Briggs, 153
Myers-Briggs Type Indicator (MBTI),
    153–154

N

National Basketball Association (NBA)
    site, 177, *179*
navigation, **211**
    internal site search tools, 205, *206*
    menus, 206–211, *207–209*
    multiple methods, 205
    self-selected, 202–204, *203*
navigation-dominant temperament, 165
neatness, 95
needs recognition, 44–45, *45*
negative, focus on, 113
negative variable interactions, 350
neocortex, 150

neomammalian brain, 150
neopallium brain, 150
new windows for video, 187
New York Barbells homepage, 77, 77
Newegg homepage, 214, 214
news feeds, 16
newsletters, 16
Nielsen, Jakob, 155–156, 192, 208
"Noes" visitors, 17–18, 18
nonparametric analysis, 335–336
    advantages, 349
    characteristics, 338–339
    disadvantages, 349–350
    full factorial, 348–349
    vs. parametric, 336
nonstationary time series, 288
normal distribution, 289–291, 290–291
normalized metrics, 315
Norman, Don, 173, 189
null hypothesis, 298

O

Oban Multilingual agency, 167
objective large numbers, 105
objective site evaluation, 6, 66, 112–113
objectivity in body copy, 195
observable behavior patterns, 155, 155
observational studies, 292
observed effects, 299
off-page search engine factors, 433–434
offers
    audience segmentation, 259–260
    introductory and trial, 95
    special, 58
    testing, 272
offline acquisitions methods, 13–14
old mammalian brain, 149
on-page search engine factors, 434
1-800-flowers site
    alternative page mock-up, 69, 69
    checkout options, 228, 229
    heat map, 70–72, 71–72
    product detail page, 68, 68
100 Things Every Designer Needs To Know About People (Weinschenk), 150
one-step sign-up, 241
one-tailed equal-variance t-tests, 295
online acquisition activities, 10–13, 11–12
online gaming sites, 79
online polls, 283
operational policies, 377
OpinionLab tool, 131
opportunity costs in insourcing vs. outsourcing, 381–382
optimizing mobile sites, 247–248, 247–248
order independence
    fractional factorial parametric testing, 344
    research, 49
orders on e-commerce catalogs
    confirmation, 232–234
    placement, 232
organization
    content, 189
    first impressions, 95

outdoor advertising, 14
output variables, 326
outside experts and media for trust, 98–101, 99–100
outsourcing
    vs. insourcing, 410–412
    testing, 380–383
overgeneralization in sampling, 284–285
overlapping responsibilities
    big companies, 374
    copywriters, 369
    graphic designers, 368
    little companies, 372–373
    marketing managers, 369
    product managers, 365
    programmers, 370
    quality assurance testers, 371
    system administrators, 367
    user experience professionals, 363–364
    webmasters, 365–366
oversampling, 282
Overstock.com site, 56–58, 56–57

P

page fold, 243–244, 244
page shell design
    accessibility, 189–191
    buttons, 191–192
    centered fixed-width designs, 176–182, 178–182
    color, 186
    graphics, 185–186
    information architecture, 189
    page sides, 183–185, 183–184
    separation of content, 176, 177
    video, 186–187, 187–188
page views per visit, 116
pages
    depth, 116
    headlines, 218
    home. See homepages
    layout, 174–176, 175
    size, 194
    structure testing, 262–263
paid endorsements, 101
paid search traffic, 121, 121
paleo-mammalian brain, 149
Pandora homepage, 103–104, 104–105
Paradox of Choice: Why More Is Less (Schwartz), 51
parallel pricing presentations, 277
parallel testing, 284
parametric analysis, 335–336
    characteristics, 336–338
    fractional factorial design, 339–340
        advantages, 343–344
        disadvantages, 344–345
        overview, 340–343
    full factorial, 346–348
Pareto Principle, 252
partners
    outsourcing, 382
    passing customers to, 234
path analysis, 253–255
pattern matching, 152
pay-per-click (PPC) model, 10, 253, 435–436
payment methods
    alternative, 231

forms of, 97–98
    insourcing vs. outsourcing, 383
peel-back ads, 11, 11
peer consensus, 101–105, 103–105
peer-to-peer recommendations, 51
perceivers in MBTI, 154
% of New Visits metric, 122
performance
    vs. positive results, 425–426, 426
    in testing, 316–319, 318
permission marketing, 41
Permission Marketing: Turning Strangers into Friends and Friends into Customers (Godin), 15–16, 41, 88
personal marketing, 41
personality types, 152–153
    Keirsey-Bates, 155–156, 155
    Myers-Briggs Type Indicator, 153–154
    Platinum Rule, 156–157
personalization, 271
personas vs. roles, 37–38
perspective in testing programs, 383–384
persuasion frameworks, 157–158
    Fogg Behavior Model, 158–160, 158
    key principles, 162–165
    unbalancing scales, 160–162
Persuasive Technology: Using Computers to Change What We Think and Do (Fogg), 158
PetSmart homepage, 97, 97
phone sales, 394
photos on homepages, 205
physical processes in parametric testing, 345
piecewise construction, 344–345
piecewise review in QA plans, 415
Pirolli, Peter, 265
pitfalls, 421
    baselines, 422
    case study, 429–433, 430–432
    data collection, 422–423
    delayed conversions, 426–429, 427–428
    inaction, 436
    search engines, 433–436
    seasonality, 424
    test costs, 424–426, 426
Plackett-Burman approach, 340
Platinum Rule, 142, 156–157
plumbing-supply company roles, 37
policies, 95, 98
politics, 375
    brand guardians, 375–376
    C-level officers, 377–378
    IT staff, 376–377
    testing, 402
polls, 283
polychromic societies, 166
pop-ups
    entry, 81–82, 82
    exit, 82
positive results vs. performance, 425–426, 426
positive variable interactions, 350
potential profit impact, 378
Power Options site, 429–433, 430–432
PPC (pay-per-click) model, 10, 253, 435–436

precise body copy, **195**
precision in statistics, **298–300**, *299*
presentations
  learning modalities factor, 152
  testing, **263**
  visual. *See* visual presentation
  web analytics, 145
price curves, **275–276**
price/profit curves, 274, *275*
price testing, **273**
  qualitative methods, **273–274**
  quantitative methods, **274–278**,
   275, 277
prices, displaying, 226
primitive brain, 149
print advertising, 14
print catalog sales, 394
printout support, 31
prioritizing
  buttons, 191
  projects, 377
privacy
  excessive information requests,
   87–92, *89–92*
  policies, 98
privacy symbols, 96
probability distribution function, 287
probability theory, **286–287**
  applied statistics, 293
  Central Limit Theorem, 291
  conversion rate, **293–295**
  landing page testing applications,
   287–289
  law of large numbers, 289
  normal distribution, **289–291**,
   290–291
  statistical methods, **291–292**
problem identification methods in
  action plans, **407–409**
problem tickets, 414
procedural changes in data
  collection, 416
product detail in e-commerce
  catalogs, **218**
  benefits, 220
  call-to-action buttons, **223–224**
  features, 220
  images, **221–222**, *222–223*
  layout and visual emphasis,
   218–219, *219*
  return policy, 220
  social proof, **224–225**, *224–225*
  upsell and cross-sell related items,
   220, *221*
product-level items, **214–215**, *214*
product listings in e-commerce
  catalogs, **215–218**, *216–217*
product managers, **364–365**
product pages, 24, *25*
product/service mix factor, 391
professionalism of design, 95
profit impact, 378
ProFlowers site, **227–228**, *227*
programmers, **370–371**
progress indicators, **241**
project-based support
  commitments, 377
prominent page parts as test
  elements, 255
promises, broken, **83–85**, *83–84*
promotions, **212–213**, *212*
prototypes, **340–341**
psychological mismatches. *See* audience
  and visitors

psychological predispositions in
  parametric testing, 345
Psychological Types (Jung), 153
public relations, 14
publishing conversion actions, 33
publishing-related sites, **28–29**
purchases
  LTV conversion actions, **393–396**
  support for, 32

Q

qualitative methods in price testing,
  273–274
quality assurance (QA)
  client-side page rendering, 310
  plans, **414–415**
  testers, **371–372**
quality control, 323
quality of search keywords, **123**
Quantcast tool, 135
quantitative methods in price testing,
  274–278, *275*
quantities, changeable, 226
questionnaires, **388–389**
questions, loaded, 285

R

R-complex, 149
radio advertising, 14
random processes, 287
random variables, **286–288**
ranking sites, 30, 33
ratings, support for, 31
rational brain, 150
Rationals temperament, 155
reading grade level, 196
real-time support options, **232**
RealAge site
  case study, **269–270**, *269–270*
  landing page test, **98–99**, *99*
recipes
  A-B split testing, 333
  client-side page rendering, 309
  fractional factorial parametric
   testing, 343, **348–349**
  full factorial parametric testing,
   346, 348
  tuning methods, 328
reciprocation in persuasion, **163**
recommendations, 51
recurring visitors, **147–148**
redundant content, 310
referrals
  client, 14
  LTV of conversion actions, 391
referred traffic, **119**
Referring Sites reports, 122
regions in third-party lead generation,
  396
registration, forced, **56–58**
registration pages, **234**
  CAPTCHAs, **235–236**, *236*
  confirmation and welcome
   e-mails, 237
  field entry and error handling,
   235–237
  third-party methods, 237
  values and benefits, **234–235**
regression analysis, 293

related products, displaying, 226
relater style in Platinum Rule, **156–157**
relevancy of search keywords, **123**
relevant marketing, 41
repeat visitors
  biased statistics from, 288
  LTV of conversion actions, 391
  rate, **122**
reports
  goals, 116, *117*
  Map Overlay, 124, *125*
  paid keyword, 121, *121*
  Top Landing Pages, 115, *115*
  top SEO pages, 115, *115*
  traffic sources, **117–118**, *118*
  web analytics, 145
reptilian brain, **149**
research
  desire stage, **47–49**, *48*
  in statistical methods, 292
  support for, 31
resources
  action plans, 388
  in-house, **404–405**
  shared, 413
  test elements, 261
restrictive test design, 345
results analysis, **418–419**
retailer catalog sites, 393
retention activities, **15–17**
return policies, 220
return visit support in multiple-page
  flows, **267**
returned leads, 397
revenue in conversion rate financial
  impact, **391–392**
reverse goal paths, 253
reversibility features, 49
reviewing
  conversion activities, 30, 33
  e-commerce catalogs, 232
reviews, 101
  expert, **197–198**
  providing, 85
  user, 51, 225, *225*
Revit Architecture homepage, 202, *203*
rewards programs, 17
rich media ads, 11
Rick Jones Pianos homepage, 94, *94*
Ries, Al, 54
risk-reward scales, **238**
*Rival Hypotheses: Alternative
  Interpretations of Data Based
  Conclusions* (Huck), 282
Rocket Surgery Made Easy
  (Krug), 197
roles
  matrix, **36–38**
  MBTI, 154
  vs. personas, **37–38**
  teams. *See* teams
rotating banner ads, **213–214**
rules in page layout, 176
Rushmore Casino homepage, 79, *79*

S

safe shopping symbols, 96
safety of visitors
  promoting, **46–47**
  transactional assurances, **95–98**,
   96–97

sales force automation (SFA) system
  intermediate conversion actions, 399
  in testing, 272
sales tax, **232**
sample reviews, 85
samples and sample sizes
  biased, **282–284**, 418
  confidence levels, **295–298**, *296–297*
  pitfalls, 423
  statistics, **298–300**, *299*
  in testing, 319–320
SandalWorld site, 66, *67*
sans serif fonts, 190
satisficing, 55
saturating goals, 315
Saxe, John Godfrey, 362
scales
  risk-reward, **238**
  unbalancing, **160–162**
ScanAlert HackerSafe trust mark, 97, *97*
scarcity in persuasion, 165
scenarios, 38
schedules
  data collection, **416**
  insourcing vs. outsourcing, 383
  test elements, 261
Schwartz, Barry, 51
scrolling, 177, **243–244**, *244*
search
  e-commerce catalog results, **215–218**, *216–217*
  internal site search
    results pages, **26–27**, *27*
    tools, **205**, *206*
  keyword relevancy and quality, **123**
  paid, **121**, *121*
  research options, 49
  space size, **328**
search dominant temperament, 165
search engine optimization (SEO)
  process, **10**
  vs. landing page optimization, **11**
  pitfalls, **433–436**
  strategy, 114
  traffic, **119–120**, *120*
search engine results pages (SERPs), 10
Sears homepage, 179, *179*
seasonal trends, **146**
seasonality factors, **424**
security
  promoting, **46–47**
  transactional assurances, **95–98**, *96–97*
  trust seals, **227–228**, *227*
SeeWhy tool, **140**
segmentation, 8
  advanced, **123–124**, *124*
  content and offer focus, **259–260**
  function and usability focus, **260**
  landing page tests, 404
  traffic sources, **145–148**, *147*
  web analytics, **144–145**
selective focus in testing, 317
self-selection
  in interest, **43**, *44*
  navigation, **202–204**, *203*
  in polling, 283
  for registration, 58
Selling the Invisible: A Field Guide to Modern Marketing (Beckwith), 54

sensation in Fogg Behavior Model, 159
sensors in MBTI, 154
SEO (search engine optimization), **10**
  vs. landing page optimization, **11**
  pitfalls, **433–436**
  strategy, 114
  traffic, **119–120**, *120*
SEOmoz site, 25, *26*
sequential testing, **284**, 292
serial pricing presentations, 277
serif fonts, 190
SERPs (search engine results pages), 10
server-side page rendering, **311–312**, *311*
servers for testing, **306–308**
service-level agreements (SLAs), 410
seven deadly design sins, 66
  broken promises, **83–85**, *83–84*
  case study, **106–109**, *106–109*
  choices, **73–75**, *73*, *75*
  identifying, 408
  information requests, **87–92**, *89–92*
  text, **86–87**, *86–87*
  trust and credibility issues. *See* trust
  unclear calls-to-action, **66–72**, *67–69*, *71–72*
  visual distractions, **76–83**, *77*, *79–80*, *82*
SF Video site
  landing page, **99–100**, *100*
  variable interactions, **353–357**, *354–356*
SFA (sales force automation) system
  intermediate conversion actions, 399
  in testing, 272
shape in parametric testing, 340
shared resources, **413**
sharing options, 233
shipping cost, 227, **232**
shipping information
  address confirmation, 232
  e-commerce catalogs, **230**
Shoes.com site, 48, *48*
shopping carts, **225–228**, *226–227*
short data collection, 284
sides, boring, **183–185**, *183–184*
Sidewiki pane, 103, *104*
sign-up pages, 25, *26*
sign-up process
  direct response pages, **246**
  limiting, **242–243**
signals in Fogg Behavior Model, 159
significance vs. importance, **297–298**
Simon, Herbert A., 40, 55
simplification
  benefits, **59**
  body copy, **196**
single goals, **314–315**
single product price elasticity model, **277–278**, *277–278*
site appearance and functionality, **388**
site performance and traffic levels, **388**
site search
  results pages, **26–27**, *27*
  tools, **205**, *206*
sitemaps, 211
SiteTuners homepage, 183, *184*
68-95-99.7 rule, **290–291**
size
  banner ads, **213**
  font, **190**
  images, 185
  pages, **194**

sample, *295–298*, *296–297*, 423
search space, 328
tests, 256, **302–303**, 410
skills and training
  big companies, **373**
  copywriters, **368–369**
  graphic designers, **367–368**
  little companies, **372**
  marketing managers, **369**
  product managers, **364–365**
  programmers, **370**
  quality assurance testers, **371**
  system administrators, **366**
  unavailable, 261
  user experience professionals, **363**
  webmasters, **365**
SLAs (service-level agreements), **410**
sleepy dog story, 160
small sample sizes, **423**
Smart Bargains site, 96, *96*
social cohesion in Fogg Behavior Model, 159
social community sites, **29**
social media traffic, **121–122**
social networking sites, **11**, *12*
social proof
  peer consensus, **102–105**, *103–105*
  in persuasion, **164**
  product detail, **224–225**, *224–225*
socializer style in Platinum Rule, **156–157**
socializing in desire stage, **51–52**
software simulation, **198–199**
Sony site, 52, *52*
sorting search results, 215
SpadeClub homepage, 79, *80*
sparks in Fogg Behavior Model, 160
sparseness, **95**
special offers, **58**
specified constraint test construction approach, **330–331**
spiders, **434**
spokespeople, 101
spot testing prices, 275
stable traffic, **148**
staging environments, **417**
staging information, **240–241**, *240*
stand-alone landing pages, **21**
standard deviation, **290–291**, 296
start small strategy, **378–379**
states of variables, 327
statistical theory, 293
statistics, **282**
  applied, **293**
  biased samples, **282–284**
  certainty, **295–298**
  cherry-picking, **282**
  confidence levels, **282**
  false causality, **285–286**
  overgeneralization, **284–285**
  precision, **298–300**, *299*
  probability theory, **286–287**
    Central Limit Theorem, **291**
    conversion rate, **293–295**
    landing page testing applications, **287–289**
    law of large numbers, **289**
    normal distribution, **289–291**, *290–291*
  results interpretation, **298**
  significance vs. importance, **297–298**
  statistical methods, **291–292**
  test length, **300–303**

stochastic processes, **287–288**, 294
storing addresses, **230**
stragglers in conversion delay, **427–429**, *427–428*
stranded parachutist scenario, 266
strategic perspective in insource testing, **384**
streaky data in parametric testing, 345
styles
    body copy, **196–197**
    font, 190
subheadlines, 70
submenus, 207
Submit Now: Designing Persuasive Web Sites (Chak), 39
subscriptions
    conversion rate financial impact, **398–399**
    support for, **32**
success criteria in action plans, **405–407**
summarization in statistical methods, 293
superior brain, 150
support
    commitments, 377
    providing, **210–211**
    systematic page flows, 264–265
support sites, **29**
supporting trust areas, 245
surprises, minimizing, **59–61**, *60*
survey tools. *See* feedback
SurveyMonkey, **131**
sweep, 257
system administrators, **366–367**
systematic page flows, **264–265**

T

t-tests, **294–295**
tabbed information, **219**
tabbed menus, 207, *208*
Taguchi method, 340
Target site
    error handling, 231, *231*
    product listing page, 216, *216–217*
task-oriented body copy, 195
tasks
    implementation plans, 414
    matrix, **38–39**
    unnecessary, **56–59**, *57–58*
teams, **361–363**
    assembling, **401–403**
    big companies, **373–374**
    copywriters, **368–369**
    graphic designers, **367–368**
    implementation plans, 413
    little companies, **372–373**
    marketing managers, **369–370**
    product managers, **364–365**
    programmers, **370–371**
    quality assurance testers, **371–372**
    system administrators, **366–367**
    user experience professionals, **363–364**
    webmasters, **365–366**
technical feasibility determinations, **376–377**
technical issues with search engines, 434

technology in testing
    changes, **322–323**
    tuning methods, 410
testing companies, 382
tests and testing
    audience changes in, **319–322**
    calls-to-action, **245–246**
    CMS for, 306
    constructing, **328–331**
    content management configurations, 308
    client-side page rendering, **308–310**, *309*
    intercept page rendering, **312–313**, *312*
    server-side page rendering, **311–312**, *311*
    cost assumptions, **424–426**, *426*
    design
        A-B split testing, 332
        full factorial parametric testing, 347
    elements, **251–252**
        audience segmentation, **259–260**
        baggage, **261**
        breadth of impact, **252–255**
        coherency, **257–259**
        granularity, **256–257**
        longevity, **260–261**
        multiple-page flows, **264–267**
        price testing, **273–278**, *275*, *277–278*
        selecting, **261–264**
        sweep, 257
        timeless testing themes, **267–273**, *268–270*
    length, **300–303**
    measuring and counting issues, **313–319**, *318*
    methods overview, **331**
    mobile sites, 249
    multivariate. *See* multivariate tests
    problem identification for, **407–409**
    servers for, **306–308**
    size
        fractional factorial parametric testing, 341, 344
        full factorial non-parametric testing, 349
        full factorial parametric testing, 347
    technology change issues, **322–323**
    terminology, **326–331**
    trust, **272–273**
    usability checks, 197
    variable interactions. *See* variable interactions
text
    ads, 11
    buttons, **192**
    color, 186
    direct response pages, **244**
    excessive, **86–87**, *86–87*, 107–108
    font, 190
    garish, 78
"The Comparable" in social proof, 102–104
"The Many" in social proof, 102–103
thinkers
    in MBTI, 154
    in Platinum Rule, 156–157

third-party e-mail lists, **12–13**
third-party lead generation, **396–397**
third-party site registration, 237
third-party validation, **98–101**, *99–100*
37Signals homepage, 42, *42*
three brain theory, **148–151**
throttling, 316, 345
Tickets.com site, **247–248**, *247–248*
TicketsNow homepage, 147, *147*
time series, 287–288
time zone issues, 146
tool-dominant temperament, 165
tooltips, **231**
top internal search keywords, **123**
top traffic pages
    high bounce rates, **115–116**, *115*
    mission-critical pages, 114, *114*
    organic search, **22–23**
    testing, 252
total solution for action, **55–56**
Townsend, Robert, 381
Toyota USA site, 181, *181*
tracking
    in data collection, **416**
    in multiple-page flows, 267
    tools, 7
tradeshows, 14
traffic
    mix, 321
    recurring, **147–148**
    volume, 7
traffic sources
    in data collection, **416**
    report, **117–118**, *118*
    in sampling, 283
    variability, **145–147**, *147*
training. *See* skills and training
transacting for action, **56–61**, *57–58*, *60*
transactional assurances, **95–98**, *96–97*
transactors, 39
translations in cultural differences, 167
transparency in insource testing, 385
trial offers, 95
triggers in Fogg Behavior Model, **159–160**
triune brain theory, **148–151**
Trout, Jack, 54
trust, **93**
    vs. anxiety, **161**
    appearance, **93–95**, *94*
    CREDO Mobile, **107–108**
    outside experts and media, **98–101**, *99–100*
    peer consensus, **101–105**, *103–105*
    testing, **272–273**
    transactional assurances, **95–98**, *96–97*
    user-generated content, 51
trust areas and seals
    direct response pages, 245
    displaying, **227–228**, *227*
tuning methods, **325**
    A-B split testing, **332–334**
    in action plans, **410–412**
    introduction, **326–331**
    multiple-page flows, **264–267**
    overview, **331**
TuningEngine technology, **348–350**
turf issues, 261
TV advertising, 14
Twain, Mark, 282

*22 Immutable Laws of Marketing:
Violate Them at Your Own Risk!*
(Ries and Trout), 54

U

UCD (user-centered design), 38–39
unbalancing scales, 160–162
unclear calls-to-action, 66–72, *67–69, 71–72*
unconstrained design, 329
underlines, 190
underlying systems in statistics, 299
undersampling, 282
uneven sampling, 319–320
unimportant landing pages, 378–379
unit normal distribution, 290
University of California site, 43, *44*
unnecessary items
eliminating, 42, *42*
tasks and action, 56–59, *57–58*
unpaired one-tailed equal-variance
t-tests, 295
unspecified constraint approach, 329
unwelcome surprises, 59–61, *60*
up-sells, 220, *221*
price elasticity model, 278, *278*
price testing, 278
warnings, 58
usability
in audience segmentation, 260
best practices expert reviews, 197–198
formal and informal testing, 197
visual attention prediction, 198–199
use cases, 38
UsedWatches.net site, 243, *244*
user-centered design (UCD), 38–39
user experience (UX) professionals, 363–364
user-generated content, 13
support for, 31
trust, 51
user reviews, 51, 225, *225*
UserTesting tool, 136–137, *137*
UserVoice tool, 132–133
UserZoom tool, 138–139
UX (user experience) professionals, 363–364

V

value-added information, 85
value of repeat sales, 391
values in testing, 313–314, 327
variability of traffic sources, 145–147, *147*
variable cost percentage (VCP), 392
variable interactions, 350–351
A-B split testing, 333–334
multivariate tests
data collection, 335
fractional factorial parametric, 341–342, 344–345, 347

full factorial
non-parametric, 349
full factorial parametric, 346, 348–349
illustrative example, 351–353, *351–352*
parametric analysis, 336–338
SF Video example, 353–357, *354–356*
spot tests, 275
variables
dependent, 291, 326
independent. *See* independent variables
in testing, 274, 326–331
values, 313–314, 327
variance, 290, 293, 337
VCP (variable cost percentage), 392
Velaro tool, 133
verifying improvement, 418–419
vertical scroll bars, 177
video
direct response pages, 245
as distraction, 78
page shell design, 186–187, *187–188*
video and interactive game content, 13
visitors. See audience and visitors
visual analysis tools, 125
AttentionWizard, 129–131, *129–130*
ClickTale, 127–128, *128*
CrazyEgg, 126–127, *126–127*
visual attention prediction, 198–199
visual distractions
banner ads, 81
clutter, 106, 108
entry pop-ups, 81–82, *82*
exit pop-ups, 82
fixes, 83
overview, 76–81, *77, 79–80*
testing, 268
visual emphasis for product detail, 218–219, *219*
visual learning modality, 151
visual presentation
accessibility, 189–191
buttons, 191–192
color, 186
embellishments and flourishes, 78
graphics, 185–186
information architecture, 189
overview, 173–174
page layout, 174–176, *175*
page shell design, 176–185, *177–184*
video, 186–187, *188*
Voltaire, 172
von Moltke, Helmuth, 421

W

walking price curves, 275–276
warnings. *See* pitfalls
web analytics, 144–145

*Web Analytics 2.0: The Art of Online
Accountability and Science of
Customer Centricity*
(Kaushik), 378
web analytics tools, 114
advanced segments, 123–124, *124*
average page depth, 116
competitive analysis, 135–136, *135*
conversion points goals, 116, *117*
direct/bookmark traffic, 118–119, *119*
e-mail enhancement, 139–140
feedback and surveys, 131–133, *132*
mission-critical pages, 114, *114*
paid search traffic, 121
referred traffic, 119
repeat visit rate, 122
SEO traffic, 119–120, *120*
social media traffic, 121–122
top entry pages with high bounce rates, 115–116, *115*
top internal search keywords, 123
traffic sources reports, 117–118, *118*
usability testing, 136–139, *137–138*
visitor demographics, 124–125, *125*
visual, 125–131, *126–130*
website performance, 133–134
web browsers, 39, 307–308
web servers, 307
web usability, 172–173
webmasters, 365–366
website performance tools, 133–134
Weinschenk, Susan, 150
welcomé e-mails, 237
well-defined action blocks, 70
"what" question about visitors, 143
"when" question about visitors, 143
"where" question about visitors, 143
whitepapers, 47
"who" question about visitors, 143
"why" question about visitors, 144
wizards, 48
words, limiting, 204
"World's Worst Website", 174, *174*
writing for web, 192
body copy, 193–196
headlines, 193

Y

Yahoo! News site, 180–181, *180–181*
Yaris car model homepage, 181–182, *182*
"Yesses" visitors, 17–18, *18*
yields in parametric testing, 341–342
YSlow tool, 134

Z

Z-scores, 295–297, *296–297*
zoomed hover-over areas, 222, *222*